QUEER CAREER

Queer Career

SEXUALITY AND WORK
IN MODERN AMERICA

◆

Margot Canaday

PRINCETON UNIVERSITY PRESS

PRINCETON & OXFORD

Published by Princeton University Press
41 William Street, Princeton, New Jersey 08540
99 Banbury Road, Oxford OX2 6JX

press.princeton.edu

All Rights Reserved

ISBN: 9780691205953
ISBN (e-book): 9780691215310

British Library Cataloging-in-Publication Data is available

Editorial: Bridget Flannery-McCoy and Alena Chekanov
Production Editorial: Ellen Foos
Jacket Design: Karl Spurzem
Production: Erin Suydam
Publicity: Kate Hensley and Kate Farquhar-Thomson
Copyeditor: Kathleen Kageff

Jacket silhouettes: Officer, waiter, worker climbing ladder / Shutterstock; nurse, executive in chair / Vexels; businesswoman by Bob Comix / Creazilla

This book has been composed in Classic Miller

Printed on acid-free paper. ∞

Printed in the United States of America

10 9 8 7 6 5 4 3 2 1

For Greta

CONTENTS

Introduction

IN THE BLUNTEST OF TERMS, we think of jobs as "good" or "bad," but that contrast hardly begins to describe our working lives.[1] The modern workplace is a realm of myriad contradictions: Some workplaces are zones of "uniforms and conformity" where compulsion reigns, norms are enforced, and identity is stripped away. At the same time, our jobs are a critical site for the formation of selfhood, so that asking someone what they "do" is tantamount to asking them who they are.[2] Some see work as our fullest realization of human creativity and cooperation; others regard it as an obstacle to our growth and happiness and wonder why we don't fight harder to escape it.[3] Occupational segregation is as much a factor as residential segregation in driving social stratification, yet workplaces also force people to come together across religious, ethnic, and racial divides.[4] Finally, while we think of work as a place apart from our intimate life,

1. Arne L. Kallenberg, *Good Jobs, Bad Jobs: The Rise of Polarized and Precarious Employment Systems in the United States, 1970s to 2000* (New York: Russell Sage Foundation, 2011).

2. Michael Selmi, "The Many Faces of Darlene Jespersen," *Duke Journal of Gender Law and Policy* 14 (2007): 468; Vicki Schultz, "Life's Work," *Columbia Law Review* 100 (2000): 1881–964. On workplaces as spaces where authentic selves can be expressed, see also Kenji Yoshino, *Covering: The Hidden Assault on Our Civil Rights* (New York: Random House, 2006).

3. On the oppressive nature of work, see especially the political theorist Kathi Weeks's provocative call for a "politics of refusal" to work and a "postwork imaginary" in her book *The Problem with Work: Feminism, Marxism, Antiwork Politics, and Postwork Imaginaries* (Durham, NC: Duke University Press, 2011). On the creative and fulfilling aspects of work, see Shultz, "Life's Work."

4. Douglas S. Massey, *Categorically Unequal: The American Stratification System* (New York: Russell Sage Foundation, 2007), 217; Cynthia Estlund, *Working Together: How Workplace Bonds Strengthen a Diverse Democracy* (New York: Oxford University Press, 2005).

it surely rivals the family in its capacity to determine multiple facets of our existence. Work is "the experience through which," according to legal scholar Vicki Schultz, "we construct coherent life stories."[5]

That work fundamentally shapes our lives is true for all of us, but it is not true for everyone in the same way. That's an obvious proposition for historians—who follow these questions over time—but we know more about certain histories than others. Labor historians, for example, formerly focused on industrial workers, but as manufacturing jobs have declined, they have shifted their attention to jobs in the expanding service sector.[6] Work has been a central concern of women's historians, who have given us rich portraits of colonial midwives, nineteenth-century seamstresses and laundresses, and early twentieth-century office workers.[7] Immigrant labor accounts for a large (and expanding) historiography.[8] Yet

5. Schultz, "Life's Work," 1927.

6. The history of labor is too voluminous to cite comprehensively, but classic works include Herbert Gutman, *Work, Culture, and Society in Industrializing America* (New York: Vintage Books, 1977); Alan Dawley, *Class and Community: The Industrial Revolution in Lynn* (Cambridge, MA: Harvard University Press, 1976); David Montgomery, *Workers' Control in America: Studies in the History of Work, Technology, and Labor Struggles* (Cambridge: Cambridge University Press, 1979); Jacquelyn Dowd Hall et al., *Like a Family: The Making of the Southern Cotton Mill World* (Chapel Hill: University of North Carolina Press, 1987); Mary H. Blewett, *Men, Women, and Work: Class, Gender, and Protest in the New England Shoe Industry 1780–1930* (Champaign-Urbana: University of Illinois Press, 1990); Earl Lewis, *In Their Own Interests: Race, Class, and Power in Twentieth-Century Norfolk, Virginia* (Berkeley: University of California Press, 1991). Studies of service work in particular include: Dorothy Sue Cobble, *Dishing It Out: Waitresses and Their Unions in the Twentieth Century* (Champaign-Urbana: University of Illinois Press, 1991); Tera Hunter, *To 'Joy My Freedom: Southern Black Women's Lives and Labors after the Civil War* (Cambridge, MA: Harvard University Press, 1997); Bethany Moreton, *To Serve God and Wal-Mart: The Making of Christian Free Enterprise* (Cambridge, MA: Harvard University Press, 2009); Jennifer Klein and Eileen Boris, *Caring for America: Home Health Workers in the Shadow of the Welfare State* (New York: Oxford University Press, 2012). Two recent works that deal with both manufacturing and service are Lane Windham, *Knocking on Labor's Door: Union Organizing in the 1970s and the Roots of a New Economic Divide* (Chapel Hill: University of North Carolina Press, 2017); Gabriel Winant, *The Next Shift: The Fall of Industry and the Rise of Health Care in Rust Belt America* (Cambridge, MA: Harvard University Press, 2021).

7. This is also a huge literature, but three foundational texts are Laurel Thatcher Ulrich, *A Midwife's Tale: The Life of Martha Ballard, Based on Her Diary, 1785–1812* (New York: Vintage, 1991); Jacqueline Jones, *Labor of Love, Labor of Sorrow: Black Women, Work, and the Family from Slavery to the Present* (New York: Basic Books, 1985); Alice Kessler-Harris, *Out to Work: A History of Wage-Earning Women in the United States* (New York: Oxford University Press, 1982).

8. See, for example, John E. Bodnar, *Immigration and Industrialization: Ethnicity in an American Mill Town, 1870–1940* (Pittsburgh, PA: University of Pittsburgh Press, 1977); Zaragosa Vargas, *Proletarians of the North: A History of Mexican Industrial Workers in Detroit and the Midwest* (Berkeley: University of California Press, 1993); Cindy Hahamovitch, *No Man's Land: Jamaican Guest Workers in America and the Global History*

productive labor's "categoric occlusions"—those worlds of work "marginal to wage labor"—remain a challenge for historians, as do other omissions.[9] When several years ago I heard a leading historian of capitalism call for a "fuller accounting of diverse forms of labor," I, as a historian of sexuality, perked up my ears.[10] He was specifically referring to the need to integrate histories of slavery into histories of political economy, but he could have been describing the paucity of our knowledge about gay workers as well.

Simply put, there are few other work experiences about which we know less.[11] Indeed, four decades into the project of LGBT history, this is still a seriously understudied area of inquiry.[12] The reasons are multiple, but some of the explanation is simply bad timing. The field of labor history was, for example, entering a quiet period at the precise moment when

---

of Deportable Labor (Princeton, NJ: Princeton University Press, 2003); Moon Ho Jung, Coolies and Cane: Race, Labor, and Sugar in the Age of Emancipation (Baltimore: Johns Hopkins University Press, 2006); Lori A. Flores, Grounds for Dreaming: Mexican Americans, Mexican Immigrants, and the California Farmworker Movement (New Haven, CT: Yale University Press, 2016); Ana Raquel Minian, Undocumented Lives: The Untold Story of Mexican Migration (Cambridge, MA: Harvard University Press, 2018); Natalia Molina, A Place at the Nayarit: How a Mexican Restaurant Nourished a Community (Berkeley: University of California Press, 2022).

9. Zachary Schwartz-Weinstein, "The Limits of Work and the Subject of Labor History," in Rethinking U.S. Labor History: Essays on the Working-Class Experience, ed. Donna T. Haverty-Stacke and Daniel Walkowitz (New York: Continuum, 2010), 290.

10. The historian was Sven Beckert, speaking at a state-of-the-field session called "The Return of Political Economy," at the 2012 annual meeting of the Organization of American Historians in Milwaukee, WI.

11. This holds true not just for historians but across the social sciences more generally. In 2004, Belle Rose Ragins described gay and lesbian workers as "one of the largest, but least studied minority groups in the workforce." Belle Rose Ragins, "Sexual Orientation in the Workplace: The Unique Work and Career Experiences of Gay, Lesbian, and Bisexual Workers," in Research in Personnel and Human Resources Management, ed. Joseph Martocchio (Bingley, UK: Emerald Books, 2004), 35.

12. To the best of my knowledge, books in the field of LGBT history that are centrally about the workplace include Allan Bérubé, My Desire for History: Essays in Gay, Community, and Labor History (Chapel Hill: University of North Carolina Press, 2011); Phil Tiemeyer, Plane Queer: Labor, Sexuality and AIDS in the History of Male Flight Attendants (Berkeley: University of California Press, 2013); Miriam Frank, Out in the Union: A Labor History of Queer America (Philadelphia: Temple University Press, 2014); Ryan Patrick Murphy, Deregulating Desire: Flight Attendant Activism, Family Politics, and Workplace Justice (Philadelphia: Temple University Press, 2016); Elspeth H. Brown, Work! A Queer History of Modeling (Durham, NC: Duke University Press, 2019). Studies that treat early twentieth-century queer working-class cultures include George Chauncey, Gay New York: Gender, Urban Culture, and the Making of the Gay Male World, 1890–1940 (New York: Basic Books, 1994); Peter Boag, Same-Sex Affairs: Constructing and Controlling Homosexuality in the Pacific Northwest (Berkeley: University of California Press, 2003); Nayan Shah, Stranger Intimacy: Contesting Race, Sexuality, and the Law in the North American West (Berkeley: University of California Press, 2011). David Johnson's study of the Lavender Scare is more of a

LGBT history gained traction and legitimacy in the academy.[13] That the history of capitalism *was* exploding at the same time that the history of sexuality simultaneously peaked could have led to productive collaborations. But historians of capitalism often defined their approach as a flight from the social and cultural history that had previously been dominant in the historiography, a fervent drive toward the "top" and away from the "bottom."[14] Trenchant critiques of these tendencies aside, historians of sexuality have themselves been somewhat dismissive of the workplace as a site of inquiry.[15] That is especially remarkable when one considers that the historian John D'Emilio, in an early well-known article in the field, hypothesized that gay identity was itself shaped by the development of capitalism. He showed how industrialization untethered queer men and women economically from family units. Some of these individuals then migrated to cities; they took on wage labor in the expanding urban economy; and, by the late nineteenth century, they began to form gay subcultures.[16] Many scholars,

---

political and cultural history of the federal purge than a book about work per se. David K. Johnson, *The Lavender Scare: The Cold War Persecution of Gays and Lesbians in the Federal Government* (Chicago: University of Chicago Press, 2006). The same is true of Stacy Braukman's study of McCarthyism at the state level in *Communists and Perverts under the Palms: The Johns Committee in Florida, 1956–1965* (Gainesville: University Press of Florida, 2012). Allan Bérubé's history of gays and lesbians in the World War II–era military deals with work but is not explicitly a labor history. Allan Bérubé, *Coming Out under Fire: The History of Gay Men and Women in World War II* (New York: Free Press, 1990).

13. Labor history has revitalized more recently, and I wonder here about renewed possibilities. One promising work in the pipeline is Joshua Hollands's 2020 dissertation, "Work and Sexuality in the Sunbelt: Homophobic Workplace Discrimination in the US South and Southwest, 1970 to the Present" (PhD diss., University College London, 2020). Hollands's dissertation won the 2021 Herbert Gutman Prize for outstanding dissertation from the Labor and Working-Class History Association.

14. Sven Beckert, "History of American Capitalism," in *American History Now*, ed. Eric Foner and Lisa McGirr (Philadelphia: Temple University Press, 2011), 314–35.

15. Such critiques include Nan Enstad, "The 'Sonorous Summons' of the New History of Capitalism, or, What Are We Talking about When We Talk about the Economy," *Modern American History* 2 (January 2019): 83–95; Amy Dru Stanley, "Histories of Capitalism and Sex Difference," *Journal of the Early Republic* 36 (Summer 2016): 335–41; Ellen Hartigan-O'Connor, "The Personal Is Political Economy," *Journal of the Early Republic* 36 (Summer 2016): 335–41. I appreciate as well Geoff Eley's notion that setting social histories at "the bottom" against histories of capitalism at "the top" is a "false antinomy," and his recognition that the "largest of analytical questions" can be "brought down to the ground." Eley, "No Need to Choose: History from Above, History from Below," *Viewpoints Magazine*, June 27, 2014, https://www.viewpointmag.com/2014/06/27/no-need-to-choose-history-from-above-history-from-below/.

16. John D'Emilio, "Capitalism and Gay Identity," in *Powers of Desire: The Politics of Sexuality*, ed. Ann Snitow, Christine Stansell, and Sharon Thompson (New York: Monthly Review Press, 1983), 100–116.

most notably George Chauncey in *Gay New York*, then documented the emergence and growth of these urban subcultures.[17] Yet D'Emilio's original insight, while strikingly brilliant, did not lead to broader inquiry into the relationship between work and gay life more generally. A more far-reaching examination of the place of employment in the queer past seems instead to have been continuously circumscribed by a widely shared assumption that the workplace was part of the "straight world" in which people passed, and that the "homosexual world," as the psychologist Evelyn Hooker wrote in the mid-1960s, was "largely one of leisure time and recreational activities."[18] Historians of sexuality have followed Hooker's lead, tending to check in after five p.m., directing their attention to the street and the bar. As a result, we know a considerable amount about working-class cultures, but very little about the workplace itself.[19]

Because of the way that work is, in the words of one sociologist, "situated in human experience," this is a gap in our historical understanding that is particularly vital to address.[20] When, more than a decade ago, I began studying the working lives of queer people in the postwar United States, I certainly started with the firm conviction that this was valuable research to attempt; but I had also fully bought in to the notion that work was an arena in which gays historically had tried to vanish and that digging up the evidence might be very tough going. Determined to try, I started where anyone who was working on the postwar period with little confidence in what the archives might yield would begin—with oral histories. Because I thought the period before gay liberation would be especially difficult to recover, I began to look specifically for gays and lesbians born in the 1930s and 1940s who were willing to speak with me about their experiences on the job. Those working lives, which spanned the 1950s into the 1990s, map temporally onto the rise and fall of standard employment

17. Chauncey, *Gay New York*.

18. Evelyn Hooker, "Male Homosexuals and Their Worlds," in *Sexual Inversion*, ed. Judd Marmor (New York: Basic Books, 1965), 94.

19. George Chauncey's assertion that on New York streets "queers constructed public identities quite different from those they maintained at work and elsewhere in the *straight world*," is illustrative of trends in the broader field for its separation of the gay world (on the streets) from the world of work. George Chauncey, "Gay Men's Strategies of Everyday Resistance," in *Major Problems in the History of American Sexuality*, ed. Kathy Peiss (Boston: Houghton Mifflin, 2002), 359 (emphasis mine).

20. Andrew Abbott, "Sociology of Work and Occupations," in *The Handbook of Economic Sociology*, 2nd ed., ed. Neil J. Smelser and Richard Swedberg (Princeton, NJ: Princeton University Press, 2005), 325.

that I also assumed would be central to my story.[21] I conducted my first interviews in 2011 and ended up doing more than 150 of them. What jumped out at me during those initial conversations was something I had not expected to hear. More often than I heard stories about elaborate ruses to conceal sexual identity at work, I heard from informants that they assumed their bosses and coworkers suspected, or even knew, about them. This degree of visibility and knowability surprised me, and it made me wonder if the archives would be more promising than I had initially anticipated.

That turned out to be true. Once I knew to look for it, the paper trail left by and about gay people in their employment, going back to the midtwentieth century, was voluminous. I drew upon substantial social scientific research that purported to explain why gays seemed to gravitate toward certain occupations, but not others. I read legal documents in which gay workers sued over government jobs, security clearances, and licenses that had been denied or revoked because of homosexuality. Organizational records revealed the concerted efforts to secure better working conditions made first by the homophiles, then by gay liberationists, and finally by the modern gay rights movement, from the Gay Activists Alliance in the 1970s to the National Gay Task Force and Lambda Legal. I also relied on the homophile, liberationist, and mainstream press, memoirs, and personal papers, as well as union and corporate records. I was well into the project before I let go of my fear of impending scarcity, my worry that it was just a matter of time before the archival trail would go cold. My first discovery was just how much evidence there was. This really wasn't a "hidden history" after all.[22]

———◆———

The contours of that history, as its shape became ever more clear, have required a reconsideration of the primary lens through which historians have considered gay employment, when they have considered it at all: that of the Lavender Scare. As I elaborate further in chapter 1, this brutal episode in the 1950s, when thousands of gay and lesbian civil servants were

21. On the standard employment relationship as a feature of the postwar era and its relationship to a gendered division of labor, see Marcel van der Linden, "San Precario: A New Inspiration for Labor Relations," *Labor: Studies in Working Class History of the Americas* 11 (Spring 2014): 15.

22. This phrase alludes to the title of an early and important collection: Martin Duberman, Martha Vicinus, and George Chauncey Jr., eds., *Hidden from History: Reclaiming the Gay and Lesbian Past* (New York: New American Library, 1989).

purged from the federal bureaucracy, has conditioned historians' thinking about gay people in employment more generally. The prevalent notion is that gay people at midcentury were in deep hiding on their jobs, and if an employer caught wind of an employee's homosexuality, they were immediately fired. That routinely happened in the government during these years, and sometimes outside the government as well. But this is a partial view, based on a particularly dramatic flash point in a particular sector, that doesn't fully capture the experience of work for many gay people at midcentury. While fear of job loss was a pervasive anxiety during these years, the workers portrayed in this history handled that fear in a variety of ways. My research has found that not all gay people, especially those employed in the private sector, were engaged in deep hiding in their jobs at midcentury. First of all, there was a "queer work world" that overlapped with the secondary labor market populated by women and people of color in low-paid, low-status work where gay people could be open and where nonnormative gender expression was sometimes affirmed on the job. Journalists, social scientists, and other midcentury observers of those who were openly employed noted "clustering" in certain kinds of "queer" occupations and in service jobs more generally. Many gay people, however, were employed in the "straight work world," in relatively better jobs, but in positions that did not affirm queerness and often repressed it. Yet even there the spectrum ranged from secrecy to discretion, with a good number of gay employees adopting something akin to what the sociologist Erving Goffman termed "covering." Goffman described covering as the effort "to keep [one's] stigma from looming large," in order to "ease matters for those in the know."[23] Covering was the opposite of "flaunting"—a term used to describe gay indiscretion, usually with a twist of gender transgression—but it rarely required an elaborate performance. As it turns out, many employers were happy to "look the other way." Employment relations during these years were, in fact, regularly characterized by an unspoken "bargain" between employers and employees—a mutual pact neither to reveal nor to pry.

The Lavender Scare then only partly illuminates this era. We need an alternative explanation that does not overgeneralize based on the public sector but rather relates the public- and private-sector experiences to one another and captures the range of ways gay people appeared at work during this period. In order to make sense of the many workplaces where

23. Erving Goffman, *Stigma: Notes on the Management of Spoiled Identity* (New York: Simon and Schuster, 1963), 102–4. The legal scholar Kenji Yoshino has made it his mission to "pull Goffman's term 'covering' out of academic obscurity and press it into the popular lexicon, so that it has the same currency as terms like 'passing' or 'the closet.'" See Yoshino, *Covering*, 194.

queerness was less covert, less concealed than the Lavender Scare frame-work would lead us to expect, it may be helpful to begin to think about gay work as a *form of labor*. The sociologist C. Wright Mills admonished us long ago to stop talking about "this job" or "that job" and to start think-ing about work systemically.[24] Women's historians and labor historians—among others—have given us an account of women's labor, for example, that *is* systemic. From them, we know that at midcentury employment relations were structured around the family, and that the heterosexual family form was valuable to capital in two ways. First, women's unwaged work in the home was necessary to the task of social reproduction. Second, the heterosexual family was itself used as a form of labor control.[25] After all, working men increasingly surrendered labor militancy in exchange for a generous "family wage" that would support their wives and children. In making that bargain, employers shored up the power of male workers over wives in exchange for their submission on the shop floor.[26] The expansion of the family wage system, which was one of the hallmarks of the "Fordist regime" that characterized work from the end of the World War II into the 1970s, was expensive and cumbersome for employers, but, in a booming postwar economy, the stability it bought was worth the price.[27]

Once we recognize gay people as more of a presence than an absence in the workplace—and if we are thinking systemically about work—we

24. C. Wright Mills, *White Collar*, quoted in Weeks, *Problem with Work*, 1, 3.

25. The "heteropatriarchal nuclear family," Gabriel Winant has recently elaborated, "was mass production capitalism's instrument for obtaining and reproducing a stable workforce." Winant, *Next Shift*, 14. (Stable and compliant, I might emphasize.)

26. Women's relegation to the secondary labor market helped to construct "women's 'primary' commitment as devotion to home and family," such that the circumscribed roles of women in the labor market and women in the family were mutually reinforc-ing. Ruth Milkman, "'Redefining Women's Work': The Sexual Division of Labor in the Auto Industry during World War II," *Feminist Studies* 8 (Summer 1982): 338–40. On the "family wage" more generally, see Nancy MacLean, "Postwar Women's History: The 'Second Wave' or the End of the Family Wage," in *A Companion to Post-1945 America*, ed. Jean-Christopher Agnew and Roy Rosenzweig (Malden, MA: Blackwell, 2006), 235–59; Alice Kessler-Harris, *In Pursuit of Equity: Women, Men, and the Quest for Economic Citizenship in 20th Century America* (New York: Oxford University Press, 2001); Marissa Chappell, *The War on Welfare: Family, Poverty, and Politics in Modern America* (Phila-delphia: University of Pennsylvania Press, 2010), 5–15. The systemic thinking by feminist historians on women's work is indebted to earlier theorizing by socialist feminists, espe-cially those associated with the "dual systems" approach. See, for example, Heidi Hart-mann, "The Unhappy Marriage of Marxism and Feminism: Toward a More Progressive Union," *Capital and Class* 8 (1979): 1–34.

27. David Harvey, *The Conditions of Postmodernity: An Enquiry into the Origins of Cultural Change* (Malden, MA: Blackwell, 1990), 125–40; Jacob S. Hacker, *The Great Risk*

also have to ask about the *other* bargain at midcentury. How do we understand the bargain between many employers and gay workers to neither see nor be seen? It's obvious why this arrangement made sense for understandably apprehensive gay employees, but for employers? Why look the other way? The appeal of gay workers at midcentury, I argue, was that of a vulnerable labor force—*one whose consciousness was shaped by the specter of the government purges, and who commonly knew of other queer people who had lost jobs.* These workers could be underpaid relative to the level of skill and responsibility their jobs demanded, easily pushed out with downturns in the business cycle, and expected to quietly walk away when fired.[28] They would also stay in jobs where they felt safe, even when they were mistreated. These dynamics played out in many different kinds of employment, but especially in white-collar jobs and corporate offices. Across the straight work world, gay people also brought assets to their jobs that employers recognized and valued: They were contingent, easy to move, and both perceived and treated as unattached from family units. As a result, they potentially alleviated some of the pressure of the Fordist breadwinner model at a time when many labor arrangements were still expensive, cumbersome, and inflexible. In sum, they were harbingers of the "post-Fordist" transformation of work that was still several decades in the future. As long as gay employees were discreet and did not attract negative attention, then, there were many reasons for employers to avoid seeing what they didn't want to see.

Because queerness (in contrast to race) is "transversal to class"—meaning that queer people do not occupy a single class position but are distributed "throughout the class structure"—it is sometimes assumed that they have experienced cultural animus but not economic exploitation.[29] This study takes aim at this assumption, arguing, as one social theorist recently put it, that the "liabilities of homosexuals are hardwired into

---

Shift: The New Economic Insecurity and the Decline of the American Dream (New York: Oxford University Press, 2006); Linda McDowell, "Life without Father and Ford: The New Gender Order of Post-Fordism," *Transactions of the Institute of British Geographers* 16 (1991): 400–419. The idea of the family wage had its origins in the nineteenth century in the American context. See MacLean, "Postwar Women's History," 238.

28. "Hiding on the Job," *Gay Liberator*, October 1, 1971, 4.

29. According to Melinda Cooper, "Queerness is rather transversal to class, cutting across the stratification of race and gender." Melinda Cooper, *Family Values: Between Neoliberalism and the New Social Conservatism* (New York: Zone Books, 2017), 159; see also Judith Butler, "Merely Cultural," in *Adding Insult to Injury: Nancy Fraser Debates Her Critics*, ed. Kevin Olson (Brooklyn, NY: Verso, 2008), 49.

relations of production."[30] Those dynamics were explicitly called out by gay liberationists beginning in the early 1970s. "Our bosses know we're gay" but pretend not to notice, one liberationist tract explained. For that, "we are profoundly grateful, as we are *expected to be*." As a result, this writer lamented, gays performed work that others would not tolerate.[31] Other liberationists took aim specifically at the way the criminalization of sexual behavior and gender transgression outside of the workplace licensed queer vulnerability within it. Yet rules against homosexuality, another liberationist noted, did not prevent homosexuals from being hired, "nor were they intended to." What such prohibitions achieved was "to force the homosexual to be not only discreet about homosexuality but also relatively docile on the job."[32] We might of course critique the liberationists for their shared tendency to caricature the sinister boss; even at midcentury homophobia was not universal, and some employers likely did not care one way or another. Yet it is notable that even tolerant and understanding employers benefited from *the system* of gay labor the liberationist writers described. One employer, for example, noted that he had "interviewed many homosexuals," and hired some of them, "always on the basis of their abilities and my employment needs." While he expressed no conscious desire to benefit from their insecurity, he also observed that the gays he hired had worked "harder than most," which he surmised they did in order to overcome stigma and "prove their worth as individuals."[33]

Whatever the attitude of various employers toward their employees, the bargain that defined employment relations more broadly did begin to break down in the 1970s and 1980s, as some gay people heeded the liberationists' call to reject its terms. This development was enabled first by a terrible economy in which there was simply less to lose and then by a deadly epidemic that had the same effect. More and more, gay people yearned to be not only seen but also acknowledged. Outside the workplace, this occurred with alacrity as gay culture exploded across these decades. Inside the workplace, the pace of change was slower. This had something

30. This is actually Nancy Fraser's skeptical formulation of Judith Butler's position in their contentious (and wonderful) exchange. See Fraser, "Heterosexism, Misrecognition, and Capitalism: A Response to Judith Butler," in Olson, *Adding Insult to Injury*, 62.

31. Mike Silverstein, "The Gay Bureaucrat: What They Are Doing to You" (1971), in *Out of the Closets: Voices of Gay Liberation*, ed. Karla Jay and Allen Young (New York: New York University Press, 1992), 166.

32. "Hiding on the Job," 4.

33. Peter J. Myette, "Employing the Homosexual," 1972, "Sexual Minorities and Employment" folder, box 1, William J. Canfield Papers, University Archives and Special Collections, Northeastern University, Boston, MA.

to do, I argue, with the way that gay people were mostly left out of the civil rights achievements of these years. In contrast to other groups that suffered from discrimination on the job, queer workers gained no underlying blanket protection; in fact, no other minority group has had so little claim on formal legal protection.[34] Not only was there no equivalent to the 1964 Civil Rights Act for sexual minorities, but the local and state laws that did exist were often passed so quietly that people didn't always know about them, and even when they did, many gay employees were unwilling to invoke the law's protection in one place only to then find themselves exposed later in another locale.[35]

Yet, outside the regular mechanisms of civil rights laws, workplaces partially opened to gay workers, and clearer expressions of identity gradually became possible by the end of the twentieth century. How did that happen? One explanation has to do with the distinction between civil rights law and civil rights culture: the civil rights imaginary increasingly included gay people, in other words, even if civil rights laws did not. Both the African American freedom struggle and the women's liberation movement affected the rights consciousness of many gay people, changing their sense of what they were entitled to in the workplace. While this growing rights consciousness did not emerge alongside robust legal tools, and safeguarding by the state remained elusive, this study documents the responsiveness of business to demands that queer employees increasingly made for protection and recognition. While some might interpret this shift as a response to the discovery of gay consumers, that played only a minor role. Rather, I argue that business was out ahead of both the government and labor unions in protecting and otherwise demonstrating a receptivity

34. Gay experience, I argue, cannot simply be assimilated to other civil rights trajectories. The sociologist John Skrentny has usefully made this point as well. "The words 'homosexual' or 'gay' in the context of American politics connote both a minority-like status and yet a separation from other minorities," Skrentny wrote in 2002. "Gays therefore did not find strong advocates in the government, as did other groups, and the logic of client politics or anticipatory politics never extended to them." John D. Skrentny, *The Minority Rights Revolution* (Cambridge, MA: Harvard University Press, 2002), 315. Coalition with other civil rights groups was also not easily achieved. As late as 1994, the Leadership Council on Civil Rights would endorse the omnibus gay civil rights bill (the Employment Non-discrimination Act, ENDA) only tepidly, making clear that not all member organizations supported the legislation. See Chai R. Feldblum, "The Federal Gay Rights Bill: From Bella to ENDA," in *Creating Change: Sexuality, Public Policy, and Civil Rights*, ed. John D'Emilio, William B. Turner, and Urvashi Vaid (New York: St. Martin's, 2000), 179.

35. Norma M. Riccucci and Charles W. Gossett, "Employment Discrimination in State and Local Government: The Lesbian and Gay Male Experience," *American Review of Public Administration* 26 (1996): 175, 185.

to gay workers by the early to mid-1990s in part because of the apparent way that these employees were in sync with and even had prefigured the employment regime of late capitalism.

Just as Sven Beckert recently argued that the emergence of *industrial* capitalism was "built upon older social hierarchies" (in his case, patriarchal relations in the household), a similar claim might be made about the ways in which *postindustrialism* (or post-Fordism) was built in part on the economic position of queer people at midcentury.[36] Many attributes that later came to be associated with post-Fordism—short-term, precarious work arrangements that enabled employers to shed responsibility for family units—were the same ones that, going back as far as the 1950s, could also be identified with gay labor. One could of course make a similar argument about women and workers of color, but queer workers were even more predictive because of the way they represented precarity in primary- as well as secondary-sector jobs (the corporate office as well as the retail shop) and because of their perceived lack of dependents. To be clear, I do not claim that queer people were *more* precarious than women and people of color, and many were positioned at the intersection of these identities. The point is rather to highlight the ways that gay workers offered capital a midcentury lesson in structuring employment relations without regard to family attachment—even in primary-sector jobs for which the breadwinner/caregiver model was paradigmatic—and, relatedly, to note that queer people were among the first precarious workers *across* the class spectrum, for example, in middle-class jobs dominated by white men.[37] In secondary-sector employment long associated with contingent and fragile jobs for women, people of color, and immigrant workers, we should only notice that queer people were also present there among the precarious.[38]

---

36. Sven Beckert, *Empire of Cotton: A Global History* (New York, Vintage, 2014), 188.

37. Queer workers then preview the precarity that did not really hit many white-collar workers until the 1980s and 1990s. The sociologist Erin Hatton has made a distinctive though parallel argument that by the 1970s temporary agencies had begun to introduce ideas of contingency into primary-sector employment, including in "breadwinner jobs." I don't disagree with Hatton but see gay employment as a precursor even to the development she was describing (and also note how many queers at midcentury were working as temps). See Erin Hatton, *The Temp Economy: From Kelly Girls to Permatemps in Postwar America* (Philadelphia: Temple University Press, 2011).

38. Earlier examples of structuring employment relations without regard to family attachment involved immigrant labor, although not in primary-sector employment. I further explore the analogy between immigrant and queer labor in chapter 2.

My aim here is to integrate sexuality into the history of capitalism, as well as into labor history, picking up the conversation that John D'Emilio began in 1983 when he published "Capitalism and Gay Identity."[39] Capitalism seemed to produce, following D'Emilio, gay identity and, in a fascinating double move, the eventual means to exploit that identity. I also hope to help nudge the prevailing narrative of postwar US history from its focus on consumption and affluence toward production (i.e., the workplace) and precarity. But, more than anything else, this book is a continuation of my earlier work *The Straight State*, which told the story of the government's policing of homosexuality over the first half of the twentieth century.[40] That I see these two projects as linked is itself an evolution in my thinking; for quite a while, I saw them as totally distinct. If my first book was "bringing the state back in," I initially thought that this project was "pushing the state back out." It was to be a shift, in other words, from the state to the market. Some years later, I realized I was wrong about this, and how conceptually intertwined these two books are. I now see the relationship between *The Straight State* and *Queer Career* as a diptych or even as a series. From a temporal standpoint, *The Straight State* mostly covers the first half of the twentieth century, and *Queer Career* addresses the second. The two works complement each other as well, in that the first book is about the state discovering queer people and writing anti-homosexualism into the architecture of the law, while this book is about capital taking advantage of that aggressive state policing.[41] *It is about the systematic exploitation of state-created legal vulnerabilities*. And, to the extent the market is shot through by the state, this book is actually *still* a history of the straight state, but in a new period of state formation that is more characterized by the hallmarks of neoliberalism.[42]

---

39. A recent book that integrates the history of sexuality and the history of capitalism, but focuses on consumption rather than work, is David K. Johnson, *Buying Gay: How Physique Entrepreneurs Sparked a Movement* (New York: Columbia University Press, 2019).

40. Margot Canaday, *The Straight State: Sexuality and Citizenship in Twentieth-Century America* (Princeton, NJ: Princeton University Press, 2009).

41. Because my first book was focused on national citizenship, I was also focused on federal policy (and policing). As I elaborate in the chapters that follow, in the employment context, state and local policing also matters.

42. Relevant here is the sociologist Erin Hatton's identification of "status coercion," "found anywhere an employer has power over the workers' social position," as a "new mechanism by which the state has expanded its punitive power in the context of neoliberalism." Erin Hatton, *Coerced: Work under the Threat of Punishment* (Berkeley: University of California Press, 2020), 16, 20. On the history of neoliberalism more generally, see Gary Gerstle, *The Rise and Fall of the Neoliberal Order* (New York: Oxford University Press, 2022).

Yet, there are ways that *Queer Career* is not just a sequel but also a revision of my earlier work, as the topic of the workplace enables me to probe some aspects of the history of sexuality that my first book did not. One of the issues with writing about state regulation that I did not realize when I began that project is that when the state policed queerness, it was almost always targeting men. So, despite my own deep commitments as a feminist historian, *The Straight State* was predominantly focused on male experience. This problem plagues the history of sexuality more generally, because it relies so heavily on the archival traces left by state policing, even when historians look at leisure and nightlife.[43] When I began to conceptualize this book, I thought much more deliberately about sites from which to write a queer history that would *not* marginalize women. It soon became obvious to me that the workplace was such a site. After all, lesbian breadwinners needed better, higher-paying jobs than married women to survive economically, and they sometimes "violated gender norms" to obtain them.[44] By

43. Margot Canaday, "LGBT History," *Frontiers* 35 (2014): 11–19. This essay is part of a forum on the twenty-fifth anniversary of John D'Emilio and Estelle Freedman's foundational text *Intimate Matters: The History of Sexuality in America* (New York: Harper and Row, 1988). Two recent exceptions to the dearth of work on lesbians are Lauren Gutterman, *Her Neighbor's Wife: A History of Lesbian Desire within Marriage* (Philadelphia: University of Pennsylvania Press, 2019); and Susan S. Lanser, *The Sexuality of History: Modernity and the Sapphic 1565–1830* (Chicago: University of Chicago Press, 2014). Older, classic works on lesbian history include Carroll Smith-Rosenberg, "The Female World of Love and Ritual: Relations between Women in Nineteenth-Century America," *Signs* 1 (Autumn 1975): 1–29; Blanche Weisen Cook, "The Historical Denial of Lesbianism," *Radical History Review* 20 (Spring 1979): 60–65; Lillian Faderman, *Odd Girls and Twilight Lovers: A History of Lesbian Life in Twentieth-Century America* (New York: Columbia University Press, 1991); Elizabeth Lapovsky Kennedy and Madeline D. Davis, *Boots of Leather, Slippers of Gold: The History of a Lesbian Community* (New York: Penguin Books, 1993); Estelle Freedman, *Maternal Justice: Miriam van Waters and the Female Reform Tradition* (Chicago: University of Chicago Press, 1996). See also Lisa Duggan, *Sapphic Slashers: Sex, Violence, and American Modernity* (Durham, NC: Duke University Press, 2000); Martha Vicinus, *Intimate Friends: Women Who Loved Women, 1778–1928* (Chicago: University of Chicago Press, 2004); Marcia Gallo, *Different Daughters: A History of the Daughters of Bilitis and the Rise of the Lesbian Rights Movement* (New York: Carroll and Graf, 2006).

44. M. V. Lee Badgett and Mary C. King, "Lesbian and Gay Occupational Strategies," in *Homo Economics: Capitalism, Community, and Lesbian and Gay Life*, ed. Amy Gluckman and Betsy Reed (New York: Routledge, 1997), 78. "Lesbians had a higher stake than heterosexual married women in accessing well-paid jobs, since lesbians did not have access to 'family wages' through husbands," the economist Julie Matthaei elaborated. "Furthermore, lesbians had already crossed gender lines in other ways . . . and were less fearful of losing their 'womanhood' and attractiveness to men if they took on 'men's jobs' than were heterosexual women." Matthaei, "The Sexual Division of Labor, Sexuality, and Lesbian/Gay Liberation: Toward a Marxist-Feminist Analysis of Sexuality in U.S. Capitalism," in Gluckman and Reed, *Homo Economics*, 155.

necessity, as one team of sociologists concluded in the 1960s, lesbians were "seriously committed to work."[45]

At the same time that I have set out here to write a history of gays and lesbians in the postwar workplace that does not subordinate female to male experience, I also have aspired to write about *people* in a different register than I did in my first book. Yes, there are people in *The Straight State*, but I was interested in them only insofar as they were caught in the apparatus of state policing. When my colleague Dirk Hartog read a draft of that manuscript, he said I talked about the people in the book and told their stories in a very cold way. I recognized the truth of this charge but ultimately decided there was little I could do about it. After all, the book was fundamentally about bureaucracy, which is impersonal by its nature. But I have not been similarly hampered in *Queer Career*; so I have engaged with a more human side of the practice of history, determined to produce scholarship that "feels" as much as it "thinks."

More than anything else, conducting oral histories has enabled me to better elucidate the human side of this story, to explore work as a "sort of life," rather than what Studs Terkel so memorably called a "Monday through Friday sort of dying."[46] I'm aware, however, that historians sometimes greet oral histories with a degree of skepticism, even when that skepticism comes with the disclaimer that written sources are also biased and need to be read critically.[47] So I should explain how I did my oral histories and identify what they add to this study: The 156 interviews I conducted as part of this research fall into two subgroups. Roughly one-third of them were carried out with individuals who emerged as actors in the story as I did archival research, who were interviewed specifically about their roles in one of the episodes the book takes up. For example, I interviewed many nurses who helped staff the first designated AIDS ward in the country, as well as the individuals who pushed AT&T to recognize the country's first gay and lesbian employee resource group. When I cite interviews with those individuals, they are identified by name. A larger group of interviews—just over one hundred—was conducted as part of what I think of as a "cohort study" of individuals born mostly during the 1930s

45. William Simon and John H. Gagnon, "The Lesbians: A Preliminary Overview," in *Sexual Deviance*, ed. Simon and Gagnon (New York: Harper and Row, 1967), 270.

46. Studs Terkel, *Working: People Talk about What They Do All Day and How They Feel about What They Do* (New York: New Press, 1972), xi.

47. There is a huge literature on the promise and also the pitfalls of working with oral history. I find especially illuminating many of the essays in Robert Perks and Alistair Thompson, eds., *The Oral History Reader* (New York: Routledge, 1998).

and 1940s, whom I spoke to about their working lives. I made anonymity a default condition of the second group; some informants preferred that, and some didn't care, but I treat this cluster of interviews uniformly.[48] Because of the age of many informants, I conducted the vast majority of these interviews in person in urban centers around the country—I did clusters of interviews in Washington, DC; New York; Atlanta; Lansing; Detroit; Houston; Ft. Lauderdale; Boston; Cambridge, Massachusetts; Buffalo; and the Bay Area. I also did telephone, and eventually Skype or Zoom, interviews with many individuals in smaller towns and cities as well.

I found interview subjects in a variety of ways and took care that they represented a wide range of socioeconomic positions. At one end of the spectrum, I took advantage of a year in residence at the Radcliffe Institute in Cambridge, Massachusetts, to use Harvard's large gay alumni network to find potential informants. At the other end of the spectrum, the social service agency Services and Advocacy for LGBT Elders (SAGE) allowed me to attend their $2 drop-in dinners in midtown Manhattan as well as their events in Harlem to talk about my research and find interview subjects.[49] SAGE DC and SAGE Atlanta also helped me find informants. I placed an ad in the lesbian feminist periodical *Lesbian Connection*— still, as in the 1970s, arriving in a plain brown wrapper and "free to all lesbians"—to find women who had used that publication to go "back to the land" in the 1970s and ended up in Oregon, Arkansas, and elsewhere. Once I had identified an interview subject, I relied on snowball sampling to find a larger network, whether of blue-collar lesbians in Houston, gay autoworkers in Detroit, or lesbian deans of social work who vacationed on Cape Cod. I was cognizant too that it was important to record the experiences of those who might be reluctant to speak to me, as I surmised they might have had a different trajectory through the workplace than, for example, a liberationist would have had. At SAGE dinners, I paid as much attention to those who did not approach me as those who did. One elderly woman, for example, told me she would consent to an interview only if I could introduce her to MSNBC host Rachel Maddow! I never produced Maddow, but after several entreaties, she finally allowed me to interview her. Throughout the project, I struggled to identify LGBT people of color in the right age range who were willing to be interviewed.

48. I have sorted anonymous interviews by location and then assigned a numeric code to each; I identify the interviewee by number, with year, and with city unless the interview was conducted via telephone, Skype, or Zoom, in which case that is noted.

49. SAGE was founded in 1978. Originally, the acronym stood for Senior Action in a Gay Environment.

Roughly 10 percent of my interviews are with informants of color, mostly African Americans. I have supplemented my own interviews with research in other oral history collections and archival sources to draw some meaningful conclusions about how race matters in the working lives I recount here.[50] Interviews with transgender subjects in this age range were more difficult to arrange; I interviewed five trans women and two trans men in this age cohort. These conversations were fascinating, but the picture that emerges from them is hardly definitive. The greatest lacunae in my collection of oral histories, however, are the voices of the generation that succumbed to AIDS. So many times in the course of my research, I went in search of contact information only to find an obituary.

For the interviews that I was able to arrange, conversations typically lasted around two hours each. I began by simply asking people to narrate their work histories, first situating themselves by telling me the year they were born, where they grew up, and the work their parents did. Then I asked them to tell me about their educational and work backgrounds, most often beginning with graduation from high school. In addition, I usually asked several more pointed follow-up questions: How had they handled sexuality at work? How had they connected to a gay world, and did their employment have any bearing on how they did so? If an individual experienced harms in the workplace as a result of being gay, what were they? What positive consequences, if any, had they experienced? I asked what occupations informants would have identified as substantially closed to them as gay people, and what occupations seemed especially open. I inquired what they remembered observing about other gay people in their workplaces. For men who married, I asked if they viewed their marriages as connected in any way to career ambition. For women who married, I asked about the material difficulties of leaving the marriage. I asked about involvement with labor unions and professional associations. Among many other questions, I asked about memories of the AIDS epidemic as it first appeared on the work site.

As the historian Michael Frisch has pointed out, oral histories tend to produce such an overwhelmingly intuitive response that the specific value of oral histories can be obscured.[51] The value of this methodology for this study is multifaceted but easy enough to articulate. In analyzing the interviews, I am especially interested in aggregate patterns across

50. For example, the Rochella Thorpe Oral History Project Files, 1992–95, Collection 7607, Rare and Manuscript Collections, Cornell University, Ithaca, NY.

51. Michael Frisch, "Oral History and *Hard Times*: A Review Essay," in Perks and Thompson, *Oral History Reader*, 32.

many working lives, as well as "a cross section of the subjectivity of the group."[52] And, in contrast to historians who use oral histories primarily to fill a vacuum in archival evidence, I often read these oral histories against or in tandem with archival evidence.[53] That not only validates people's memories about events that happened a long time ago, but it also corrects either the archival record, or more likely, my own faulty reading of it. The triangulation of archival and oral history sources, in other words, can enhance the interpretation of both types of material.

Of course, these interviews are valuable for many other reasons as well. They helped me to construct a national history, even if the fact that so many gay people were migratory during this period nonetheless leads to a kind of hazy sense of place. Interviews support the notion that the very sharp divide we now imagine between socially conservative "red states" and socially liberal "blue states" is, in some ways, a fairly recent development. Into the 1970s and 1980s, queer people faced a surprising amount of discrimination in big cities like San Francisco and New York, which are often perceived as safe havens. Indeed, I even heard some informants opine that southern cities could be safer for gay people in the 1950s and 1960s because there wasn't enough of a critical mass there and police weren't really very interested in them, in sharp contrast to places like New York.[54]

The very life course of this cohort is also important in that it maps onto the narrative arc of the book itself. My informants entered the labor market during the years of the Lavender Scare (or "the bargain," as I define the same era); they worked through the liberation and AIDS eras and retired just as diversity was becoming a stated value in industry. Their working lives tell us a lot about the labor regimes they experienced over time. Members of this cohort entered the labor force during the years when

52. Alessandro Portelli, "What Makes Oral History Different," in Perks and Thompson, *Oral History Reader*, 67. I also like Portelli's formulation that subjectivity is, in his words, "the business of history."

53. Ana Raquel Minian's inspiring interviews with undocumented immigrants come much closer to filling a significant void in archival sources. "Migrants' experiences made it hard for them to preserve documents," she has observed. "When crossing the border illegally, they carried as little as possible; once in the United States, they relocated often and left many of their documents behind." Minian, *Undocumented Lives*, 239. Natalia Molina turned to oral histories for a similar reason in crafting her portrait of the Mexican immigrants who worked in her grandmother's restaurant in Echo Park in Los Angeles. "This is a book about a place and a people that have no archives—what I call the 'underdocumented.'" Molina, *Place at the Nayarit*, xiii.

54. Interview subject 74, interview conducted via telephone, 2013. See also John Howard, *Men Like That: A Southern Queer History* (Chicago: University of Chicago Press, 2001).

high productivity was coupled to the relatively high wages that fueled mass consumption, when unions were powerful, and when many workers experienced fairly stable employment. This cohort was for the most part still employed *after* 1975, when deindustrialization decimated manufacturing, the service sector burgeoned, and unions were undermined, while real wages fell and standard terms of employment declined. "Individuals last longer than do the social structures of the work world," the sociologist Andrew Abbott has observed, "so it is to individuals, by themselves and as a cohort . . . that we must look for the deep historicality of the world of work."[55]

Above all, the distinctive value of oral history sources may lie in their orality. The fullness of this—to my ear, the wonderful way many queer people *sound*—tends to be lost when it moves to the written page, but not all of it.[56] The intonation imparts subtleties of meaning that become part of the interpretation. So, for example, one of my informants, an African American man, was remembering his early working years and remarked: "I was a typist, and I wanted to type." Except he didn't just state this; he joyfully exclaimed it: *"I was a typist,"* his voice rose, *"and I wanted to type!"*[57] And the exuberant, almost breathless, proclamation that I heard in this man's voice—*"I was a typist, and I wanted to type!"*— helps me to formulate an argument about the complexity of "queer jobs" that were low in pay and status but also sometimes affirmed a queer identity in a way that made them simultaneously exploitative and rewarding. So what we hear in a speaker's voice can guide us toward more nuanced readings of the past, leading us, for example, toward an understanding of the workplace as a site where queer people experienced not only great vulnerability but also the deepest kind of meaning.

———◆———

What I hope this book offers then is threefold: a persuasive historical account of gay workers across changing employment regimes in the postwar United States; embedded within that account, a "thick description" of the long history of queer precariousness at work; and finally, an *affective* labor history. Regarding the last of these, as British historians especially

55. Abbott, "Sociology of Work and Occupations," 311–12.

56. Don Kulick, "Gay and Lesbian Language," *Annual Review of Anthropology* 29 (2000): 243–85; Michael Schulman, "Is There a Gay Voice?," *New Yorker*, July 10, 2015, https://www.newyorker.com/culture/culture-desk/is-there-a-gay-voice.

57. Interview subject 16, New York, NY, 2012 (emphasis mine).

have emphasized, work was "a deeply emotional experience."[58] Of course, some of the feelings I have needed to sort out in writing this book belong not to my informants but to me, and the many career narratives I've recorded over the past ten years have led me to reflect much more deeply on my own work history, and to consider both its dissonances and its resonances with the working lives of the historical subjects of this book.[59] I do not remember thinking, as many of my informants several decades older did, that being gay meant that I could not *become anything*. What I do remember was the belief that what was most consequential to me even as a college student—understanding queer lives past and present—was not academically serious. I ended up choosing American studies as my major at the University of Iowa simply because it enabled me to supplement a "rigorous" track of conventional political science and history courses with more personally meaningful ones in feminist and queer studies. Although these courses were technically all part of a single major, in my mind the two tracks represented a completely bifurcated course of study. Because I didn't view the subjects that resonated with me most deeply as leading toward an academic career, I certainly didn't see myself as headed for graduate school, nor did I take the necessary steps to prepare myself for that possibility. Still, I was as academically focused as you could be without any real sense of direction, and a conversation I had during my senior year with one of my professors about the inroads feminist scholars had made in the discipline of history stayed with me.[60]

58. Arthur McIvor, *Working Lives: Work in Britain since 1945* (Hampshire, UK: Palgrave Macmillan, 2013), 75. As the historian Clare Langhamer has observed: "Thinking more broadly about feelings at work allows us to explore the ways in which social relations underpin relations of production, to take a category of cultural history and engage with it in social and economic terms." Langhamer, "Feeling, Women, and Work in the Long 1950s," *Women's History Review* 26 (2017): 79. On the "deeply human character of economic life," see also Emma Griffin, *Bread Winner: An Intimate History of the Victorian Economy* (New Haven, CT: Yale University Press, 2020), 23.

59. On autobiography and history, see the introduction to Lizabeth Cohen, *A Consumers' Republic: The Politics of Mass Consumption in Postwar America* (New York: Alfred A. Knopf, 2003), 5–7; David R. Roediger, *The Wages of Whiteness: Race and the Making of the American Working Class* (London: Verso, 1991), 3–5; Susan Porter Benson, *Household Accounts: Working-Class Family Economies in the Interwar United States* (Ithaca, NY: Cornell University Press, 2007), 2–6. More recently and more expansively, see Susan Lee Johnson, *Writing Kit Carson: Fallen Heroes in a Changing West* (Chapel Hill: University of North Carolina Press, 2020).

60. That professor was the political scientist Sally J. Kenny. I was fortunate too that both Sally Kenney and the historian of Mexico Charles Hale thought to pull me aside and tell me I should think about graduate school. In large state schools especially, those

As significant was what happened on the path I took every day from my apartment to the main campus, and the shortcut I discovered that took me through the law school. In the stairwell of the law school one day I met my partner, Rachel, who was trying to create a group for gay law students, but no one (in the early 1990s) would join. She berated me for not signing up for her group, I explained that I was not a law student, and somehow we ended up shooting pool in a bar. When she graduated from law school, she returned home to San Francisco to sit for the California bar and begin working, and I followed her there after I completed my degree. Because the economy was in a deep recession, I could not find a job, even in a coffee shop. I ended up doing an unpaid internship with the San Francisco Commission on the Status of Women, mostly tracking legislation in Sacramento. But we couldn't afford to live there on Rachel's meager salary in a plaintiffs' civil rights firm, and our credit card debt was mounting with each passing month. I was also reading feminist history in my free time, and after about a year, I saw a path to graduate school that made sense to me.

I did enough investigation to decide that the University of Wisconsin was the perfect program given my interests, but not enough investigation to realize that establishing residency is not something graduate students generally need to do. I asked Rachel to leave her job and move to Madison with me so that I would be a Wisconsin resident in anticipation of eventually attending graduate school. She reluctantly agreed, and I assured her she would love Madison. It was not helpful that almost the first thing that happened when we arrived was being denied an apartment we really wanted to rent because, as the landlord said to us, "our lifestyle grieved God's heart." We recovered; Rachel began to study for the Wisconsin bar exam, and I looked for work. I hoped to get a job with the State of Wisconsin and began to take civil service exams, but recognizing that getting a state job would take some time, I immediately signed up with a temp agency as a "Kelly Girl."

My first assignment was doing reception and clerical work at a small insurance company in a suburb a few minutes outside of Madison. After about a week, the office manager asked me if I would like to be considered for a permanent job. A permanent job meant not sharing my paycheck with Kelly Services while I waited for a civil service position to come through, so I agreed to bring in a current resume the next day. I don't

---

conversations are so important, and I am still grateful to both of them for their generosity and kindness.

know why it didn't occur to me to "de-gay" that resume, but I didn't erase my year in San Francisco, omit my internship with the Commission on the Status of Women, or change the names of the gay organizations I had been active with during college. I just handed the unedited version over to my prospective employers the next morning. From my perch at the front desk, I thought I saw the office manager show my resume to the head of the company, and I worried that their conversation seemed to last much too long. When I got home that night, I received a call from my contact at Kelly Services, who told me the insurance company had abruptly terminated my contract with them. I was instructed not to report to work the following morning.

One might think that with temporary work, it's easy come and easy go, but I slumped down on the couch as soon as I got off the phone and began to cry. "What if I am actually unemployable?" I remember saying out loud. Rachel, who is twelve years my senior, assured me that I *was* employable, adding that one day I would laugh about this experience. I soon had another assignment from Kelly Services—but this time I was driving an hour from Madison to work in a cramped, windowless office providing support for a mean and incompetent man who was working on a development campaign for a small-town hospital. Even in the world of temporary work, this was a *bad* assignment. But I stuck it out until I got a call to interview for a position with the state. The job was working in the Personnel Division of the Wisconsin Department of Corrections, investigating discrimination and harassment complaints made by correctional and probation and parole officers. I immediately called the person at the San Francisco Commission on the Status of Women who handled complaint investigations for the city. She carefully explained their procedures to me, and at the interview I sounded like I knew what I was doing. I was offered a position.

I learned a lot in that job; it was challenging and occasionally even rewarding. But it was also truly depressing to spend so much time inside Wisconsin prisons, and while the Personnel Division was predictably full of gay people, no one said it out loud, so days spent in the central office were somewhat depressing too. Perhaps because by this point I imagined myself eventually going to graduate school, I was "out" in the sense that I talked about Rachel freely. I also wore Doc Martens shoes to work on Fridays, which I think my straight coworkers had even more trouble getting used to, but it was my compensation for feeling like I had to wear a skirt whenever I went into a prison to conduct an investigation. This was what "dressed up" and "professional" meant in Wisconsin in the early 1990s, and it was probably the most alienating aspect of the job for me.

In a huge state agency of around five thousand people, I did not imagine that important people in the central office would have noticed me in my Friday Doc Martens, offering chipper reports from my ground-floor cubicle on weekend outings with Rachel.[61] That was naive—a fact I realized only after Rachel and I registered as domestic partners with the City of Madison. This was a relatively recent innovation, and a Milwaukee newspaper called to ask if they could feature us in a story about Madison's domestic partner ordinance. We were thrilled and happily complied. After the story ran, with several large photographs of us, then state (and now US) senator Tammy Baldwin called Rachel at her office to thank her for being visible. I didn't expect that anyone at my job would even see the story, and initially that seemed to be the case. Some days later—maybe a week?—I was finishing a report on an investigation concerning a probation and parole officer. My boss reviewed it and asked if I would run it up to the director of probation and parole. I had never met this high-ranking official, nor ventured anywhere near his office on one of the top floors of the building. He was away, and so was his secretary, so I walked into his office, intending to place the document on his chair. It was then that I saw that the *only* thing on the director's desk was the clipping of the story from the Milwaukee newspaper featuring Rachel and me.

This discovery was chilling. Because it was days after the story had run, it didn't seem like the clipping had just casually landed on this man's desk. But what did it mean? Had the article been passed around among the agency's leadership? Sent to the head of probation and parole by the Milwaukee office? I never found out, but in retrospect I don't think I was ever in danger of losing my job. Wisconsin was one of the only states in the nation at that time that had a gay rights law, although it's relevant to the story that unfolds in the coming chapters that I don't think I knew about that law at the time.[62] If I had stayed, though, I believe my career options would have been circumscribed and advancement would have been more difficult. My openness as a lesbian was, of course, only part of the difficulty. Around the same time, I started walking home from work with a friendly young man who had been hired at the same time as I had with a very similar background. His job was less demanding than mine, but as he casually let slip one night on our way home, he was making a lot more money than I was.

61. The total number of Wisconsin Department of Corrections employees in 1995–96 was 5,413. Lawrence S. Barish, ed., *State of Wisconsin 1995–1996 Blue Book* (Madison, WI: State Legislative Reference Bureau, 1995–96), 401.

62. State and local civil rights laws tend to underprotect in general. Nan D. Hunter, "Sexuality and Civil Rights: Re-imagining Anti-discrimination Laws," *New York Law School Journal of Human Rights* 17 (2000): 572–73.

Lesbians are never just gay people in their jobs; we are also always women as well. That was it for me at the Department of Corrections.

So I applied to graduate school in history at the University of Wisconsin, and to six or seven other schools just in case. My lack of clear direction as an undergraduate dogged my application process, and only the University of Minnesota admitted me. As a graduate student, the main quandary of my undergraduate years—whether my academic work could fit with an interest in queer life—was one I bracketed. I didn't even consider studying the history of sexuality during the first several years I was in graduate school. By then I had plenty of models of brilliant scholarship in that field: for example, I read George Chauncey's book *Gay New York* in my second quarter at Minnesota. So the question was no longer whether queer history could be serious intellectual work. It obviously could! But my antenna was already up about professional issues, and I ascertained that doing a dissertation in the history of sexuality might be a risky move in terms of my future employment.

I was trained at Minnesota in the history of women and gender— training that is foundational for me, but in a subfield that had already established its legitimacy in the academy. As I began to look about for a dissertation topic, I found myself intrigued by the histories of gender and citizenship that were being produced in the late 1990s and early 2000s by some of the top scholars in the field. Their work was inspiring, but also intimidating. What was left for me to say? I floundered for a distressingly long time without finding my own project. Then I read Linda Kerber's magisterial study of gender and citizenship *No Constitutional Right to Be Ladies*. The last chapter of that book is about the gendered obligation of military service, and in that context Kerber wrote just a couple of sentences about the paradoxes of gay and lesbian citizenship.[63] As I read that passage, I immediately sensed that I had found a dissertation topic, and I felt the personal pull of a project that gathered in one place the overriding intellectual concerns about both sexuality and politics that had been with me since college but had until then seemed unassimilable. But I still had to get over my fear of doing a project like this, and that fear kept me even longer from committing. I ultimately decided that a risky dissertation was better than no dissertation, which seemed to be where I was otherwise headed, and I finally got started.

There were a few other bumps along the way. When faculty at Minnesota nominated me for a fellowship from the graduate school, for

63. Linda K. Kerber, *No Constitutional Right to Be Ladies: Women and the Obligations of Citizenship* (New York: Hill and Wang, 1998), 300.

example, the History Department's director of graduate studies wrote in his letter of nomination that projects "as political" as mine *were not good history*.[64] After the first campus interview I had, the chair of the search committee called one of my advisers to tell her that I had done well but that no job offer would be forthcoming. The department interviewing me, she explained, thought that I was "a Martian." A Martian? The call was well intentioned, but I remember wondering then if I had made a huge mistake, and if I was, again, simply unemployable. I'm certain the fact that my project engaged the history of the state helped me feel a bit safer; in some sense, it was my own form of covering. I leaned into that even harder when I went back out on the job market the following year, and that probably helped condition the positive response I eventually got. So did changing times. I was incredibly lucky to finish my dissertation just after the Supreme Court struck down sodomy laws in the *Lawrence v. Texas* decision and as states began to legalize gay marriage. It was crystal clear at that moment that LGBT issues were matters of national concern, not trivial or strange. Hiring committees broadened their outlook. There were only a few years between that shift and the financial crisis of 2008, which precipitated the collapse of the academic hiring market, especially in humanities disciplines like history.[65] But I was fortunate to be on the market during that short, hopeful window, and I was lucky to get a very good job with colleagues who have always recognized me as a person and valued my scholarship. In my academic life, in fact, I ultimately got what I couldn't seem to figure out how to have as a younger person. I was able to be integrated, a whole person, and to "follow the principle," as the European intellectual historian Paul Robinson opined, "that you should write about things that really matter to you."[66] I could go to work without, as gay liberationists had once lamented, *always having "a piece missing."*[67]

64. I learned of this letter only when the subsequent director of graduate studies called me in to show it to me because she felt I should know it was in my file (emphasis mine).

65. Benjamin Schmidt, "The Humanities Are in Crisis," *Atlantic*, August 23, 2018, https://www.theatlantic.com/ideas/archive/2018/08/the-humanities-face-a-crisisof-confidence/567565/.

66. Paul Robinson, "Becoming a Gay Historian," in *Becoming Historians*, ed. James M. Banner Jr. and John R. Gillis (Chicago: University of Chicago Press, 2009), 250. On career narratives of lesbian and gay academics more generally, see Toni McNaron, "Poisoned Ivy: Lesbian and Gay Academics from the 1960s through the 1990s," in *Feminist Generations: Life Stories from the Academy*, ed. Hokulani K. Aikau, Karla A. Erickson, and Jennifer L. Pierce (Minneapolis: University of Minnesota Press, 2007), 67–86.

67. Transcript, folder 14, box 83, Barbara Gittings Papers, Manuscripts and Archives Division, New York Public Library, New York, NY (emphasis mine).

———

This is not a particularly dramatic career narrative, especially in contrast to some of the stories I heard from my informants about their experiences in prior decades. I think I am probably fairly typical of my age cohort, and also fairly typical of LGBT academics more generally, for whom, as the pioneering anthropologist Esther Newton put it, "scholarly and personal coherence" has been and sometimes still can be a particular hurdle.[68] But I write this here partly because it's been on my mind all the years I've been working on this project, and perhaps also to make myself vulnerable after so many informants have made themselves vulnerable in front of me. Above all, in the context of professional norms that still evidence some discomfort about or distrust of the "private reasons" we are drawn to an area of study, I want to be clear that *Queer Career* is, for me, a deeply personal book.[69] I don't think that fact compromises my ability to ask good historical questions or to interpret evidence carefully, but ultimately readers will decide for themselves.

There are a few other aspects of this study that the reader needs to know about in order to proceed. The first is some explanation of language and scope. Anyone who works in this subfield knows that in some way, the words we employ will always fail us. I mostly use "gay," "lesbian," or sometimes "queer" to describe the subjects of this book. These words were used throughout the period I am writing about, although I am aware that "queer" is for some of my subjects a painful word that calls up memories of childhood taunts. The fact that the word was reclaimed by a younger generation and even deemed "subversive" has not fully removed its sting. I use it because it is the one historically accurate referent that applies equally to men and women and captures both the same-sex eroticism and the gender nonconformity that are entwined in many (but not all) of the working lives I try to capture here.[70]

I do not use "LGBT" until the discussion of the very late twentieth century, when that acronym came into general usage. I should be clear as well that transgender experience is only lightly treated in this book. That was not my intention when I began, but I struggled to find enough

68. Esther Newton, *My Butch Career: A Memoir* (Durham, NC: Duke University Press, 2018), 17.

69. Ibid., 114.

70. Siobhan B. Somerville, "Queer," in *Keywords for American Cultural Studies*, 2nd ed., ed. Bruce Burgett and Glenn Hendler (New York: New York University Press, 2014), 203–7.

material to adequately depict this historical experience in relation to the workplace. Yet, while trans men and women populate this study somewhat sparsely, my thinking about gender normativity is deeply indebted to academic trans studies. Moreover, I emphasize transgender work experiences in the epilogue with the hope that future historians may be able to treat this subject more comprehensively than I have here.[71]

Next, a "roadmap" for the reader: The book is divided into three parts, each with two chapters. Part 1 is entitled "Gay Labor" and offers an ethnography of gay and lesbian employment in both the "straight" (chapter 1) and the "queer" (chapter 2) work worlds during the early 1950s and 1960s. The bargain of discretion and obliviousness that I have already described as hegemonic for straight jobs did not apply in the low-wage, low-status jobs that often affirmed gay people's identity in the queer work world, but the boundary between those two realms was quite porous. That permeability mattered: fear of being relegated to the queer work world secured the vulnerability of gay workers in the straight world, making them desirable employees for those employers willing to close their eyes to what may have been in front of them.

Part 2, "Law and Liberation," examines the 1970s as a fulcrum of change when the bargain of midcentury began to break down. The most significant legal reform for gay employment rights in the twentieth century was the lifting of the ban on gay civil servants in 1975, which in many ways ended the vestiges of the Lavender Scare. That reform, explored in chapter 3, was largely the result of a sustained fight by a government astronomer who was fired from his job in the mid-1950s, refused to go quietly, and then devoted his life to this legal battle. The policy change Frank Kameny eventually won, as he himself recognized, was not as monumental as it is sometimes represented to be, partly because of the continuing use of security clearances against gay people, and even more so because the vast majority of Americans worked in the private sector during these years.

---

71. Contemporary accounts do exist, such as sociologist Kristen Schilt's study *Just One of the Guys? Transgender Men and the Persistence of Gender Inequality* (Chicago: University of Chicago Press, 2010); Anne Balay, *Semi Queer: Inside the World of Gay, Trans, and Black Truckers* (Chapel Hill: University of North Carolina Press, 2018); Michelle Esther O'Brien, "Trans Work: Employment Trajectories, Labour Discipline and Gender Freedom," in *Transgender Marxism*, ed. Jules Joanne Gleeson and Elle O'Rourke (London: Pluto, 2021). There is also a rich historical literature on nineteenth-century cross-dressing and its relationship to wage work. Exemplary is Claire Sears, *Arresting Dress: Cross-Dressing, Law, and Fascination in Nineteenth-Century San Francisco* (Durham, NC: Duke University Press, 2015). See also Emily Skidmore, *True Sex: The Lives of Trans Men at the Turn of the 20th Century* (New York: New York University Press, 2017).

Still, Kameny's sustained activism created ripples that helped set the stage for the politics of liberation. Chapter 4 considers the liberationist period outside of government employment, when the emancipatory impulse went beyond individual declarations on the job, however risky, to collective projects to remake the workplace as well. Across the decade, employers responded to gay people's sudden yearning to be seen with bewilderment, and the smattering of municipal ordinances that were passed by liberationists and their allies by the late 1970s did little in practice to guard against growing employer animus. Historians have focused more on the freeing aspect of these years rather than their overall precariousness, but these elements were inextricably intertwined.

Part 3, "Civil Rights in a Neoliberal Age," concerns the 1980s and 1990s. The AIDS era ushered in not just a medical epidemic but a legal one, as gays and lesbians faced an upsurge in employment discrimination as a result of the fear of HIV/AIDS and its strong association with gay people. The epidemic, and the legal needs it created, spurred the rise of gay lawyering, both for solo practitioners and for nonprofit gay legal organizations. Ironically, though, gay rights lawyers probably had the least success in the arena of employment. Eventually growing rights consciousness in the face of continuing state hostility caused gay people to turn from the state to business for protection, and the final chapter examines the quest for gay employment rights inside the corporate sector, as well as that sector's surprising responsiveness to those demands. By century's end, the bargain that had been shattered by liberation and AIDS was not exactly reconstituted, but employers and their gay employees found a new equilibrium during these years that once again positioned the latter as potentially desirable subjects of capitalism.[72]

The sharp divide between the straight and queer work world that structures part 1 of the manuscript is also present but somewhat less pronounced in parts 2 and 3, as more open expressions of sexuality gradually became somewhat acceptable in the straight world from the 1970s onward. Yet parts 2 and 3 still each maintain a separation between mainstream work cultures (chapters 3 and 6) that were slowly changing, and more alternative "queer" work worlds (taken up in portions of chapters 4 and 5), where work was openly queer, underpaid, and often quite labor intensive. As part of the scope of chapters 4 and 5, I slow down to provide detailed "workscapes" of a few alternative work cultures to highlight the

---

72. On "the historical specificity of capitalism's investment in formations of sexuality," see Meg Wesling, "Queer Value," *GLQ* 18 (January 2012): 107.

ways that queer people created workplaces for themselves, found profound meaning, and sometimes even formed surrogate families on the job (at a moment when many gay people were alienated from families of origin).[73] In chapter 4, for example, my broader exploration of the relationship between gay liberation and work is recounted in my discussion of lesbian feminist attempts to create an alternative economy during these years as represented by lesbian businesses such as Olivia Records and Diana Press. In chapter 5, I devote considerable attention to the work of nurses on the AIDS ward at San Francisco General Hospital as a way of keeping affect and feeling centered in the project, as well as knitting the legal and medical epidemics together (nurses remained especially vulnerable to employment discrimination many years into the AIDS crises). In both chapters, it may seem odd to devote so many pages to these workplaces that each employed a relatively small number of people. Yet Olivia Records and Diana Press illustrate a much broader movement to create a separate lesbian work culture, whose significance has been largely missed in the historiography because it was undercapitalized, operated in the shadows of the mainstream economy, and was dispersed across the landscape in ways that has made it seem less important than it actually was.[74] For all three "workscapes," moreover, it's not the scale of the organization but the scale of the experiment (*the scale of their thinking*) that is important. Moreover, each of these chapters (4 and 5) centrally involves women and helps to rebalance chapters (3 and 6) that focus on national security and corporate sectors and, as a result, tilt more toward men's employment. It so happens that in subfields that tend to marginalize women's experience, as LGBT history does, concentrating on women can sometimes create narrative challenges. I hope the reader will nonetheless agree with me that these are worthwhile trade-offs to make.

As concerns the broader temporal movement of the book, decades are generally sloppy containers, and so the six chapters themselves are chronologically staggered, with a slightly overlapping historicity across them. And while most historical narratives foreground change over time, I hope readers will note how much stasis and continuity there is in this story.

---

73. The concept of the "workscape" is from Thomas Andrews, *Killing for Coal: Labor's Deadliest War* (Cambridge, MA: Harvard University Press, 2008).

74. But see Alexandra Ketchum, *Ingredients for Revolution: American Feminist Restaurants, Cafes and Coffeehouses, 1972–2022* (Montreal: Concordia University Press, forthcoming); Finn Enke, *Finding the Movement: Sexuality, Contested Space, and Feminist Activism* (Durham, NC: Duke University Press, 2007); Joshua Clark Davis, *From Head Shops to Whole Foods: The Rise and Fall of Activist Entrepreneurs* (New York: Columbia University Press, 2017).

The balance of continuity and change has been one of the hardest things to sort out about this project. I have listened to informants talk about the 1950s and 1960s with the feeling that I was hearing about a completely lost world, and simultaneously a sense that the scene was oddly familiar. I recognized, for example, quite a bit of what these informants ascribed to mid-century in my coworkers from the early 1990s. How could both things be true? I hypothesize that it has to do with the fact that enormous cultural change for queer people happened without much in the way of accompanying legal protection.[75] This fact sets the gay experience sharply apart from the experiences of women or African Americans, for whom these things happened in tandem.[76] This of course makes the gay experience a particularly useful case for thinking through the question of whether and how civil rights laws matter, an issue that I return to in the epilogue.

One last note: Some readers may question my use of the word "career" in the title of a book that purports to be about working-class as well as professional jobs. I appreciate that potential objection, but to my ear the word contains multitudes. I think, for example, of C. Vann Woodward's *The Strange Career of Jim Crow* to denote the South's racialized system of stratification, violence, and oppression.[77] Writing just a few years after Woodward, the sociologist Howard Becker used "deviant careers" to describe the lifeways of society's "outsiders."[78] Neither usage maps tightly onto what I am up to here, but there are some resonances. Because the

75. In 1979, legal scholar Rhonda Rivera drafted what came to be seen as a truly canonical study of the legal status of gay people at the time. Twenty years later, in 1999, she was asked to update that essay to reflect "progress" in the law. She assessed the forward gains over that span of time as extremely limited. My own view of legal developments over these years accords with Rivera's. See Rhonda R. Rivera, "Our Straight-Laced Judges: The Legal Position of Homosexuals in the United States," *Hastings Law Journal* 30 (March 1979): 799–955; Rhonda R. Rivera, "Our Straight-Laced Judges: Twenty Years Later," *Hastings Law Journal* 50 (1999): 1187–88.

76. I am referring here to the temporal proximity of the African American freedom struggle and women's liberation to the legal protection achieved by Title VII of the Civil Rights Act of 1964. The Equal Employment Opportunity Commission was initially more responsive to complaints based on race, but by 1969 the agency began to treat complaints based on sex like complaints based on race. Hugh Graham Davis, *The Civil Rights Era: Origins and Development of National Policy* (New York: Oxford University Press, 1990), 211–32; Kessler-Harris, *In Pursuit of Equity*, 246. On the longer arc of civil rights struggle, see especially Kate Masur, *Until Justice Be Done: America's First Civil Rights Movement, from the Revolution to Reconstruction* (New York: W. W. Norton, 2021).

77. C. Vann Woodward, *The Strange Career of Jim Crow* (New York: Oxford University Press, 1955).

78. Howard Becker, *The Outsiders: Studies in the Sociology of Deviance* (New York: Free Press, 1963).

trajectory of the book also tracks what the sociologist Gerald Davis has more recently termed "the death of the career," I also employ the word to underscore that looming development.[79] Yet above all, I use "career" in the book's title to assert that, as with professionals, some working-class people also earned their livelihoods in the kinds of positions to which they attached closely and meaningfully across the arc of the life course. *I was a typist, and I wanted to type!*

79. Gerald Davis, *The Vanishing American Corporation: Navigating the Hazards of a New Economy* (San Francisco: Berrett-Koehler, 2016), 123, 144.

PART I

Gay Labor

CHAPTER ONE

"The Homosexual Does Cope Fairly Successfully with the Straight World"

DEFINING GAY LABOR AT MIDCENTURY

HISTORIANS AND SOCIOLOGISTS rely on a few, commonly used short-hand phrases to describe conditions for workers in the 1950s and 1960s United States. Sometimes this period is referred to as the "glory years" or a "golden age," alternatively, as an "age of security."[1] These phrases all gesture toward the same rosy constellation of factors: a booming postwar economy in which workers offered loyalty to their employers, receiving high wages and benefits as well as job security in return. Sustained growth across this period meant that jobs were easy to get. While white-collar workers benefited the most from postwar prosperity, the working class also experienced a significant rise in living standards in exchange for rejecting shop-floor militancy as a tactic. Both white- and blue-collar working men expected a breadwinner's wage with which they could support a family, as well as the formation of long-term attachments between employers and

---

1. Andrew Abbott, "Sociology of Work and Occupations," in *The Handbook of Economic Sociology*, 2nd ed., ed. Neil J. Smelser and Richard Swedberg (Princeton, NJ: Princeton University Press, 2005), 311; Stephen Marglin and Juliet Schor, eds., *The Golden Age of Capitalism: Reinterpreting the Postwar Experience* (Oxford: Clarendon, 1990); Arne Kallenberg, *Good Jobs, Bad Jobs: The Rise of Polarized and Precarious Employment Systems in the United States, 1970s to 2000s* (New York: Russell Sage, 2011), 22.

employees and opportunities for advancement plentiful enough "to enable workers to construct orderly and satisfying career narratives."[2]

From the perspective of gay history, these tropes (whether the "glory years" or an "age of security") seem seriously off kilter.[3] This is especially true when one considers the shorthand that historians of sexuality have most commonly used to describe these years: namely, "the Lavender Scare." That term, which has become nearly hegemonic for thinking about gay life in the 1950s and 1960s, refers to the purge of gays and lesbians from the federal government that began in the late 1940s. Modeled after the military's own witch hunt, it culminated with President Eisenhower's 1953 executive order that named "sex perversion" as a ground for termination not only from government service but also from private industry for companies that held government contracts.[4] The idea that gay people were so vulnerable to blackmail that their employment might compromise national security was offered as justification for the firing of more than five thousand federal civil servants for homosexuality, as well as the refusal to hire many, many more. Historians now estimate that far more people were fired from the government for homosexuality as "security risks" during this period than for alleged Communist ties.[5]

2. Kallenberg, *Good Jobs, Bad Jobs*, 3.

3. From the perspective of women's history, the period was also not exactly a glorious "golden age." The family wage that guaranteed male breadwinners high wages to support families simultaneously cemented women's position as low-wage workers in secondary labor markets. On the history of the family wage, see especially Alice Kessler-Harris, *In Pursuit of Equity: Women, Men, and the Quest for Economic Citizenship in 20th Century America* (New York: Oxford University Press, 2001); Nancy MacLean, "Postwar Women's History: The 'Second Wave' or the End of the Family Wage," in *A Companion to Post-1945 America*, ed. Jean-Christophe Agnew and Roy Rosenzweig (Malden, MA: Blackwell, 2002), 235–59. Nor were these glory years for people of color: "The male-headed household formed the elementary institution of the public-private welfare state," according to Gabe Winant. "The subjects of this order, the persons it recognized most fully, were the heterosexual white men who held most factory jobs and headed most working-class households. African American men held a real foothold within this world, but it was small, confined, and eroding." Gabriel Winant, *The Next Shift: The Fall of Industry and the Rise of Health Care in Rust Belt America* (Cambridge, MA: Harvard University Press, 2021), 13.

4. Allan Bérubé, *Coming Out under Fire: The History of Gay Men and Women in World War II* (New York: Plume, 1991), 269.

5. David K. Johnson, *The Lavender Scare: The Cold War Persecution of Gays and Lesbians in the Federal Government* (Chicago: University of Chicago Press, 2004), 166–67. On the Lavender Scare, Johnson's study is the definitive account. See also John D'Emilio, "The Homosexual Menace: The Politics of Sexuality in Cold War America," in *Passion and Power: The Politics of Sexuality in Cold War America*, ed. Kathy Peiss and Christina Simmons (Philadelphia: Temple University Press, 1989), 226–40; Robert Dean, *Imperial Brotherhood: Gender and the Making of Cold War Foreign Policy* (Amherst: University of Massachusetts Press, 2001).

The methods employed during the witch hunt were extreme—the slightest trace of gender inversion, a roommate's phone calls at the office, or even a specious tip from a disgruntled coworker could subject federal workers to intrusive scrutiny. Investigators checked credit and police records, interviewed friends and acquaintances extensively, and engaged in direct surveillance, hoping to follow a suspect's footprints right to a gay bar, bathhouse, or cruising area.[6] In some cases, the post office might even monitor a civil servant's mail for physique magazines, gay "pen-pal" clubs, or other telltale signs.[7] The FBI reported morals arrests to the Civil Service Commission, which also maintained a database of those fired for homosexuality so they would not be reemployed by other federal agencies.[8] The results were devastating for those who lost jobs—especially for women and African Americans of both sexes. Opportunities for government employment far surpassed anything else available to them, making the likelihood of starting over in the private sector more remote than it was for white men. One woman economist "with New York–type ambition" was, for example, devastated by her removal from the Treasury Department.[9] Another man remembered the lengths that African American gays and lesbians would go to in order to protect their government jobs, even attending parties in male-female pairs and then separating once inside the door. He recalled this strategy as a marked feature of Black gay life in Washington during the years when federal anti-homosexualism was at its height.[10]

Even more generally, the social ecology of the capital city was deeply affected by the gay purges. One woman's clearest memory of life in Washington during the 1950s was how quiet people were on city buses, afraid to speak to one another.[11] The Lavender Scare also spread beyond Washington as state and local governments began going after state employees, those with professional licenses, and especially university and secondary teachers who were suspected of being homosexual. Large purges were conducted in Florida, Idaho, Iowa, Massachusetts, North Carolina, Texas, Michigan, Oklahoma, New York, and California, among other places.[12]

6. Johnson, *Lavender Scare*, 73.

7. John D'Emilio, "Homosexual Menace," 62.

8. Johnson, *Lavender Scare*, 81.

9. Interview subject 71, Sebastopol, CA, 2011.

10. Interview subject 10, Washington, DC, 2013.

11. Johnson, *Lavender Scare*, 156.

12. A useful compendium is provided in Brad Sears, Nan D. Hunter, and Christy Mallory, "Documenting Discrimination on the Basis of Gender and Sexual Orientation in State Employment" (UCLA Law School, Williams Institute Report, 2009), chapter 5. On

Because they were so targeted, teachers and civil servants exhibited the most extreme passing behaviors during these years. People in these types of jobs tended to be more likely to date or even marry another gay person of the opposite sex, to "de-gay" an apartment, or to keep gay life and gay community at a drastic distance.

The brutality of the Lavender Scare is undeniable, but like the "age of security" or the "glory years," it also misses the mark as a shorthand for this period. One-fifth of the entire American workforce was employed either by the federal government or by private employers who contracted with the government. All those people, most of whom were neither gay nor suspected of being so, had to take loyalty or security oaths.[13] But that leaves four-fifths who were less directly affected. Moreover, these purges were in many ways local events. Only in Washington, DC, was the Lavender Scare all pervasive, and perhaps in the handful of state governments that were similarly overtaken by anti-homosexualism. The work of the Johns Committee in Florida, which led to the removal of untold numbers of secondary teachers and university professors, was for example horrific but also somewhat singular in its duration and scope at the state level.[14]

Precisely because the particular impact of the Lavender Scare (in Washington, DC, and in some states) was so intense, however, the civil service purge has been understandably distorting for historians. Many accounts characterize the relationship between homosexuality and employment at midcentury as one of sharp repression, as a witch hunt or crackdown that sent gay people into deep hiding. This image is not wholly inaccurate, but it is a partial view, applicable primarily to government employees (and some government contractors). Elsewhere, the midcentury employment regime for sex and gender nonconformists is not best understood in terms of episodic crackdowns or dramatic flashpoints, even while those crackdowns did foster an intensifying sense of danger that shaped employment relations everywhere. Away from the heart of the Lavender Scare, however, the manifestations were distinct enough that we might reconceptualize the gay work experience not as something repressed and hidden but rather as a *form of labor* in the same way one might talk about the

university purges, see also Lillian Faderman, *The Gay Revolution: The Story of the Struggle* (New York: Simon and Schuster, 2015), 40. On large purges at the University of Florida and at the University of Michigan, see "Homosexual Purges at Two Universities," *Mattachine Review* 6 (March 1960): 18–20.

13. Johnson, *Lavender Scare*, 137.

14. Stacey Braukman, *Communists and Perverts under the Palms: The Johns Committee in Florida, 1956–1965* (Gainesville: University Press of Florida, 2012).

history of women's work or immigrant labor, for example. This kind of lens *is* possible: despite constituting "one of the largest, but least studied, minority groups in the work force," gay labor is not actually an absence or an invisibility.[15] It is not something cloaked and veiled that we can never see. Rather it is a kind of presence, perhaps unspeakable but still somewhat knowable, not just to us but also to midcentury Americans, gay and straight, employers, employees, coworkers and colleagues.

That visibility and knowability was *especially* true in the occupations that make up what I call the "queer work world," which is considered in the next chapter. These were the stereotypically gay occupations as well as other casual, temporary, low-paid, low-status work, often in the service sector, where gay people clustered in part because they could generally be fairly open. As one man said about these years, "I was always looking for low-paying jobs where I could be myself."[16] Some did not choose to be in this world but were forced into these kinds of jobs after encountering employment difficulties in mainstream occupations. But many other gay people, possibly the majority, actually worked in those mainstream occupations that I designate here as the "straight work world." For these workers, who are the focus of this chapter, the civil services purges and the related increase in policing of gay life that commenced in the 1950s certainly loomed as a threat.[17] At the most extreme, an encounter with the vice squad in a bar or a cruising area could result in a gay man or lesbian losing their position, and an arrest record might make reemployment in a straight job difficult.[18]

15. Belle Rose Ragins, "Sexual Orientation in the Workplace: The Unique Work and Career Experiences of Gay, Lesbian, and Bisexual Workers," in *Research in Personnel and Human Resources Management* 23 (Bingley, UK: Emerald Books, 2004), 35.

16. Interview subject 49, Atlanta, GA, 2012.

17. The growing military-industrial complex enhanced that vulnerability. If more "employees of business establishments come under scrutiny of the Government because of contracts for military equipment or services," lamented George Henry, who founded an agency to help homosexuals in trouble with the law, "then the closing of additional avenues of employment for homosexuals becomes an even greater social problem." George W. Henry, MD, "The Fifteenth Annual Report of the George W. Henry Foundation," 1963, folder 1, box 11, Mattachine Society Project Collection, ONE National Gay and Lesbian Archives, Los Angeles, CA. On the increase of policing in the 1950s, George Henry's assistant Alfred Gross observed "much greater police vigilance and corresponding activity." Alfred Gross, "Understanding the Homosexual," *Crime and Delinquency* 1 (1955): 140. See also Anna Lvovsky, *Vice Patrol: Cops, Courts, and the Struggle over Urban Gay Life before Stonewall* (Chicago: University of Chicago Press, 2021).

18. Police practices varied, but in some locales the morals squad routinely informed the employers of those arrested. John Logan, "You're Fired! Thousands of Homosexuals in America Face Inward Terror of Hearing Their Employer Say These Two Words,"

The queer and straight worlds of work at midcentury were thus inter-dependent, not only because gay people moved back and forth between them, but because knowledge of the way they could be banished condi-tioned behavior on the job for those who maintained a perch in the straight work world. They were not hidden and safe but somewhat exposed and deportable. Their vulnerability made them exploitable in particular ways, and some midcentury employers appreciated and took advantage of their *precarity in an age of security*. It is at least partly for this reason, I argue, that some employers welcomed the presence of sex and gender noncon-formists in mainstream occupations, and why the relationship between employee and employer in these jobs was not usually defined by elaborate hiding by the employee and cluelessness on the part of the employer, but rather by a shared commitment to downplay what the sociologist Erving Goffman called the "evidentness" of stigma.[19]

Gay workers during these years thus may have been as much desired as they were disavowed. Capital, abetted by law, "produces subjects accommo-dated to its own needs."[20] This was a vulnerable and intimidated work force for whom job loss stood as the greatest fear. And yet, as sociologists Martin Weinberg and Colin Williams concluded of this period, "*the homosexual does cope fairly successfully with the straight world*."[21] The phrase "coping fairly well" of course sets low expectations; it says surviving rather than thriving. Not incidentally, it also offers a useful guiding precept for explor-ing gay life inside mainstream occupations during the American economy's glory years. This then may finally be a useful shorthand for the period.

Mattachine Review 2 (June 1956): 27–29. One reader of the *Mattachine Review* elaborated that "they [the police] even go to the places where they [the arrested] are employed and call them off the job. . . . They then are held as long as the police desire to hold them and generally cost the respective employee his job (which the police clearly envision because of their actions)." "Readers Write," *Mattachine Review* 7 (July 1961): 27. Sometimes police did not directly report arrests but newspapers reported on the arrest, which might also result in job loss. In another instance, a man was recognized by the court attendant who then "had me fired from a good job." Letter from "Mr. B., Philadelphia," *ONE* 2 (June 1963): 30.

19. Some employers "welcomed" while others only tolerated queer employees. The point here is less about the degree of toleration or hostility among midcentury employers than that they benefitted from the subordinate position of queer workers irrespective of their own attitudes. On "evidentness," see Erving Goffman, *Stigma: Notes on the Manage-ment of Spoiled Identity* (New York: Simon and Schuster, 1963), 48.

20. Meg Wesling, "Queer Value," *GLQ* 18 (2011): 17.

21. Martin S. Weinberg and Colin J. Williams, *Male Homosexuals: Their Problems and Adaptations* (New York: Penguin, 1975), 126 (emphasis mine). While the publication date of this study is 1975, the data for the US portion of the book (which also covers the Nether-lands and Denmark) is from the mid-to-late 1960s (see pp. 47 and 65).

What was the landscape of gay labor? One of the challenges of attempting something of a bird's-eye view of gay people's work experiences across the 1950s and 1960s, rather than focusing in on a single occupation or industry, is that individuals' experiences on the job—their points of entry into a position, their coping strategies once there, ambitions thwarted or realized—all varied somewhat. That's true even within the crude division between a straight work world and a queer one made in this chapter and the next. Still, in the aggregate certain patterns are clear, and it's possible to sketch a composite portrait drawn from archival records and published sources, as well as numerous interviews I conducted with the cohort born in the 1930s and early 1940s. Some members of that group, who entered the labor market during the 1950s and early 1960s, interestingly set themselves apart from the generation that preceded them. More than one informant noted, for example, that they struggled especially with men born in the 1910s and 1920s "who were so gay" that "*it got in the way of their work.*" One man born in the 1930s remembered thinking of this older generation: "why can't they be more serious?"[22] This man's "seriousness" was undoubtedly conditioned by his own experience of being entrapped by the vice squad in a public restroom in New Orleans and consequently kicked out of the military as a very young man, and then enduring a long stint in temporary jobs in San Francisco, before working his way back toward a straight job.[23] Being removed from the military for homosexuality usually brought substantial vocational derailment, perhaps even more so for women with their very limited opportunities for employment during these years. One young woman, for example, was kicked out of the Marine Corps for homosexual tendencies in the mid-1950s. Before she was discharged, she learned she had placed third out of three hundred women for entry into air traffic school. She later reflected that it had taken her years to understand "what was taken from me."[24] Being sent home from college for homosexuality could be as significant a setback. One college student, called in by the dean of women on suspicion of lesbianism, remembered feeling terrified. "I was counting on a college degree," she recalled. "I was a lesbian. I wasn't going to get married. No one was going to support me."[25]

22. Interview subject 70, Santa Rosa, CA, 2011; interview subject 87, Cambridge, MA, 2011; interview subject 26, New York, NY, 2011 (emphasis mine).

23. Interview subject 70, Santa Rosa, CA, 2011.

24. Interview subject 101, Houston, TX, 2011.

25. James Sears, *Lonely Hunters: An Oral History of Lesbian and Gay Southern Life, 1948–1968* (New York: Basic Books, 1997), 89.

For those who made it through college or a tour of duty without being investigated, the career trajectory was still marked from the beginning for those who understood themselves as either sex or gender variants during these years.[26] Coming to terms with their homosexuality, some reported, could be an emotional barrier to focusing on a career. One Florida man described the experience of "going crazy" and not being able to finish their education as rather common among gay men of his generation.[27] The homophile activist Barbara Gittings ascribed her flunking out of Northwestern University after her first year to a similar dynamic.[28] A contemporary of Gittings reported that she left her graduate program after a year because "she was too anxious about who she was to focus on studying."[29] Several others reported believing that "a homosexual must not excel": "shame kept them from focusing on a career," and they had "no clear direction."[30]

For some women in particular, the barriers might be less psychological than purely economic. Sexist hiring practices and low wages literally kept lesbians trapped in marriages to men.[31] Sources of advice were

26. One midcentury study showed that the greatest number of students seeking personal adjustment counseling were those who had occupational interests "opposed to those most culturally acceptable for their sex": young men who were drawn to nursing, for example, or young women whose ambition made them feel restless inside traditional women's occupations. Samuel Osipow and James Gold, "Personal Adjustment and Career Development," *Journal of Counseling Psychology* 8 (1968): 442–43. The term "sex variant" was popularized by the sexologist George Henry in *Sex Variants: A Study of Homosexual Patterns* (New York: Hoeber, 1941). The term continued to be used into midcentury and encompassed not only those with same-sex erotic desires but sometimes gender nonconformists as well. It was also a term queer people used to describe themselves. "Because the term *variance* offered an interpretive fluidity and openness," the historian Jennifer Terry has explained, "it was appealing to so-called sex variants themselves, especially when compared to the more rigid belief that sexual inverts or homosexuals were of an entirely different and inferior order." Jennifer Terry, *An American Obsession: Science, Medicine, and Homosexuality in Modern Society* (Chicago: University of Chicago Press, 1999), 221. On midcentury uses of the term *variant*, see, for example, an editorial that described the homophile publication ONE as aiding "in the social integration of the sexual variant." Lyn Pedersen, ONE 6 (May 1, 1958): 4.

27. Interview subject 46, Atlanta, GA, 2012.

28. Kay Tobin and Randy Wicker, *The Gay Crusaders* (New York: Paperback Library, 1972), 208.

29. Faderman, *Gay Revolution*, 140.

30. The Seventeenth Annual Report of the George W. Henry Foundation, April 1, 1965, folder 147, box 13, Foster Gunnison Papers, Archives and Special Collections, Thomas J. Dodd Research Center, University of Connecticut–Storrs; interview subject 35, New York, NY, 2012; interview subject 41, New York, NY, 2011.

31. The prospect of losing custody of their children was another barrier for lesbian mothers who wanted to leave heterosexual marriages. Daniel Rivers, *Radical Relations: Lesbian Mothers, Gay Fathers, and Their Children in the United States since World War II* (Chapel Hill: University of North Carolina Press, 2013), 84.

also extremely limited. One woman who grew up in the 1930s and 1940s remembered being given a copy of *The Well of Loneliness*, the 1928 lesbian novel, by her PE teacher, who told her she should also be a gym teacher.[32] For women, few other tracks were even available. "I just couldn't see past teaching," said one woman.[33] Often the advice offered—to both sexes— was about what *not* to be. "I wanted to be a nurse," one man admitted, "but I was told that was for gays, so I did something else."[34] Another man who was interviewing for a teaching position was correctly "read" by the school superintendent, who told him that he couldn't be in such close proximity to students and should be a librarian instead. At that point, the aspiring teacher had never even touched another man. "Being gay put up road-blocks," he said: "Don't be this, and don't be that."[35]

Some of those roadblocks came from the growth of personnel and human resource offices at midcentury and the more elaborate screening methods they utilized. To be clear, personnel officers were not doing the deep detective work of their counterparts in the military and the civil ser-vice; they were predominantly interested in screening out only the "obvious types" who might embarrass the company.[36] An unconventional gender pre-sentation, for example, might lead one's resume to be flagged with the letters "HCF," short for "high class fairy."[37] An address in a Bohemian part of town or too much time already logged in unconventional work settings also raised flags. "Bill, just one more question before you leave," one would-be salesman was asked in 1965. "Because you have been in summer theatre work, I think I should ask it. Are you inclined to be a homosexual?"[38] Besides blocking

32. Interview subject 71, Sebastopol, CA, 2011.

33. Interview subject 45, Atlanta, GA, 2012.

34. Comment from an audience member during a talk at Services and Advocacy to Gay Elders (SAGE), New York, NY, 2012.

35. Interview subject 34, New York, NY, 2012. Another man who had a homosexual incident in his background was steered by a vocational counselor in 1960 away from teach-ing toward barbering. "Homosexual Denied Employment," 1964, folder 16, box 1063, Rec-ords of the American Civil Liberties Union, Seeley Mudd Library, Princeton University, Princeton, NJ.

36. "Employment Discrimination against Homosexuals," presented by the Gay Activ-ists Alliance to the New York City Commission on Human Rights, July 10, 1970," folders 1–2, "Fair Employment," box 16, Records of the Gay Activists Alliance, Manuscripts and Archives Division, New York Public Library, New York, NY.

37. Appendix, "On Economic Discrimination," circa 1970, folder 2, box 16, Records of the Gay Activists Alliance.

38. "Employment Discrimination against Homosexuals," presented by the Gay Activists Alliance to the New York City Commission on Human Rights, July 10, 1970," folders 1–2, "Fair Employment," box 16, Records of the Gay Activists Alliance. In his own job search, the diarist Donald Vining carefully "refrained from mentioning that my Yale Studies were in drama." Donald Vining, *A Gay Diary*, vol. 1, *1933–1946* (New York: Hard Candy, 1996), 260.

employment altogether, the personnel office could prevent advancement to "straight" work within a single firm. "I was employed by a company with a retail and a wholesale operation," one man explained. The retail side of the business was gay and poorly paid. The wholesale side was straight and better remunerated. "I had been assigned to retail work and had done very well, more than doubling the record of any other retail person. I wanted to change to the wholesale section because it offered greater opportunity for money and advancement. [But] when I asked about a transfer I was told that . . . I was better suited to retail."[39]

———————

Despite these sentries along the border that separated the queer and straight worlds of work, many pursued a straight job during these years. As with the retail salesman trying to move to wholesale, some wanted to be there because of the pay and respectability and sometimes to protect the "investments" they had already made in "education, training, and vocational development."[40] But it was also a decision to navigate lifelong risk. They hedged their bets in part by sharing information about where to work. Acquaintances directed one man toward "friendly" companies in the financial district in San Francisco where you certainly "would not say you were gay, you would not do anything overt, but you probably would not be fired if anyone found out." Sexuality there was merely "background noise."[41] The more general precepts, applicable in almost any locale, were also well known, partly because they were shared widely through the homophile press. For starters, job applicants should not be too forthcoming about problems in one's background. As the employment service of the Mattachine Society, one of the earliest gay rights organizations, cautioned: "Arrive at answers that will fit the need and still not provide more information than is required."[42] Beyond that, most understood that

39. Project Open Employment, "Employment Discrimination Survey," folder 35, box 97, Records of the National Gay and Lesbian Task Force, Rare and Manuscript Collections, Cornell University, Ithaca, NY.

40. Jeffrey Escoffier, "Stigmas, Work Environment, and Economic Discrimination against Homosexuals," *Homosexual Counseling Journal* 2 (January 1975): 14.

41. Interview subject 131, interview conducted via telephone, 2015.

42. Mattachine Society, Employment Referral Information, undated (circa 1965), folder 12, box 2, Mattachine Society Project Collection. On the history of the Mattachine and other early "homophile" groups, see especially John D'Emilio, *Sexual Politics, Sexual Communities: The Making of a Homosexual Minority in the United States, 1940–1970* (Chicago: University of Chicago Press, 1983).

acquiring and retaining jobs in the private sector was far easier than for jobs in the public sector.[43] And positions in large corporations, with a culture of anonymity, could be easier to negotiate than those in the midsize, more family-oriented ones.[44] Most also knew that teaching was one of the riskiest occupations—but one that many lesbians pursued anyway because it, along with other public-sector employment, offered the highest pay to women. "Wouldn't they be [safer] in private industry?" the lesbian activists and pioneers Phyllis Lyon and Del Martin queried of lesbians in public employment, before answering their own question: "Not all women are satisfied with mediocre jobs at mediocre pay."[45]

If government jobs entailed the greatest risk—and any occupation that required licensing by the government or bonding could also be dangerous—self-employment was by far the safest.[46] It's no accident that so many of the early homophiles (and later liberationists) worked for themselves.[47] But if self-employment was impossible, then the next best option was to find a job where one spent a lot of time alone. One woman said that the solitary nature of the job was what drew her to a position delivering mail.[48] Another saw the same advantage in accepting employment as a bookkeeper.[49] Jobs that involved a lot of travel could have nearly the same effect, in that those who were out on the road would be less closely observed by coworkers.[50] Travel had the added benefit of providing opportunities to explore a city's gay scene after hours in a way that would be more difficult closer to home. The historian Nick Syrett has

43. Weinberg and Williams, *Male Homosexuals*, 323.

44. Interview subject 69, San Francisco, CA, 2011. Some had a different take on the impact of business size, however. Dorr Legg of the homophile organization ONE warned a job seeker to avoid the "big outfits. These customarily are staffed by devising all manner of probing application forms. A smaller firm, especially one that is rather new, quite often will be less fussy and may not even ask the sort of questions which bring on troubles." Letter to Dear Friend, January 5, 1970, folder 16, box 90, Social Service Division and Satellite Offices Records, ONE, Inc. Records, One National Gay and Lesbian Archives.

45. Del Martin and Phyllis Lyon, *Lesbian/Woman* (San Francisco: Glide, 1972), 196.

46. JK to the President, June 1, 1966, Correspondence Files, folder 11, box 42, ONE, Inc. Records; case intake form, October 29, 1962, Social Sciences Division, folder 10, box 90, ONE, Inc. Records.

47. Faderman, *Gay Revolution*, 86, 141, 213, 218. Also noteworthy, one scholar "interviewed 55 gays and lesbians who were leaders in the gay and lesbian movement. All, it turned out, were self-employed or owned their own businesses." Marny Hall (citing earlier research by Russo), "The Lesbian Corporate Experience," *Journal of Homosexuality* 12, nos. 3–4 (1986): 62.

48. Interview subject 103, Houston TX, 2013.

49. Interview subject 23, New York, NY, 2012.

50. "The Invert and His Job," *Mattachine Review* 1 (May–June 1955): 15.

documented, for example, the lives of married midwestern businessmen who created an erotic queer world for themselves while traveling on business.[51] Business travel held a similar allure for those who were beginning to explore transgender identity. One executive, who later transitioned to female but was living as a man at the time, remembered traveling during these years with lingerie in her suitcase wrapped like a present for her wife. She could experiment with female dress in the privacy of her hotel room in a way that was at that moment still impossible at home.[52]

Those who did not have the luxury of working by themselves, or using travel to create a buffer, followed strict codes of behavior on the job. Gays occasionally constructed elaborate fronts; one individual actually wrote to a homophile organization to ask if they had a referral service for gay men who needed female dates for office parties.[53] Yet, far less emphasis was placed on appearing straight than on not being overtly homosexual. Those who didn't seem clearly one or the other circled around one another carefully, quietly gathering evidence. If "you suspected someone was gay," one man elaborated, "you might approach." One might then have lunch, begin to "develop a quiet friendship," and send out subtle feelers, like mentioning a gay bar to see if there was a response. "These were pretty safe things to do, because straights didn't know about these bars," he recalled. But "there was also an unspoken agreement about how to behave." "It was very business-like. You used a low voice."[54]

Once past the exploratory stages, workplace friendships that did develop often required cover. A group of lesbian teachers at a newly established school started a cheerleading squad and a drama club. If anyone from the school saw them together at work, or in town, their colleagues would assume they were meeting about the squad or the club. "It gave us a reason to be together."[55] Protective codes of behavior extended from the workplace to other public spaces. The writer Marijane Meaker was at a Greenwich Village bar with four other lesbians one night when the television producer David Susskind came in with his female assistant. "We all

51. Nicholas Syrett, "A Busman's Holiday in the Not-So-Lonely-Crowd: Business Culture, Epistolary Networks, and Itinerant Homosexuality in Mid-Twentieth-Century America," *Journal of the History of Sexuality* 21 (2012): 121–40.

52. Interview subject 106, interview conducted via telephone, 2015. I use female pronouns here to affirm this woman's authentic gender identity even though it conflicts with her actual presentation when this episode occurred.

53. JF to ONE, Inc., December 11, 1968, Social Service Division, folder 14, box 90, ONE, Inc. Records.

54. Interview subject 35, New York, NY, 2012.

55. Interview subject 90, Provincetown, MA, 2011.

knew Jackie," Meaker recalled. One of the women at Meaker's table had "had an affair with her, and I'd joined her table at gay bars many times." Nevertheless, "none of us looked their way. Mum was the word in situations like that, always."[56]

Wherever a person found themselves along that spectrum of occupational risk, getting by in the straight work world also meant using gay networks when they were available and when it was safe. Early homophile organizations created employment bureaus, and business owners occasionally wrote in with offers to hire those who'd lost jobs.[57] The Mattachine's employment service reported being hampered because some gay employers were reluctant to take the risk, but employment services made the transaction safer for both parties by agreeing to never mention "homosexuality" when the contact was made and to practice discretion.[58] Even as they sometimes tiptoed, these services were merely formalizing a more general instinct. Gays often "tend to hire other gays as employees, either through friendship connections or due to sympathy for gays generally," one study reported. "An obvious consequence of this process is that gays may tend to be clustered, not only in certain lines of work but within certain firms."[59] That finding seemed to hold not only in the white-collar office but in blue-collar settings as well. "Believe it or not," a Mr. T. wrote to a homophile magazine in 1964, "We have a gay construction crew. The operator is an Italian fellow who . . . employs about 20 men. . . . The guys are old and young, black and white."[60] As Mr. T.'s comment suggests,

56. Marijane Meaker, *Highsmith: A Romance of the 1950s* (San Francisco: Cleis, 2003), 106.

57. "What Does Mattachine Do?," *Mattachine Review* 3 (April 1957): 20. Besides the Mattachine, the homophile organization ONE created a Social Services Division that offered employment counseling. "Case History," ONE 9 (February 1961): 27–28. The Daughters of Bilitis and the Society of Individual Rights (SIR) also had employment placement services, as did the George Henry Foundation. Glide Memorial Church in San Francisco established a Committee for Fair Employment Practices. See ad for SIR's employment services in *Vector* 3 (February 1967): 9; "The Right to Work," *Vector* 5 (January 1968): 9.

58. See "SIR's Gay Jobs Bureau," *Vector* 8 (October 1972): 21. Early gay activist Dick Leitsch reported that "the Mattachine Society ran into that sort of reverse discrimination a few years ago when we tried to set up an employment service. Many gay men in hiring positions said, 'I'm the only homosexual in my company. If I bring in another one, he might start camping or otherwise give me away. I can't take chances.'" Leitsch quoted in "Playboy Panel Discussion: Homosexuality," *Playboy*, April 1971, 180. More ominously, "when a homosexual employee runs up against an employer who is a latent or repressed homosexual, a vicious situation can ensue about which nothing much can be done." "Job Hunting Doesn't Need to Be a Problem," *Ladder* 1 (March 1957): 6.

59. Joseph Harry and William B. DeVall, *The Social Organization of Gay Males* (New York: Praeger, 1978), 160.

60. Mr. T. to Letters, ONE 12 (December 1964): 28.

gay networks could be interracial. Indeed, because of the access to white social capital that these connections provided, African Americans sometimes identified homosexuality as a *positive* factor in furthering a career during these years.[61] Along with jobs, informal training, advice, and mentoring were provided across not only race but class lines, so the movement between queer and straight work worlds entailed not only downward but occasionally upward mobility. "Thus," one sexologist observed in 1966, "a slum urchin may through a series of partners or patrons be taught a trade or even graduate to a white-collar job."[62] Gay employment networks, it should be said, were rarely cross-gender, and women in general were less likely to be in positions to help one another. But that happened too, for example, in the case of teachers being able to place friends or partners in their school.[63]

Gay networks could, of course, backfire, placing people in jeopardy. One man was asked by his boss to hire a project manager, and he tried to do it through a gay contact at a mainstream employment agency. When the prospective hire came to the interview wearing a white puffy pirate shirt with a pink scarf (this was the mid-1960s), this man decided he was taking a risk he should not be taking.[64] Another man tried to get his effeminate roommate a job in his financial services company; his roommate was not hired, and then he was fired himself.[65] One also had to be careful with existing coworkers, to avoid the borderline cases who themselves had only a tenuous perch in the straight work world. To protect their employment, gays could, in fact, be very cool to one another. One man recalled running into a colleague at a gay bar who had steadfastly refused to pick up on his signals in the office, ignoring the many hints he dropped. "Don't you ever tell anyone that you saw me here," the coworker implored.[66]

───────

Fear of job loss could alienate gay people from others like them in the workplace, but it also shaped behavior out in the world. Some only participated

61. Alan P. Bell and Martin S. Weinberg, *Homosexualities: A Study of Diversity among Men and Women* (New York: Touchstone, 1978), 148. (Research for this work was conducted in the 1960s; see p. 9.)

62. Paul Gebhard, "Homosexual Socialization," *International Congress Series* 150 (1966): 1029.

63. Interview subject 71 and interview subject 72, Sebastopol, CA, 2011.

64. Interview subject 83, Boston, MA, 2011.

65. Fair Employment Committee to Mr. Terry Connelly, approximately 1970, folders 1–2, "Fair Employment," box 16, Records of the Gay Activists Alliance.

66. Interview subject 35, New York, NY, 2011.

in the gay world guardedly. Men were more likely than women to risk ven-
turing into a gay bar or restaurant, but they often didn't talk very openly
when they were there. "You got a first name . . . never asked anybody what
they did," remembered one pharmacist of these years.[67] Successful men with
a lot to lose were, in fact, far more likely to go to a public restroom for a
sexual encounter than to the bar; if questioned, their presence could always
be excused by saying they had just wandered in to use the facilities.[68] Notably, one San Francisco resident observed that for men looking for "hanky
panky," the most likely destinations were restrooms in the *financial district*
that presumably filled a need for businessmen who might not venture out to
gayer areas of town like North Beach, the Tenderloin, or South of Market.[69]

Evidence suggests that lesbians often felt they had to be even more
careful. Some crossed state lines to patronize gay bars, and "even so you
left as much ID as you could at home. Maybe you hid your driver's license
in your bra."[70] The lesbian clientele at the bars comprised "a higher pre-
ponderance of secretaries" than teachers or other professionals.[71] The
latter groups tended to socialize in private, often with women who had
as much to lose as they did. One woman described her rules for hosting
parties during these years: Only those who were in jobs they would have
lost immediately "would get into this house. . . . So school teachers and
military officers" came.[72] More strikingly, there were even some lesbians
who would not acknowledge they were homosexual even to the other lesbian couples in their social circles. "We could have lost our jobs," one said,
explaining her reticence to say the word "lesbian" or "homosexual" out loud.
"We needed to make money."[73] The one silver lining for lesbians was that

67. Interview with Hector Navarro, conducted by Paul Gabriel, 1998, Oral History
Project 98-30, GLBT Historical Society of Northern California, San Francisco, CA.

68. Laud Humphreys, *Tearoom Trade: Impersonal Sex in Public Places* (Chicago:
Aldine/Atherton, 1970), 96–97.

69. Interview with Bill Plath, conducted by Paul Gabriel, 1997, Oral History Project
97-24, GLBT Historical Society of Northern California.

70. Interview subject 90, Provincetown, MA, 2011.

71. Interview with Bill Plath, conducted by Paul Gabriel, 1997, Oral History Project
97-24, GLBT Historical Society of Northern California. Internal Revenue Service auditor
Charlotte Coleman was one exception. Her friends had warned her that she had a good job
and shouldn't go to the bars. But "she needed to go." She was spotted in the bars, and "that's
how the IRS got me." She was, she remembered, "crushed when I lost my job." She later
became a bar owner in San Francisco. Interview with Charlotte Coleman, conducted by Paul
Gabriel, 1997, Oral History Project, 97-023, GLBT Historical Society of Northern California.

72. D. Johnson, *Lavender Scare*, 152.

73. Interview subject 103, Houston, TX, 2013; interview subject 104, Edison, NJ, 2014.
See also J. Sears, *Lonely Hunters*, 106.

their overall economic oppression as women gave them cover for living together. One informant remembered how, when he was growing up in Washington state, the two women librarians in his town lived together without attracting suspicion. The town's gay male teacher was, by contrast, "alone and forlorn."[74] Similarly, women editors in New York could easily share an apartment; male editors might each take an apartment in the same building, but they would not live together.[75]

Yet, in general, for men and women alike, vocational achievement often carried with it a profound loneliness. One woman with her own advertising business carefully avoided patronizing gay establishments or "having anything to do with the gay scene" because it might hurt her business. Only years later did she finally allow herself to appear in a publicly gay space for the memorial service of a prominent New York City public official, which was held at NYU in Greenwich Village. As she took her seat, "it hit me that for the first time in my life, I was in a room full of gay people," she recalled. "I was absolutely overwhelmed with longing."[76]

Alienation also characterized relationships with straight coworkers. Most gays kept socializing with coworkers to a minimum during the 1950s and 1960s. "You can't get too close to people at work," one woman said. "It gets too complicated. You start going out and they want to know too much about you."[77] "We all knew where the boundaries were," said another woman who began teaching in a small town in rural Maryland in the mid-1960s but lived and socialized with a circle of lesbian teachers in northern Virginia. She remembered cordoning off her job from the rest of her life; she rarely ventured out into the community she worked in, or made an effort to know the local families.[78]

The need to create a buffer between one's work and one's gay life not only was isolating but could hurt one's prospects on the job. As one sociologist observed, "When career advancement depends on informal contacts, it may be negatively affected because these informal links are severed."[79] The lesbian magazine the *Ladder* declared it "sad but true" that "promotions go

74. Interview subject 87, Cambridge, MA, 2011.

75. Interview subject 138, interview conducted via telephone, 2016.

76. Interview subject 33, New York, NY, 2012.

77. William Simon and John H. Gagnon, "The Lesbians: A Preliminary Overview," in *Sexual Deviance*, ed. Simon and Gagnon (New York: Harper and Row, 1967), 272.

78. Interview subject 90, Provincetown, MA, 2011.

79. Escoffier, "Stigmas, Work Environment, and Economic Discrimination against Homosexuality," 14–15. "The problem of the deviate in a job situation which puts great emphasis on the social sub-organization can be most difficult," opined a 1955 piece, "The Invert and His Job," *Mattachine Review* 1 (May/June 1955): 15.

more readily to the 'good mixers' and we are therefore at a disadvantage."[80] Indeed, while gays operating within the straight world were anxious about being fired, many were also resigned to being held back.[81]

The straight world of work was a world of severely curbed ambition— this was one of its most pronounced characteristics. "Once you were in a job where you felt accepted and safe," one man recounted, "you would not push up the ladder. Why risk it? People who were not gay took chances I didn't feel I could."[82] In those years, sheltering in place was a common survival strategy. Another man whose homosexuality became known to the airline he worked for realized then that he would never become a sales representative, a promotion he had hoped for. "I just adjusted my expectations," he said, settling into his job in customer service, grateful not to have been fired. The president of the University of Florida, who was a family friend, at one point asked this man if he didn't want a better job. The customer service representative responded that he was not a "big achiever" like his brother, but later he remembered that "it made me feel bad to say that because I [did want] more." He admitted that, as a gay man, "I didn't feel like I could have more."[83]

That clear sense of limits even shaped the aspirations of those who were, apart from their sexuality, quite privileged. Dr. Howard Brown, who later became one of the founders of the first nationwide gay rights organization (the National Gay Task Force), remembered thinking for a long time that *homosexuals could not be doctors*.[84] Another man said that he *could* imagine himself a doctor, "but never chief of surgery." For one thing, he would not have a wife to go to cocktail parties with.[85] Many gay men did of course marry during these years. Relatively few of these decisions were exclusively about work, but for a subset of professionals they occasionally were. One New York City advertising executive, for example, was poised to become a named partner of a thriving agency in the mid-1960s. He was

80. Jo Harper, "The Lesbian at Work," *Ladder* 13 (April–May 1969): 6.

81. Richard Zoglin, "The Homosexual Executive: What It's Like to Be Gay in a Pin-Striped World," in *Gay Men: The Sociology of Male Homosexuality*, ed. Martin P. Levine (New York: Harper and Row, 1979), 74 (the original version was published in the July/August 1974 issue of *MBA*).

82. Interview subject 69, San Francisco, CA, 2011.

83. Interview subject 46, Atlanta, GA, 2011. Another man, who had been fired from his job, also adjusted his expectations. "You find out you shouldn't have been there," he said, explaining his mental state in the aftermath. "The place you were fired from wasn't the right place for you." Interview subject 38, New York, NY, 2011.

84. Howard Brown, *Familiar Faces, Hidden Lives: The Story of Homosexual Men in America Today* (New York: Harcourt Brace Jovanovich, 1976), 65 (emphasis mine).

85. Interview subject 70, Santa Rosa, CA, 2011.

living a gay life in Greenwich Village at the time. The existing partners said there was just one condition: he had to get married. He agreed; and his future partners used a headhunter to find him a wife, who was herself a VP at a rival advertising agency.[86] Marriage was also explicitly part of the career calculus of a publisher who explained his decision to marry during these years as inseparable from his career ambition. Heterosexual marriage, he elaborated, like putting on a tie every day and getting the early train to the office, was "part of a package."[87] Those ideas, moreover, were broadly enough imprinted that many gays during these years internalized an opposition between "being queer" and "being something."[88]

———————

Marriage and ambition of course were inversely coded for women, but even for single women, career options were still very limited. Most did not imagine themselves as doctors, much less as chiefs of surgery. As late as the 1970s, even after occupations had begun to open somewhat under the pressure of the women's liberation movement, 70 percent of all women still worked in just four fields: teaching, nursing, social work, and as secretaries.[89] Nonetheless, many lesbians were, as a pair of sociologists concluded in the 1960s, "seriously committed to work."[90] That commitment was spoken in different registers by working-class and middle-class women, but it was palpable for both. So, for example, the writer Joan Nestle remembered of these years that "it was always working-class clear to

86. Interview subject 86, Cambridge, MA, 2011.

87. Interview subject 42, New York, NY, 2011. See also letter to ONE from Mr. T., a married lawyer in Cleveland who was the lover of another married man: "We do not hate our wives, on the contrary, we are fond of them. But we are not about to fight the world and jeopardize our jobs." Letter to the Editors, ONE 10 (October 1962): 30. Lesbians also married during these years, sometimes owing to the lack of good economic options, and sometimes as a more deliberately protective move. One lesbian lawyer, for example, married a male friend when she found herself being investigated by the state bar association for homosexuality, "to throw investigators off track." Case intake form, August 11, 1960, Social Service Division, folder 7, box 90, ONE, Inc. Records. On the history of lesbians in heterosexual marriages, see Lauren Gutterman, *Her Neighbor's Wife: A History of Lesbian Desire within Marriage* (Philadelphia: University of Pennsylvania Press, 2019).

88. This theme runs through the annual reports of the George Henry Foundation. They can be found in folders 147–48, box 13, Foster Gunnison Papers. This notion that if you were gay, you couldn't "become anything" was also a theme in many of the interviews I conducted with those who grew up during these years.

89. Sandra Schwartz, "Determinants of Occupational Role: Innovation among College Women," *Journal of Social Issues* 28 (1972): 178.

90. Simon and Gagnon, "Lesbians," 270.

me that I had to earn my living in a very concrete way to make my erotic survival possible."[91] About her entry into working world, the historian Lillian Faderman similarly observed that "the more satisfying women were to me, the more important it was for me to prepare for a career since I was forever closing the option—apparently so prized by other women—of being supported by a husband."[92]

Yet this association between lesbians and workplace ambition was, as one 1968 study noted, a problem for "all women who took work seriously."[93] The career woman "was defined by many of the stereotypical characteristics that are found in the stereotype of the lesbian."[94] One remarkable midcentury study even rated career women low on a scale for heterosexuality, opining that they worked in order to avoid sexual relationships with men.[95] The way that ambitious professional women and lesbians were considered overlapping types, however, sometimes assisted younger women looking for mentors in both career and personal matters. One student at the University of Miami, for example, got involved with the dean of women's office in the mid-1960s. She and a friend were fascinated by a national gathering of women deans held at their university. In observing the way the deans interacted, "it seemed . . . that there was an attraction between them—but, of course, they were trying not to make it obvious to [us,]" this student remembered. "Georgia and I, who were starved for role models of professional women, picked up on it."[96] Was it the deans' professional achievement or the erotic energy between them that was so exciting to these two college students? It seems likely it was the way they were intertwined, giving them hopes for an independent and erotically charged future at great variance with the feminine mystique on offer to so many of their peers.[97]

For this set of professional women, managing one's appearance was as important as concealing emotional ties to other women. One woman

91. Joan Nestle, *A Fragile Union: New and Selected Writings* (San Francisco: Cleis, 1998), 129–30.

92. Lillian Faderman, *To Believe in Women: What Lesbians Have Done for America—A History* (Boston: Houghton Mifflin, 1999), 331.

93. Simon and Gagnon, "Lesbians," 269.

94. John H. Gagnon and William Simon, *Sexual Conduct* (Chicago: Aldine, 1973), 203. This volume was a lightly revised version of their 1967 study "The Lesbians: A Preliminary Overview."

95. Donald Hoyt and Carroll E. Kennedy, "Interest and Personality Correlates of Career-Motivated and Homemaking-Motivated College Women," *Journal of Counseling Personality* 5 (1958): 47.

96. J. Sears, *Lonely Hunters*, 104.

97. Betty Friedan, *The Feminine Mystique* (New York: Norton, 1963).

remembered that even women who "were drill sergeants would come striding down the hallway wearing heels and little button earrings."[98] The navy-blue suits and pumps were "as much a requisite uniform as butch and femme dress in the gay bars. It was crucial in the middle-class lesbian subculture to behave with sufficient, though never excessive, femininity."[99] It was also advisable for single career women to have a script ready to narrate the chance circumstances that left them "married" to the company. "I expected to be raising a family," one female executive said to a journalist in 1960. "Things didn't work out that way. I took to the bank, and the bank took to me."[100]

If deftly handled, being "read" as a career woman during these years—as long as one was not seen as overly "masculine" or "driving"—could have benefits.[101] After all, many employers dreaded training young women only to see them abandon their jobs for marriage and family. This assumption sometimes gave women who were perceived as permanently single an advantage over women whose marital prospects were not yet regarded as exhausted.[102] For this reason, one woman who was frustrated at being passed over for promotion by men at her firm in the mid-1960s considered telling her boss she was a lesbian. She worried about the firm's reaction, though, and eventually decided against it.[103]

So lesbians worked hard for the company but simultaneously kept their own aspirations in check. Outside of the family wage economy, lesbians' economic position was in some ways different from that of other women, but they were also ordinary, facing the same constraints and obstacles as other women workers. Many informants reported, for example, being hemmed in by the same kind of harassment, limited job opportunities, and low pay that also hampered their heterosexual coworkers. That lesbians were simultaneously uniquely vulnerable and also exploited in ways that would be familiar to all women is illustrated by the story of one woman who was purged from the Department of Commerce in the late 1950s. Years later, she remembered how that event conditioned her response to unwanted

98. Interview subject 8, Washington, DC, 2013.

99. Lillian Faderman, *Odd Girls and Twilight Lovers: A History of Lesbian Life in Twentieth-Century America* (New York: Columbia University Press, 1991), 181.

100. Mary Anne Guitar, "The New Cool Way of Getting Ahead," *Mademoiselle*, September 1960, 162.

101. Robert Sanford Coe, "The Personality and Adjustment Characteristic of Females in Various Occupational Groups" (PhD diss., University of Houston, 1957), 15.

102. See Escoffier, "Stigmas, Work Environment, and Economic Discrimination against Homosexuality," 15.

103. Simon and Gagnon, "Lesbians," 269–70.

advances from "executives bored with their wives." So, she remembered, she "played that game," thinking "I don't want to be fired again. I don't want to lose what I have."[104] Other lesbians contended that the struggles of women were fundamentally *their* struggles. As one woman wrote in 1968 to the homophile activist Foster Gunnison, "What has held me back all my life is being a woman."[105] It's hardly surprising, then, that the lesbian deans of women at the University of Miami schooled their young charges not on how to handle their erotic interest in other women, but on how to deal with the pervasive sexism ahead: "One dean was very quick to point out that she had the same responsibility as the dean of men, and yet her salary and influence were less," one remembered. "Their advice to us was to strive to be the most polished, poised, and highly educated professional you can possibly be, because the higher your level of education, the more likely you are to overcome some of these disparities."[106] The *Ladder*, the publication of the Daughters of Bilitis (DOB), the early lesbian rights organization founded a few years after the Mattachine, read a lot like any other liberal feminist periodical from the mid-to-late 1960s.[107] The magazine's editor emphasized the "economic side," noting that the concern of the Daughters was "no longer with homosexuality exclusively as it was with the problems of women in a male dominated society."[108] The DOB president also stressed their differing economic positions in distinguishing the interests of lesbians and gay men by the late 1960s. What mattered most to gay men was police harassment and "the legal proscription of sexual practices, and for a relatively few the problem of disproportionate penalties for acts of questionable taste such as evolve from solicitations, wash room sex acts, and transsexual attire." What mattered most to lesbians, by contrast, was "job security and career advancement."[109]

104. Interview with Madeleine Tress, conducted by Len Evans, 1983, box 1, Len Evans Papers, GLBT Historical Society of Northern California.

105. Rita LaPorte to Foster Gunnison, November 13, 1968, in Daughters of Bilitis Correspondence, folder 97, box 10, Foster Gunnison Papers.

106. J. Sears, *Lonely Hunters*, 104.

107. See, for example, Dorothy Lyle, "The Basic Bias," *Ladder* 11 (February 1967): 2–5; Dorothy Lyle, "Without Representation," *Ladder* 11 (August 1967): 2–4; Susan Fontaine, "A Time of Sowing," *Ladder* 13 (August–September 1969): 11–12; "Hint at Sex Bias in Jobs," and "A Better Deal for Women" (in "Cross Currents"), *Ladder* 11 (November 1966): 22. On the history of the Daughters of Bilitis, see Marcia M. Gallo, *Different Daughters: A History of the Daughters of Bilitis and the Rise of the Lesbian Rights Movement* (New York: Carroll and Graf, 2006).

108. "The Life of the Lesbian," *Ladder* 11 (April 1967): 4.

109. Shirley Willer, "What Concrete Steps Can Be Taken to Further the Homophile Movement?," *Ladder* 11 (November 1966): 17–18.

The fact that lesbian issues on the job overlapped so much with issues
faced by all women has led to a common refrain, then and now, that gay men
had it "worse" on the job than lesbians did. The treatment of gay men after
all appears to have been more distinct from that of heterosexual men than
the treatment of lesbians was from that of heterosexual women. But closer
scrutiny suggests that gay men may *not* have had a harder time in their
workplaces than lesbians. It is telling that lesbians clearly had a "greater
instinct for self-preservation" than gay men, that their practice of discretion was far more pronounced.[110] "A problem we lesbians have that the guys
don't is our inordinate fear of discovery," the activist Rita LaPorte wrote in
1968. "I have met lesbians who didn't dare breathe a word even to me that
they were such [and] I attribute [that] to the fact that it is still a man's
world . . . and a tough uphill struggle . . . to get somewhere."[111] The need
for discretion was likely exacerbated by the fact that the best employment
options for women were in the public sector, which was far more dangerous
during these years than the private sector. Even as white-collar jobs in the
private sector where beginning to open up for women during these years,
men's employment options were still far greater.[112] "[Gay] men were much
better off," one lesbian stated simply. "They had their jobs."[113]

While women had few avenues to better-paying jobs dominated by men,
the gay men who worked in traditionally female occupations experienced
advantages there. What sociologists call the "glass escalator" effect, whereby
men are pushed to the top of traditionally female professions, seems to have
been well in place at midcentury.[114] "Gay men sure did move up quick as
nurses," one woman recalled.[115] And if a gay man was fired, he had better
options to find another job than a lesbian would. He also was more likely
to have money in the bank to cover his setback, and if he was dependent
on a lover during a long period of unemployment, then he was dependent
on another *male* wage earner. Even though men were certainly careful at

110. Jess Stearn, *The Grapevine: A Report on the Secret World of the Lesbian* (New York:
Doubleday, 1964), 13.

111. Rita LaPorte to Barbara Gittings, August 1, 1968, folder 1, box 4, Frank Kameny
Papers, Manuscript Reading Room, Library of Congress, Washington, DC.

112. Elizabeth Lapovsky Kennedy and Madeline D. Davis, *Boots of Leather, Slippers of
Gold: The History of a Lesbian Community* (New York: Penguin Books, 1993), 115.

113. Interview subject 95, interview conducted via telephone, 2013.

114. See Christine L. Williams, "The Glass Escalator: Hidden Advantages for Men in
the 'Female Professions,'" *Social Problems* 39 (August 1992): 253–67.

115. Interview subject 29, New York, NY, 2013. Another remembered that in her job
with the airlines, "the gay guy made twice what I did." Interview subject 94, interview conducted via telephone, 2013.

work, there was no lesbian equivalent to gay men "dropping a hairpin" (to subtly announce themselves to other gay men); this was a mode of expression that was not available to most women.[116] The clear exception was the butch lesbian in blue-collar work, but *she still did a man's job for a woman's wage*. The gay men standing next to her on the assembly line made more money. None of this is to deny that gay men faced difficult circumstances, but the notion that they had it "worse" than lesbians is a racialized and gendered assertion that these workers couldn't access their regular privilege as (presumably white) men. It's also certain, as the economist Julie Matthaei has noted, that occupational segregation by sex did not just benefit married men, whose wives were held in low-wage jobs and therefore limited in their ability to leave a marriage. Unmarried men, including gay men, were also indirect beneficiaries of occupational segregation as well as direct beneficiaries of "women's low wage provision of services to business."[117]

———————

Matthaei's shrewd analysis prompts a shift of attention from this (thus far) mostly experiential account of the way gay men and lesbians navigated on their jobs—how they began their working lives, intuited or shared tacit knowledge, managed risks, connected to or kept their distance from a gay world—toward more structural questions about gay labor and the way it fit into the schema of midcentury employment relations. Most obviously, in between the poles of intensified policing of the gay leisure world and the ravages of the Lavender Scare, an extremely vulnerable workforce made its way every day to the office, the hospital, the factory, and the school. Gay people were vulnerable because, despite the assumed salience of the idea of the "closet," many were at least somewhat visible to employers and bosses.[118]

116. This was true even as women were more dependent on the workplace to meet other women because of the way that lesbian institutions were often harder to locate in the outside world. On the terminology of "dropping a hairpin" to indicate gay men dropping clues about themselves for other gay (but not straight) people to observe, see George Chauncey, *Gay New York: Gender, Urban Culture, and the Making of the Gay Male World, 1890–1940* (New York: Basic Books, 1994), 6–7.

117. Julie Matthaei, "The Sexual Division of Labor, Sexuality, and Lesbian/Gay Liberation: Toward a Marxist-Feminist Analysis of Sexuality in U.S. Capitalism," in *Homo Economics: Capitalism, Community, and Lesbian and Gay Life*, ed. Amy Gluckman and Betsy Reed (New York: Routledge, 1997), 170–71.

118. Fascinatingly, the diarist Donald Vining in 1968 referred to "the closet" as "new jargon" that was not used in "my day." Donald Vining, *A Gay Diary*, vol. 4, *1967–1975* (New York: Pepys, 1983), 35.

Gayness may not have been very "speakable" during these years, but it was at least partially seeable and knowable. Most obviously, those with either bad military discharges or arrest records were often exposed to their employers. And arrests in particular were a relatively common attribute of gay life during these years; nearly all gay people knew someone who had been arrested in connection with a bar raid or entrapment, and quite a few had been arrested themselves. One midcentury study estimated that 30 percent of gay men and 12 percent of lesbians had arrest records.[119]

It was not the uptick in arrests alone that made people more knowable, moreover, but rather the way that new methods of policing created an ethnography of queer life that eventually made its way into general knowledge. As the morals squad increasingly focused on entrapment, police were required to scrutinize and master the ways midcentury homosexuals performed queerness through appearance and conversation. As the historian Anna Lvovsky described in her brilliant analysis of the *visible, invisible* homosexual of the 1950s and 1960s, vice officers became "leading students of the gay world that had sprung up in American cities following World War II."[120] The popular press relied on these police experts as their sources in crafting the many exposes of homosexual life that exploded in print culture during these years: "New York's Middle Class Homosexuals" in *Harper's*, "Homosexuality in America" in *Life*, "Growth of Overt Homosexuality in City Provokes Wide Concern" in the *New York Times*, and "Homosexual in America" in *Time* were some of the genre's classic statements. With many other in-depth stories in the *Washington Post*, the *Chicago Daily News*, the *Atlanta Constitution*, and *Greater Philadelphia Magazine*, the cumulative media coverage helped to make the gay world more legible to straight Americans.[121]

119. "DOB Questionnaire Reveals Some Comparisons between Male and Female Homosexuals," *Ladder* 4 (September 1960): 11.

120. Lvovsky, *Vice Patrol*, 143, 149, 225–56. Social science was another source of knowledge about gay life during these years. See, for example, many of the essays in Simon and Gagnon, *Sexual Deviance*. A useful analysis is provided in Gayle Rubin, "Studying Sexual Subcultures: Excavating the Ethnography of Gay Communities in Urban North America," in *Deviations: A Gayle Rubin Reader* (Durham, NC: Duke University Press, 2011), 310–46.

121. Lvovsky, *Vice Patrol*, chapter 6; William J. Helmer, "New York's Middle Class Homosexuals," *Harper's Magazine*, March 1963, 85–92; Paul Welch, "Homosexuality in America," *Life*, June 26, 1964, 66–74, 76–80; Robert C. Doty, "Growth of Overt Homosexuality Provokes Wide Concern," *New York Times*, December 17, 1963, 33; "Homosexual in America," *Time*, January 21, 1966, 40–41; Jean M. White, "Those Others: A Report on Homosexuality," *Washington Post*, January 31, 1965, E1 and E3; Lois Wille, "Chicago's Twilight World: The Homosexuals—a Growing Problem," *Chicago Daily News*, June 20, 1966, 4; Dick Herbert, "They Meet without Fear in 'Gay' Bars around the City," *Atlanta*

Even for those who weren't following the newspapers, other factors made homosexuality more visible during these years. Remaining single past a certain age, for example, was itself considered a telltale sign in an era with historically high marriage rates.[122] A gay man described his coworker's chilly response to his offering a job to a single man: "Bob asked me if [the new hire] was married. When I said he was single, Bob said, 'I thought so' with something of a leer which I coldly ignored. Thinking back," the narrator conceded, "I guess he probably is queer."[123] What is significant here is the equivalence, revealed in Bob's leering look, between being unmarried and being "queer." Thirty seems to have been the magic age when an adventurous bachelor might begin to be seen as "a little off," or when the office girl was suddenly reinterpreted as a "career woman." Beyond that, there was also what the sociologist Donald Webster Cory described as the gay person's own conflicted need to simultaneously conceal and reveal at midcentury, that is, to remain as covert as possible while also dropping the clues that enabled gay people to be recognized "in order to find companionship, friendship, affection, understanding, and physical partners." And finding others only enhanced the assumption *"even . . . at work"* of "mannerisms, method of speech, and other traits from each other, in much the same manner as members of a ghetto community of an ethnic character might do." Cory elaborated on the "very definite type of haircut," the "tonal modulation," the "handshake," and the walk, "far from effeminate, [but] almost militaristic, consisting as it does of a bringing of the heels down in a sharp, clacking, almost Prussianistic manner. It is possible," Cory concluded, "in a few extreme cases, to close one's eyes and hear a gay person walking down the street."[124]

While Cory was focused on men, others also noticed the "obviousness" of lesbians.[125] The need to both conceal and reveal might explain the way the historian Alix Genter has described the lesbian's professional attire at midcentury: "crisp, tailored women's suits with slim skirts" that could

---

Constitution, January 3, 1966, 1, 10; Gaeton J. Fonzi, "The Furtive Fraternity," *Greater Philadelphia Magazine*, December 1962, 20–23, 48–65.

122. On marriage rates, see Elaine Tyler May, *Homeward Bound: American Families in the Cold War Era* (New York: Basic Books, 1999), 14–15.

123. Donald Vining, *A Gay Diary*, vol. 2, *1946–1954* (New York: Pepys, 1980), 348. Vining reported as well a related conversation from 1953: "[They] were discussing Garbo and Cynthia's husband said, 'All this time she's never married? Well, I say people who never marry are queer'" (465).

124. Donald Webster Cory, "Can Homosexuals Be Recognized?," ONE 1 (September 1953): 10–11 (emphasis mine).

125. Stearn, *Grapevine*, 6.

simultaneously signal professional decorum and slight gender variance from the other women in the office.[126] The original draft of Helen Gurley Brown's 1964 *Sex and the Office* (the follow-up to *Sex and the Single Girl*) included details on lesbian sexuality, which, according to her biographer Jennifer Scanlon, Brown saw as "integral to office politics." She was quite peeved that her publisher eventually made her cut the material, remarking that the "the lesbian thing just seems part of the office to me."[127] Brown's observation suggests the visibility and knowability of even professional lesbians, with their exacting practices of discretion.

Whether male or female, public officials worked harder than anyone else to stay under the radar as homosexuality seemed to become more discernible. Dr. Howard Brown, New York City's Health Services administrator under Mayor Lindsay, had his partner, Thomas, move out of their apartment once he was appointed to his post. Brown's caution did not prevent a *New York Times* reporter from including him on an "accurate" list of every gay person prominent in the Lindsay administration. As Brown's contact recited the names on the list, Brown "listened, stunned. Our supposedly private lives were, if not yet public knowledge, no longer secret." Brown resigned his position with the city before his secret came to light.[128] Particularly in government jobs, the visibility and knowability of homosexuality meant a lot of ruined or damaged careers. But there was also no perfect correspondence between an employer's awareness or suspicion about an employee and job loss—sometimes one followed the other, sometimes not.

Away from the public sector, what seemed to govern the employment relation was what one midcentury observer referred to as a kind of collusion, or a bargain.[129] Generally speaking, many employers agreed to try not to "see," while many employees agreed to try not to be "seen." This bargain meant that the most "obvious types" would not make it past an initial interview, and anything that caused serious embarrassment to the company could be grounds for termination. But for nearly everyone else, "so long as the employee's sexual proclivities . . . do not result in the molestation of other employees, customers, or clients," observed the homophiles'

---

126. Alix Genter, "Appearances Can be Deceiving: Butch-Femme Fashion and Queer Legibility in New York City, 1945–1969," *Feminist Studies* 42 (2016): 610.

127. Jennifer Scanlon, *Bad Girls Go Everywhere: The Life of Helen Gurley Brown, the Woman behind Cosmopolitan Magazine* (New York: Penguin Books, 2009), 133–35.

128. Brown, *Familiar Faces, Hidden Lives*, 15.

129. Merle Miller, *On Being Different: What It Means to Be a Homosexual* (New York: Random House, 1971), 4–5.

ONE magazine in 1963, "many employers are happy to pretend they know nothing at all about the matter."[130] Another author spoke of a "tacit understanding" on "both sides" that, even when homosexuality is suspected, "the subject is best ignored."[131] Those contemporaneous assessments line up well with the recollections from innumerable informants that during these years bosses and coworkers either knew or strongly suspected that they were homosexual, and yet they often continued to hold their position.[132]

———◆———

We know why employees accepted this bargain, but what did employers gain by doing so? The answer may lie in the sociologist Andrew Abbott's caution that we not treat workers as an undifferentiated mass. Economic sociologists and labor historians have disaggregated the experiences of women workers or racial and ethnic minorities, Abbott has observed, but have done too little to appreciate the full diversity of forms of labor.[133] Yet gay people also brought distinct attributes to their places of employment. The lesbian activists and authors Lyon and Martin saw that clearly:

> [Lesbians] have a single-minded attitude toward their careers since they know . . . there is no husband in the background on whom they can depend. Often, as the "single" woman in an office, they are available for overtime or weekend work where those with families can't spare the time. They can be more flexible with relation to vacation schedules since they don't have to go while the children are out of school. Lesbians usually don't spend long periods on the telephone talking to their lovers, nor do they spend time flirting with the girls in the office. . . . And, finally . . . most Lesbians, rather than waiting for a man to come around to do the heavy work, would move their typewriters or files themselves.[134]

130. "Case History," *ONE* 2 (November 1963): 7.

131. Zoglin, "Homosexual Executive," 71.

132. On the general knowability of homosexuality during these years, see also Cory and LeRoy's chapter on the "better-adjusted homosexual." They wrote, "From factory workers to business executives, these people are not unlike their coworkers. . . . Their lives are quiet and unnoticed usually, with but a small amount of not-too-malicious gossip: 'I wonder about him.' They are friendly with wide circles of people, including many heterosexuals, most of whom 'know the score' but leave the gap between their lives unarticulated." Donald Webster Cory and John P. LeRoy, *The Homosexual and His Society: A View from Within* (New York: Citadel, 1963), 213.

133. Abbott, "Sociology of Work and Occupations," 309.

134. Martin and Lyon, *Lesbian/Woman*, 193. They are drawing on Harper, "Lesbian at Work," 4–8.

Lyon and Martin knew what employers knew as well; that gay employees could be advantageous hires.[135] Despite the image of the homosexual as an unstable, unreliable employee, this was true of men as well as women. "It is likely that gays have more to give their jobs due to freedom from familial obligations," one study found.[136] Many noted that gays were likely to stay in jobs that felt safe to them.[137] But they were simultaneously available to work split shifts, to put in extra hours, to be transferred to a different part of the country, or to travel for the company on a moment's notice.[138] They could also be underpaid relative to their level of responsibility and skill—with women because they weren't men, and with men because they weren't breadwinners supporting a wife and children.[139]

Under the terms of the bargain, then, gay employees were literally a bargain. The employers' "reluctance to know" makes even more sense when considering the attributes of the gay workforce in relation to the broader contours of employment relations during these years.[140] In the Fordist era, employers sought an accord with labor, offering stable and secure employment, as well as high wages and benefits, in exchange for limiting strikes, stoppages, and other forms of labor militancy.[141] At the heart of what workers were offered was the so-called family wage—a wage that was "indexed . . . to the costs of maintaining a wife and children at home."[142] This arrangement, which also relegated women to a lower-paid, secondary labor market, subtly made family relations a key element of labor control: it put a male worker's gendered interest in controlling the labor power of his economically dependent wife at odds

135. Martin and Lyon, *Lesbian/Woman*, 193; see also Rita Bass-Hass, "The Lesbian Dyad: Basic Issues and Value Systems," *Journal of Sex Research* 4 (May 1968): 116.

136. Harry and DeVall, *Social Organization of Gay Males*, 163.

137. This was a common refrain in interviews I conducted.

138. See Bass-Hass, "Lesbian Dyad," 116; Harry and DeVall, *Social Organization of Gay Males*, 163. Traveling jobs, as the *Mattachine Review* noted in 1955, also helped gays remain hidden. "Invert and His Job," 15.

139. Certain mainstream occupations, like publishing, in which a lot of gay men worked, were low-paying relative to skill and educational level. See also Escoffier, "Stigmas, Work Environment, and Economic Discrimination against Homosexuality," 10.

140. Harry J. Cannon, "Gay Students," *Vocational Guidance Quarterly* 21 (March 1973): 184.

141. Daniel Bell, "The Treaty of Detroit," *Fortune*, July 1950, 53–55; David Brody, *Workers in Industrial America: Essays on 20th Century Struggle*, 2nd ed. (New York: Oxford University Press, 1993).

142. Melinda Cooper, *Family Values: Between Neoliberalism and the New Social Conservatism* (New York: Zone Books, 2017), 10.

with his class interest in joining together with women workers against the boss.[143]

Familial relations thus underlay employment relations. This not only was true among blue-collar workers but made its way up the class structure. Corporations also rewarded their managers with steady, secure jobs with excellent benefits to support their families during these years. White-collar workers especially began to be regarded as fixed costs by corporations, and relatively invulnerable to swings in the business cycle.[144] This labor regime was generally sustainable because of the unprecedented productivity of the economy during the 1950s and 1960s. But the system was also cumbersome and expensive. By the 1970s, when productivity began to slump, employers began to alter the terms of their social contract with labor, gradually withdrawing their commitment to high benefits and steady employment, and demanding more flexibility from employees.[145]

Even before that happened, employers looked for ways that they could make Fordism less costly and more nimble. If heterosexuality was valuable to employers in helping to maintain labor control though the family wage, homosexuality was valuable in suggesting ways to ease the strains and expense of that arrangement. There was always a secondary labor market, of course, populated by women, immigrants, and racial minorities, which absorbed some of the costs and inflexibility.[146] But in order to buffer the jobs of permanent employees in the primary labor market, employers also valued a peripheral workforce *within* that sector.[147] Gays were one obvious source, a Fordist pressure-release valve: trapped and exploitable, like married men,

143. Although she was writing specifically about occupational segregation by sex during the World War II period, my thinking here is indebted to the sociologist Ruth Milkman's classic essay "Redefining Women's Work: The Sexual Division of Labor in the Auto Industry during World War II," *Feminist Studies* 8 (Summer 1981): 337–72.

144. Kallenberg, *Good Jobs, Bad Jobs*, 24.

145. David Harvey, *The Condition of Postmodernity: An Enquiry into the Origins of Cultural Change* (Malden, MA: Blackwell, 1990), 138, 147–50. More generally, see also Jacob Hacker, *The Great Risk Shift: The New Economic Insecurity and the Decline of the American Dream* (New York: Oxford University Press, 2008); Gerald Davis, *The Vanishing American Corporation: Navigating the Hazards of a New Economy* (San Francisco: Berrett-Koehler, 2016).

146. "The primary labor market segment was made up of good jobs (that is, well-paying, relatively secure jobs that were associated with job ladders in large firms)," the sociologist Arne Kallenberg has explained; the secondary segment "consisted of bad jobs (that is, relatively insecure jobs associated with low-wage employment and the absence of job ladders and opportunities for advancement to better jobs)." Kallenberg, *Good Jobs, Bad Jobs*, 11.

147. On this point, see, for example, Erin Hatton, *The Temp Economy: From Kelly Girls to Permatemps in Postwar America* (Philadelphia: Temple University Press, 2011). Hatton associated this development particularly with temporary workers in the 1970s, but I would

but without the costs incurred by families. Contemporaries referred to them "in various states of economic precariousness," as the "last hired and the first fired."[148] Another described gays as a "relatively well-educated, cheap labor force."[149] They were the guest workers of the corporate office: inexpensive, moveable, and easily eliminated.

———◆———

Their vulnerability and their low expectations were key. Gay people knew they could be had "for less," as one lesbian remarked.[150] Another man explained that because "our bosses know we're gay," but pretended not to notice, gays worked hard, "without a thought of reward."[151] If their services were no longer needed, those who were pushed out of their jobs seldom protested their removal. One man, asked for his resignation, was assured that "it has nothing to do with the conduct or quality of my work on the job. . . . So it must have been some aspect of my sex life." Without further information, "I figured upon it for a half an hour . . . and decided not to fight it." Resignation, he concluded, "was the very best way out—no branding, no publicity, no fuss and feathers (*my* feathers)."[152] Many seemed to share this inclination. "Lawyers who have represented homosexuals have told us," the Council on Religion and the Homosexual reported in 1965, "that most homosexuals . . . will not fight their cases through the courts."[153] Even a short blurb in the homophiles' ONE magazine that wondered about the possibility that those who experienced discrimination

---

argue that gays were employed as contingent workers in primary-sector jobs even earlier than that.

148. George W. Henry, MD, to Judge Bromberger, December 31, 1947, "Sex Offenders, 1947" folder, box 62, Records of the Society for the Prevention of Crime, Rare Books and Manuscripts Library, Columbia University, New York, NY. "In times of recession . . . members of variant or minority groups tend to be the hardest hit," stated an editorial in ONE magazine. Lyn Pedersen, ONE 6 (May 1, 1958): 4.

149. Project Open Employment, "Employment Discrimination Survey," folder 35, box 97, Records of the National Gay and Lesbian Task Force.

150. Interview with Betty Deran, conducted by Len Evans, 1983, box 1, Len Evans Papers. This sentiment was also reflected in many of the interviews I conducted.

151. Mike Silverstein, "The Gay Bureaucrat: What They Are Doing to You" (1971), in *Out of the Closets: Voices of Gay Liberation*, ed. Karla Jay and Allen Young (New York: New York University Press, 1992), 166.

152. Thomas Painter Notebooks, series 2, C.1, February 16, 1956, Kinsey Institute, Indiana University, Bloomington.

153. "The Council on Religion and the Homosexual: A Brief of Injustices," ONE 13 (October 1965): 8.

might contact the Equal Employment Opportunity Commission was pessimistically captioned: "Us too? (But don't kid yourself.)"[154]

The ease with which they could be pulled in or pushed out, their lower cost, their flexibility, and their tendency to stay where they were safe all help to explain what otherwise seems inexplicable: midcentury employers' at least occasional expression of a positive desire for gay workers. With lesbians, the preference was sometimes stated almost directly. One bank president demanded, "Where can I find a career woman?"[155] For both men and women, moreover, there were consistent counterexamples to the expected narratives of serious career setbacks resulting from the discovery of homosexuality, even under what seemed like the most damaging circumstances. "The undesirable discharge is not the hazard it is supposed," two women from the personnel field told members of the Mattachine Society at a 1957 meeting.[156] "I have met quite a number of men who have gay discharge records from the service," one man wrote to ONE magazine in 1961. "Most have stopped worrying about it and have done something for themselves."[157] An advice columnist wrote to a veteran that she knew of "a number of young men with a problem similar to yours who did get jobs— not entirely to their liking—but jobs with salaries, once they made up their minds that they would find work in spite of an undesirable discharge."[158] That some employers appeared willing to employ those with unfavorable service records was one sort of marker of these employees' appeal. Another was the fact that the homophiles' various employment bureaus seemed to regularly work through and with mainstream agencies.[159] One employment agency that initially placed an ad in a gay paper only inadvertently was surprised at how "placeable" these gay workers were (but also

154. "Tangents: News and Views," ONE 14 (February 1966): 25.

155. Frances M. Fuller and Mary B. Batchelder, "Opportunities for Women at the Administrative Level," *Harvard Business Review* 31 (January–February 1953): 112. I would argue that the single career woman and the lesbian were functionally almost indistinguishable, and that ambitious career women were coded as deviant during these years.

156. "Bread and Butter Tips: Homosexuals Can Get Jobs—and Keep Them!," *Ladder* 3 (December 1957): 17. See also Mr. S., "Who Says Undesirable?," ONE 9 (July 1961): 31.

157. "Letters," ONE 9 (March 1961): 29.

158. Blanche M. Baker, MD, "Toward Understanding," ONE 8 (February 1960): 25.

159. "Since we learn of few jobs to which we can refer persons directly," the Mattachine Society wrote, "we therefore must rely . . . on services which established employment agencies can perform for job seekers." "Mattachine Society, Inc.—Employment Referral Information," circa 1960, Mattachine Society Project Collection, folder 12, box 2, ONE, Inc. Records. The DOB's forum on "employment and the homosexual" included a manager of an employment agency. "Job Hunting Doesn't Have to Be a Problem," *Ladder* 1 (March 1957): 5. See also Brown, *Familiar Faces, Hidden Lives*, 163–64.

how underemployed).[160] And Hartford's "H. Project," a quasi-religious group organized to help homosexuals "adjust to their condition" through employment and "friendship," held a dinner for the personnel officers of several area businesses, mostly in insurance, to frankly discuss "the whole matter of homosexuality." The personnel officers responded to the invitation "with enthusiasm."[161]

One company told the Mattachine Society that while it was "always in the public eye," it would not automatically terminate an employee for homosexuality. "His actual job and time on the job play a very important factor [as to] how much the company can tolerate."[162] Many of the other businesses the Mattachine surveyed in 1965 were not as relaxed, but the homophile Barbara Gittings reported that the Philadelphia architecture firm she worked for knew of her activism in a lesbian rights organization. Two years after she had left her job, dissatisfied with the man who replaced her, they asked her to come back.[163] Yet another man reported that his employer had been "particularly helpful" after he got into legal trouble for homosexuality. "I have one of those employers who shrugs off the idea that he has a homosexual employee," he said, "with 'I hire for work.'"[164] Even more telling is one man's account of being hired at IBM in 1963 despite having just lost his job as a schoolteacher because he had been arrested in a public restroom. The man listed the arrest on his application for the job at IBM. He was offered and accepted employment anyway. Soon after he started his job, "IBM removed the arrest question from the standard application form." When he pointed this out to his manager, the man later recalled, "he snipped it off my application form, kept in my personnel jacket. Presumably," he concluded, within the company "no other record exists."[165]

160. Testimony by Dr. Ralph Blair before City Council's General Welfare Committee on Bill 475, City Hall, Friday, December 17, 1971, Homosexual Community Counseling Center folder, box 83, Barbara Gittings Papers, Manuscripts and Archives Division, New York Public Library.

161. Minutes, "Project H. Meeting," October 20, 1966, folder 3, box 1, Canon Jones Papers, Special Collections, Central Connecticut State University, New Britain, CT.

162. 1965 Survey, folder 29, box 3, Records of the Mattachine Society of New York, Manuscripts and Archives Division, New York Public Library.

163. Barbara Gittings to Frank Kameny, February 6, 1967, folder 14, box 3, Frank Kameny Papers.

164. JH to ONE, Inc., November 12, 1957, Social Services Division, folder 5, box 90, ONE, Inc. Records.

165. Project Open Employment, "Employment Discrimination Survey," folder 29, box 97, Records of the National Gay and Lesbian Task Force. IBM was certainly not singular. "My employer, a major national corporation, knows that I am gay," one man reported in the

This mounting body of evidence suggests something of a liminal space in between untarnished possibility and a totally ruined life. This was the space where many gay people, in fact, lived out much of their working lives. To be clear, *this was not freedom from discrimination but rather a distinct form of it.* With no legal protection against an aggressively hostile state, gay people were ripe for employer exploitation. The law licensed their exploitation; sometimes it was accompanied by employer animus, at other times by a genuine feeling of toleration. Either way the price was right, and the logic is quite different from the Lavender Scare and the tropes that commonly explain these years as characterized by extreme secrecy and hiding. Yet such a system could also exist only because of the Cold War purges, could exist only in a world where it was commonplace "among homosexuals" to learn "that someone of the group has lost a job."[166] This helps to make sense of the seeming paradox that gay people concurrently reported that job loss was their single greatest fear and also that they did "cope fairly successfully" with the straight world.[167] Both things were true simultaneously; really, there was no contradiction between them.

The dynamic is encapsulated especially well in one lesbian economist's experience of learning that her security clearance investigation had revealed her homosexuality and she was on the brink of being fired from the Treasury Department. Her immediate boss, who was sympathetic to her plight, helped set up an interview for her with some private-sector economists from New York. She was fortunate that he was willing to help, and also that the New York firm was not looking for someone to do government work. But she still had a strategy to ensure the needed outcome: she asked her boss *to be sure that the prospective employer knew about the clearance problem.* This was shrewd on her part. For the New York company, "the clearance problem" was not an impediment, but rather an opportunity to get a highly skilled economist at a significantly reduced price. "They knew the only reason they could hire me was because of that clearance," she recalled. For the economist, the job offer came much more

---

homophile publication *Vector*, "yet, I still have my job." "My Boss Knows," *Vector* 5 (January 1969): 29.

166. Logan, "You're Fired!," 27–28.

167. Dennis Altman, *Homosexual: Oppression and Liberation* (New York: Outerbridge and Dienstfrey, 1971); and Don Teal, *The Gay Militants* (New York: Stein and Day, 1971); both cited in Donald Alan Brown, "A Study of the Educational and Vocational Decision-Making of Four Groups of Homosexuals" (PhD diss., University of Michigan, 1973); Williams and Weinberg, *Male Homosexuals*, 126.

quickly than she had expected, and was an "end to my desperation." But it was also "a lesser job than I would have taken" otherwise.[168]

In sketching out the key elements of gay employment as a form of labor during these years then, the following attributes are foremost: Gay workers were as visible as they were hidden; they were valuable because they vulnerable, but also because they were cheap, unattached, and highly moveable; they brought, in other words, a useful element of precarity and flexibility to sectors of the economy that were generally structured by security and rigidity. If an employee brought unfavorable attention to an employer, or even if production slowed, they were also highly deportable— often to jobs far more peripheral than the one that the lesbian economist purged from the Treasury Department was extremely lucky to obtain. The knowledge that gay workers carried with them and shared with one another pertained not only to how to navigate safely across the straight work world, but how to survive in the queer one as well. "It seems to me that there ought to be any number of $35-a-week jobs in Miami that you could get and they wouldn't care who you were or what you were connected with at that price," one friend wrote another in the wake of his termination. "Dishwashing, janitoring, god knows what else. . . . Think about it."[169]

168. Interview with Betty Deran, conducted by Len Evans, 1983, box 1, Len Evans Papers. (The timing of this incident seems to be late 1950s or early 1960s.) The economist Madeleine Tress, also interviewed by Evans in the 1980s, agreed that those purged from the government often ended up in occupations below their skill level (and presumably at lower wages). Tress ended up "in a field I would not have gone into." Interview with Madeleine Tress, conducted by Len Evans, 1983, box 1, Len Evans Papers. After the astronomer Frank Kameny was purged from the government, the "progressive minded" president of a thermal electronics laboratory, "fully aware of [Kameny's] predicament," was pleased to hire him. Notably, however, the job paid him on a week-to-week basis and offered him only "a fraction of other, similarly qualified physicists' salaries." Eric Cervini, *The Deviant's War: The Homosexual vs. the United States of America* (New York: Farrar, Straus and Giroux, 2020), 106.

169. Foster Gunnison to Dick Inman, October 1, 1966, folder 24, box 3, Foster Gunnison Papers.

CHAPTER TWO

"The Ones Who . . . Had Nothing to Lose"

DAYS AND NIGHTS IN THE QUEER WORK WORLD

SO HOMOSEXUALS DID "COPE fairly successfully with the straight world," in part because they constituted a vulnerable, exploitable labor force that was a bargain for employers accustomed in these years to otherwise paying a lot to maintain loyalty and quietude among their employees.[1] Fear was key; it was maintained by the fact that being fired for homosexuality was a common enough occurrence that gay people routinely knew people who had lost their jobs. The default advice was usually to resume one's working life in a different kind of job: "Surely, there must be small business concerns like privately owned gas filling stations, lunch counters, handyman and errand service . . . where there is not such a detailed investigation of your past experience," one homophile columnist suggested to "JK" in 1960.[2] A New Mexico schoolteacher who was fired in 1964 reported being "resigned to waiting tables."[3] An executive, with presumably more resources than JK or this schoolteacher, decided in the wake of his

---

1. The assertion that homosexuals coped well is from Kinsey Institute field research from the mid-to-late 1960s. The results were published in Martin S. Weinberg and Colin J. Williams, *Male Homosexuals: Their Problems and Adaptations* (New York: Penguin, 1975), 126.

2. Blanche M. Baker, MD, to JK, "Toward Understanding," ONE 8 (February 1960): 25.

3. Mr. Kenyon to the President, June 1, 1966, "Correspondence," folder 11, box 42, One, Inc. Records, One National Gay and Lesbian Archives, Los Angeles, CA.

termination to head to the West Coast to open a "small florist's shop."[4] Likewise, a woman who was fired from her job as an auditor for the IRS redirected her business acumen toward opening a gay bar in San Francisco.[5]

This chapter is about those other kinds of jobs—"open naturally to homophiles"—in what I call the queer work world.[6] Much of what we think we know about gay people and employment during the 1950s, 1960s, and early 1970s comes from observations made about this world. Social scientists, journalists, and others noted high rates of self-employment, and that homosexuals congregated as well in certain kinds of "queer occupations" (which cut across class), and in service occupations more generally.[7] The queer work world was regularly stigmatized as downwardly mobile and workers within it often portrayed as unreliable.[8] Jobs tended to be low paying, and often temporary; according to one homophile publication, this arena offered "peripheral employment . . . in jobs that [were] always unstable."[9] While such descriptors are helpful, the queer work world is perhaps most easily characterized by what it was *not*. Simply put, these were the jobs that fell outside the straight world of work. So they tended to affirm rather than negate gay identity: because one could be open in them, or they enabled some form of gender transgression, or there were simply lots of other gay and gender-variant people around. Sometimes one feature predominated, sometimes all three coexisted. But the queer work world was not in any economic sense a "sector" like manufacturing, retail, or banking. It was rather an idea in the minds of gay people, both a "trap" and a "refuge."[10]

When those who had lost jobs in the straight world landed in the queer work world, they joined denizens who had been there all along. Some would stay only long enough to get a strategy and begin their climb back toward higher-status positions in the straight world. But alongside

4. Howard Brown, *Familiar Faces, Hidden Lives: The Story of Homosexual Men in America Today* (New York: Harcourt, Brace, Jovanovich, 1976), 151–52.

5. Interview with Charlotte Coleman, conducted by Paul Gabriel, 1997, Oral History Project, 97-023, GLBT Historical Society of Northern California, San Francisco, CA.

6. "Editorial," ONE 6 (May 1958): 4.

7. Freddy Lee Myrick, "Structure and Function of Deviant Economic Institutions" (PhD diss., University of Texas, 1972), 88–90; Joseph Harry and William B. DeVall, *The Social Organization of Gay Males* (New York: Praeger, 1978), 160.

8. Harry and DeVall, *Social Organization of Gay Males*, 157.

9. "Editorial," ONE 6 (May 1958): 4.

10. Allan Bérubé, *My Desire for History: Essays in Gay, Community, and Labor History*, edited and with an introduction by John D'Emilio and Estelle B. Freedman (Chapel Hill: University of North Carolina Press, 2011), 265.

these temporary sojourners in the queer work world were the permanent residents who either were too visibly queer to pursue jobs in the straight world or simply chose not to. Here I borrow terminology from the immigration context purposively. There are strong parallels between gay and immigrant labor, for at least two reasons. First, both types of workers were often perceived as advantageous hires because they were sometimes viewed as unencumbered by dependents—with queer people because whatever the reality of their attachments they often presented as functionally single at work, and with certain immigrant groups because families were left behind in sending countries.[11] Second, and as importantly, for both groups, the potentially illegal status of the workforce shaped working conditions. Gay people shared with certain immigrants, in other words, a presumptive status as "illegal" persons, and this licensed exploitation and otherwise shadowed their movement through the working world.[12] Either might be an arrest away from losing their hold on the lives they

11. Cindy Hahamovitch's study of Jamaican guest workers is a key text for my thinking here. Hahamovitch has argued that these workers appealed to employers not only because of their lack of legal protection but also because they had no dependents in the United States. Hahamovitch, *No Man's Land: Jamaican Guest Workers in America and the Global History of Deportable Labor* (Princeton, NJ: Princeton University Press, 2013). Linda Gordon identified a similar dynamic for Mexican workers in Arizona mining towns during the early twentieth century, whose families were in Mexico, which made them "employees from heaven." See Linda Gordon, *The Great Arizona Orphan Abduction* (Cambridge, MA: Harvard University Press, 1999), 57. Other gender-skewed migrations—of Chinese men in the nineteenth century, for example—would have been appealing to employers for similar reasons. Of course some immigrants emigrated with families (and some queer people had dependents, for example, many lesbians with children). For a nuanced discussion of gender ratios among immigrants, see Donna Gabaccia and Elizabeth Zanoni, "Transitions in Gender Ratios among International Migrants, 1820–1930," *Social Science History* 36 (Summer 2012): 197–221.

12. Immigration restriction—initially of the Chinese and other Asians in the late nineteenth century; then with the Johnson-Reed Act of 1924 and the national origins quota system it created; and finally, and most dramatically, with the severe contraction of quotas for immigrants from Mexico and Latin America after 1965—"generated" illegal immigration. The "presence of large illegal populations in Asian and Latino communities has historically contributed to the construction of those communities as illegitimate, criminal, and unassimilable," the historian Mae Ngai has argued. For the undocumented, Ngai remarked on "the psychological and cultural problems associated with 'passing,' . . . community vulnerability and isolation, and [undocumented people's] use . . . as a highly exploited or reserve labor force." Mae M. Ngai, *Impossible Subjects: Illegal Aliens and the Making of Modern America* (Princeton, NJ: Princeton University Press, 2004), 2, 3, 58, 260–63. See also Erin Hatton's useful discussion of the "status coercion" directed at guest workers and the undocumented—"employers can convert workers into criminals (illegal aliens) by exposing their illegality." Erin Hatton, *Coerced: Work under the Threat of Punishment* (Berkeley: University of California Press, 2020), 15.

had created. Some gays of course possessed race (as well as class) privilege, and so the parallel to some immigrant communities should not be overstated.[13] Gay people could be deported from their good jobs in the straight world into the queer world of work. They were not deported out of the country, and their formal status as citizens remained intact.[14] Still, it is noteworthy that so many of the jobs that were predominantly gay in the preliberation era, for example, in restaurant kitchens, are now often predominantly held by immigrants. This may be a key, then, to unlocking some of the mystery of the queer work world.[15]

There are other parallels besides those to immigrant work that are also important to understanding the queer work world. Most obviously, some of the defining features of this world—jobs characterized by low pay, limited opportunities for advancement, and service work, as well as the insecurity of "last hired, first fired"—also defined the work of people of color and women during these years.[16] The queer work world was thus an overlapping one and somewhat more mixed in terms of race and gender than the straight work world. The work that was regarded as distinctly "queer," moreover, was sometimes explicitly racialized; it involved *white* men doing the kinds of service work that African Americans usually

13. Immigrant communities varied as well in the privilege they might claim along lines of race or class. For example, "Europeans and Canadians tended to be disassociated from the real and imagined category of the illegal alien," Mae Ngai has argued, "which facilitated their national and racial assimilation as white American citizens." Ngai, *Impossible Subjects*, 58.

14. Queer immigrants, however, *were* deported out of the country during this period—often as "psychopathic personalities." Margot Canaday, *The Straight State: Sexuality and American Citizenship in Twentieth-Century America* (Princeton, NJ: Princeton University Press, 2009).

15. In making an analogy here between queer and immigrant work, I do not intend to obscure the work histories of those who were both (queer and immigrant). On this point, see Natalia Molina's recent discussion of the numerous gay men who were immigrants from Mexico who worked in her grandmother's restaurant in Echo Park in Los Angeles. Interestingly, Molina recently identified a workplace dynamic for these men very similar to what I describe as "the bargain" operating in the straight work world. In Molina's study, it was "'puede ser pero no ver' (you can be it but not look it)." Natalia Molina, *A Place at the Nayarit: How a Mexican Restaurant Nourished a Community* (Berkeley: University of California Press, 2022), 117. See also Ana Raquel Minian, *Undocumented Lives: The Untold Story of Mexican Migration* (Cambridge, MA: Harvard University Press, 2018).

16. "Last hired . . . first fired" appears in "Editorial," ONE 6 (May 1958): 4; George W. Henry, MD, to Judge Bromberger, December 31, 1947, "Sex Offenders, 1947" folder, box 62, Records of the Society for the Prevention of Crime, Rare Books and Manuscripts Library, Columbia University, New York, NY.

performed.[17] It was also gendered to the extent that men served female customers, for example, as hairdressers or designers, or performed work normally reserved for women.[18] The one job JK was able to find after being kicked out of the military was as a typist.[19] Similarly, women in the queer work world often performed work that was associated with men and masculinity; for example, one who "wanted mechanical work" and felt "happiest when she had a hammer in her hand."[20]

The open inversion of gender norms meant of course that this was a world that was especially visible to outsiders. Many of these workers were not trying to avoid being seen, at least not to the same extent as in the straight work world. "I am a pansy," one man proclaimed to his boss at midcentury, "and I don't have to pretend to nobody!"[21] Those who did not conform to conventional notions of masculinity or femininity, moreover, generally understood that their appearance and manner changed the contours of a job search.[22] "When you were . . . effeminate and had long hair, it was hard to get a job in an office," one African American drag queen remembered of his working life during the 1950s. "So you became a foot messenger, because you could look the way you wanted."[23] Similarly, a group of men who "weren't going anywhere" within a 1960s publishing firm dressed "very gay"—which probably meant tight pants, fuzzy sweaters, and sneakers.[24] Butch lesbians went to work in men's clothes, sometimes

17. Bérubé, *My Desire for History*, 264. White gay men were ship stewards, Bérubé pointed out, doing work that "on land, in trains, hotels, and wealthy homes was often 'colored' work." See also Phil Tiemeyer, *Plane Queer: Labor, Sexuality, and AIDS in the History of Male Flight Attendants* (Berkeley: University of California Press, 2013), 16.

18. Anthony Eschbach, "Gay Men's Work," in *A Book of Readings for Men against Sexism*, ed. Jon Snodgrass (Albion, CA: Times Change, 1977), 205–6.

19. JK to Blanche M. Baker, MD, "Toward Understanding," *ONE* 8 (February 1960): 25.

20. Betty Falek, Placement Director of the Vocational Foundation Bureau, to Mr. Schaefer, September 12, 1952, "1952" folder, box 6, Records of the Society for the Prevention of Crime.

21. Maurice Leznoff and William A. Westley, "The Homosexual Community," in *Sexual Deviance*, ed. William Simon and John H. Gagnon (New York: Harper and Row, 1967), 189 (reprinted from *Social Problems* 3 [April 1956]: 257–63).

22. A survey of five hundred San Francisco employers by the American Civil Liberties Union concluded that employers' concern about sexuality centered on "whether one 'appeared' to be homosexual rather than the orientation itself." "An Employers' Survey by ACLU: Just Don't Look Gay," *Vector* 7 (June 1971): 17.

23. Interview subject 16, New York, NY, 2012.

24. Interview subject 41, New York, NY, 2011; "Growth of Overt Homosexuality in City Provokes Wide Concern," *New York Times*, December 17, 1963, 33. The uniform that police wore to entrap gay men was, according to Steven Rosen, "tight pants, sneakers, and polo sweaters." See Rosen, "Police Harassment of Homosexual Women and Men in New York City, 1960–1980," *Columbia Human Rights Law Review* 12 (1980–81): 169.

riding Harley Davidsons to get there.[25] These visual indications of homosexuality, which often repelled gay people in the straight work world, had the opposite effect in the queer work world and helped to create the clustering that was so widely reported in the press at midcentury.[26] Employed in jobs where they could dress in a way that felt authentic and enjoy the company of others like them, these workers took advantage of the "refuge" aspect of the queer work world.[27]

Yet their freedom did not come cheap. Career pathways that were circumscribed in the straight work world were entirely closed in the queer work world, and many felt blocked. "I lived shabbily in every way . . . without much hope," remembered one man who struggled to regain his footing after he lost his job with the State Department in the early 1960s.[28] Perhaps even more commonly than a feeling of hopelessness, those in the queer work world registered a sense of aimlessness, or a lack of interest in work. "I never had a plan about work, and I never worried about it," a Texas woman who worked alongside other women in light electronics assembly remembered.[29] Another lesbian recalled of the 1960s, "If I had a job, I did, and if I didn't, I didn't."[30] College-educated Donald Vining began his working life as a desk clerk at the YMCA before moving on to low-level office jobs. His partner held similar kinds of employment. "Fortunately," he wrote in 1967, "I am not seriously disturbed by Ken's lack of success or my own," adding, "I am not cut out to advance."[31] For some, the trade-off one made between safety on the job and low pay and poor working conditions was quite explicit. "If I'm not taking the good job," one 1950s butch lesbian demanded, "*what the fuck can you do to me*, what can you do to me? You can't threaten my job if I'm making a dollar five an hour instead of four fifty, five an hour, what can you do to my dollar five an hour

25. Donald Webster Cory, *The Lesbian in America* (New York: Tower, 1964), 92–93; Leslie Feinberg, *Stone Butch Blues* (Los Angeles: Alyson Books, 1993), 100, 174.

26. "Homosexuals naturally gravitate to those circles where they are more or less accepted," reported the *Mattachine Review* in 1956. D. J. West, "Should Laws Be Changed," *Mattachine Review* 2 (April 1956): 28.

27. Bérubé, *My Desire for History*, 265; Cory, *Lesbian in America*, 92–93.

28. Project Open Employment, "Employment Discrimination Survey," folder 36, box 97, Records of the National Gay and Lesbian Task Force, Rare and Manuscript Collections, Cornell University, Ithaca, NY.

29. Interview subject 99, Houston, TX, 2013.

30. Interview subject 52, Lansing, MI, 2012.

31. Donald Vining, *A Gay Diary*, vol. 4, *1967–1975* (New York: Pepys, 1983), 22.

job? Get me fired? Say 'that's a queer working for you?'"[32] This notion of forgoing a "good job" for not having to worry about being discovered was not by any means limited to the working class. Gays from across the occupational spectrum wrote to the employment services that the homophile organizations operated in search of more compatible employment. One Pennsylvania chemist, for example, "tired of the complete hypocrisy," sought employment "in full time data processing, as a homophile."[33] And the Daughters of Bilitis offered to place lesbians in positions "in which the employers know they are gay, thus freeing them from all fear of exposure."[34]

———◆———

While various features of the queer work world are broadly applicable across many types of occupations, in order to get a sense of the sprawling complexity of this universe, a spatial survey might usefully begin with the lower-level white-collar and service jobs that were routinely held by queer people.[35] This sector of the economy was expanding, and the relative looseness made it easier for both men and women to come in and out. "Jobs were easy to get," remembered one lesbian bookkeeper of these years.[36] Temporary agencies in particular employed a lot of gay people.[37] One man remembered that at a time when the dominant cul-

32. Elizabeth Lapovsky Kennedy and Madeline D. Davis, *Boots of Leather, Slippers of Gold: The History of a Lesbian Community* (New York: Penguin Books, 1993), 87 (emphasis mine).

33. JC to ONE, Inc., December 11, 1969, folder 16, box 90, Social Services Division and Satellite Offices Records, ONE, Inc. Records.

34. "Editorial: Economic Independence for Gays," *Newsletter of the Homophile Action League* 2 (March–April, 1970), in folder 7, box 95, Frank Kameny Papers, Manuscript Reading Room, Library of Congress, Washington, DC.

35. Harry and DeVall, *Social Organization of Gay Males*, 157.

36. Interview subject 23, New York, NY, 2012.

37. Two midcentury writers observed, for example, many "queens" circulating in temporary jobs as "busboys, waiters, bartenders, hairdressers, and hospital orderlies." Donald Webster Cory and John P. LeRoy, *The Homosexual and His Society: A View from Within* (New York: Citadel, 1963), 71. On temporary work during this period as "women's work," and the deliberate effort by the temporary industry to portray temporary work as feminized, see Erin Hatton, *The Temp Economy: From Kelly Girls to Permatemps in Postwar America* (Philadelphia: Temple University Press, 2011). The related association between temporary work and queer work appears to have been long lasting. For example, informants reported to two sociologists in the 1990s that "temps are usually women or homosexual men," or "most of the people [in temporary work] that I know have either been gay men or women. Or lesbian

ture placed a high premium on marriage and the steady job that went along with it, working as a temp might in itself be considered a mark of queerness, a sign that one was a little "kooky." This man established relationships with temporary agencies that enabled him to move back and forth between low-level office jobs in San Francisco and New York in the 1950s. He could come into New York on a Friday, for example, and line up a job for Monday. He would rent an inexpensive room on the Upper West Side and enjoy the "pretty busy" bars in the neighborhood in his off hours.[38] This particular setup exemplified what the sociologists William Simon and John Gagnon observed more generally—that "low pay and limited opportunities for advancement" within lower white-collar and service jobs actually "facilitated a homosexual life," which was their main compensation.[39] Not everyone shared Simon and Gagnon's matter-of-fact view of this phenomenon, however. Another team of sociologists observed, with considerably more judgment, that the limited work commitments required by lower white-collar and service jobs allowed gays to "devote large amounts of time to the hedonistic culture of the gay world, that is, to boozing and cruising, maintaining irregular hours, and traveling to other cities to 'make the scene.'"[40] That criticism was even sometimes leveled from within the gay world: "A surprising number [of us] never hold any one job for long," one reader of the *Mattachine Review* lamented in 1956. "Though persons of wide culture and discrimination, [many] hold menial positions and steadfastly avoid engaging in any sort of work that would demand a greater share of responsibility and growth."[41]

The description certainly fit Donald Vining, who had a degree from West Chester State College, had studied at the Yale University School of Drama, and was a voracious reader and keen intellect, an avid theater lover and international traveler. When he arrived in New York, Vining worked briefly as a sales clerk in a department store, then moved to a position staffing the front desk at the YMCA Sloane House, a lively queer cruising scene.[42] It was known there that he was gay; he discussed his social life

women." See Kevin D. Henson and Jackie Krasas Rogers, "Male Clerical Temporary Workers Doing Masculinity in a Feminized Occupation," *Gender and Society* 15 (April 2001): 229–30.

38. Interview subject 26, New York, NY, 2012. When jobs became scarcer many years later, all the movement hampered his employment prospects. The same temporary agency eventually placed him, and he spent the last years of his working life as a cashier.

39. William Simon and John Gagnon, "Homosexuality: The Formation of a Sociological Perspective," *Journal of Health and Social Behavior* 8 (September 1967): 108.

40. Harry and DeVall, *Social Organization of Gay Males*, 157.

41. Letter from Mr. J.P.L., *Mattachine Review* 3 (June 1956): 34.

42. On gay clerks at the YMCA more generally, see John Donald Gustav Wrathall, *Take the Young Stranger by the Hand: Same-Sex Relations and the YMCA* (Chicago: University

with his coworkers and was occasionally teased by his boss: "Mr. Henry . . . said, 'I don't know but what I better arrange for you two to have the same nite off together.'"[43] Vining spent several years at Sloane House, briefly considering moving on but hesitating. The job at the YMCA "contributes to my happiness," he wrote. "I see hundreds of people, mostly men, [have] nothing difficult to do, [and] time to write."[44]

Within a few years, though, Vining had moved on to a "farcical" office position with the Phillippine (*sic*) Desiccated Coconut Corporation. Although he described the office as "a stinking hole," he stayed more than two years, resigning in 1949 to take an extended trip in Europe.[45] He struggled a bit to find work when he returned, with one potential employer stating that he was "a poor employment risk, with all his background."[46] Whether she was referring to the fact that he "up and left his job to go to Europe" or the fact that he had declared his homosexuality and been classified 4f by the military is not clear. But at age thirty he went back to work for his former employer—this time cutting and packing coconuts "with two negroes."[47] When he was arrested for "groping a fellow" in the park, he seemed less worried about the consequences for his job than about the opera ticket he wouldn't be able to use and about missing his first two Italian lessons.[48] While Vining was in jail, his partner, Ken, called the coconut company to tell them Vining had left town to care for his sick father. After his release, Vining told his employer that he had actually been arrested but lied about the reason. He was let go.[49]

After several weeks collecting unemployment, Vining scored well on the clerk-typist test for Columbia University and was hired by the Development Office.[50] As was true across the queer work world, an arrest might cost one a job but generally did not prevent reemployment in similar lines of work. Other than the low salary, Vining thought the Columbia position was "the perfect job for me."[51] Indeed, he stayed in that office for the remainder of his career, and he eventually got Ken hired to work with him. This step is especially notable because Ken was somewhat effeminate in

of Chicago Press, 1998), 170.

43. Ibid., 172.

44. Donald Vining, *A Gay Diary*, vol. 1, *1933–1946* (New York: Hard Candy, 1996), 504.

45. Donald Vining, *A Gay Diary*, vol. 2, *1946–1954* (New York: Pepys, 1980), 26, 131.

46. Ibid., 225.

47. Ibid., 225–26.

48. Ibid., 237.

49. Ibid., 243.

50. Ibid., 272, 269.

51. Ibid., 269.

appearance.[52] As he weighed the decision, Vining noted that "being so much together, we might be the subject of talk up there (as we no doubt are already among the office workers)."[53] Vining was not worried about losing his job, nor was he concerned that he and Ken should make an effort to conceal the fact of their relationship. Rather, he recognized that Ken was already known as gay to his immediate coworkers and that fact would be more widely known once he started his job. Yet he decided it was worth it to have Ken in a job he would be happier in. Years later, he and Ken were still working together. They were "well met, for if either of us had been too successful we would have left the other behind," Vining concluded. "I wouldn't give my life with Ken for any amount of power or success."[54]

Bois Burk, in Berkeley, California, had a similar employment history. Burk was the son of an internationally known educator who served as president of the San Francisco State Normal School, which later became San Francisco State University.[55] Like Donald Vining, Burk had a college degree, in economics from UC-Berkeley, but went right from college to being an office boy and running errands for an insurance company. After some years, he began another low-level job as an equipment clerk for the Physical Education Department at his alma matter, where he stayed for the next thirteen years. This lack of momentum might have been due to a 1946 arrest for lewd vagrancy, which, as was typically the case, *could* have presented an issue at his job at the university.[56] The fact that Burk maintained employment after his arrest (and Vining was reemployed after his) is telling, as is the fact of those arrests in the first instance. For it was often these "little people in various states of economic precariousness" who were *most* likely to be arrested

52. Ibid., 289, 463.

53. Ibid., 478.

54. Vining, *Gay Diary*, 4:22–23.

55. Finding Aid for Papers of Bois Burk, GLBT Historical Society of Northern California.

56. "Bois Burk Employment Record," folder 7, and "Bois Burk Arrest," folder 8, both in box 1, Bois Burk Papers. Burk was arrested under section 647.5 of the California Penal Code pertaining to "every lewd or dissolute person or every person who loiters in or about public toilets or public parks." For those who lost positions, this type of arrest was generally not a bar to eventual reemployment in other clerical or low-level office jobs, but it could take some savvy to navigate. One 1967 study, for example, noted that while 75 percent of employment agencies would not refer someone with an arrest record (whether or not there was actually a conviction), one-fourth of them would. So it was important to know whom to approach. Terry Calvani, "Discrimination on the Basis of Arrest Records," *Cornell Law Review* 56 (February 1971): 471 (citing the 1967 report of the President's Commission on Law Enforcement and Administration of Justice).

in a subway toilet or a park.[57] In part, that's simply because there were lots of queer people in these kinds of "little" jobs. The San Francisco chief of police, for example, kept a list of the occupations of homosexuals he had identified in his city, and many were office clerks or in retail; only a small number of elite occupations were included.[58] Relatedly, only 18 of 493 felony and 48 of 475 misdemeanor charges for homosexuality involved professional men, UCLA's massive study of the policing of consensual homosexuality revealed. Even when professional men were arrested, "silk stocking communities [tended to] 'protect community members,'" often allowing these men to plead guilty to less suspicious charges or allowing "private police" to handle the matter discreetly.[59]

Accordingly, it was the "clerk or bookkeeper, on a small salary, whose sole security is his job, who makes the choicest victim" of blackmailers in the case of arrest.[60] This happened to Burk, who had the misfortune of encountering a figure he initially thought was a cop again in 1951. The detailed notes he wrote about the episode began:

> Propositioned in can, terminal SF. Fellow said he had a room nearby. I told him that I didn't do it his way and he said that would be all right. He did hurry me. Well-dressed, slick talker, 25, but clothes had many spots. Said that he was in a hurry and . . . led me into the can of Foster's on corner and said that it would be alright and he stood against [stall] door with his back but anyone could look over. We both had our hands on each other's penis. A fellow came in to pee and soon he came over and looked in and said, "all right fellows, I saw you, come on out." [61]

57. George W. Henry, MD, to Judge Bromberger, December 31, 1947, "Sex Offenders, 1947" folder, box 62, Records of the Society for the Prevention of Crime.

58. Despite the description of the survey as determining "the extent of homosexuality in all phases of the educational and professional fields; federal employment, state, county, and city government; the arts and sciences; and private industry," the occupations most commonly listed (by far) were "clerk," "office worker," "salesman," or "saleswoman." There were also many whose employment was connected to the queer leisure world—bars or bathhouses, for example. The survey included just a handful of attorneys, physicians, or college professors. See box 1, series 1, "Vice Investigation, 1954–1959" folder, Thomas Cahill Papers, San Francisco Public Library, San Francisco, CA.

59. "The Consenting Adult Homosexual and the Law: An Empirical Study of Enforcement and Administration in Los Angeles County," *UCLA Law Review* 13 (1966): 740–41; Alfred E. Gross to Charles Cook, November 3, 1949, "Sex Offenders, 1949" folder, box 62, Records of the Society for the Prevention of Crime.

60. "The Homosexual in Society—an Address Given before the Seminar of the Brooklyn Division of the Protestant Council on Friday, June 20, 1947," 12, "Sex Offenders, 1947" folder, box 62, Records of the Society for the Prevention of Crime.

61. "Picked up by S.F. Plainclothes man," folder 8, box 1, Bois Burk Papers.

Burk was still working in the Physical Education Department at the university, a fact that the supposed cop zeroed right in on. During extensive questioning, the officer "asked about . . . job and where I worked. I first said education department and clerk." The questioner wasn't satisfied with this. "He later asked more details and exact office where I could be found," adding that "'downstairs in the locker room' didn't make an impression on him the way it did for the officer in '46." The cop told Burk that "he was impressed with my job, a long resident, a good job, and didn't like to see me in San Quentin." He asked Burk for "ten dollars in an envelope to give to the Foster Management." The cop then gave Burk "the impression of coming over to the office tomorrow." By the time he left, Burk was sure the alleged cop had memorized where the clerk worked, "especially Office 2A." Sure enough, the next morning the "clean-cut fairly young so-called cop was back." Burk had his doubts but wasn't sure, wondering, "what if the cop was real and the other guy was a decoy?" Real or not, the officer told Burk that the fine for a felony could be as high as $1,000. Having been arrested before, Burk puzzled, "why did he say it was a felony and not a misdemeanor?" The cop had a plan to work with a judge who could fix things up, and he just needed Burk to withdraw $335 from his bank account to pay the judge. It was a small fortune; Burk complied.[62]

Whether the cop was real or not, he knew Burk's employment was the place to apply pressure. But was it Burk's existing job that was important to protect, or the future opportunities that another arrest would foreclose? A subsequent police investigation of stealing in the university locker room was what finally revealed Burk's record, as the police detective in charge checked Burk's background and then informed his boss about the clerk's past.[63] The police, Burk recalled, "put pressure on my boss to let me go." His boss allowed him to resign "for personal reasons." He left with a positively glowing letter of reference, which described his departure as voluntary. But he also had a letter from his psychiatrist to show to prospective employers. It identified him as a "frank homosexual" but stated that "he had his life well under control," exhibited "no anti-social behavior," and

62. Ibid.

63. Ibid. Burk took a polygraph in connection with the investigation during which the investigator said if Burk was thinking about something else, it would obscure what they wanted to find out about stealing, and so they asked him about sex. He told them "about the '54 and '55 histories." These are the histories he kept of his sexual life that he eventually shared with Alfred Kinsey.

"could be employed in any capacity." Initially, the letter worked. He was hired as an office supply clerk at roughly the same rate of pay. But when he was laid off from that job in 1958, reemployment seemed to become more difficult, despite another very positive reference.[64]

Burk then applied for a clerk's job with the federal government. He was asked to explain the 1946 arrest and responded that his sex life "was more adjusted" than in the past, and that he had worked around college youth for thirteen-and-a-half years without incident. He added that there were "many single people in government today who are leading good lives and are good workers." A month later he was informed, unsurprisingly, that owing to "gross immoral conduct" he "did not meet the standards required for the competitive federal service." A series of temporary jobs followed: He was a process server, sold his own blood plasma, delivered phone books, was an election clerk, was paid as a research subject taking various drugs for the UC Medical School, and conducted a house-to-house survey for a New Zealand beer company, among other jobs. By 1961, he had secured an intermittent position as a clerk with the State of California, filing unemployment claims for an hourly rate. In 1963, he put in an application for permanent employment with the state, but as it was on the heels of another run-in with the police after an erotic encounter "in the company of three negroes" in the Oakland railroads, he was not successful.[65]

While Burk's personal papers indicate an active gay life—both regular cruising activity and involvement in homophile organizations—they reveal less about how he felt about his own employment history. Still it seems notable that he saved a number of positive letters of reference he received from employers, all the way back to his summer job in high school as a filling station attendant.[66] Also significant is the disparity between his employment trajectory and those of his three brothers, who earned

64. "Surveys and Interviews of BB," folder 6; "B.B. Employment Record," folder 7; "Arrests of BB and Others," folder 8: all in box 1, Bois Burk Papers.

65. "Arrests of BB and Others," folder 8, box 1, Bois Burk Papers. The racial dynamics of this incident are interesting because the police seem as bothered by Burk's being in Oakland with African Americans as with the sexual dynamics of the encounter. Relatedly, one white woman reported that her employer found out about her relationship with an African American woman and threatened to fire her. According to this informant, the problem was not that she was gay, rather "it was the interracial relationship." This was in Delaware in the 1960s. Folder 20, box 1, Rochella Thorpe Oral History Project Files, 1992–95, Collection 7607, Rare and Manuscript Collections, Cornell University.

66. "BB Employment Record," folder 7, box 1, and description in Finding Aid, Bois Burk Papers.

doctorates and went on to have prominent careers in science.[67] But, as was typical of his generation, being as invested as Burk was in a gay life often meant not being very invested in a career.

———

Beyond the office environments where Vining and Burk worked, many service-sector jobs were especially associated with effeminacy and attractive to some gay men as they were able to be more open in them than in jobs in other sectors. One San Diego man remembered, for example, how free he felt when was "reborn" as a hairdresser in the mid-1960s. "I reveled in the knowledge that there were other choices to be made besides the dreary, boring, frightened life I was leaving behind," he wrote.[68] Race operated in interesting ways in these settings—queer men of color seemed to be especially visible in many kinds of service jobs. One white New Orleans man remembered, for instance, the African American and Filipino "fairies" who worked in his father's restaurant in the 1950s, remarking that his father "was not hostile" to them.[69] A Black informant similarly recalled that the young man who shampooed in his mother's beauty parlor was "a sissy" but widely accepted.[70] In more upscale environments, however, queer men of color may have been pushed into the background. In expensive hotels and restaurants, for example, being waited on by white gay men marked the experience as an elite one and was what "made the hotel exclusive," one Atlanta concierge explained.[71] These men were sometimes derided as "pretentious ribbon clerks," "striving for gentility," and compared to an equally derided Black bourgeoisie that tended, in two sociologists' troubling account, to "parody the attributes of respectability

67. See Find a Grave entry for Frederic L. Lister, https://www.findagrave.com/memorial /65780083/frederic-lister-burk; and Norval Burk, https://www.findagrave.com/memorial /121074022/norval-foster-burk; and Wikipedia entry for Dean Burk, https://en.wikipedia .org/wiki/Dean_Burk.

68. Eschbach, "Gay Men's Work," 205.

69. Interview subject 51, interview conducted via telephone, 2012.

70. Interview subject 24, New York, NY, 2012. The Black community, this man thought, had "more tolerance for sissies."

71. Interview subject 42, Atlanta, GA, 2012. The historian Phil Tiemeyer has documented an association between gay stewards and the exclusiveness of air travel that goes back to the 1930s. (He did not specify the race of the stewards.) "The companies hiring men actively sought to ensconce the steward in the 'gay' leisure world that these passengers already knew. Thus stewards were servile but also sophisticated and fashionable. Their natural good looks could be used to sell air travel [and] . . . promote air travel as glamorous." Tiemeyer, *Plane Queer*, 40.

of the dominant group."[72] Yet employers clearly and consistently valued these workers. Their queerness was less often something to hide (or even to put up with) than it was to package and brand. One informant remembered "unbridled affection" between the men on the cruise ship he worked on, and a generally "very open environment" for gay men on the staff that probably confirmed the "anything-goes" allure of the boat for passengers. The owner of the cruise line clearly preferred gay men on the ship to dance with and attend to unescorted ladies on vacation.[73] It is notable as well that the historian Allan Bérubé referred to the work of white gay men on ships servicing passengers as work that was "on stage."[74] It was a public performance, in contrast to the work of men and women of color who toiled out of sight below deck. A similar logic might have been at work at Dayton's department store, which was reportedly seeking to hire "swishy gays" in sales positions, and in the general openness of many department stores to employing (especially white) gay men as salesmen.[75]

The service sector was also full of women, but whether white or Black there was nothing "queer" about their presence, and they did not stand out. Where women did stand out was in the service-sector jobs associated with men. Driving a taxi was a common occupation for lesbians during these years. One woman in Buffalo thought half the drivers in the cab company she worked for were lesbians. The owner liked to hire lesbians—it was a transient job, but the lesbian drivers tended to stay. "Got any friends?" he would ask. "Send them in." For her part, the job didn't interfere with her going to the bars, which she did every night. And she could dress the way she wanted. During those years, she wore pants, a shirt, and a binder to work.[76]

———

Factories were another place where women could wear men's clothes, and these jobs attracted butch lesbians and other gender-variant people. Manufacturing may seem a surprising stop on this tour of the queer work world, especially because it was a locus of breadwinner masculinity and

72. Harry and DeVall, *Social Organization of Gay Males*, 156–57.

73. Interview subject 42, Atlanta, GA, 2012.

74. Bérubé, *My Desire for History*, 265.

75. "We seek individuals with the professional expertise and creative energies needed to achieve our company objectives," Dayton's personnel counselor said. "Honeywell Admits Job Bias, Betty Crocker Says Gays Welcome," *Gay News* 1 (August 31, 1970): 1.

76. Interview subject 97, Buffalo, NY, 2013.

by the mid-1970s had become a far more hostile environment for sex and gender nonconformists. Indeed, factory jobs are often considered one of the more dangerous and unwelcome workplaces for sexual minorities.[77] But in the 1950s and 1960s, factory work often allowed queer people to be nearly as open as in the service sector. One hint of this comes from the sociological observation reported in Leznoff and Westley's classic 1956 essay: for gay people, overtness and covertness were very clearly correlated with occupational rank, and individuals tended to conceal more as they ascended the class structure.[78] The dynamic was nicely captured by an informant:

> My promotions have made me more conscious of the gang I hang around with. You see for the first time in my life I have a job that I would really like to keep and where I can have a pretty secure future. I realize that if word were to get around that I am gay, I would probably lose my job. . . . I don't want to hang around with Robert any more or any of the people who are like Robert. I don't mind seeing them once in a while at somebody's house, but I won't be seen with them on the street anymore."[79]

While this pattern is quite familiar, it's notable that Westley and Leznoff's theorem about covertness and occupational rank did not make an exception for craft, operative, or other manufacturing positions. Neither did the sexologist George Henry, whose foundation in New York brought him into regular contact with gay people. While he noted that it was common to associate homosexuals with "clerks, male stenographers, hairdressers, and other semi-skilled" workers who "are removed from the rough and tumble of 'he-men,'" his study of "underprivileged homosexuals" led him to conclude that there was "an appreciable number of homosexual coal-heavers and truck-drivers," adding, "we certainly know a fair number of homosexual factory workers."[80] One factor that facilitated

77. See, for example, Badgett and King's more contemporary findings that "people in the professional and technical occupations hold more tolerant attitudes [about homosexuality], regardless of the measure, and those in the craft and operative occupations are the least tolerant." M. V. Lee Badgett and Mary C. King, "Lesbian and Gay Occupational Settings," in *Homo Economics: Capitalism, Community, and Lesbian and Gay Life*, ed. Amy Gluckman and Betsy Reed (New York: Routledge, 1997), 80.

78. Leznoff and Westley, "Homosexual Community," 184–96.

79. Ibid., 192.

80. George W. Henry, "Research Proposal," 6, in folder "H," Official Files 1937–54, Records of Superintendent Winifred Overholser, Records of St. Elizabeth's Hospital, entry 54, RG 418, National Archives and Records Administration, College Park, MD.

openness in this sector was that many of these jobs were unionized, and unions generally protected workers from being fired for reasons that were treated as arbitrary under the terms of their contracts. According to one African American lesbian factory worker in Detroit, workers counted on that fact.[81] Similarly, a white lesbian from Texas who worked at Western Electric remembered, "We worked in the shop, and we belonged to the union, and *we couldn't be fired.*"[82]

Given that these were years marked by a strong economy and a booming manufacturing sector, many employers probably were not inclined to fire these workers anyway. A promotion to a position as foreman was a different matter, however, and the hope of advancing might have kept some white gay men from being more expressive at work. But, as in the service sector, African Americans and women (of all races) had no such incentive. "A Black man was not going to be promoted," one Detroit autoworker who spoke openly about his boyfriend to his coworkers reflected, "so he was not going to be fired."[83] Other African Americans agreed that being gay at work "was not a big deal" because "you weren't taking anyone's job." The far bigger issue was "how you carried yourself in the Black community and family."[84] This generalization held across occupational settings, but it seems especially true that African Americans in manufacturing jobs found the workplace to be a much freer space than their families. Another African American man remembered "tons of drag queens" who pushed carts in the garment industry because they "wanted to be around the dresses." In that industry, he had his hair colored and wore tight clothes and "looked gay" at work.[85] In the auto plants during these years, African Americans were also campier and more open on the assembly line. One informant remembered many African Americans who were gay there, but only one white gay man.[86]

Black and white women understood as well that employers were happy to have butch women working men's jobs and earning women's wages.[87]

---

81. Folder 6, box 1, Rochella Thorpe Oral History Project Files.

82. Interview subject 100, Houston, TX, 2013 (emphasis mine). A woman was terminated in 1961 after the cover illustration she drew for the lesbian magazine the *Ladder* somehow ended up in her boss's hands. The AFL-CIO fought the discharge, and she was reinstated. Letter from Kerry in New Hampshire, *Ladder* 5 (April 1961): 23. The importance of the union for helping butches to "carve out a niche" in the factory is also a theme in Feinberg, *Stone Butch Blues*, 75.

83. Interview subject 54, Detroit, MI, 2012.

84. Interview subject 10, Washington, DC, 2013.

85. Interview subject 28, New York, NY, 2012.

86. Interview subject 54 and 56, Detroit, MI, 2012.

87. Interview subject 17, New York, NY, 2012.

"I did not feel vulnerable at work," remembered one butch woman of her job during the 1950s. She had a position deburring metal; she kept a picture of her girlfriend on her work bench and wore men's clothes to her job.[88] Numerous women reported being hassled by police on the street for wearing "fly front trousers" or other masculine apparel, but being left alone by their bosses.[89] "I never had any problem with work," reported one woman who worked in factories and also as a bell hop, because "pants was the norm" in those jobs.[90] By the 1950s, according to the historical anthropologists Kennedy and Davis, butches wanted to go *everywhere* in men's clothes. The boldness of these women, who became less and less willing to tone down their appearance, was certainly aided by the boom in manufacturing jobs during these years.[91] When, by contrast, factories began to lay off workers or close, a few of these lesbians went back to wearing women's clothes; more commonly, they stopped working and were supported by femme girlfriends.[92]

Yet even in the best of times, while employers did not seem to care, there were still other employees to deal with. One man remembered "a hipper atmosphere then" and "coworkers who embraced anything presented to them," but many men and women said dealing with coworkers in these jobs did, in fact, require "a strategy." This usually meant a "defensive posture," being ready to come back with a quip in the case of verbal harassment and even to be physically intimidating if necessary.[93] One man remembered asking a trans woman at Ford if she got hassled. The woman had "huge hands and fists" and responded to his query, "*they wouldn't dare*."[94] In her interviews with Detroit autoworkers, the historian Miriam Frank also learned of a trans woman named Buddy who worked at Chrysler in the late 1960s. "She wore a do-rag like Little Richard, color coordinated to her outfit, and cheap perfume you could smell eight feet away. You had to wear leather shoes at the plant. Buddy's were white go-go

88. Interview subject 101, Houston, TX, 2013. Deburring is the process of removing small imperfections from machined metal parts.

89. Interview subject 99, Cleveland, TX, 2013; interview subject 100, Houston, TX, 2013; interview subject 17, New York, NY, 2012.

90. Interview with Rusty Brown, conducted by Len Evans, 1983, box 1, Len Evans Papers, GLBT Historical Society of Northern California.

91. Kennedy and Davis, *Boots of Leather, Slippers of Gold*, 82–83.

92. Ibid.; Feinberg, *Stone Butch Blues*, 143. The homophile magazine ONE asserted that jobs were more difficult to get for those women who adopted butch dress and style. Frankie Almitra, "Why Not Compromise," ONE 7 (May 1959): 16.

93. Interview subjects 54 and 56, Detroit, MI, 2012.

94. Interview subject 54, Detroit MI, 2012 (emphasis mine).

boots." But Buddy's path through the Chrysler plant was also eased by the fact that she was extremely strong with "great big biceps."[95]

Gay men, too, performed toughness at work.[96] They also engaged in a sexual negotiation with other men at work during these years that resembled the trade/fairy paradigm that the historian George Chauncey depicted as hegemonic for the early twentieth century. In that paradigm, "normal" sexual behavior for men was based on gender rather than sexual object choice, so a masculine man (trade) could play the insertive role with a feminine partner (male or female) and still be considered "regular." Only the "passive" (male) party was considered a "fairy." Although Chauncey found that paradigm was beginning to fade in middle-class culture by World War II, it appears to have lingered on among some working-class men, at least until midcentury and perhaps beyond.[97] For example, one autoworker, who was "perceived as a queen," reported having sex with men at his plant "who didn't think of themselves as being gay."[98] Another gay factory worker recalled being approached for sex by men at work who, by contrast, felt shame and "definitely didn't want others to know." He had a place in the plant where he went to meet them. One of his regulars he called "Miss Five Dollars," because this man wanted to be given some money "for things to feel okay," but he didn't want very much![99]

Sexual encounters in the factory between women may have also occurred, but evidence of them is sparse. What seems consistent across male and female experience is that women too sometimes needed "a strategy." The extreme harassment and violence commonly encountered by women in nontraditional jobs was probably more characteristic of the mid-to-late 1970s, when government programs encouraged employers to hire women for typically male jobs at the same time that employment in manufacturing jobs began its irreversible decline.[100] In the 1950s, when

95. Miriam Frank, *Out in the Union: A Labor History of Queer America* (Philadelphia: Temple University Press, 2014), 37.

96. Interview subject 56, Detroit, MI, 2012.

97. The substitution of the homo-hetero binary for a world once divided between fairies and "normal" men occurred unevenly and is difficult to date with precision. It was definitely underway by the 1930s and 1940s, and Chauncey noted that "exclusive heterosexuality became a precondition for a man's identification as 'normal' in middle-class culture at least two generations before it did so in much of Euro-American and African-American working-class culture." George Chauncey, *Gay New York: Gender, Urban Culture, and the Making of the Gay Male World, 1890–1940* (New York: Basic Books, 1995), 13–14.

98. Frank, *Out in the Union*, 37.

99. Interview subject 56, Detroit, MI, 2012.

100. See chapter 8 of Nancy MacLean, *Freedom Is Not Enough: The Opening of the American Workplace* (Cambridge, MA: Harvard University Press, 2006).

there were both fewer women in nontraditional occupations and more jobs, women were probably not seen as a threat in the way they were later. During the early postwar period, then, it was possible for lesbians to sometimes be treated "like one of the guys" on the factory floor.[101] Achieving a comfortable relationship with coworkers was often a matter of "proving oneself" in the job. Working on "male turf," explained Jess, the butch/trans protagonist in Leslie Feinberg's autobiographical novel about queer working-class life at midcentury, required working "with dignity, as though the job was effortless." It also meant ignoring insults—"he-shes at high noon!"—and "dropping one's eyes" when one needed to get around the men.[102]

Things were easier in the factory positions that were held almost exclusively by women, such as light assembly. But anywhere, Feinberg reports, "it took a while for a new person to be accepted into the community of a plant. Before co-workers invested their caring in you they wanted to know if you were staying. Many workers never came back after the first day, or couldn't make quota." The bonds that did form were especially tight among lesbians in plants that were large enough to allow a subculture to develop. "If this were a big plant," Jess, the narrator in *Stone Butch Blues*, speculated, "I would be one of many he-shes, so many we would have our own baseball or bowling teams within the factory complex. There, I would probably have bound my breasts at work, worn a white T-shirt with no jacket, and found my place among our own smaller societal structure within the life of the plant."[103]

Feinberg's lightly fictionalized account of Buffalo closely matches the reality described by other narrators. One trans man, for example, remembered working with many butch women in a glass factory in a small Illinois town during the late 1950s and early 1960s. At that time, he understood himself as a butch lesbian but went further in appearance than the others did, with a crew cut and "men's everything." The work required speed and dexterity, and if you could do it, "you were as valid as the next person," he

101. Cory, *Lesbian in America*, 92–93.

102. Feinberg, *Stone Butch Blues*, 76. I describe Jess as "butch/trans" to avoid claiming Jess as either lesbian or transgender in a queer milieu where there was not, to borrow Julian Gill-Peterson's language, a "clear separation between the categories." Gill-Peterson's reference was to the early twentieth century, but I think the dynamic lingers somewhat at midcentury as well. See Julian Gill-Peterson, *Histories of the Transgender Child* (Minneapolis: University of Minnesota Press, 2018), 13. Also relevant is Jen Manion's construct of the "transbutch" as a "gendered embodiment that is both butch and trans." Jen Manion, "Transbutch," *TSQ* 1 (May 2014): 1–2.

103. Feinberg, *Stone Butch Blues*, 77.

remembered.[104] A Houston woman recalled working during those years in an electronics assembly plant that also employed many lesbians. The lesbians all wore jeans, hung out together at work, and then went together to the bar afterward. For her, it was a seamless integration. "Work, the bar, and home were all in a straight line," she remembered.[105]

⸻

The relationship between the gay bar and the job seemed to parallel in some ways the cultural theorist Paul Gilroy's description of the dichotomization of work and leisure in Black culture. In response to exclusion from primary labor markets, Gilroy has argued that Black cultures "announce and celebrate their exclusion [via] patterns of consumption [whereby] the night time is the right time. The period allocated for recovery and reproduction is assertively and provocatively occupied instead by the pursuit of leisure and pleasure."[106] Moreover, that "occupation" is explicitly sexual: "the black body is reclaimed from the world of work and celebrated as an 'instrument of pleasure rather than labor.'"[107] Gilroy's analysis has resonances with the queer work world. One informant remembered, for example, that he might or might not show up at his clerical job depending on whether or not something was going on at the gay bar the night before. If there was, "I had to be there!" regardless of whether he was supposed to work the next day. On so many mornings, he remembered lyrically, "I was going up the stairs of my brownstone, when I should have been coming down."[108] Another woman, explaining her own erratic work history, remarked, "For working class women, our lives were in the bars."[109]

104. Interview with Jude Patton, conducted via Zoom, 2020.

105. Interview subject 99, Cleveland, TX, 2013.

106. Paul Gilroy, *There Ain't No Black in the Union Jack: The Cultural Politics of Race and Nation* (Chicago: University of Chicago Press, 1991), 210. Gilroy's work referred to contemporary Britain in particular. A similar argument specific to the United States was made by Robin D. G. Kelley, *Race Rebels: Culture, Politics, and the Black Working Class* (New York: Free Press, 2004), 43–51.

107. Gilroy, *There Ain't No Black in the Union Jack*, 202–3. Gilroy is quoting Herbert Marcuse here.

108. Interview subject 16, New York, NY, 2012.

109. Interview subject 36, New York, NY, 2012. While Gilroy's tone was perhaps somewhat celebratory, we shouldn't miss that for many, participating in the queer leisure world while attempting to cobble together a living was exhausting. Marge McDonald, a young lesbian living in a small town in Ohio in the 1950s, felt driven by loneliness to go out every night but wrote in her journal, "I don't get nearly enough rest. I get to bed at 2 or 3 or sometimes 4 and get up at 6:30 to go to work. I take pills to keep me going." Excerpt from

And the psychologist Evelyn Hooker, writing in the early 1960s, famously described "the homosexual world" as "largely one of leisure."[110]

Gilroy's depiction of work and leisure in contemporary Black culture does not fit the queer work world perfectly, however. Like Hooker's framing of the gay world as a "leisure world," it misses the extent to which the gay bar was an economic as well as a sexual node.[111] Bars were important workplaces in their own right, and they were also places where people went to make the connections that led them to jobs. For this reason, the bar will be the penultimate stop on this tour of the queer work world.

It is striking how many small towns and communities supported gay bars in the 1950s and 1960s, and also that big cities had so many.[112] There were an estimated seventy bars in Manhattan operating in the late 1960s, and between fifty and seventy-five in San Francisco.[113] Evelyn Hooker counted sixty gay bars in Los Angeles in 1961.[114] These bars differed quite a lot by locale during this period. They were far more likely to be controlled by organized crime in New York than in San Francisco, for example.[115] Whether mob operations or not, as time went on, gay bars

Marge McDonald's diary, July 2, 1955, box 1, Marge McDonald Papers, Lesbian Herstory Archives, Brooklyn, NY.

110. Evelyn Hooker, "Male Homosexuals and Their Worlds," in *Sexual Inversion*, ed. Judd Marmor (New York: Basic Books, 1965), 94.

111. On the gay bar as a *prepolitical* space as well, see Kennedy and Davis, *Boots of Leather, Slippers of Gold.*

112. Bars in smaller towns and cities were more likely to be racially and gender integrated. Interview subject 31, New York, NY, 2012. The sociologists Donald Black and Maureen Mileski noted that bars in smaller towns and cities were "more democratic," and a single gay bar might serve men and women, rich and poor, old and young. Donald Black and Maureen Mileski, "The Social Organization of Homosexuality," *Journal of Contemporary Ethnography* 1 (July 1972): 91.

113. Weinberg and Williams, *Male Homosexuals,* 59, 79.

114. Evelyn Hooker, "The Homosexual Community," in Simon and Gagnon, *Sexual Deviance,* 173.

115. Police harassment of bars, including raids and entrapment of bar patrons, happened in both cities, but with considerable variation as well. In San Francisco, the historian Nan Boyd has documented a period of persecution of gay establishments prior to 1951, then several years of relative quiet, and then a resurgence of aggressive policing beginning in the mid-1950s. Nan Alamilla Boyd, *Wide Open Town: A History of Queer San Francisco to 1965* (Berkeley: University of California Press, 2003), 114–47. In New York City, Mayor Wagner's tenure was extremely repressive toward gays. His successor, Mayor Lindsay, ended the practice of entrapment and liberalized policing. But still crackdowns did occasionally occur during the Lindsay years, for example, the police raid on the Continental Baths in 1969. Rosen, "Police Harassment of Homosexual Women and Men in New York City," 159–90. See also Anna Lvovsky, *Vice Patrol: Cops, Courts, and the Struggle over Urban Gay Life before Stonewall* (Chicago: University of Chicago Press, 2021).

everywhere were becoming more insular and gays less likely to share space with heterosexual customers.[116] The larger cities featured even greater specialization.[117] There were lesbian bars, "leather" bars, "nellie" bars ("for an effeminate atmosphere"), and "hustler" bars, according to the Kinsey Institute's Martin Weinberg and Colin Williams.[118] San Francisco even had a bar in the Embarcadero area—Maurice's—that catered to the "queens" in the merchant marine. "They would get off the ship with 9 or 10,000 [dollars] paid out in cash," one man remembered. "They would go to Maurice's and they would drink it down. When they ran out of money, they would go back to work."[119]

Everywhere they existed, whatever niche they catered to, these establishments provided critical economic (as well as erotic) functions. They were often the first stop for migrants to a big city looking to get established. Bars were thriving in San Francisco, the police chief's detail investigating homosexuality in the city noted, in part because so many newcomers were there seeking "legitimate" employment.[120] Evelyn Hooker described bars as "communication centers" for "practical problems such as finding a job."[121] Nancy Achilles's mid-1960s ethnography of gay bars described the "neighborhood" bars in particular as "message reception centers," and "loan office[s]."[122] A man who became a legal secretary remembered getting excellent career advice in the gay bar he frequented: to learn the electric typewriter.[123] Another recalled that gay doctors used the bars as a way to build a patient base that enabled them to be more open in their medical practices than would have been possible otherwise.[124] Other accounts emphasized the social welfare functions that bars provided, such as "passing the piss pot" for a patron who faced illness, unemployment, or other difficulties.[125] That

116. Boyd, *Wide Open Town*, 56, 125.

117. Ibid., 70; Weinberg and Williams, *Male Homosexuals*, 63. On the specialization of bars more generally, see Nancy Achilles, "The Development of the Homosexual Bar as an Institution," in Simon and Gagnon, *Sexual Deviance*, 229.

118. Weinberg and Williams, *Male Homosexuals*, 45. (Their data is from fieldwork conducted between 1966 and 1969; see pp. 47 and 65.)

119. Interview with Bob Ross, conducted by Paul Gabriel, 1998, Oral History Project, 98-012, GLBT Historical Society of Northern California.

120. "Memorandum, July 31, 1956, 6, folder 17, box 1, Thomas J. Cahill Papers. On Cahill's investigation, see Lvovsky, *Vice Patrol*, 151–52.

121. Hooker, "Homosexual Community," 178.

122. Achilles, "Development of the Homosexual Bar," 230, 242.

123. Interview subject 32, New York, NY, 2012.

124. Interview subject 79, Cambridge, MA, 2011.

125. Interview with Bob Ross, conducted by Paul Gabriel, 1998, Oral History Project, 98-012, GLBT Historical Society of Northern California.

kind of assistance was especially important for the denizens of the queer work world who were less likely than those in mainstream occupations to have access to health care or other more generous forms of welfare state provision.

"Passing the piss pot" was but one form of economic exchange that occurred among bar patrons. The bar—"with its wide cross-section of occupational and socio-economic levels"—was the institution that was perhaps most responsible for the economically porous nature of gay life.[126] While some professionally successful individuals fell from the straight work world into the queer work world after an arrest or another mishap that cost them a job, others were pulled toward the straight work world by connections they made in gay bars. According to the sexologist Paul Gebhard, opportunities to "rise both socially and economically" were "not infrequent."[127] Another midcentury commentator concurred that the "social mobility which is offered to a young man by the homosexual world is much greater than he would have in the heterosexual world."[128] Yet, while the strong economy may have made the 1950s and 1960s the golden age of queer cross-class economic assistance, an opposite phenomenon was occurring among women. Women who aspired to the middle class saw good, white-collar jobs begin to open to them. Unwilling to risk those positions, they were more discreet than ever before.[129] Professional women were, in fact, somewhat less likely to venture into gay bars than professional men, and also less likely to engage in cross-class mentoring and uplift than their male counterparts there.[130]

The gay bar was not just a place to meet an employer; it was also an employer in its own right. One lesbian distinguished between the respectable people who patronized the bars "now and then," and the "dykes and

126. Hooker, "Homosexual Community," 179.

127. Paul H. Gebhard, "Homosexual Socialization," *International Congress Series* 150 (1966): 1029.

128. Martin Hoffman, *The Gay World* (New York: Bantam Books, 1968), 152.

129. Kennedy and Davis noted that this phenomenon made the lesbian world even more starkly divided by class. The strong economy, they showed, had an opposite effect on working-class women, who assumed they could always find another job. This meant tough bar lesbians became "more willing to risk exposure," while their middle-class counterparts were becoming more careful and taking fewer chances. Kennedy and Davis, *Boots of Leather, Slippers of Gold*, 145.

130. Interview with Bill Plath, conducted by Paul Gabriel, 1997, Oral History Project 97-24, GLBT Historical Society of Northern California. When professional women went to the bars, they were more likely to travel some distance to attend a bar in a different community from the one they worked in.

drag queens" who worked in the bars, lived in the same apartment build-
ings, ate together, and shared a closed social and economic world.[131]
Inside that world, the position of the bartender was the most coveted;
as bars specialized and competed for narrower segments of the market-
place, they became "the bar's most valuable asset."[132] At the most basic
level, the bartender physically represented the segment of the homosexual
market that the bar was competing for; bartenders were a visual marker
of the bar's brand. "The bartender in the leather bar will be a rough looking individual, dressed accordingly; in the faggot bar, the person mixing
the drinks does so with a limp wrist. A female behind the bar indicates a
primarily Lesbian clientele," the ethnographer Nancy Achilles explained
in the 1960s. There were also more subtle distinctions: "In the discreet gilt
and mahogany bars of the financial district, the bartenders wear black ties
and speak with Oxford accents; in the neighborhood bars, slacks and sport
shirts are the rule."[133]

Mixing drinks was less important than attracting and retaining customers. As one job advertisement stated, bartenders must "either have
a following or the personality to build one." If a bartender left one bar
and went to another, the bar's customers usually followed. This could be a
helpful survival strategy when a bar was shut down, because it was rather
easy to find a new spot, install the same bartender, and begin again. Alternatively, if one didn't like the character a bar had taken on and wanted to
change what kind of bar it was, changing the bartender was usually far
simpler and more effective than changing the décor or the menu.[134]

By the early to mid-1960s in San Francisco, an increasing number of
bar owners were actually gay people themselves, who began to colonize
ownership of gay bars by neighborhood. There were lesbian-owned bars
in North Beach, and then lesbian- and gay-owned bars on Polk Street and
in the Tenderloin, a skid row area of the city populated in part by "formerly middle class" homosexuals who were down on their luck.[135] It didn't
take a great deal of money to open one of these simple, sawdust-floor

131. Interview with Blue Lundeen, conducted by Quinn, 1989, 114, box 1, Blue Lundeen
Papers, 83-04, Lesbian Herstory Archives.

132. Achilles, "Development of the Homosexual Bar," 239; see also interview with Blue
Lundeen, conducted by Quinn, 1989, 72, box 1, Blue Lundeen Papers.

133. Achilles, "Development of the Homosexual Bar," 241.

134. Ibid., 239–41. See also Kennedy and Davis, *Boots of Leather, Slippers of Gold*, 149.

135. Appendix, "On Economic Discrimination," circa 1970, folder 2, box 16, Records of
the Gay Activists Alliance, Manuscripts and Archives Division, New York Public Library,
New York, NY; interview with Bob Ross, conducted by Paul Gabriel, 1998, Oral History

establishments, and bar owners often tended to pool money and go in as partners. Some gay owners got loans from the companies that owned the cigarette machines. If a proprietor had already lost a liquor license after being shut down by the state liquor agency, then they were barred from reapplying, so a lot of bars were held in the names of sisters and lovers.[136]

As more gay owners entered the business, bars could be fairly protective of gay people, trying to shelter patrons from the police as well as hire those who wandered in with troublesome situations. The women's bar Mona's, for example, hired lesbians who had been turned away by their families. Jose Sarria, whose drag performance later became a San Francisco institution, was hired at North Beach's Black Cat after he was arrested in a hotel restroom and lost his teaching job.[137] The Tavern Guild, San Francisco's collective organization of gay bar owners, created a fund to assist bartenders who were chronically rendered unemployed by frequent bar closings.[138]

Some found employment not in gay bars per se but in the gay restaurants and coffee shops that sprang up in and around gay bars, such as on New York's Upper East Side.[139] In some locales, a liquor license required that food also be served in the same venue, so bar owners created restaurant concessions, which added to the number of employees and could also draw patrons to the bars. "Show me a restaurant with cheap food," one man remembered of these years, "and I'll show you a lot of gay people."[140] The nightclubs that emerged in San Francisco beginning in the 1940s borrowed from burlesque and vaudeville traditions; they employed not only waitstaff but dancers and performers as well.[141] Drag performances at the Black Cat attracted both gay and straight audiences "seeking a taste of San Francisco's Wild Side," according to the historian Nan Boyd.[142] On

---

Project, 98-012, GLBT Historical Society of Northern California. Lesbians were opening their own bars by the early 1950s in San Francisco. See Boyd, *Wide Open Town*, 132.

136. Interview with Bob Ross, conducted by Paul Gabriel, 1998, Oral History Project, 98-012, GLBT Historical Society of Northern California.

137. Boyd, *Wide Open Town*, 65, 58–59, 68.

138. Ibid., 224. On antipathy between the Tavern Guild and unions, see George Mendenhall, "The Unions and the Tavern Guild," *Vector* 11 (March 1975): 50–51.

139. Weinberg and Williams, *Male Homosexuals*, 61.

140. Interview with Tom Redmon, conducted by Len Evans, 1984, box 1, Len Evans Papers. Redmon also noted that restaurants served a more important social function for gay men in the 1950s and 1960s than later. It was rare to have someone home, he remembered. You would take someone to dinner at a restaurant, and possibly to the baths, but rarely home.

141. Boyd, *Wide Open Town*, 49.

142. Ibid., 56–58.

the other side of the country, the lesbian pulp writer Marijane Meaker asked a taxi driver to take her to a gay bar when she first arrived in New York from the Midwest. The driver took her to the 181, a "commercial/ touristy" gay nightclub on Second Avenue. The waiters, Meaker wrote, "were major butches . . . [and] all of the entertainers were male transvestites who appeared in ball gowns singing, 'balls, balls, how I love balls.'"[143] Mona's in San Francisco also featured butches in tuxes as waiters, and the titillating performances at Finocchio's were legendary and attracted a steady stream of tourists.[144]

For the trans women who performed at Finocchio's, this was more than just a job. The actress Aleshia Brevard was first taken to the night club by a man she was involved with and "instantly felt she had to be there." At the time, she was preoperative, and just beginning to find her way in this world. After Brevard was hired as a member of the chorus, another dancer at the club took her under her wing. Brevard viewed her job as an impersonator as a step in the process that prepared her financially and emotionally for her medical transition. She eventually became a headliner at Finocchio's but left after three years to have her surgery performed under the care of the eminent sexologist Harry Benjamin. It was common, she remembered, for trans women to dance at Finocchio's just long enough to earn the money for surgery and then leave. As a result, Finocchio's eventually preferred hiring cross-dressers to trans women because they tended to stay on the job.[145]

Despite the fact that the "pay was okay," Brevard remembered feeling exploited and disrespected there. When she wanted to leave, the owners tried to stop her by telling her she was contractually bound to keep dancing. Finocchio's also had a rule that performers couldn't come to or leave the club as women, which prevented Brevard from living full-time as a woman. She had a little skull cap that she wore out of the club. The customers would hang around to watch performers leave as male, which was humiliating. That policy "was an example of how Finocchio's did not respect the performers," Brevard remembered.[146] Similarly, Tony Manriquez, an impersonator who danced at the club in the late 1950s, remembered it as relatively well paid and very "glamorous," and was

143. Marijane Meaker, *Highsmith: A Romance of the 1950s* (San Francisco: Cleis, 2003), 36.

144. Boyd, *Wide Open Town*, 68, 77; interview with Blue Lundeen, conducted by Quinn, 1989, 63, box 1, Blue Lundeen Papers.

145. Interview with Alicia Brevard, Scotts Valley, CA, 2013.

146. Ibid.

grateful for help with hair and makeup from a more experienced performer who looked out for Manriquez. Like Brevard, though, Manriquez
remembered the club as unduly restrictive. "We were not allowed to
drink. We were not allowed to go to gay bars or be caught in a situation
that would look bad for the club." Still the contrast between Finocchio's
and other (often mob-owned) establishments was sharp. Manriquez dif-
ferentiated Finocchio's from the My-O-My club in New Orleans and the
82 Club in New York City, where performers were hit and badly abused.
"Someone wanted to quit," Manriquez remembered hearing. "And this
guy took a shovel and beat this drag queen. [At Finocchio's], I never had
to go through that."[147]

Strict codes of respectability at Finocchio's undoubtedly had to do with
the club's Prohibition-era ties with the sex trade and an effort to "legiti-
mize" its business while maintaining its titillating tourist appeal.[148] In
other bars, prostitution remained a central part of the place's economic
life. This was particularly true in several lesbian bars, where lesbians and
prostitutes regularly shared space.[149] But lesbians also engaged in sex
work themselves, often using "mixed" or "street" bars where straight and
gay comingled as a base for operations. Sometimes, prostitutes in these
bars were femmes who supported their butch girlfriends, who worked
irregularly or not at all.[150] Despite occasional complications, femmes who
were prostitutes were seldom stigmatized within working-class lesbian
communities.[151] For one thing, many women who dated butches were
married to men, and some bar-goers saw little difference between these
women and those who were sex workers.[152] Simply put, it was not easy
for working-class lesbians to free themselves economically from sexual

147. Interview with Tony Manriquez, conducted by Don Romesburg, 2000, GLBT Historical Society of Northern California.

148. Boyd, *Wide Open Town*, 77.

149. Kennedy and Davis referred to the rough bars that lesbians shared with prostitutes
and pimps as "street" bars. Kennedy and Davis, *Boots of Leather, Slippers of Gold*, 71–72.
In San Francisco, Tommy's 229 in North Beach and Blanco's in Manilatown were two of
the bars where lesbians and prostitutes coexisted. Boyd, *Wide Open Town*, 88. On the historic linkages between prostitutes and lesbians, see Joan Nestle, *A Restricted Country* (San
Francisco: Cleis, 1987), 154–75.

150. Interview subject 97, Buffalo, NY, 2013; interview subject 138, interview conducted
via telephone, 2016. "Sister-in-lawing" was the term for butches who had more than one
woman prostituting for (and living with) them. Interview with Blue Lundeen, conducted
by Quinn, 1989, 70, box 1, Blue Lundeen Papers.

151. "In general, prostitution was an accepted occupation for fems," Kennedy and Davis
have argued. See *Boots of Leather, Slippers of Gold*, 98–99.

152. Ibid., 98.

relationships with men, whether licit or illicit. Prostitutes earned good money, and their work enabled them to spend time with their butch partners in the bars, and sometimes even support them in style, as with one African American woman in Detroit who earned enough to open a charge account for her lover at Richman Brothers, the men's fine clothing store.[153] For some femmes, then, this was an appealing alternative to secretarial work, waitressing, or retail.[154]

Just as femmes who supported butches through prostitution were not censured, butches who did not work were often accepted. Gay people in the bars generally had the idea that it was "for squares" to go to school or have a career, one lesbian remembered.[155] That butches in particular did not have jobs "was normalized," one Buffalo lesbian who frequented the bars recalled. Butches "were too self-conscious" to appear in women's clothing in order to get work. "It was difficult to go in and apply for a job."[156] Another Buffalo lesbian, who had done well on the civil service exam, refused to dress for the interview, and "wouldn't . . . go."[157] Even factory jobs might require toning down masculine attire for the actual interview; one butch remembered managing this by wearing culottes to her interview, and then jeans once she had the job.[158] After securing a position, freedom to wear men's clothes was one of the job's few perks— factory work for butches tended to be low paid, "and the bosses worked the hell out of you."[159] In working-class lesbian communities during these years, there was a general sentiment that "butches went through a lot" at the hands of the police, and as targets of violence on the street and in

153. Folder 5, box 1, Rochella Thorpe Oral History Project Files; interview subject 138, interview conducted via telephone, 2016.

154. Interview subject 138, interview conducted via telephone, 2016. It was far less common, but a few butch lesbians also used the bar to turn tricks themselves. This *was* stigmatized, according to Kennedy and Davis. "Whereas all other ways of hustling money from straight men enhanced butches' reputations as bold survivors, turning tricks met with strong disapproval from other butches." Kennedy and Davis, *Boots of Leather, Slippers of Gold*, 101.

155. Interview with Blue Lundeen, conducted by Quinn, 1989, 71, box 1, Blue Lundeen Papers.

156. Interview subject 97, Buffalo, NY, 2013. In a more middle-class, suburban milieu, the journalist Jess Stearn noted that "the butches looked feminine at times. The explanation was simple. 'They all have jobs . . . and so while they can cut their hair short and bob or shingle it, they can't afford to look mannish.'" Jess Stearn, *The Grapevine: A Report on the Secret World of the Lesbian* (Garden City, NY: Doubleday, 1964), 239.

157. Kennedy and Davis, *Boots of Leather, Slippers of Gold*, 87.

158. Interview subject 17, New York, NY, 2012.

159. Kennedy and Davis, *Boots of Leather, Slippers of Gold*, 87.

mixed bars as well.[160] Femmes had an easier path through the world, so it made sense to some that they be the primary breadwinners, even if the role entailed sex work.[161]

Male sex work was also sometimes based in the bars. The ethnographer Nancy Achilles described the dark, narrow passages that were common in hustler bars.[162] Working in hotels and in more respectable establishments like New York's Astor Bar, a hustler would get dinner and better money.[163] But hustling often spilled out on city streets in areas around seedier bars, and hustlers adopted the protective dress of juvenile delinquents, "zippered jackets and tight jeans."[164] Times Square was an infamous "sore spot," although by the 1950s prostitution there was becoming less gay, and some male hustlers had moved to East Fourteenth Street in the Village and around the antiques shops on Third Avenue on the Upper East Side.[165] Bayfront Park in Miami was another area where hustlers could be found in the 1950s and 1960s, as was Pershing Square in Los Angeles, "Skid Road" in Seattle, and the lower Polk and especially the "Meat-Rack" in the Tenderloin neighborhood of San Francisco, where young hustlers waited "outside these bars, especially around closing time."[166]

The Tenderloin was also a center for trans sex workers, who according to historian Mack Friedman, faced extraordinary violence but also usually commanded a significantly better wage than male hustlers.[167] This was

160. Interview subject 138, interview conducted via telephone, 2016. On the violence directed at butches, see Kennedy and Davis, *Boots of Leather, Slippers of Gold*, 149, 171. This is also a pervasive theme of Feinberg's autobiographical novel *Stone Butch Blues*.

161. The prolonged lesbian feminist debate about whether butch-femme relationships at midcentury parodied or subverted heterosexuality (and whether they should therefore be derided or celebrated) seems to have focused on the aesthetic and romantic aspects of this cultural formation and missed the profound economic inversion at its center.

162. Achilles, "Development of the Homosexual Bar," 259.

163. Mack Friedman, *Strapped for Cash: A History of American Hustler Culture* (Los Angeles: Alyson Books, 2003), 116; Brown, *Familiar Faces, Hidden Lives*, 160.

164. Achilles, "Development of the Homosexual Bar," 243; Cory and LeRoy, *Homosexual and His Society*, 93. Lesbians who worked as prostitutes were also not strictly based in the bars. In Detroit, for example, one woman remembered lesbians who were "working the bus station," as prostitutes in the mid-1960s. Folder 15, box 1, Rochella Thorpe Oral History Project Files.

165. Friedman, *Strapped for Cash*, 114. Friedman also noted the influx of Puerto Rican hustlers on the Upper East Side. See also "Dear Mr. Cook," May 1, 1949, "1947" folder, box 62, Records of the Society for the Prevention of Crime.

166. Weinberg and Williams, *Male Homosexuals*, 79. See also Robert W. Deisher, Victor Eisner, and Stephen Sulzbacher, "The Young Male Prostitute," *Pediatrics* 43 (June 1969): 939; John Reccy's semiautobiographical novel *City of Night* (New York: Grove, 1963).

167. Friedman, *Strapped for Cash*, 125. Friedman thought (citing letters between the sexologists Harry Benjamin and William Masters) that a date with a performer at Finocchio's (usually made through a waiter) could be arranged for around $50. The higher

significant because for trans women undergoing transition during these years, employment "was the hardest part of the change," as one explained. References were especially difficult. "If we have ever worked, it was as a man . . . and we are often out of work for as long as the change process takes, and that can mean years."[168] Transitioning often led to sharp downward mobility, and for working-class women especially, dancing and sex work were two of the most likely jobs after surgery.[169] The sexologist Harry Benjamin "told 'his girls' that if they did the sex change they would have to kiss their financial futures goodbye," Aleshia Brevard remembered. But her own career was an exception. After leaving Finocchio's to have surgery in 1962, she performed in an act in Hawaii for servicemen that was "transsexual headliners."[170] Eventually, she returned home to Tennessee, went to school, and then embarked on a successful career as an actress, appearing with Don Knotts in *The Love Gods* in 1969, earning roles as a regular on the *Red Skelton Show*, *The Partridge Family*, and finally on the soap opera *One Life to Live*, among other performances. Her career was in what she called "deep stealth," since neither agents, nor directors, nor fellow actors knew about her past.[171]

Brevard's work in theater takes us to one last stop on this tour of the queer work world: the queer professions, such as in the arts, decorating, hairdressing, and in libraries, where gay people clustered. The idea that certain professions were predominantly queer is itself very old and most likely preceded the firm consolidation of homosexuality as a category, which historians associate with the early twentieth century.[172] In 1897,

price was because these women were, according to some, considered exotic. Certain young gay hustlers "who ordinarily might not have cross-dressed" did so in order to command a higher wage. Friedman, *Strapped for Cash*, 124–25.

168. Florence Salomone, "Jobs, Dates, or Maybe Marriage?," *Herald Statesman*, September 24, 1970, https://search-alexanderstreet-com.ezproxy.princeton.edu/view/work/bibliographic_entity%7Cbibliographic_details%7C2078197.

169. Interview with Lynn Conway, Ann Arbor, MI, 2015.

170. Interview with Aleshia Brevard, Scotts Valley, CA, 2013. According to one sociologist's study of seventeen trans women (who transitioned medically in the 1960s), openly performing "as a sex change" was not uncommon. See Thomas Kando, *Sex Change: The Achievement of Gender Identity among Feminized Transsexuals* (Springfield, IL: Charles C. Thomas, 1973), 46–59.

171. Interview with Aleshia Brevard, Scotts Valley, CA, 2013.

172. "The sodomite had been a temporary aberration," Foucault famously wrote. "The homosexual was now a species." Michel Foucault, *The History of Sexuality*, vol. 1 (New York: Vintage, 1990), 43.

the sexologist Havelock Ellis connected, for example, "certain avocations including literature, medicine, acting, and hairdressing," to sexual inversion.[173] Regardless of which specific professions were counted as queer at any particular moment, these occupational stereotypes were commonly deployed about gay people, and the idea that homosexuality was expressed vocationally was pervasive in both social science and popular culture by the mid-twentieth century.[174]

Occupational stereotypes could draw people in and be protective. So, in 1947, one man decided to become a hairdresser simply because "he wanted a profession that would put him in the gay world."[175] An antiques dealer described being gay as "presumed and accepted" in his line of work.[176] Like the military's list of gay bars that were "off limits," even negative images of gay decorators and librarians steered queer people to those professions to find others like them. And "where homosexuals gravitate," heterosexuals shy away, "so that certain types of employment are the almost exclusive domain of cliques of sexual deviants," the *Mattachine Review* observed.[177] Those cliques were mostly left alone in pockets of relative safety. Research conducted in the early 1970s found that those in "stereotypically homosexual occupations" were the least likely to experience difficulties in their jobs as a result of being gay.[178]

Yet the safety of "stereotypically homosexual" professions was not guaranteed. Many had state licensing requirements with moral conduct provisions. The reach of the law was different, then, for a librarian or a nurse than for someone who worked at a soda fountain or in an electronics assembly plant. As a result, many nurses "kept it quiet."[179] One remembered how

173. Havelock Ellis, *Sexual Inversion* (London: F. A. Davis, 1897), 294. It is interesting that medicine is included on this list—Ellis believed that sexual inverts were drawn to the medical profession (and to hairdressing) because they desired close physical contact with patients and clients.

174. See, for example, Harry Haselkorn, "The Vocational Interests of a Group of Homosexuals" (PhD diss., New York University, 1952). This idea was also reflected in midcentury psychological instruments, especially Strong's Vocational Interest Blank, which identified certain occupational interests with "passive" homosexuality. E. K. Strong, *Vocational Interests of Men and Women* (Stanford, CA: Stanford University Press, 1943), 240.

175. Daniel Rivers, *Radical Relations: Lesbian Mothers, Gay Fathers, and Their Children in the United States since World War II* (Chapel Hill: University of North Carolina Press, 2013), 29.

176. Project Open Employment, "Employment Discrimination Survey," folder 28, box 97, Records of the National Gay and Lesbian Task Force.

177. D. J. West, "Should Laws Be Changed," *Mattachine Review* 2 (April 1956): 18.

178. Marcel T. Sahir and Eli Robins, *Male and Female Homosexuality* (Baltimore: William L. Wilkens, 1973).

179. Interview subject 29, New York, NY, 2012.

much less open she was at her job in the hospital than she had been when she worked in restaurants before nursing school.[180] A Black male librarian recounted very developed networks among gay men and lesbians at his job, but other African American librarians warned him not to associate too openly with them.[181] Perhaps most strikingly, one dancer who left the drag world to become a "legitimate" dancer had to give up certain aspects of his appearance, such as plucking his eyebrows, which were crucial for drag but not acceptable in mainstream dance companies. In the dance world during those years, he remembered, "it was okay to be gay as long you didn't seem [it] onstage. You had to be able to butch it up."[182]

Even though professional dancing, nursing, or being a librarian required greater caution than working in a bar or as a clerk, these jobs were still part of the queer work world. Unlike jobs in the straight work world, these positions brought gay people together, were associated with homosexuality, and sometimes enabled unconventional gender expression. As a result, they affirmed the gay people who worked in them. The straight work world could be summed up in one man's succinct statement: "I couldn't wait to leave the office and be who I was."[183] Everywhere in the queer work world, people were who they were. Librarians and nurses may have kept it quiet, but they densely populated their professions and were among the very first to organize in the early 1970s. The dancer above had to "butch it up" on the stage, but the straight women in the company knew who the gay men were and loved dancing with them.[184]

Jobs are critical in the formation of selfhood—and not just for the dancer, the librarian, or the nurse described above. Rather, this could be said to apply to nearly all jobs. In the queer work world in particular, though, it was especially true for the kinds of work that the literary critic Meg Wesling has called "playful work"; these were jobs that by their nature refused the "alienating or estranging effects of labor."[185] Think of the women who performed at Finocchio's; the drag queens pushing carts around the garment industry because they wanted to be around the dresses; the gay stewards camping with each other on cruise ships; or the man who proclaimed joyfully, "I was a typist, and I wanted to type!"[186] Yet

180. Interview with Marcy Fraser, San Francisco, CA, 2015.
181. Interview subject 19, New York, NY, 2012.
182. Interview subject 28, New York, NY, 2012.
183. Interview subject 35, New York, NY, 2012.
184. Interview subject 28, New York, NY, 2012.
185. Meg Wesling, "Queer Value," *GLQ* 18 (2012): 111.
186. Interview subject 16, New York, NY, 2012.

jobs also affirmed identity in work that could in no way be associated with play, or even with a subaltern sexuality finding its exuberant channel. This was true, for example, in the blue-collar factory jobs that seem to exemplify Marx's definition of estrangement, a person doing work that "does not affirm himself but denies himself."[187] Yet, butch women working factory jobs in the 1950s received validation—from otherwise lousy working conditions—that was not culturally available anywhere else. In explaining to a bereft straight male coworker why she was leaving the small bindery where they had worked together for a job in the steel mills, the narrator in *Stone Butch Blues* said, "You don't understand what it would mean for me to work in a steel mill, do you? . . . All we [butches] have is the clothes we wear, the bikes we ride, and where we work."[188] In an even starker contrast to most descriptions of factory work during these years, Feinberg had Jess say, "I felt free. Free to explore what freedom meant." And then Jess concluded without irony, "I looked at my watch. It was time to go to work."[189]

It would be of course easy to romanticize this world of work, to celebrate the freedom that people like Jess (or, really, Feinberg) may have felt as they punched in on the assembly line, a testament to the resilience and creativity with which vulnerable people made their way in the world. But even when work in the queer work world could be affirming, it was also always quite exploitative. The queer work world, moreover, was part of a labor system connected (by aggressive state policing and the void of legal protection) to the straight work world. Those worlds could seem separate, but they touched all the time, at work and outside of it, in the blurry spaces between work and leisure. They touched, for example, when Howard Brown, then a young doctor who would later become New York City's commissioner of health, learned that the attractive man he had met in the bar and was excited to be going home with was a hairdresser. *His reaction was to flinch*. This sort of spasmodic, instantaneous, involuntary reaction was followed later by a more conscious decision: to drop the man because he "did not want to be seen with a hairdresser."[190] There is no mention of effeminacy, and his reaction at first seems strange. Disconnected from

187. Karl Marx, "Economic and Philosophic Manuscripts of 1844," in the *Marx-Engels Reader*, ed. Robert C. Tucker (New York: Norton, 1978), 74; on estrangement (and its relationship to alienation), see Wesling, *Queer Value*, 109.

188. Feinberg, *Stone Butch Blues*, 100. I use female pronouns for Jess here because this is what Feinberg most often used for her. See Jacob Klein, "Queer History and *Stone Butch Blues*," Jewish Women's Archive, June 2, 2017, https://jwa.org/blog/queer -history-and-stone-butch-blues.

189. Ibid., 47.

190. Brown, *Familiar Faces, Hidden Lives*, 51.

effeminacy and its misogynistic association with weakness in men at mid-century, it seems that what made Howard Brown flinch was only the fact that the man held a visibly queer job, that he belonged, in the parlance of the time, with *"the ones who . . . had nothing to lose."*[191] Did the hairdresser remind this very ambitious man of the hazards that endangered his own opportunity? The queer world of work posed a threat for those who were not in it and was yet another vector by which desire shaped the working life, and the working life shaped desire.

191. Meaker, *Highsmith*, 137 (emphasis mine).

PART II

Law and Liberation

CHAPTER THREE

"I Have Brought the Very Government . . . to Its Knees"

THE CAMPAIGN TO END THE BAN ON FEDERAL EMPLOYMENT

WHAT SET THE ASTRONOMER and eventual gay rights pioneer Frank Kameny apart from other gay men was not his 1956 arrest in the men's room at the Key Terminal in San Francisco. There was also nothing so unusual about his subsequent termination from his government job with the Army Map Service, in accordance with a 1953 executive order barring those with "sexual perversion" from the federal service.[1] Rather, the first sign that Kameny was atypical was his refusal to acquiesce to what for many in similar circumstances amounted to a generational survival strategy: he did not seek refuge in the queer work world. His refusal to do so was immediate and quite explicit. "I was NOT going to throw away my training and abilities on some menial job," Kameny seethed, "even if I starved first."[2]

---

1. The Civil Service Commission was charged with enforcing President Eisenhower's 1953 executive order (10450) that named "sexual perversion" as a condition that required removal from the federal service. (Kameny's job with the Army Map Service was a civilian position.) The purge of homosexuals from the federal government, however, actually began with President Truman's Loyalty Program in 1947. See David K. Johnson's definitive account, *The Lavender Scare: The Cold War Persecution of Gays and Lesbians in the Federal Government* (Chicago: University of Chicago Press, 2004).

2. Franklin E. Kameny to the Mattachine Society, May 5, 1960, 5, folder 1, box 44, Frank Kameny Papers, Manuscript Reading Room, Library of Congress, Washington, DC.

He starved. "Literally not merely figuratively." He recalled living on as little as twenty cents a day, and sleeping on his side because it was less painful with his protruding rib cage.[3] He initially sought another job in astronomy, a profession he had set his heart on even as a small child.[4] "I am trying desperately to rebuild a professional career which was badly shattered in mid-course," he wrote.[5] And as an astronomer "at the commencement of the space age," his resume initially received a strong response. "I was flown in luxury for interviews all over the country . . . treated with great deference, and 'wooed' with great care," Kameny remembered. Until prospective employers learned Kameny would not be able to get a security clearance. Then their interest evaporated, and in the meantime Kameny's unemployment compensation ran out.[6] His correspondence from those years exposes a bleak material existence during an era usually associated with affluence—his teeth were a mess, his clothes were disheveled, his house in disrepair.[7] One visitor remembered the springs on Kameny's sofa poking through the worn upholstery.[8] An avuncular Kameny offered a fellow homophile struggling with unemployment advice on "how to live on no income" and "how to fend off your creditors," sardonically remarking that "I am *very* experienced."[9] He cautioned another man who was also fired from federal employment because of homosexuality that he "may find the going rough *at first*."[10] But nearly twenty years after his arrest, Kameny was still describing himself as "perpetually on the brink of financial disaster."[11]

What kept Kameny from going completely over the brink was that he eventually found short-term and usually low-level technical work to keep

3. Franklin E. Kameny, "More Entrapment," *Los Angeles Advocate*, July 1968, 11; William N. Eskridge, *Dishonorable Passions: Sodomy Laws in America, 1861–2003* (New York: Viking, 2008), 137.

4. Franklin E. Kameny, "An Informal, Condensed Autobiography," folder 11, box 43, Frank Kameny Papers.

5. Franklin E. Kameny to JL, July 31, 1962, folder 5, box 136, Frank Kameny Papers.

6. Franklin E. Kameny to the Mattachine Society, May 5, 1960, p. 4, folder 1, box 44, Frank Kameny Papers.

7. See especially letters from Frank Kameny's mother, who constantly worried about the state of his finances, folders 3–6, box 1, Frank Kameny Papers.

8. Interview with Harvey Friedman, Washington, DC, 2013.

9. Frank to Dick, June 25, 1966, in *Gay Is Good: The Life and Letters of Gay Rights Pioneer Franklin Kameny*, ed. Michael G. Long (Syracuse, NY: Syracuse University Press, 2014), 133–34.

10. Franklin E. Kameny to JLS, May 28, 1968, folder 7, box 43, Frank Kameny Papers (emphasis mine).

11. Franklin E. Kameny to DBG, January 26, 1976, folder 10, box 92, Frank Kameny Papers.

himself afloat, sometimes with "progressive" employers who were kind about his predicament but still pleased to get Kameny at a fraction of the cost of "other, similarly qualified physicists." Yet whenever cutbacks came, without a security clearance, Kameny was usually the first to go.[12] As time wore on, Kameny gave up on ever fully returning to the world of science.[13] Instead, Kameny mobilized to fight the injustices responsible for his plight. Here he revealed more of his maverick nature. People who were fired for homosexuality in the 1950s and early 1960s rarely protested.[14] Lawyers were reluctant to help, or at the least very expensive to retain.[15] The ACLU still believed that homosexuals might be unsuitable employees and that the government's position did not pose a civil liberties issue.[16] Most gay people would not have complained about these matters because, as the Gay Activists Alliance later reflected in a policy paper, there was nowhere to lodge a complaint. "When brutality and discrimination did come down on an individual his only recourse was to pick up the shattered pieces of his life and try to make the 'best of it.'"[17]

These anecdotal assertions are borne out by a larger body of data. For example, the records of midcentury loyalty and security investigations of federal employees were divided by National Archives staff into "thin" and

12. Eric Cervini, *The Deviant's War: The Homosexual vs. the United States of America* (New York: Farrar, Straus and Giroux, 2020), 106, 133.

13. In later years, Kameny also scraped by on speaking fees when he was able to get them. On Kameny's erratic and precarious employment history, see Cervini, *Deviant's War*, especially 43, 51, 55, 88–89, 106, 128, 132–33, 163, 165, 206, 221, 228, 273–74, 288–89, 291, 348.

14. The Chicago attorney and activist Pearl Hart lamented the "sense of guilt in relation to . . . personal conduct" and wished for "a stronger will to fight back" among homosexuals who ran into legal trouble. See Pearl Hart to the Mattachine Society of New York, January 12, 1962, folder 1, "Legal Matters," box 4, Records of the Mattachine Society of New York, Manuscripts and Archives Division, New York Public Library, New York, NY. The Council on Religion and the Homosexual concurred that "most homosexuals will not fight their cases." "A Brief of Injustices," *ONE* 13 (October 1965): 8.

15. On lawyers who would handle gay matters but for "fantastic sums," see unsigned letter to Boston Area Council, folder 1, box 4, Records of the Mattachine Society of New York.

16. Herbert Monte Levy, Staff Counsel, ACLU, to Mrs. Thomas Dillingham, September 20, 1955, "Exclusion of Homosexuals," folder 2, box 887, Records of the ACLU, Seeley Mudd Library, Princeton University, Princeton, NJ.

17. "'A Homosexual Bill of Rights,' Presented by the Gay Activists Alliance to the New York State Legislature," February 1, 1971, folder 40, box 165, Records of the National Gay and Lesbian Task Force, Rare and Manuscript Collections, Cornell University, Ithaca, NY. "Homosexuals have historically been reluctant to face the potential costs and public exposure of litigation," one lawyer said. Todd Mitchell to Wisconsin Civil Liberties Board, June 20, 1973, Saransky folder, box 2986, Records of the ACLU. See also Irving Kovarsky, "Fair Employment for the Homosexual," *Washington University Law Quarterly* 1971 (Fall 1971): 543.

"thick" files. The "thin" files were the cases in which people named in an investigation basically disappeared in the aftermath, without much additional information. The "thick" files involved those in which people fought their terminations, sat through administrative hearings, and appealed decisions. While the thin files were destroyed, there are approximately two thousand thick files from these years stored at the National Archives.[18] A roughly 20 percent sample (four hundred cases) revealed just two cases pertaining to homosexuality.[19] Historians believe more civil servants were purged for homosexuality than for political subversion during these years, and even the hard numbers that are known for select agencies suggest there ought to be many more cases in this sample that concerned homosexuality.[20] But these are the "thick" files—*the cases of those who protested*. As a 1953 memorandum elaborated, 114 State Department separations for sexual deviation were officially recorded as resignations because named employees were "afraid" to request a hearing. "These individuals resigned when confronted with the evidence," this observer concluded; "the publicity factor is a strong one."[21]

So Kameny's fighting instinct was rare during this period. But if his rights consciousness was distinct, it was nonetheless still a work in progress. His initial efforts to appeal his termination by the Army Map Service were, for example, more pragmatic than principled. As part of that

18. Most of the cases are from the late 1940s through the early 1960s. "Analysis and Appraisal of the Civil Service Commission, Regular Sized Investigative Case Files at the Washington National Records Center," tab D of "Selective Index to Documents Relating to Appraisal of Average CSC Personnel Security Case Files" (in author's possession). I'm grateful to historian Landon Storrs for providing me with this document. The "thin" files—which would have provided definitive data on the number of civil servants who were terminated for homosexuality during these years—were ironically destroyed within weeks of the 1975 decision by the Civil Service Commission to end its outright ban on gay employees. See "Minutes of the Proceeding of the US Civil Service Commission," June 25, 1975, box 58, RG 146, National Archives and Records Administration, College Park, MD.

19. Oversize Personnel Security Investigation Case Files, RG 478, National Archives.

20. For example, from May 28, 1953 to June 30, 1954, 618 civil servants were terminated or resigned owing to charges related to sex perversion. US Civil Service Commission, *1954 Annual Report* (Washington, DC, 1954), 135. The historian David Johnson estimated that around one thousand had been fired by the State Department alone by the early 1960s, and probably five thousand across the federal government. Within the State Department, Johnson observed, "the highest profile cases may have involved suspicion of communism, but the majority of those separated were alleged homosexuals." Johnson, *Lavender Scare*, 76, 166.

21. Memo from Washington, DC, Office, to Alan Reitman, "Federal Employee Security Program," October 6, 1953, "Freedom of Belief, Expression, and Association, Loyalty and Security, 1940–1969" folder, box 876, Records of the ACLU.

appeal, he wrote to Benjamin Karpman asking the eminent psychiatrist to submit a statement on his behalf. Kameny did not come close to presenting himself as gay to Karpman, noting instead that "I have been seeing a great deal of one particular young woman. I would be pleased to marry her," although "I'm not sure of her feelings." In the statement Karpman subsequently provided, he concluded that Kameny's history of sexual experimentation was, in fact, evidence of a *scientific* rather than a homosexual nature: "From a scientist with a large element of inquisitiveness and experimentation in his psychological make up, and of a liberal, open minded . . . civilized attitude on most questions," Karpman wrote, "such experimentation is rather to be expected . . . and cannot be taken to be indicative of his orientation."[22] By 1958, Kameny was dealing directly with the Civil Service Commission (CSC), asking them to evaluate his sexual "irregularity" in the context of the "*whole person*."[23] After the CSC denied his appeal, Kameny wrote to the secretary of defense. He did not appeal on behalf of "the civil liberties of all homosexuals," as biographer Michael Long recognized, but only asked that the government "treat him as a distinct individual."[24]

Still, if Kameny did not make "gay is good!" his slogan for several years, he quickly moved to a more affirmative position.[25] With the help of an attorney, he became the first gay person to take on federal employment policy in court. By the time he wrote the Mattachine Society of New York to request financial help with his legal expenses, he was directly challenging the CSC's characterization of homosexuality as immoral and arguing that its actions constituted illegal discrimination under the Fourteenth Amendment.[26] After Kameny lost his case at the district and appeals court levels, his lawyer resigned but left Kameny with a pamphlet on how to write a petition for a writ of certiorari before the US Supreme Court. Kameny then wrote and filed his own petition, "phoning the Court itself

22. Franklin E. Kameny to Dr. Karpman and statement from Dr. Karpman, undated, approximately late 1957 or early 1958, folder 4, box 44, Franklin Kameny Papers.

23. Franklin E. Kameny to Mr. Ellsworth, 1958, in Long, *Gay Is Good*, 25–27 (emphasis in the original).

24. Franklin E. Kameny to Mr. McElroy, June 1, 1959, in Long, *Gay Is Good*, 29–32.

25. "Gay Is Good" was unanimously adopted at the 1968 conference of the North American Conference of Homophile Organizations. It was an outgrowth of Kameny's position that homosexuality was not a sickness. The Mattachine of Washington adopted the "anti-sickness resolution" in 1965. Kay Tobin and Randy Wicker, *The Gay Crusaders* (New York: Paperback Library, 1972), 98–99.

26. Franklin E. Kameny to the Mattachine Society, May 5, 1960, folder 1, box 44, Frank Kameny Papers.

whenever I needed further guidance."[27] Years later he recalled that "writing it forced me to formulate my ideas on gay rights," including the then novel assertion that discrimination against homosexuals was analogous to discrimination based on race or religion.[28] The Civil Service Commission was dismissive of this claim: "I think we can dispose of the constitutional question rather quickly," the agency's general counsel scoffed.[29] But as Kameny labored "long and hard on his constitutional right," he began a rigorous "course of informal, on-the-job training in law, which opened the door to an informal, unofficial, but enormously productive career as a 'lawyer without portfolio.'"[30]

——◆——

Unsurprisingly, the Supreme Court denied cert, "thus throwing out the window 3½ years of my life and much money," Kameny lamented at the time.[31] But the lawsuit—in addition to providing Kameny with a legal education of sorts—was by no means a waste of effort. The publicity provided a spark. A civil servant named Bruce Scott, who had been fired by the Department of Labor in circumstances that were very similar to Kameny's, read a short article about Kameny's court case in a homophile publication. Scott was nearly fifty years old and had struggled to find work in the aftermath of his termination. He called Kameny to commiserate. Soon after, in the fall of 1961, Kameny and Scott joined with a few others to found the Mattachine Society of Washington (MSW). That organization became more forceful than prior homophile organizations in advocating for the civil rights of homosexuals, taking particular aim at employment

27. Franklin E. Kameny, "Government v. Gays: Two Sad Stories with Two Happy Endings, Civil Service Employment and Security Clearances," in *Creating Change: Sexuality, Public Policy, and Civil Rights*, ed. John D'Emilio, William B. Turner, and Urvashi Vaid (New York: St. Martin's, 2000), 191.

28. Ibid.; "Petition for a Writ of Certiorari," in *Kameny v. Brucker* (October 1960) (no. 676), 50–51. See also Jeffrey Kosbie, "Contested Identities: A History of LGBT Legal Mobilization and the Ethics of Impact" (PhD diss., Northwestern University, 2015), 74.

29. L. V. Meloy, General Counsel, to John W. Macy, September 21, 1962, in "Chapter 7" of Office of General Counsel (OGC) files, Civil Service Commission records, Mattachine Society of Washington, https://mattachinesocietywashingtondc.org/the-deviants-trove/.

30. Kameny, "Government v. Gays," 191.

31. Franklin E. Kameny to WL, July 24, 1961, folder 1, box 44, Frank Kameny Papers. Kameny's own legal battle continued. In 1969, some twelve years after his firing, Kameny initiated another lawsuit against the Department of Defense to fight the denial of his security clearance. Franklin E. Kameny to Ralph J. Temple, January 4, 1969, "Correspondence 1959–1969" folder, box 45, Frank Kameny Papers.

discrimination by the federal government.[32] Most notably, the group organized pickets in front of the White House, the Pentagon, the State Department, and the Civil Service Commission to protest the government's discriminatory employment policies.[33]

The Mattachine Society of Washington eventually leveraged its picketing to force a face-to-face meeting with the Civil Service Commission.[34] Kameny and his colleagues sat down with agency officials at a moment of peak CSC hostility. An internal memo revealed that the agency "leaned over backwards" to remove homosexuals, applying their own "emotional reactions and moral standards" to a population they deemed "uniquely nasty."[35] Sitting down in person did not make a dent in the CSC view of things, and the disappointing end result of that meeting was the CSC's renewed statement that it had to comply with "existing mores" regarding homosexuality.[36] Yet in the meantime, Kameny had already authored a pamphlet—"How to Handle a Federal Interrogation"—which advised civil servants to "sign no statements," "say nothing," and get counsel.[37] Kameny plastered these pamphlets up on State Department and Pentagon bulletin boards, placing them in holders labeled "Take one!"[38]

Kameny's growing expertise rippled across gay Washington. An employee of the Library of Congress remembered that he knew immediately what to do when he was unexpectedly called into an investigation; he didn't admit anything, didn't sign anything. "We had all been prepared by Frank Kameny," he explained. "If you were in a gay professional milieu in DC, you knew how to handle it. [This] was discussed at dinner

32. David L. Aiken, "Gay Is Now Okay in 2.6 Million Jobs," *Advocate*, July 30, 1975, 4; Lillian Faderman, *The Gay Revolution: The Story of the Struggle* (New York: Simon and Schuster, 2015), 147.

33. John D'Emilio, *Sexual Politics, Sexual Communities: The Making of a Homosexual Minority in the United States, 1940–1970* (Chicago: University of Chicago Press, 1983), 164–65.

34. Franklin E. Kameny, "U.S. Government Hides behind Immoral Mores," *Ladder* 10 (June 1966): 17–20.

35. John W. Steele to O. Glenn Stahl, November 17, 1964, in "Chapter 7" of Office of General Counsel (OGC) files, Civil Service Commission records, Mattachine Society of Washington, https://mattachinesocietywashingtondc.org/the-deviants-trove/.

36. In other arenas, CSC chair John Macy was quite progressive, noting that the commission planned "a renewed attack on prejudice itself . . . with the goal of eradicating every vestige (of prejudice) from the Federal Service." The irony was not lost on Frank Kameny. See Kameny, "U.S. Government Hides behind Immoral Mores."

37. East Coast Homophile Organizations, "How to Handle a Federal Interrogation," folder 24, box 19, Papers of Phyllis Lyon and Del Martin, GLBT Historical Society of Northern California, San Francisco, CA.

38. Tobin and Wicker, *Gay Crusaders*, 101.

parties."[39] Kameny also provided direct advice. "You are free to phone at any hour of the 24, however late," he characteristically told a caller seeking assistance.[40] And he increasingly represented gay civil servants as lay counsel at the administrative level. In those settings, he touted his lack of formal legal training as an asset. "Attorneys are not a privileged class in our society," he snapped at a CIA lawyer who had attempted to put Kameny in his place. "I am not a second-class citizen subordinate to attorneys-as-first-class citizens." Kameny reminded his opponent that as a non-attorney *he* could not be disbarred. That "give[s] me a considerably enhanced freedom of action . . . over accredited attorneys," Kameny crowed. "It is a freedom in which I exult."[41]

Indeed, during these years, Kameny honed what could only be described as a politics of annoyance. In the earliest hearings in which he appeared, the Civil Service Commission attempted to bar Kameny from the proceedings, telling him he could not be in the room but only down a long corridor a full city block away. Kameny instructed his client to request to see him after every question, and the two of them then together drafted a written response to each query, no matter how simple or routine. As a result, the "employee got his exercise for the day (two blocks of walking per question)," and the proceedings dragged on for hours.[42] Kameny had made his point. Eventually, "the infuriated bureaucrats gave in and [Kameny] took a seat beside the gay person he was counseling."[43] He was full of such stunts: sending copies of Kafka to government lawyers, or addressing correspondence to them as "Pervert" Smith or "Pervert" Jones because they were, he explained, perverting the law.[44] Throughout, he claimed that he behaved not as an "amateur lawyer trying to act like [a] professional . . . , but as a professional human being . . . trying to teach our [government] to be the same."[45]

39. Interview subject 13, Washington, DC, 2013.

40. Franklin E. Kameny to DD, May 5, 1969, folder 13, box 19, Frank Kameny Papers.

41. Franklin E. Kameny to Edmund Cohen, CIA Office of General Counsel, October 23, 1977, folder 5, box 34, Frank Kameny Papers.

42. Franklin E. Kameny to JA, August 18, 1983, folder 11, box 13, Frank Kameny Papers.

43. Tobin and Wicker, *Gay Crusaders*, 107.

44. Franklin E. Kameny to William P. Berzak, September 13, 1973, folder 13, box 41, and DH Jr. to Franklin E. Kameny, February 6, 1967, folder 7, box 17, both in Frank Kameny Papers. In returning Kafka's *The Trial* to Kameny, the hearing examiner opined that "the aforesaid book is irrelevant and immaterial and accordingly should not be included in the record in the applicant's case."

45. Franklin E. Kameny to SP, March 7, 1969, "Correspondence 1959–1969" folder, box 45, Frank Kameny Papers.

Despite his many extralegal flourishes, Kameny believed that change would ultimately come through the courts—he called trying to change cultural attitudes without accompany legal change "punching at pillows"—and so he and Bruce Scott were cultivating relationships with lawyers from the National Capital Area Civil Liberties Union (NCACLU).[46] Scott and Kameny regularly attended chapter meetings, but the real breakthrough occurred when the unemployed Scott took a job as a secretary for the NCACLU. This personal connection made it easier for Kameny and Scott to persuade the NCACLU to help Scott sue the government.[47] Scott's case was also a good one for the ACLU affiliate to make an initial foray—well ahead of the national organization—into gay employment rights. Scott had been at the Department of Labor for seventeen years when he was required to get a security clearance. That process turned up an arrest for loitering nearly ten years prior, and his boss suggested he resign. His past record, however, followed him into his attempts to find employment in the private sector, his home was foreclosed, and he endured several difficult years.[48] In 1961, then a member of the Mattachine, he reapplied for a federal job with the Department of Labor. He passed the qualifying exams but was soon under investigation for homosexuality.[49] Scott refused to answer the Civil Service Commission's questions about his sex life, which he said was "like religion, a private affair."[50] In his claim to a right of sexual privacy, Scott followed other homophile activists who had begun to articulate such a right a few years prior. So had a handful of liberal lawyers, but Scott was nonetheless deemed unsuitable for government employment because of "immoral conduct." The CSC refused to specify the precise content of the charges against Scott.[51]

Scott's initial lawsuit against the government, filed in 1963, was not successful. Maintaining the judiciary's tradition of deferring to administrative

46. Tobin and Wicker, *Gay Crusaders*, 97; Kameny, "Government v. Gays," 192. On the ACLU's policy on homosexuality, see Kosbie, "Contested Identities," chapter 5.

47. Cervini, *Deviant's War*, 87–88, 110–11, 119–20.

48. Johnson, *Lavender Scare*, 156–58.

49. Franklin E. Kameny, draft of "U.S. Government Clings to Prejudice," folder 14, box 3, Frank Kameny Papers.

50. "Homosexuality as Bar to U.S. Job Challenged," *Washington Evening Star*, April 24, 1963, A-2.

51. Franklin E. Kameny, draft of "U.S. Government Clings to Prejudice," folder 14, box 3, Frank Kameny Papers. On the claim to sexual privacy among homophiles and liberal lawyers, see Clayton Howard, *The Closet and the Cul-de-Sac: The Politics of Sexual Privacy in Northern California* (Philadelphia: University of Pennsylvania Press, 2019), 55, 160. See also Sarah E. Igo, *The Known Citizen: A History of Privacy in Modern America* (Cambridge, MA: Harvard University Press, 2018).

findings, the district court upheld the CSC decision to refuse to qualify Scott for federal employment.[52] "Homosexuality is immoral under the present mores of society and is greatly abhorrent to the great majority of Americans," Judge Hart of the US District Court of the District of Columbia opined.[53] Scott appealed, and "the Court deliberated for an unusual period of six months." Scott expected to lose, but when Chief Justice David Bazelon of the DC Court of Appeals ruled, he reversed the lower court's decision.[54] Bazelon, one of the judiciary's liberal giants, stated that the CSC's determination that Scott had engaged in immoral conduct would not only bar him from federal employment but also damage his employment prospects more generally. He ruled that the government was therefore obligated to specify the conduct it labeled immoral and "state why that conduct related to 'occupational competence or fitness.'"[55] Noting that the ruling did not, as Scott had hoped, strike down the disqualification of homosexuals from government service, Kameny called it a "partial victory."[56]

The court's requirement of specificity was important, however, because it meant that the government had "to do far more work on each case, and often leaves them with no case at all, because they cannot obtain sufficient specificity."[57] For its part, the CSC regarded the ruling as a "shocker" and set out to try to figure out how to "offset" it.[58] For starters, the government *did* have specifics on Bruce Scott, who was made eligible for federal employment again only to have the government reinitiate an investigation

52. Rhonda R. Rivera, "Our Straight-Laced Judges: The Legal Position of Homosexuals in the United States," *Hastings Law Journal* 30 (March 1979): 814.

53. Franklin E. Kameny, draft of "U.S. Government Clings to Prejudice," folder 14, box 3, Frank Kameny Papers. The district court decision was unpublished, but see *Bruce C. Scott v. John W. Macy*, Civil Action no. 1050-63, U.S. District Court for the District of Columbia, 1963, in folder 38, box 9, Mattachine Society Project Collection, ONE National Gay and Lesbian Archives, Los Angeles, CA; Deviant's Archive, https://thedeviantsarchive .org/archive/scott-v-macy/.

54. Franklin E. Kameny, "U.S. Government Clings to Prejudice," *Ladder*, January 1966, 22–24.

55. *Scott v. Macy*, 349 F.2d 182 (U.S. Court of Appeals, D.C. Circuit, 1965). On Bazelon's impact, see Marilyn Berger, "Bazelon Dies at 83; Jurist Had Wide Influence," *New York Times*, February 21, 1993, 38.

56. Franklin E. Kameny, draft of "U.S. Government Clings to Prejudice," folder 14, box 3, Frank Kameny Papers.

57. *Scott v. Macy* also gave federal job applicants (not just probationary or permanent employees) standing to sue. Franklin E. Kameny to the *Advocate*, February 10, 1969, folder 9, box 1, Frank Kameny Papers.

58. L. V. Meloy, General Counsel, Memo: Case of Bruce G. Scott, August 13, 1965, in "Chapter 7" of Office of General Counsel (OGC) files, Civil Service Commission records, Mattachine Society of Washington, https://mattachinesocietywashingtondc.org/the -deviants-trove/.

into his suitability a week later. He fought the CSC in court once again. This time, however, the CSC made sure to give Scott several pages of evidence. With that, the same district court judge who had initially ruled against him once again found Scott unsuitable for federal employment. Scott appealed and was somewhat vindicated by Judge Bazelon's 1967 opinion (in *Scott* II), but it was vague enough to leave Scott dispirited.[59]

Just a few years later, Judge Bazelon's decision in *Norton v. Macy* was far more definitive. Norton was a well-regarded budget analyst for NASA who was arrested in a gay cruising area in Washington, DC. First DC police and then NASA's security chief questioned Norton all night long. The budget analyst denied being a homosexual, but NASA fired him anyway. In his 1969 ruling, Bazelon expressed concern for the due process rights of government employees, especially where "dismissal imposes a 'badge of infamy' disqualifying the victim from any further [government] employment, [and] damaging his prospects of private employ." Bazelon acknowledged in some circumstances an employee's immoral conduct could be grounds for dismissal, but the burden was on the government to "demonstrate some 'rational basis' for its conclusion that a discharge 'will promote the good of the service.'"[60] This soon came to be known as the "rational nexus" test. There had to be a clear connection, in other words, between the offensive conduct and the efficiency of the government agency before a removal was legally permissible.

The government could not pass this test with regard to Clifford Norton. Bazelon pointed out that Norton's "duties did not bring him into contact with the public, and his fellow employees were unaware of his 'immorality.'" He was, moreover, an "extremely infrequent offender" who "neither openly flaunts nor carelessly displays his unorthodox sexual conduct."[61] Indeed, Norton's own tendencies toward discretion were on display in a letter that he wrote Kameny immediately after the landmark ruling in his case. He was worried, he confessed, that his family might read about his case in the newspaper and thereby discover his homosexuality. Kameny was utterly disgusted with him. "You have fought the very government of the United States and won," Kameny fumed in a letter to Norton. "You have bearded the lion in his den. And you're still running from your family???!!!"[62]

---

59. Scott worried that that the CSC was "free to try a third time to bar me from the eligible registers for which I have otherwise qualified." Cervini, *Deviant's War*, 219, 238–39, 286–87.

60. *Norton v. Macy*, 417 F.2d 1161 (U.S. Court of Appeals, D.C. Circuit, 1969).

61. Ibid.

62. Franklin E. Kameny to Clifford Norton, July 11, 1969, Norton folder, box 29, Frank Kameny Papers.

Despite Kameny's disappointment in Norton the man, *Norton* the decision initially seemed to provide an expansive logic that would open up federal employment and even have an impact beyond it. In *Morrison v. State Board of Education*, the California Supreme Court ruled that before the plaintiff's teaching license could be revoked, the state had to show how Morrison's homosexual conduct demonstrated impaired job fitness.[63] Like Norton, Morrison did not admit to being a homosexual, and other cases involving teachers seemed to turn on this same issue of openness. "When the homosexual act is an isolated one . . . the nexus required for dismissal has not been found," the legal scholar Ellen Levine wrote; "conversely, when the individual has acknowledged homosexuality . . . job impairment has been found."[64]

With regard to the federal work force, the Civil Service Commission's immediate response to the ruling in *Norton* was intransigence. Frank Kameny complained to colleagues at the national ACLU, which had changed its policy on the federal employment of gay people in the wake of *Scott v. Macy*, that the CSC was "making a dead letter of the decision."[65] And the flip side of *Norton's* "rational nexus" standard was that, while the government had to show how homosexuality impaired the functioning of the government, homosexuality could still be grounds for dismissal. As one lawyer wrote, this offered a "heckler's veto over expressions of gender and sexuality with which [some] are uncomfortable."[66] A series of court decisions interpreted *Norton* as *allowing* discrimination against federal employees based on homosexual conduct or status.[67] The decision in Richard Schlegel's case was especially egregious. The court of claims distinguished his case from Clifford Norton's because while the latter case involved "merely an advance," Schlegel was alleged to have committed a homosexual act at least four times. "Any school boy knows that a homosexual act is immoral, indecent, lewd, and obscene," Judge Skelton asserted

63. *Morrison v. State Board of Education*, 1 Cal. 3d 214, 461 P.2d 375, 82 Cal. Reporter 175 (1969).

64. Ellen Levine, "Legal Rights of Homosexuals in Public Employment," *Annual Survey of American Law* 1978 (1978): 459, 490.

65. Franklin E. Kameny to Ralph J. Temple, September 6, 1971, folder 4, box 16, Frank Kameny Papers. In addition to the *Scott* decision, the national ACLU began to oppose the ban on gay employees as a result the NCACLU's position on homosexuality, as well as Kameny's agitation through the Mattachine Society. Cervini, *Deviant's War*, 239.

66. William Rubenstein, ed., *Lesbians, Gay Men, and the Law* (New York: New Press, 1993), 261.

67. Norma Riccucci and Charles W. Gossett, "Employment Discrimination in State and Local Government: The Lesbian and Gay Male Experience," *American Review of Public Administration* 26 (June 1996): 177.

in upholding Schlegel's dismissal from his civilian position in the Department of the Army. "If activities of this kind are allowed to be practiced in a government department," the opinion continued, "the efficiency of the service will in time adversely be affected."[68]

Of course, Schlegel hadn't practiced any sexual behavior *in* his government office. Several more years went by before the courts issued a decision that would force the government to uphold "the plain meaning of *Norton.*" It did so through a class action suit that challenged the government's policy of per se exclusion of homosexuals. In *Society for Individual Rights, Inc. v. Hampton*, the court ordered the CSC to "cease excluding or discharging from government service any homosexual person whom the Commission would deem unfit for government employment solely because the employment of such a person in the government might bring that service into contempt."[69] In the wake of this decision, the commission had no alternative but to change its policy. Frank Kameny got a call directly from the CSC's general counsel Anthony Mondello—they were in almost daily contact anyway, Kameny remembered, because of the number of cases he had before the CSC at that time.[70] Mondello conceded that pressure from Kameny had been a factor along with broader trends, but that the court's opinion in *Society for Individual Rights, Inc. v. Hampton* had accelerated the announcement.[71] In December 1973, the CSC issued proposed regulations to all federal agencies and requested comments. Both Kameny and the ACLU opined that the commission's response was, they felt, "hostile and grudging."[72] ("As a historical statement, that is accurate," Mondello more or less conceded the point: "I don't think anybody would believe that the Civil Service Commission would do this on its own.")[73] Moreover, news of the policy reversal spread unevenly, and the General Accounting Office warned of inconsistencies across the government.[74] To take one

68. 416 F.2d 1378 (U.S. Ct. of Cl., 1969); see also *Vigil v. Post Office Department*, 406 F.2d 921 (10th Cir., 1969); *Richardson v. Hampton*, 345 F.Supp. 600 (D.D.C., 1972).

69. *Society for Individual Rights, Inc. v. Hampton* 63 F.R.D. 399 (N.D. Cal., 1973).

70. Interview with Frank Kameny, conducted by Eric Marcus, June 3, 1989, Washington, DC, https://makinggayhistory.com/podcast/episode-1-5/.

71. David L. Aiken, "U.S. Asks Job Rules Keyed to Performance," *Advocate*, January 2, 1974, 24.

72. ACLU of the National Capital Area, "Comments on Proposed Revision of Civil Service Commission Suitability Regulations," January 10, 1974, folder 5, box 42, and Franklin E. Kameny to JK, April 14, 1974, folder 10, box 6, both in Frank Kameny Papers.

73. Aiken, "Gay Is Now Okay in 2.6 Million Federal Jobs," 4.

74. Gregory B. Lewis, "Lifting the Ban on Gays in the Civil Service: Federal Policy toward Gay and Lesbian Employees since the Cold War," *Public Administration Review* 57 (September/October 1997): 392.

example, a librarian employed by the Library of Congress was investigated for homosexuality in 1974, following the navy's investigation of a man with whom he had been involved. Despite the fact that the library's inquiry began several months after the CSC's initial notice of policy change, the experience was severe enough that this man later reflected that he "understood how a person could commit suicide."[75]

When the CSC issued its final guidelines for evaluating the suitability of individuals for federal employment in July 1975, it had more clearly embedded the "rational nexus" into government policy.[76] On balance, it seemed a significant advance. "I have brought the very government of the United States to its knees," Kameny boasted to his mother.[77] Immoral conduct had been entirely eliminated as grounds for dismissal. Permissible grounds for dismissal were limited to "criminal, dishonest, or notoriously disgraceful conduct."[78] Yet Kameny soon worried about "the element of notoriety," which he fretted "seems to be an element for keeping Gays 'in the closet.'" The notorious conduct provision, he continued, "is a kind of 'sleeper' which has potential for abuse."[79] Kameny's fears seemed well grounded when, less than a year later, the Ninth Circuit Court of Appeals upheld the firing of a man named John Singer from his clerk-typist job at the EEOC.[80] Singer—who changed his first name to Faygele, the Yiddish word for "little bird" that also meant "gay," as his case made its way through the courts—had placed a "gay power" sticker on his car, applied for a marriage license to marry another man, and kissed a man in public,

75. Interview subject 13, Washington, DC, 2013. Technically, a notice of proposed rulemaking is only a notice that the agency is considering changing its policy rather than a change in the policy itself. So it's not the fact that the librarian was investigated during this period that is surprising, as much as the severity of the investigation he faced at this time.

76. Sarah Collins, "Homosexual Rights: An Issues Overview," Congressional Research Service (April 18, 1980), 2, folder 7, box 2, Frank Kameny Papers.

77. Frank Kameny to Mother, August 2, 1975, folder 4, box 1, Frank Kameny Papers.

78. Rivera, "Our Straight-Laced Judges," 822.

79. Franklin E. Kameny, "Homosexual American Citizens and Federal Employment," Presentation for the National Gay Task Force White House Conference, March 26, 1977, "NGTF Federal Employment" folder, box 27, Costanza Files, Jimmy Carter Presidential Library, Atlanta, GA.

80. The irony that it was the EEOC was not lost on Frank Kameny. "Incidentally, some people in the Office of the General Counsel here in Washington are very much embarrassed by this case," Kameny wrote to Singer's attorneys. "They feel that the case represents a violation by the government of everything that the EEOC is trying to accomplish and for which it stands." Franklin E. Kameny to Arnold Pedowitz and Ronald Kessler, August 29, 1974, folder 9, box 32, Frank Kameny Papers.

among other affronts.[81] In district court, the US attorney representing the CSC argued that Singer had shown "'a proclivity, almost a compulsion, for publicity,' and that any reasonable employer would be concerned about this."[82] That the appeals court ruled that such "flaunting" could cause embarrassment to the federal service such that Singer's removal was justified suggests the limits of the commission's revised policy.[83] "The court sloughed off the First Amendment aspects of the case and called them homosexual conduct," Singer's attorney complained. Despite the changed policy, then, the ruling meant that as soon as gays "get any publicity, they can't work for the federal government."[84]

Even for more reticent employees, however, the new CSC guidelines provided only partial protection for two reasons. First, not all federal agencies were covered by the CSC guidelines. The FBI, the CIA, and the National Security Agency; the Federal Reserve Board; the Tennessee Valley Authority and the atomic energy agencies; and the Foreign Service all had their own separate policies in place.[85] As Kameny pointed out, these agencies "remained adamant in continuing to exclude Gays," and each was "very much a law unto itself, in these matters."[86] Second, the revised suitability standards did not apply to the guidelines for security clearances for federal employees and for employers who contracted with the government. Security clearance policy remained restrictive for gay people for much longer. Not only that, but the government was requiring a higher and higher proportion of its employees to obtain clearances, including those who never came within miles of a government secret. Some suspected that this was a backdoor way to circumvent the liberalization of CSC policy regarding homosexuality. Kameny explained that "agencies are now using the greater freedom which they still possess in respect to security clearances to eliminate gay employees through clearance denials, when they feel that direct [disqualification] on the basis of homosexuality is no

81. Singer changed his full name to Faygele Ben-Miriam to emphasize both his Jewish and his gay/feminist identity. Ben-Miriam meant "son of Miriam." Gary Atkins, *Gay Seattle: Songs of Exile and Belonging* (Seattle: University of Washington Press, 2003), 125.

82. Arthur Evans, "Court Won't Bar Equal Opportunity Firing," *Advocate*, January 31, 1973, 12.

83. *Singer v. U.S. Civil Service Commission*, 429 U.S. 1034 (1977).

84. "Set-Back for Employment Rights," *Advocate*, April 21, 1976, 10.

85. Aiken, "Gay Is Now Okay in 2.6 Million Jobs," 4.

86. Franklin E. Kameny, "Homosexual American Citizens and Federal Employment," Presentation for the National Gay Task Force White House Conference, March 26, 1977, "National Gay Task Force-Federal Employment" folder, box 27, Costanza Files.

longer possible." He feared this "gradual growth of evasive tactics" across the federal bureaucracy.[87]

———

In a myriad of ways, difficulties in obtaining a security clearance wreaked havoc on gay employment. Frank Kameny reported, for example, that "very much to the point is a recent Department of the Army case, in which the Army General Counsel's Office pointed out the individual could not be fired on the basis of his declared homosexuality. The Army then denied him a security clearance on the ground, solely, of 'admitted homosexuality.'"[88] In the private firms that held government contracts, clearance problems could also lead to job loss, although larger companies that were sympathetic and had enough nonclassified work were sometimes able to reassign an employee, often at a lower rate of pay. Because the consequences could be so severe, many gay people avoided the government's security apparatus, refusing to apply for promotions or compete for jobs that would require a clearance.[89] But sometimes even when one stayed in the same position, job requirements changed such that one was compelled to put in for a security clearance or upgrade a lower-level one. One particular Senate investigation, for example, required those staffing the committee to obtain access to CIA materials, which meant a gay lawyer was among those asked to obtain the highest-level security clearance. "You have to understand this is not a regular background check," this man's boss explained to the staff. "So, anything that is going to cause you any problems, just tell me and I will take your name off the list and that will be the end of it." The lawyer waited thirty minutes before going to tell his boss that he was gay. But that was not "the end of it." The senator in charge of the committee told the man he was a political liability and needed him to find another job. "It was Christmas time," the lawyer recalled, and "for the first and only time in my life, I considered suicide."[90]

Security clearances were thus another aspect of the government's exclusionary apparatus during these years. They moved along a track different

87. Ibid.

88. Ibid. This was part of a larger pattern, Kameny argued, of eliminating gay civil servants through clearance denials.

89. Interview subject 69, San Francisco, CA, 2011. On the risks of promotions that entailed higher level clearances, see "One Loses Her Job, Another Her Daughters," *Advocate*, February 13, 1974, 2.

90. Interview subject 120, interview conducted via telephone, 2015.

from the suitability provisions that had undergirded the Civil Service ban, although both were grounded in the same McCarthy-era executive order (10450) that had established the government's "loyalty-security program" in the 1950s. Yet with the decisions in *Scott*, *Norton*, and *Society for Individual Rights, Inc. v. Hampton*, courts had gradually narrowed the focus of EO 10450 to apply only to "sensitive positions and access to classified information, and not to federal employment across the board."[91] The same logic, moreover, that had exempted the national security agencies from the liberalization of CSC policy in 1975—that homosexuals were security risks rather than unsuitable per se—shored up the government's policy of denying security clearances across all agencies.

Specifically, the executive order established that security clearances could be denied based on any "criminal, infamous, immoral, notoriously disgraceful conduct," or "sexual perversion."[92] While that standard governed all security clearance cases, the executive order simultaneously created a highly decentralized system. Each department or agency was to have its own procedure for vetting employees. In practice this meant, as Frank Kameny later complained, "a chaotically fragmented . . . internally inconsistent system in which . . . there are as many independent security clearance programs as there are Federal Departments and agencies, each with its own independent investigative and adjudicative facilities, each with its own regulations . . . for the issuance and denial of clearances." Agencies did not always recognize one another's clearances, and they used different terms to designate clearance levels. Without any centralization across the government, the security clearance apparatus was so illogical, so inconsistently managed, and so byzantine in its operations that it was not a security program at all, Kameny charged, but only a "social and sexual conformity program."[93]

The starkest division, however, was not in the way this or that agency handled its clearances but rather between the various protocols for civil servants and those provided for private-sector employees who needed clearances to work on government contracts. Federal employees who required a clearance could find themselves drawn into a process where investigative and adjudicative functions were merged, decisions were issued as informal oral statements, and there was no meaningful appeal

91. Franklin E. Kameny to Leonard Hirsch, "Security Clearances for Gay Federal Employees," January 3, 1994, folder 5, box 57, Frank Kameny Papers.

92. Franklin E. Kameny, "Gays and the U.S. Civil Service," *Vector* 9 (February 1973): 8.

93. Franklin E. Kameny to Leonard Hirsch, "Security Clearances for Gay Federal Employees," January 3, 1994, folder 5, box 57, Frank Kameny Papers.

process. But as a result of the 1959 Supreme Court decision in *Greene v. McElroy*, industry's security clearance procedures *were* standardized, providing private-sector employees with evidentiary hearings, written decisions, and an appeal mechanism.[94]

As a result of these standardized procedures (and the written evidence they produced), the clearance process is easier to follow on the industrial side. Initial applications were handled by the Defense Industrial Security Clearance Office (DISCO) in Columbus, Ohio, which had the authority to approve clearances outright. Applications that looked questionable were forwarded on to the Industrial Security Clearance Review Office (ISCRO) in Washington, DC, whose director usually assigned a case to its Screening Board for additional investigation.[95] Arrest, court, and credit records were scoured, as well as the records of other state and federal agencies. For higher-level clearances, record checks were followed by interviews with coworkers, neighbors, and family members. Finally, the applicant would be interviewed as well. This proceeding was usually "adversarial," and investigators were looking for any derogatory information they could use.[96] "Joe was interviewed twice by government agents," one man wrote to Frank Kameny in 1968. "Each time there were three in number and the interrogation lasted the greater part of the day. . . . They didn't have much difficulty in tripping him up."[97] If the Screening Board denied the clearance, it issued a written "Statement of Reasons" justifying its decision. The applicant then responded to the statement in writing and could request a hearing in order to present evidence and cross-examine witnesses. The decision of that hearing examiner could then be appealed by either the applicant or the government agency to yet another government board. Only after exhausting all those layers of bureaucracy would a clearance applicant have access to the courts.[98]

94. Ibid. Security Clearances for private industry were governed by Executive Order 10865, issued in 1960.

95. On process, see especially Kathleen M. Graham, "Security Clearances for Homosexuals," *Stanford Law Review* 25 (February 1973): 407–8; Marshall McClintock and Kim R. Smith, "National Security Clearances and Gay People," 1984, folder 2, box 66, Frank Kameny Papers.

96. E. Carrington Boggan, Marilyn G. Haft, Charles Lister, and John P. Rupp, *The Rights of Gay People: An American Civil Liberties Handbook* (1975; New York: Discus, 1983), 64; McClintock and Smith, "National Security Clearances and Gay People," 1984, folder 2, box 66, Frank Kameny Papers.

97. Joe, this correspondent also reported, was fired from his job shortly after his clearance denial. Edward G. Hefter to Frank Kameny, March 24, 1968, folder 9, box 5, Frank Kameny Papers.

98. McClintock and Smith, "National Security Clearances and Gay People," 1984, folder 2, box 66, Frank Kameny Papers; Graham, "Security Clearances for Homosexuals," 407–8.

At the administrative level, the government's logic was consistently and impenetrably circular, undercutting the sense that procedural protections made favorable outcomes any more likely for employees in private industry. "Largely window dressing," Frank Kameny eventually concluded.[99] The government (not only ISCRO, but the federal agencies where civil servants fought denials) relied on three main justifications to support clearance denials during these years. By far, the most prevalent was the idea that homosexuals were security risks who could not be trusted with classified information because they were vulnerable to blackmail. In part because of the "bureaucratic tendency for policies to become derationalized," government officials were unmoved by the argument that the government's own practices created the potential susceptibility to blackmail among gay workers.[100] They were also not persuaded by the lack of any evidence that any gay person had ever been blackmailed into betraying government secrets. Nor did it matter that applicants who were openly homosexual could not be blackmailed.[101] Instead, the government insisted that being openly gay actually made employees more easily identifiable to blackmailers, and they might succumb to blackmail to protect another person (perhaps a lover who was not as open?).[102] Shifting their focus from the person under scrutiny to the potential associate, the authorities called this hypothetical situation "third party blackmail."[103]

The criminal status of homosexual conduct provided an independent rationale for denying security clearances. It made no difference to the government whether or not an employee had actually been arrested under a state sodomy statute, nor did it matter that by the late 1960s criminal

99. Franklin E. Kameny, undated memo, in "Gay Rights: Memos, Correspondence, Clippings, 5/75–8/78" folder, box 4, Costanza Files.

100. Franklin E. Kameny to AR, July 29, 1969, folder 15, box 16, Frank Kameny Papers.

101. Franklin E. Kameny, undated memo, "Gay Rights: Memos, Correspondence, Clippings, 5/75–8/78" folder, box 4, Costanza Files; interview with Harvey Friedman, Washington, DC, 2013. In the most egregious example of all, a government physicist who had a sexual encounter with a man who later tried to blackmail him said, "Well, go ahead and report me to the FBI." The thwarted blackmailer did phone the FBI. As a result, the physicist (who had just rebuffed a blackmail attempt!) had his clearance revoked and was subsequently terminated from his job. He was then turned down by over one hundred prospective employers because of his clearance denial and ended up on welfare. "Misc. Homosexuals: *Grimm v. Laird*" file, box 2985, Records of the ACLU.

102. For example, one applicant's openness "would only serve to accentuate [his] susceptibility as a target for possible efforts to obtain classified information in an improper manner." See Appeal Board, Industrial Security Clearance Review Office, "Memorandum of Reasons," July 15, 1970, folder 5, box 37, Frank Kameny Papers.

103. Franklin E. Kameny, "Gays, Blackmail, and Security," 3, folder 5, box 57, Frank Kameny Papers.

prosecutions for homosexual offenses were beginning to decline. The logic was, in Frank Kameny's summation, "the law is the law is the law." With or without an arrest, "anyone who knowingly and continuingly violates the criminal law when it suits his convenience to do so and when he finds that law onerous and burdensome, is likely to be just as cavalier with respect to the security regulations if he finds compliance with them inconvenient, onerous, and burdensome."[104] This rationale, which Kameny thought was the hardest one to beat, actually bled right into the third justification: that homosexuals were untrustworthy and exhibited poor judgement. Examining officers viewed going to a gay bar or restaurant, for example, as demonstrating the "poor judgement" that made an individual a questionable security risk. "Who knows who you might meet there? Foreign agents?"[105] Kameny advised those who found themselves caught in this vortex, as well as the lawyers who assisted them, not to expect to win at the administrative level. Examiners issued determinations "consisting of many pages of utter drivel. . . . They will repeat themselves like a broken phonograph record."[106]

The Industrial Security Clearance Review Office denied that it relied on a per se exclusion of homosexuals during these years and made a great show of "giving the citizen every possible opportunity to make his case."[107] But litigation some years later unearthed a 1962 memo outlining just such a blanket policy: "Proof of recent homosexual activities establishes conclusively . . . that the applicant cannot be granted access authorization," declared the Department of Defense in the first paragraph. "In some instances," the memo continued, "the applicant acknowledges the status, recognizes that it is publicly known, and argues that since the applicant cannot be blackmailed, he presents no security risk." Yet this was not the checkmate it seemed. For "in this case, Department counsel will have little to do but emphasize the proof that the applicant is a homosexual; the Field Board will act in accordance with established policy as stated in the [first] paragraph": "The [homosexual] applicant cannot be granted access authorization."[108]

104. Franklin E. Kameny to Arnold H. Pedowitz, February 24, 1975, folder 9, box 32, Frank Kameny Papers.

105. Interview with Harvey Friedman, Washington, DC, 2013.

106. Franklin E. Kameny to KB, March 6, 1991, folder 7, box 58, and Franklin E. Kameny to AR, July 29, 1969, folder 15, box 16, both in Frank Kameny Papers.

107. Franklin E. Kameny to AR, July 29, 1969, folder 15, box 16, Frank Kameny Papers.

108. Franklin E. Kameny, undated memorandum, "Gay Rights—Memos, Correspondence, Clippings, 5/76–8/78" folder, box 4, Costanza Files. Further evidence of the department's "pro se" exclusion of homosexuals during these years was offered during the

Well before Frank Kameny put his hands on that memo, he understood that the point of fighting security clearance cases at the administrative level was not to win. It was to "lay the groundwork" for a court case and to draw the public's attention to the issue.[109] Security clearance hearings became an increasingly larger part of Kameny's portfolio by the late 1960s, when civil servants and private-sector employees first appeared to challenge their denials. Their emergence at that time probably had to do with the progress being made with the Civil Service Commission more generally, as well as the resulting spotlight on Kameny.[110] As with his campaign to end the CSC ban, Kameny's stake in the security clearance issue was personal. Years after he had concluded his court fight protesting his termination from the government, he was still actively fighting to have restored his own security clearance, revoked after he was fired from the Army Map Service.[111] His efforts were stymied by regulations that stipulated that the government would not process a security clearance application unless the applicant was on the payroll of a company that required access to classified information. "However, if any employer thinks there's anything unorthodox in the applicant's background, which might make issuance of a clearance questionable, he just won't hire," Kameny explained. "The applicant can't get (or have processed) a clearance until he gets a job, but he can't get a job until he gets a clearance."[112]

Fortunately, Kameny had found another calling. He began to help clients—most of whom were men given the types of jobs that required clearances—through the administrative stages of appealing security clearance denials, sometimes even charging modest fees for his time.[113] There

---

deposition of the director of ISCRO who stated that in his twenty years in the position he could not think of a single case where a clearance had been granted to a homosexual. *Wentworth v. Laird*, 348 F.Supp. 1153 (D.D.C., 1972).

109. Franklin E. Kameny to AR, July 29, 1969, folder 15, box 16, Frank Kameny Papers.

110. Testimony of Kathleen Buck, US Congress, Senate, Permanent Subcommittee on Investigations, *Hearings on Federal Government Security Clearance Programs*, 99th Cong., 1st sess., April 16–18, 25, 1985, 709.

111. Tobin and Wicker, *Gay Crusaders*, 110.

112. Franklin E. Kameny to Dick Leitsch, April 3, 1966, folder 10, box 6, Frank Kameny Papers.

113. The predominance of men among Kameny's clients likely reflected greater vulnerability (as well as greater discretion) among lesbians, which made them less likely to fight dismissals and denials, as well as gendered discrepancies among those who would be in jobs that required security clearances in the first place. In addition, most of those who

were more of them than Kameny could handle alone. He soon brought in
fellow activist Barbara Gittings, the founder of the New York chapter of the
Daughters of Bilitis who had recently become frustrated with the compla-
cency of the homophile movement, to serve as co-counsel.[114] As Kameny
worked alongside Gittings, his technique reached full flower. He was more
bombastic than ever; one official even referred to him as "abusive."[115]
When the Department of Defense moved to disqualify Kameny as counsel,
for example, he wrote twenty-two singled-spaced pages moving to "disqualify THEIR counsel."[116] As he had in his battle with the CSC, Kameny
continued to use the mail prodigiously, sending his adversaries pointed
letters and, especially, books. Kameny was horrified, for example, to see
the pop psychiatrist Edmund Bergler's antigay diatribe, *1000 Homosexuals*, in the office of Frederick Tilton, chair of ISCRO's Appeal Board. He
promptly sent Tilton a copy of the psychotherapist George Weinberg's
Society and Healthy Homosexuals.[117] Perhaps to Kameny's surprise, Tilton responded with a gracious letter of acknowledgment: "I was intrigued
by your reference to the Bergler book because I had completely forgotten I
had it. Had you looked inside the book, you might have noted its purchase
price was $1.98." The book was acquired many years prior, Tilton added,
and its "excellent condition attests to its lack of use."[118] On another occasion, Kameny responded to the invasive sexual questions a hearing examiner asked of one of his clients by sending the examiner both "verbal and
pictorial" books to satisfy his "morbid curiosity" about what homosexuals
did. "We went on to say that while we lauded and encouraged such efforts

---

ended up in test case litigation (whether challenging the Civil Service Commission ban or
security clearance policy) were those with ties to the (predominantly male) Mattachine.

114. Around the time Gittings began working with Kameny on security clearance cases,
Gittings was removed as editor of the *Ladder*, the official publication of the Daughters of
Bilitis. The organization's board believed Gittings was too militant and too provocative.
Marcia M. Gallo, *Different Daughters: A History of the Daughters of Bilitis and the Rise of
the Lesbian Rights Movement* (New York: Carroll and Graf, 2006), 131–32; Faderman, *Gay
Revolution*, 84–89.

115. "For Official Use Only," undated memo, folder 5, box 19, Frank Kameny Papers.

116. Frank Kameny to Mother, March 12, 1975, folder 3, box 1, Frank Kameny Papers.

117. The book, published in 1972, argued that homosexuality was not a psychological disorder. Weinberg also coined the term "homophobia" in the 1960s. William Grimes,
"George Weinberg Dies at 87; Coined 'Homophobia' after Seeing Fear of Gays," *New York
Times*, March 22, 2017, https://www.nytimes.com/2017/03/22/us/george-weinberg-dead
-coined-homophobia.html.

118. Franklin E. Kameny to Mr. Frederick A. Tilton, January 22, 1977, and Frederick
Tilton to Mr. Franklin E. Kameny, January 25, 1977, both in folder 7, box 58, Franklin
Kameny Papers.

by the Examiner to arouse (and to satisfy) his prurient interests and to learn more about homosexuals and homosexuality," Kameny recounted, "we objected to his efforts to make [my client's] personal life the vehicle for such efforts."[119]

Kameny's genius above all was his use of publicity, which he articulated as a "marked departure from the traditionally accepted approach in matters involving homosexuals and homosexuality—covertness, secrecy, and a shunning of publicity."[120] Here the former astronomer's tactics synced up well with other gay activists who were also starting to reject privacy—and its association with the "closet"—as a discourse for their politics.[121] Kameny's offensive in this regard was actually double pronged. First, Kameny sought to expose the abuses of hearing examiners, threatening them with what he called "an ordeal by publicity." He stated his intention to publish examiners' "Statements of Reasons" with his own commentary so the public could understand the injustice and "slovenly reasoning" of these decisions. All officials involved would be named so they could not hide beyond a cloak of anonymity. Kameny cautioned the Defense Department to let its examiners know of his plan. "We, ourselves, have been dismayed to find that material which we wrote for private reading was published," he warned.[122] Relatedly, he pushed to have the hearings themselves opened to the public, which was finally fought in the courts and won in 1974.[123] "I intend to play to the gallery in showing up the program for the shoddy farce and travesty that it is," Kameny announced in anticipation of the first open hearing.[124] And he persuaded other lawyers who were doing security clearance cases—still few and far between because taking security clearance work during these years was taken as a sign one was gay—to adopt similar techniques.[125] Lawyer Harvey Friedman, who was inspired by and learned from Frank Kameny, tried, for example, to make examiners feel he would expose what went on during clearance hearings by having a friend who was a court reporter appear with his stenotype at

119. Frank E. Kameny, "My Sex Life Is None of the Government's Goddamned Business," *Vector* 6 (October 1970): 11.

120. Franklin E. Kameny to JL, March 20, 1968, folder 5, box 59, Frank Kameny Papers.

121. Howard, *Closet and the Cul-de-Sac*, 264.

122. Franklin E. Kameny to JL, March 20, 1968, folder 5, box 59, Frank Kameny Papers.

123. See Kameny, "Government v. Gays," 201–2.

124. Franklin E. Kameny to RF, May 28, 1974, folder 10, box 3, Frank Kameny Papers.

125. Interview with Harvey Friedman, Washington, DC, 2013. "You are quite correct in saying that competent defense counsel is difficult to find for these cases," Kameny wrote to an associate. "It is, in fact, largely non-existent." Franklin E. Kameny to HMS, April 25, 1969, folder 10, box 9, Frank Kameny Papers.

these hearings. The court reporter was usually kicked out, but the political theater sent a message.[126]

The other aim of Kameny's publicity strategy was to clearly refute the idea that clients could be blackmailed. "Shouting it from the rooftops," was the best defense against this charge, but not all clearance seekers were ready for that.[127] One scientist, who eventually fought his case through the courts, said he wanted to be known "as a physicist, not a homosexual."[128] Kameny worked with such reticent clients, sometimes persuading them that they needed to go home within a specified number of days to tell their families that they were gay.[129] With clients who were involved with Mattachine or in other ways more inclined toward openness, Kameny had far more room to maneuver. At one hearing, he announced: "We, including specifically Mr. Wentworth, come into this hearing with our heads high, proud of our homosexuality and proud to be homosexuals."[130] And when clients were willing, Kameny and co-counsel Gittings began to stage what he called "our productions."[131] He and Gittings would call a press conference to be held in the corridors of the Pentagon. They and their client would show up in suits and dresses wearing large "Gay Is Good" buttons, publicly announce the individual's name, and declare that he or she was a homosexual who intended to go right on being one. If they got press coverage, they would make sure news stories were entered into the record as evidence.[132] Sometimes they were quite successful at attracting the attention of mainstream news outlets: several newspapers across the country, including the *New York Times*, ran stories about Benning Wentworth's security clearance case, for example.[133] Kameny admitted to a fellow lawyer that calling a press conference to get media attention represented

126. Interview with Harvey Friedman, Washington, DC, 2013.

127. Mattachine Society of Washington, "Comments, Suggestions, and Recommendations Regarding Proposed Revisions to 5 CFR Part 731," January 2 1974, 9, folder 5, box 42, Frank Kameny Papers.

128. "Determination of Examiner Charles Klyde, in re: GWG," 9, "Misc. Homosexuals" folder, *Grimm v. Laird*, box 2985, Records of the ACLU.

129. Franklin E. Kameny to LB, March 15, 1984, folder 11, box 13, Frank Kameny Papers.

130. From Judge Robb, concurring in part, dissenting in part, in *Gayer v. Schlesinger*, 490 F.2d 740 (D.C. Circuit 1973).

131. Franklin E. Kameny to Florence Jaffy, June 20 1969, folder 2, box 6, Frank Kameny Papers.

132. Franklin E. Kameny to Renee C. Hanover, January 14, 1971, folder 11, box 40, Frank Kameny Papers.

133. Will Lissner, "Homosexual Fights Rule in Security Clearance," *New York Times*, November 26, 1967, 17D; Charlayne Hunter, "Homosexual Presses a Security Clearance Fight," *New York Times*, August 20, 1969, 38C.

a radical course, but unless you "kill the blackmail allegation, and 'kill it good,' you will get nowhere administratively or judicially."[134]

The government had tricks of its own, including using the investigation to invade the employee's privacy in a thinly veiled attempt to humiliate and shame. The general counsel for the CSC fretted privately about investigators "who show a lustful and salacious interest in the specifics of what might well be the private sexual activity of applicants."[135] His worry was a prescient one, as ISCRO and other government investigators routinely asked questions that one civil servant later described as "pornographic."[136] The questions the Defense Department posed to one man, for example, included: "With regard to a particular act: were you the insertor or were you the receptor? Were there any other acts which you found sexually stimulating? . . . Did you, in concert with your partner, do anything to cause your arousal or his arousal? . . . Was there any mutual masturbation? Was there any anal penetration? When you have a homosexual experience, is it fellatio?"[137]

Kameny skillfully blocked the government's attempt to turn his own strategic use of publicity against his clients. "He admitted to a continuing on-going pattern of homosexuality," Kameny reported of one client in 1972, "but refused to supply details as to 'who does what with which to whom in bed.'"[138] At Kameny's urging, another client refused to answer the Defense Department's interrogatories, declaring instead that "I have engaged in, I engage in, and good luck and good health permitting, intend to continue to engage in homosexual . . . acts as frequently as circumstances and my

134. Franklin E. Kameny to AR, July 29, 1969, folder 15, box 16, Frank Kameny Papers.

135. Anthony Mondello, General Counsel, CSC, to Robert J. Drummond Jr., FBI Director, September 19, 1973, in "Chapter 7" of Office of General Counsel (OGC) files, Civil Service Commission records, Mattachine Society of Washington, https://mattachinesocietywashingtondc.org/the-deviants-trove/.

136. Lilli M. Vincenz, "Otto Ulrich, Quiet Freedom Fighter," Rainbow History Project, www.rainbow.history.org/html/Ulrich2.htm.

137. Mattachine Society of Washington, "News Release—Wentworth Case," November 17, 1969, folder 5, box 37, Frank Kameny Papers. Another set of questions posed by government investigators: had the clearance seeker "ever engaged in acts of oral copulation-fellatio; anal copulation . . . with other males"; "how many such acts had occurred"; "whether such acts were engaged in private"; "how many different persons were involved?" Consolidated Brief for Defendants-Appellants (D.C. Circuit), *Richard L. Gayer v. Melvin R. Laird* (No. 71-1934), and *Otto H. Ulrich v. Melvin R. Laird* (No. 71-1935), 13–14, folder 3, box 36, Frank Kameny Papers.

138. Franklin E. Kameny to JF, September 8, 1972, folder 8, box 3, Frank Kameny Papers.

desires and whims make it possible, and in my sole view, appropriate."[139]
During hearings and before examining boards, Kameny underscored the
department's line of questioning as an offensive invasion of privacy: "What
in the hell is the American government doing asking questions like this of
ANY of its citizens?" Moreover, he excoriated the discriminatory way this
technique was being applied.[140] No such questions were regularly asked
of clearance applicants who were heterosexual, even though, as Kameny
proclaimed, "passion pits" at movie theaters and "lovers' lanes" were regular scenes of heterosexual sexual acts that were considered as "American
as apple pie."[141] These hearings could be over in as little as ten minutes,
with Kameny and Gittings declaring the questions irrelevant to the safeguarding of classified information, and hearing examiners declaring that
the questions should have been answered and denying the clearances on
these grounds.[142]

———————

This was the state of play when Kameny handed several cases, "constructed with loving care," off to the ACLU.[143] Otto Ulrich, Richard (Dick)
Gayer, and Benning Wentworth were all employed in private industry and
had security clearances suspended after their homosexuality came to light.
Ulrich and Gayer had listed their membership in homophile organizations
on their applications for security clearances; Wentworth was named by a
man being investigated by the navy. In subsequently ruling that all three of
their clearances be restored, Judge Pratt of the DC District Court did not
say that homosexuality was irrelevant to an employee's ability to protect
state secrets, but rather that the onus was on the government to demonstrate how it compromised the "individual's judgement, stability, or
vulnerability to blackmail." What seemed most worrisome to Judge Pratt,
however, were the "probing personal questions" the Defense Department

139. Consolidated Brief for Defendants-Appellants (D.C. Circuit), *Richard L. Gayer v.
Melvin R. Laird* (No. 71-1934), and *Otto H. Ulrich and Melvin R. Laird* (No. 71-1935), 9,
folder 3, box 36, Frank Kameny Papers.

140. Mattachine Society of Washington, "News Release—Wentworth Case," November 17, 1969, folder 5, box 37, Frank Kameny Papers.

141. Franklin E. Kameny to the Screening Board of the Industrial Security Clearance
Review Division, Department of Defense, July 20, 1969, quoted in Long, *Gay Is Good*, 229.

142. Franklin E. Kameny to Arthur Warner, July 18, 1969, folder 8, box 10, Frank
Kameny Papers.

143. Franklin E. Kameny, "Homosexuals Challenge U.S. Government—Injustice Continues," *Vector* 6 (September 1970): 10.

had asked of the three men.[144] In Gayer's case, Pratt wrote that "the questions asked of plaintiff are a violation of his First Amendment right to privacy and lack the necessary nexus to a determination of whether plaintiff is effectively able to safeguard classified information."[145] The government could not seek private, personal information, in other words, without first clarifying the connection between that information and the ability to protect government secrets.[146] In his opinion in the Wentworth case, decided some months after the other two, Pratt again protested the "shocking array" of intimate questions.[147] Especially for "declared homosexuals" like Gayer, Ulrich, and Wentworth, for whom, the court believed, the blackmail issue could be set aside, "the government could not make detailed inquiries into personal life."[148]

The government appealed the three decisions, "not on the validity of the nexus requirement, but on the right of ISCRO to suspend clearance investigation procedures due to lack of information because the applicant refuses to answer questions asked by the agency."[149] The consolidated opinion that emerged in *Gayer v. Schlesinger* was, Kameny wrote, "a mixed and annoying decision, which needs much study and evaluation to see just what it means."[150] The court opined that the government could demonstrate a "nexus" between homosexuality and an inability to protect information without "direct or objective" evidence by relying on "overall common sense." The formula required, the court elaborated in language that must have made Frank Kameny pound his fists, "a nice but not-easily definable weighing of the ingredients of which the particular case is comprised." The court's "weighing of the ingredients" in this instance, however, actually led it to conclude that the revocation of security clearances for Ulrich and Wentworth had been improper. This was not due to a failure by the government to demonstrate a rational nexus, but because the questions asked "went beyond the boundaries of the permissible" and made the applicant "suffer [a] severe invasion of privacy." The government could,

144. Thomas W. Lippman, "Judge Limits U.S. Check of Homosexuals," *Washington Post*, September 14, 1971, A6; Franklin E. Kameny, "A Victory for Gayer: Security Clearance Granted by Government," *Vector* 7 (October 1971): 32.

145. *Gayer v. Laird*, 332 F.Supp. 169 (D.D.C., 1971).

146. Richard Gayer to RC, December 8, 1973, folder 7, box 22, in Frank Kameny Papers.

147. *Wentworth v. Laird*, 248 F.Supp. 1153 (D.D.C., 1972). See also "Restore Wentworth Clearance, Says Judge," *Advocate*, June 21, 1972, 1.

148. Franklin E. Kameny to EB, 1972, folder 5, box 28, Frank Kameny Papers.

149. "Security Clearance Procedure," undated, folder 5, box 58, Frank Kameny Papers.

150. Franklin E. Kameny to LC, November 19, 1973, folder 1, box 3, Frank Kameny Papers.

the court ruled, go beyond the applicant's statement that he or she was homosexual to ask "what is reasonably necessary to make a determination with respect to any criteria being invoked." But two of the three plaintiffs had been subjected to a "wide ranging fishing expedition," Judge Fahy wrote for the majority.[151]

The court came to a different conclusion with Gayer, as he had refused to answer questions the court did see as permissible. The court ordered that Gayer be given a chance to answer the questions. If he failed to do so, the revocation of his security clearance would be sustained.[152] Gayer, who had gone to law school during the intervening years and would soon be taking security clearance cases in his own practice, mulled his options and fretted about the decision. The opinion rejected, Gayer wrote, "Pratt's conclusion that the government must show a 'nexus' before it can demand answers" to inquiries like the ones he had faced.[153] And if an applicant refused to "disclose such information," the suspension of a clearance was in fact permissible.[154] So, while the rational nexus standard survived, in the security context it seemed to be diminished by the court's ruling.

Gayer v. Schlesinger remained, in Frank Kameny's estimation, "the lead case in creating practical 'nuts and bolts' security clearance law with respect to gays."[155] Surprisingly, and despite its limitations, almost immediately after the decision the overall situation seemed to improve somewhat.[156] In 1975, the Department of Defense issued its first security clearance to an openly gay man.[157] A short time later, Richard Gayer received a letter from the Defense Department declaring it "clearly consistent with the national interest to grant clearance at the SECRET level for you at this

151. *Gayer v. Schlesinger*, 490 F.2d 740 (D.C. Circuit, 1973).

152. Ibid.

153. Richard Gayer to RC, December 8, 1973, folder 7, box 22, Frank Kameny Papers.

154. *Gayer v. Schlesinger*, 490 F.2d 740 (D.C. Circuit, 1973).

155. Franklin E. Kameny to Lou and Lisa, February 18, 1991, folder 5, box 57, Frank Kameny Papers.

156. Why, with the courts still more or less on the government's side, did the Defense Department shift course? Several explanations seem plausible: Even the gradual shift in the courts was making it more work to win; there were more cases being filed as time went on; the change in CSC policy and changes in the broader culture may have also had an impact. Dick Gayer believed as well that Frank Kameny was wearing the Defense Department down. See "Gay Security Clearance Victory," press release, September 9, 1975, folder 8, box 22, Frank Kameny Papers.

157. "Gay Wins Top Secret Clearance," *Los Angeles Free Press*, February 12, 1975, 3. Otis Tabler would eventually win back pay for lost wages as a result of his clearance denial. See Kameny, "Government v. Gays," 202.

time."[158] Looking back years later, Kameny identified this moment as the turning point. He had never won security clearance cases before, but now he started to win them for his clients.[159] Neither Kameny nor Gayer was overly rosy about the broader picture. There were still several "hold-out agencies": the FBI, the NSA, and especially the CIA continued not only to deny security clearances but also to terminate gay employees.[160] In these agencies, eligibility for a security clearance and suitability for employment were inseparable.[161]

Elsewhere, gays could win clearance fights, but not without spending a significant amount of money on lawyers and enduring long delays.[162] This situation had pernicious and somewhat hidden effects. Because the clearance process was often "protracted," some employers would "not hire gays at all."[163] Also hidden was the practice of some government agencies skirting the legal process entirely by simply asking companies to quietly "withdraw" security clearance applications for their employees when homosexuality was uncovered. Government contractors knew where their "bread is buttered" and were probably pressured to comply.[164]

158. "Gay Security Clearance Victory," press release, September 9, 1975, folder 8, box 22, Frank Kameny Papers.

159. Statement by Dr. Franklin E. Kameny, Paralegal, Gay Rights Advocate on Security Clearances, in Hearings before US Congress, House, Subcommittee on Civil Service of the Committee on the Post Office and Civil Service and the Subcommittee on Civil and Constitutional Rights of the Committee on the Judiciary, 101st Cong., 1st and 2nd sess., October 19, 1989, in folder 9, box 61, Frank Kameny Papers.

160. On the "hold-out agencies," see ibid.; Franklin E. Kameny to Jim Kemper, October 27, 1978, folder 10, box 6, Frank Kameny Papers; Franklin E. Kameny to Representatives and Senators, May 13, 1987, folder 3, box 57, Frank Kameny Papers. See also *Dubbs v. CIA*, 769 F.Supp. 1113 (N.D. Cal., 1990); *Buttino v. FBI*, 801 F.Supp. 298 (N.D. Cal., 1992).

161. Kameny, "Government v. Gays," 203. The same mentality that hampered change in the security agencies was also manifest in the military, where gay and lesbian soldiers would continue to struggle through the century's end. See Randy Shilts, *Conduct Unbecoming: Gays and Lesbians in the U.S. Military* (New York: Fawcett Columbine, 1993).

162. Richard Gayer to Leo Clark, General Accounting Office, October 19, 1993, folder 2, box 40, Frank Kameny Papers.

163. Franklin E. Kameny to President Clinton's Transition Team, December 17, 1992, folder 5, box 57, Frank Kameny Papers.

164. "The employee is then told that his application has not been denied, because it was withdrawn before adjudication, and that his case does not exist and never did exist," Frank Kameny stated in prepared testimony before Congress. "The whole thing is Orwellian." US Congress, House, Committee on the Post Office and Civil Service, *Hearings on Proposed Changes to Security Clearance Programs*, 101st Cong., 1st sess., March 9, 1989, 274-75. Most of the evidence I have seen on this is from the 1980s and 1990s. Major General Hugh Overholt, for example, referred to this as an "occasional government practice" in 1990. See Major General Hugh R. Overholt to David Gavin, re: Committee on Contracting with National Security Requirements, August 16, 1990, folder 7, box 55, Frank Kameny Papers.

So, the security clearance issue was far from resolved by the mid-1970s. Kameny himself probably had no inkling of how much longer the struggle would take when in 1978 he wrote a letter to officials in the Carter White House complaining that he was growing "weary of fighting endless clearances, based upon Executive Orders and ancillary policy going back to the darkest of McCarthy Days."[165]

———

By 1978, however, it wasn't just Frank Kameny who was writing the White House about gay issues. The White House was hearing from many others, particularly from those associated with the relatively recently formed National Gay Task Force (NGTF), in relation to President Carter's plan to reorganize the Civil Service for the first time in one hundred years. The Civil Service Reform Act of 1978 (CSRA) was meant to make the federal government more efficient by placing greater emphasis on merit in compensation and advancement, and giving managers more flexibility and authority in "all phases of personnel management" including discipline.[166] Alongside those reforms was a commitment to reaffirming the "protection of legitimate employee rights."[167] Title I of the act thus set out "merit system principles" and included a statement prohibiting discrimination

———

Was it done earlier? At a minimum, government agencies obviously had a lot of leverage with contractors. One intriguing bit of evidence is Richard Gayer's statement that his employer (Sylvania) refused to provide him with a letter that stated he was laid off because of a lack of unclassified work and "that the main reason for the refusal was Sylvania's desire to avoid involvement in my suit against the DOD." Richard Gayer to Dennis M. Flattery, April 18, 1971, folder 7, box 22, Frank Kameny Papers.

165. Franklin E. Kameny to Marilyn Haft, February 3, 1978, "Gays Civil Service 10/76–4/78" folder, box 4, Costanza Files. Also relevant is the general spread of security clearances—as increasing numbers of positions required them, more and more gay people would have experienced the employment complications they introduced. One CIA employee I spoke to said that when he got his high-level security clearance with the agency in the mid-1960s, seventy-five other people held that level of clearance. When we conducted the interview (in 2013), he said that over a million held that level of clearance. Interview subject 5, Washington, DC, 2013. Frank Kameny similarly warned the Congress of a "'runaway' security clearance system . . . used to evade the protections provided to Federal employees under applicable laws and regulations." US Congress, House, Committee on the Post Office and Civil Service, *Hearings on Proposed Changes to Security Clearance Programs*, 101st Cong., 1st sess., March 9, 1989, 273.

166. Campbell Memorandum on Civil Service Reform, November 2, 1978, "Civil Service Reform" folder, box 168, Eizenstat Files, Jimmy Carter Presidential Library. See also Paul Sturm, "Carter vs. the Bureaucrats," *Forbes*, February 6, 1978, 41–45.

167. Draft message to Congress from President Carter, March 1, 1978, "Civil Service Reform" folder, box 168, Eizenstat Files.

in federal employment based on political affiliation, race, color, religion, national origin, sex, age, marital status, or "handicapping condition."[168]

Despite the earlier change in Civil Service Commission policy, homosexuality was not included in Title I. One Carter staffer noticed its absence and wrote to general counsel at the CSC "to inquire about an omission I thought might not have been considered but which may lead to complaints from the gay community." That official responded that the list of protected categories in the bill included only those approved by Congress rather than by court decisions.[169] Yet the protection that existed for gays and was codified in Civil Service regulations since 1975 had been gained as a result of lower court opinions and thus could be overturned. While omitting them from the list of protected categories would not strip gays of that existing but tenuous protection, White House staffers opined, their absence would underscore their political vulnerability, thereby sending a signal that could invite a test case by the right to "move against the gays."[170] Explicitly including gay civil servants in the legislation therefore would better protect them. White House officials debated the merits of proposing this addition to the president. Jimmy Carter was at best ambivalent, given his stated, albeit personal, "moral objection" to the gay movement. Congress, moreover, might not pass the legislation if the reform package explicitly protected gay employees.[171] One adviser wrote an informational memo to the president that made no recommendation, only warning that the draft legislation might "attract substantial criticism from the gay community because it does not contain language protecting gays against employment discrimination."[172] Two others wrote to advise Carter against including explicit language protecting gays.[173]

168. Marilyn Haft to Midge Costanza (via Seymour Wishman), "Civil Service Reform Legislation," January 24, 1978, "Gays—Civil Service Reform Legislation 7/75 to 2/78" folder, box 22, Costanza Files.

169. Ibid.

170. Marilyn Haft and Seymour Wishman, Notes from Conversation regarding Civil Service Legislation—Gay Rights, February 2, 1978, "Gays—Civil Service Reform Legislation 7/75–2/78" folder, and Seymour Wishman to Midge Costanza, "Gay Rights Inclusion in Civil Service Reform," February 14, 1978, "Gay Civil Rights 10/76–2/78" folder, both in box 22, Costanza Files. The lower court cases were *SIR v. Hampton*, 63 F.R.D. 399 (N.D. Cal., 1973) and *Baker v. Hampton*, 6 Empl. Prac. Dec. P9043 (D.D.C., 1973).

171. Wishman to Costanza, "Gay Rights Inclusion in Civil Service Reform," February 14, 1978, "Gay Civil Rights 10/76–2/78" folder, box 22, Costanza Files.

172. Margaret Costanza to the President, "Civil Service Reform Legislation and Gay Rights," February 21, 1978, "Civil Service Reform" folder, box 168, Eizenstat Files.

173. Steve Simmons and Stu Eizenstat to the President, February 25, 1978, "Civil Service Reform Legislation and Gay Rights," February 21, 1978, "Civil Service Reform" folder, box 168, Eizenstat Files.

Ultimately, Carter would not risk one of the signal reforms of his presidency on what was an emerging but still politically weak constituency. The law did not explicitly mention gays. It did, however, quietly incorporate the "rational nexus" logic from prior court decisions protecting gay civil servants. Among the enumerated "Prohibited Personnel Practices" in the CSRA was discriminating against any employee or applicant "on the basis of conduct which does not adversely affect the performance of the employee or applicant or the performance of others."[174] The legislative history was silent as to whom "Prohibited Personnel Practice #10" specifically pertained, but just as the "nexus principle" developed in the courts generally referred to gay people, so too did this provision of the CSRA.[175] The Office of Personnel Management (OPM), which replaced the Civil Service Commission, confirmed that "all of the principals involved in the passage of the CSRA believed subsection 10 of the Prohibited Personnel Practices to include a prohibition against discrimination on the basis of sexual preference," and, in fact, privately "referred to that subsection as the 'gay amendment.'"[176]

Even as "Prohibited Personnel Practice #10" extended protections that did not exist in the private sector, gay activists were, as predicted, not impressed with the amendment that dared not speak its name. White House officials acknowledged as much. One charged that gays were "blind to the effect of the Civil Service Reform Act," which was "insufficiently dramatic to satisfy [their] need."[177] Another hoped that the amendment, while not well known, would eventually be recognized as an antidiscrimination "landmark."[178] But, with Carter fighting for reelection, activists in and around NGTF instead began to demand an executive order that, some later reflected, should have been "the logical and next step," as soon as

174. US Merit Systems Protection Board, *Sexual Orientation and the Federal Workplace: Policy and Perception*, May 2014, 18, https://www.mspb.gov/mspbsearch/viewdocs.aspx?docnumber=1026379&version=1030388&application=ACROB.

175. "The nexus principle clearly has applications in Federal employment beyond employment rights for gay women and men, but the record shows that ours was the main line of cases which developed this mode of legal analysis." See Howell draft, November 30, 1992, folder 11, box 42, Frank Kameny Papers.

176. Margery Waxman to Robert Malson, "Effect of Exclusion of Intelligence-Type Agencies from Prohibited Personnel Practice," undated, "National Gay Task Force" folder, box 7, Malson Files, Jimmy Carter Presidential Library (emphasis mine).

177. Bob Malson to Stu Eizenstat, Meetings in California with Leaders of the Gay Community, May 8, 1980, "7/20/79–5/31/79" folder, box 7, Malson Files.

178. David Rubenstein to Jody Powell, "Radio Call-In Show," October 13, 1979, "Gay Rights 12/79–5/80" folder, box 56, Rubenstein Files, Jimmy Carter Presidential Library.

the revised Civil Service Commission regulations were issued.[179] Carter's team initially claimed an executive order was "under consideration" but quickly reversed course.[180] The official response to the request came from Carter campaign chairman Robert Strauss. In a letter to the codirectors of the task force, Strauss lauded the protection that was already part of that CSRA and "covered 95% of all federal workers." For those who were not covered, for example in the security agencies, he argued that an executive order would have no effect at all because those agencies were exempted from civil service rules by statute.[181] The NGTF called out the administration for "hiding behind a procedural curtain" and announced its disappointment that the administration would not issue an executive order.[182]

The election-year solution to this political impasse was a memo from OPM. Advisers initially suggested that it might go out under Carter's signature to carry symbolic value without the precedential implications of an executive order.[183] But it was instead issued by OPM director Alan "Scotty" Campbell in the spring of 1980. That memo—which fell well short of an executive order—did not attempt to soften the approach of the CIA, NSA, or FBI. Rather it simply directed heads of departments and agencies already covered by the CSRA to make clear what the law had left opaque: "Prohibited Personnel Practice #10" in fact meant that the government forbade adverse personnel actions based on sexual orientation.[184] The

179. Howell draft, November 30, 1992, folder 11, box 42, Frank Kameny Papers.

180. NGTF news release, "White House Receives Gay Rights Petition—Discusses Presidential Executive Order," December 21, 1979, "NGTF" folder, box 271, Alison Thomas's Subject Files, Jimmy Carter Presidential Library.

181. Robert Strauss to C. F. Brydon and Lucia Valeska, March 3, 1980, "Gays" folder, box 211, Eizenstat Files. The Strauss letter also "sidestepped" the question of support for a bill that would amend the Civil Rights Act of 1964 to include protection based on sexual orientation. NGTF news release, "Carter Appeals for Gay Support," March 6, 1980, "National Gay Task Force" folder, box 7, Malson Files.

182. NGTF news release, "Carter Appeals for Gay Support," March 6, 1980, "National Gay Task Force" folder, box 7, Malson Files. Frank Kameny agreed that the White House's position was misleading. "Kameny said that while an executive order would not remove a statutory exclusion, such a removal is not necessary because no existing law bans a federal agency from hiring gays. It is the policy of the individual agencies that excludes gays." See Lou Chibbaro Jr., "Carter Statement Viewed as Retreat," Blade, March 20, 1980, 4.

183. "Gays are looking for public acknowledgement by the President," adviser Bob Malson wrote to Stu Eizenstat. "Meetings in California with Leaders of the Gay Community," March 8, 1980, "Gay—Homosexuals, 7/20/79–5/31/79" folder, box 7, Malson Files.

184. Robert A. Malson to Mr. Krieger, July 30, 1980, "Gays/Lesbians 7/1/80" folder, box 7, Malson Files; Alan K. Campbell to Heads of Departments and Independent Establishments, "Policy Statement on Discrimination on the Basis of Conduct Which Does Not Adversely Affect the Performance of Employees or Applicants for Employment," April 10, 1980, "Gays" folder, box 211, Eizenstat Files.

OPM sent the letter to 119 officials urging them to issue a "strong policy statement" to their subordinates (although it is not clear whether or not they complied).[185] Perhaps as important to OPM as promulgating the previously submerged spirit of the "rational nexus" provision in the CSRA and its clear relation to gay employees was what the memo revealed about what OPM hoped still to keep quiet: it explicitly prohibited government officials from inquiring into the sexual habits and behaviors of federal employees or applicants.[186]

———◆———

The campaign to end discrimination in federal employment—a charge led by Frank Kameny but joined by the mid-1970s by many others—amounted to a halfway revolution. Certainly, it was an extraordinary breakthrough when the Civil Service Commission announced that homosexuals would no longer automatically be considered unsuitable for government employment. Yet that and the CSRA's subdued incorporation of the courts' "rational nexus" principle stood as the only significant antidiscrimination protection bestowed on gay people by the federal government until the very end of the twentieth century.[187] And while the McCarthy era was receding, palpable reminders of the old vulnerabilities remained, especially in the security clearance morass and the persistent brutality of the intelligence agencies. The CSRA provisions themselves, as one activist later reflected, were diminished by "the same kind of historical amnesia that made so many civil rights laws enacted during Reconstruction forgotten and unenforced until modern times."[188]

185. Anthony Silvestre to Ms. Alison Thomas, June 11, 1980, "Gays/Lesbians 2/8/79–6/30/80" folder, box 7, Malson Files.

186. Mike Causey, "The Federal Diary," *Washington Post*, May 14, 1980, G-2.

187. More than twenty years later, the political scientist Gregory Lewis could still write that no court had ever "ruled that homosexuality or homosexual conduct [was] necessarily irrelevant to employment decisions." Lewis, "Lifting the Ban on Gays in the Civil Service," 394. In 1998, President Clinton finally signed the executive order that gay activists had originally urged from President Carter. This was "the first executive order to state the policy of non-discrimination based on sexual orientation in Federal employment. . . . It did not, however, establish enforceable rights or remedies for employees who believed they had been discriminated against, such as the ability to proceed before the Equal Employment Opportunity Commission (EEOC)." US Merit Systems Protection Board, *Sexual Orientation and the Federal Workplace: Policy and Perception*, May 2014, 22.

188. Howell draft, 11/30/92, folder 11, box 92, Frank Kameny Papers. Late in the 1990s, it was the rediscovery of the 1980 OPM memo (by a friend of Frank Kameny's who was a "packrat") that an organization of gay federal employees (Federal GLOBE) used to say "we

Reforms quietly done had more circumscribed effects than they other-wise might have had.[189] But looking back at the development of federal employment policy during the 1970s, the quiet is significant for another reason. What are we to make of an antidiscrimination provision that spoke in such coded language? Of the government's holding on to the prohibi-tion against "notorious conduct," which Kameny contended was meant to keep gay workers in the closet? Or its discomfort with "flaunting," as well as its admonition that its officials not pry into the private lives of employees? The transition out of the McCarthy era seemed to import into government the same "don't ask / don't tell" sensibilities that had long defined gay employment in the private sector.[190] The timing was awkward. Government moved to adopt these private-sector arrangements between employers and employees—*to not see and to not be seen*—as the norm of discretion was everywhere weakening and the bargain of midcentury was just beginning to lose its cultural hold. That shift was visible in all kinds of jobs, but inside the government too. One only needs to think, for example, about the differences between plaintiffs like Clifford Norton, who worried about news of his court case finding its way to the morning paper, and the growing numbers who would, as Frank Kameny put it, "shout . . . it from the rooftops."[191]

Frank Kameny's shouting aside, sociologists who study social move-ments have argued that gay people were not a part of the rights revolu-tions of the 1960s and 1970s that so transformed the legal landscape for racial minorities and women.[192] Those accounts are mostly right; there was nothing equivalent to the Civil Rights Act of 1964 for gay people

---

have these rights" to the Clinton administration in their renewed demand for an executive order. Interview with Leonard Hirsch, founder of Federal GLOBE, Washington, DC, 2013.

189. As late as 1997, the *Washington Blade* reported that up to a quarter of the federal workforce had not been informed that antigay discrimination was against the law. Lou Chibbaro Jr., "Quarter of Federal Workers Not Told Gay Bias Is Illegal," *Washington Blade*, January 31, 1997, 1, 23–25.

190. I would argue that the idea for the military's "don't ask / don't tell" policy (enacted in 1996) had its origins in these earlier civil service reforms and court decisions, which were in turn shaped by employment practices in the private sector. The implementation of the mili-tary's policy was quite different from its rhetoric, however, and the number of soldiers purged under the "reform" increased markedly. Center for American Progress, "Don't Ask, Don't Tell by the Numbers: The Military Loses Patriotic Men and Women Every Day," May 25, 2010.

191. Mattachine Society of Washington, "Comments, Suggestions, and Recommenda-tions regarding Proposed Revisions to 5 CFR Part 731," January 2 1974, 9, folder 5, box 42, Frank Kameny Papers.

192. John D. Skrentny, *The Minority Rights Revolution* (Cambridge, MA: Harvard University Press, 2002), 3.

during these years.[193] But if they were not fully in or part of the rights revolution, they still saw it happening all around them, and it gradually began to change their sense of what they were entitled to, of what they could expect.[194] That Frank Kameny was somewhat ahead of the curve is a reminder as well of how central repression in the public sector was in shaping not only a broader sense of queer vulnerability but also concerted resistance to it. These homophile tremors would soon erupt into the liberationist earthquake.

Yet because this rights consciousness developed without much in the way of robust legal tools—especially outside of government employment— the demise of midcentury's bargain actually led to even greater precarity for the gay workforce, as the next chapter will show. But precarity is a lingering part of the story here in the arena of federal employment during the rugged and uneven transition out of the Lavender Scare years as well. The government librarian who was narrowly saved from termination by the CSC's policy reversal knew that losing a government job probably meant "ending up in a different stratum of life."[195] So when we remember Bruce Scott's partial victory against the Civil Service Commission, we should not forget that he lost his house (a house that he had designed and built himself) and became impoverished in that fight.[196] When we

193. On internal confusion within the EEOC as to whether or not Title VII of the Civil Rights Act of 1964 might cover gay or transgender workers during the law's first decade, see footnote 4 in chapter 4; Brief of Historians as *Amici Curiae* in Support of Employees in *Bostock v. Clayton County*; *Altitude Express, Inc. v. Zarda*; and *R. G. & G. R. Harris Funeral Homes v. EEOC*, Nos. 17-1618, 17-1623, 18-107 (U.S., July 3, 2019).

194. References to the African American freedom struggle were ubiquitous in the homophile press in these years, for example. Kameny was also seeing connections to the broader rights revolution. He wrote to Judge Hart (who wrote the district court decision upholding Bruce Scott's termination from the government) that "the argument that segregation is the traditional Southern way of life is no more a valid one in support of a denial of rights, dignity, and employment to Negro human beings and citizens than is the argument, presented by the government in this case, that the fact that prejudice against the homosexual is the traditional American way of [life], is justification for the denial of rights, dignity, and employment to the homosexual human being and citizen. It is for the Government to attempt to change that tradition, not to succumb to it!" Franklin L. Kameny to Judge George L. Hart Jr., January 24, 1964, folder 4, box 32, Frank Kameny Papers. On connections between gay rights and the African American civil rights movement, see Kevin Mumford, "The Trouble with Gay Rights: Race and the Politics of Sexual Orientation in Philadelphia, 1969–1982," *Journal of American History* 98 (June 2011): 49–72; Jennifer D. Jones, *Ambivalent Affinities: A Political History of Blackness and Homosexuality after World War II* (Chapel Hill: University of North Carolina Press, forthcoming).

195. Interview subject 13, Washington, DC, 2013.

196. "Reply of Bruce Chardon Scott to the United States Civil Service Commission," undated, 16, "Bruce Chardon Scott General File" folder, box 32, Frank Kameny Papers.

remember Clifford Norton, whose landmark court case established the nexus principle that became the foundation for the "gay amendment" in the CSRA as well as the OPM memorandum, we should remember his cross-country bus trip looking for work in the wake of his termination, a time when he was "down to my last four dollars." We should remember his letter to Frank Kameny—sent some thirteen years after Kameny's own firing—asking for help finding a job, and we should also remember the former government astronomer's matter-of-fact reply: "My financial situation is, if possible, even more dire than yours."[197]

Scott remembered the time when he was working on the house as a "happy period in my life."

197. Clifford Norton to Frank Kameny, July 6, 1969, and Franklin E. Kameny to Clifford Norton, July, 11, 1969, folder 5, box 29, Frank Kameny Papers. Kameny's financial precarity continued to the end of his life, when his near destitution led Washington friends to form the Kameny Papers Project to raise money to buy Kameny's extensive papers from him. That purchase—which provided Kameny with income in the last years of his life—was completed in 2006. In 2008, the Kameny Papers Project donated his extensive archive (taller than a six-story building!) to the Library of Congress. Cervini, *Deviant's War*, 385.

CHAPTER FOUR

"Trouble" Followed
"Revolutionary Action"

LESBIAN AND GAY
LIBERATION AND WORK

AS A RESULT OF THE PROFOUND sacrifices that Frank Kameny and others made, the federal government was becoming, across the 1970s, a somewhat less dangerous place for sexual minorities to work.[1] This claim is only relative, since the federal government had been by far the most hostile workplace during the 1950s and 1960s. And there were significant limits to the reform in that sector, as the last chapter has outlined, but it's also true that apart from security clearance procedures, a degree of openness was becoming possible in the government that would have been unthinkable ten or twenty years prior. One man who was a typist for the IRS by day and a drag queen by night remembered that he "flamed" at his office during the 1970s; he wore his hair in a ponytail or a topknot and came to the office in a halter top, pleated pants, sashes, and platform shoes. He also remembered other IRS coworkers coming to work in similar dress during this period, and his notion that this would not have been acceptable in many jobs in the private sector was likely correct.[2]

1. For years, Madeleine Tress, also purged by the government, felt guilty because she did not fight her termination and was eventually reemployed while Kameny, she remembered, "was starving." When in Washington for work, Tress said, "I would always try to at least put Frank in my travel plans and take him to dinner." Interview with Madeleine Tress, conducted by Len Evans, 1983, box 1, Len Evans Papers, GLBT Historical Society of Northern California, San Francisco, CA.
2. Interview subject 16, New York, NY, 2012.

Indeed, for the 80 percent of Americans who worked in the private sector in the 1970s, the typist's "obtrusiveness" would have carried risks at a time when legal protection for queer people remained especially anemic.[3] There were numerous lawsuits that attempted to stretch Title VII of the 1964 Civil Rights Act, which was revolutionizing the workplace for women and racial minorities during these years, to cover homosexuality or transsexuality.[4] Yet most of these court challenges were unsuccessful.[5] The main bright spot was a California case in which gay students at Hastings and Berkeley law schools sued Pacific Telegraph and Telephone (PT&T) for its adamant refusal to hire homosexuals. The law students claimed that they either had or would in the future seek employment with PT&T. In its ruling, the California Supreme Court rejected the argument that antigay discrimination was a form of sex discrimination, and thus covered under Title VII. What the court asserted instead was that "coming out" might be protected political activity under the state's labor code, and that PT&T's refusal to hire gay employees was a violation of the state constitution's equal protection provision (which applied to PT&T as a quasi utility). What was initially seen as a pathbreaking decision, however, was in reality something of a one-off. As the historian Katherine Turk has written, "other state courts did not follow suit, and lower California state courts

3. Lane Windham, *Knocking at Labor's Door: Union Organizing in the 1970s and the Roots of a New Economic Divide* (Chapel Hill: University of North Carolina Press, 2017), 7. On obtrusiveness, which "increases the difficulty of maintaining easeful inattention regarding the stigma," see Erving Goffman, *Stigma: Notes on the Management of Spoiled Identity* (New York: Simon and Schuster, 1963), 103.

4. During the first ten years after the passage of Title VII, gay, lesbian, bisexual, and transgender people did sometimes appeal to the EEOC for help, and the EEOC did in a few instances interpret homosexuality as coming under the prohibition on discrimination "because of . . . sex." That the EEOC occasionally treated homosexuality and transgender status expansively does not seem to have translated into robust (or even widely known) protection during this period. It *does* indicate that the word "sex" in the law may have occasionally included homosexuality and transgender status when Title VII was first enacted, contrary to the claims of those who have recently opposed including LGBT people under Title VII's protective umbrella as "unimaginable" at the law's inception. By 1975, however, the EEOC had reversed course, issuing nonjurisdiction opinions that declared that homosexuality was not covered under Title VII. That then became the "common sense" of Title VII until quite recently. See Brief of Historians as *Amici Curiae* in Support of Employees *Bostock v. Clayton County*; *Altitude Express, Inc. v. Zarda*; and *R. G. & G. R. Harris Funeral Homes v. EEOC*, Nos. 17-1618, 17-1623, 18-107 (U.S., July 3, 2019). On Title VII more generally, see Nancy MacLean, *Freedom Is Not Enough: The Opening of the American Workplace* (Cambridge, MA: Harvard University Press, 2006).

5. The leading decision was *DeSantis v. Pacific Telephone and Telegraph*, 608 F.2d 327 (9th Cir., 1979). See also *Smith v. Liberty Mutual Insurance*, 395 F.Supp. 1098 (N.D. GA, 1975); *Voyles v. Ralph K. Davies Medical Center*, 403 F.Supp. 456 (N.D. Cal., 1975).

and agencies reached conflicting interpretations of the decision."[6] Just a few years after the ruling, the legal scholar Rhonda Rivera pronounced the broader effort to use Title VII to combat discrimination based on sexual orientation to be a "dead end"; the Congressional Research Service concluded that "the federal civil rights of the 1960s and 1970s have been judicially determined to have no application in the gay rights context."[7] Efforts to achieve protection in the private sector through federal legislation, first introduced in 1974 by Congresswoman Bella Abzug, sputtered on for years. The legislation gained sponsors in Congress year by year, but prospects for passage remained almost nil.[8]

The one area apart from the federal government where, at first glance, there did appear to be legal momentum during the 1970s was municipalities. The first antidiscrimination ordinance was passed in 1972 in East Lansing, Michigan, as a result of a concerted effort by student activists at Michigan State University. The antidiscrimination measure was initially passed with an additional provision that specified that "recruitment for homosexual behavior" on the job could lead to termination. East Lansing activists were furious, and after some back and forth, the city council removed the offending language from the law.[9] A year later, antidiscrimination ordinances were adopted in San Francisco and Ann Arbor and subsequently continued to be passed in college towns and other liberal cities.[10] Progress was steady, but even in the most politically progressive

6. See Katherine Turk, "'Our Militancy Is Our Openness': Gay Employment Rights Activism in California and the Question of Sexual Orientation in Sex Equality Law," *Law and History Review* 31 (May 2013): 457–59; *Gay Law Students Association v. Pacific Telephone & Telegraph*, 24 Cal. 3d 458, 595 P.2d 592, 156 Cal. Rptr. 14 (1979).

7. Rhonda R. Rivera, "Queer Law: Sexual Orientation Law in the Mid-Eighties," *University of Dayton Law Review* 10 (1984–85): 471; Congressional Research Service, "An Overview of Legal Developments in Homosexual Rights," 1985, folder 7712, box 6, Records of the Human Rights Campaign, Rare and Manuscript Collections, Cornell University, Ithaca, NY.

8. Dudley Clendinen and Adam Nagourney, *Out for Good: The Struggle to Build a Gay Rights Movement in America* (New York: Simon and Schuster, 1999), 240–42; "NGTF on Capitol Hill: An Overview of the Program for Federal Gay Rights Legislation," in *IT'S TIME: Newsletter of the National Gay Task Force* (special bonus issue), folder 29, box 1127, Records of the ACLU, Seeley Mudd Library, Princeton University, Princeton, NJ.

9. "E. Lansing Victory," *Gay Liberator*, April 1972, 2; "Oops, E. Lansing First with Hiring Law," *Advocate*, May 10, 1972, 1; "New Gay Rights Law in E. Lansing," *Gay Liberator* 28 (July 1973): 1.

10. "New Gay Rights Law in E. Lansing," 1. The next US cities to pass antidiscrimination ordinances (through August 1974) were Washington, DC; Seattle, WA; Berkeley, CA; Detroit, MI; Columbus, OH; Minneapolis, MN; Alfred, NY; St. Paul, MN; Palo Alto, CA; and Ithaca, NY. "Gay Rights Protections in the United States and Canada," summary, *National Gay News* (January 1975 through June 1976), "National Gay Task Force—Need

places, the laws usually lacked enforcement mechanisms. "No city has yet authorized funds to ensure that laws covering discrimination against gay men and women are enforced," one journalist noted in 1975, observing as well that passage of the local ordinances generally required a quiet approach: "Most of the [gay] employment rights laws which have been passed were put through with a minimum of publicity." In Seattle, to take just one example, "members of gay organizations were not even aware that the law had passed."[11] A key activist who worked for the adoption of a gay rights ordinance in Philadelphia "adopted a 'secret' strategy of internal memos, coordinated outreach, and networking," according to the historian Kevin Mumford. Even the gay press was to be kept in the dark.[12] The utility of local antidiscrimination ordinances was undoubtedly compromised by their hushed adoption. "I have found to my distress," wrote the lawyer Matt Coles several years after the enactment of San Francisco's ordinance, "that a substantial portion of the gay community remains unaware that private discrimination against gay people is now illegal."[13]

The situation was truly a catch-22, because the discretion that enabled cities to enact such ordinances made for weak and ineffective laws. But when campaigns for antidiscrimination laws were conducted more openly, city councils failed to pass them. New York City is a prominent illustration. The Gay Activists Alliance (GAA), an offshoot of the city's Gay Liberation Front, first announced a campaign for a gay civil rights bill in the New York City Council in September 1970. At that moment, it was the first such measure in the country. After months of lobbying, the bill was introduced by four members of the city council and referred to the General Welfare Committee for consideration in January 1971. When no action had been taken by fall, one thousand GAA members marched in protest to the apartment building

---

for Federal Legislation" folder, box 28, Costanza Files, Jimmy Carter Presidential Library, Atlanta, GA.

11. "Employment Rights Roundup," *Advocate*, January 28, 1975, 9. On the quiet passage of antidiscrimination ordinances protecting gays, see "Three More Cities End Discrimination," *Advocate* 160, March 26, 1975, 6.

12. Kevin Mumford, "The Trouble with Gay Rights: Race and the Politics of Sexual Orientation in Philadelphia," *Journal of American History* 98 (June 2011): 69.

13. Matthew A. Coles to Phyllis Lyon, December 6, 1978, "Political Organizations Correspondence 1978–1979" folder, box 70, 93-13, Papers of Phyllis Lyon and Del Martin, GLBT Historical Society of Northern California. Even if one was aware of such a law, "the gay employee would have to be rather brave" to use it, two sociologists opined. "It is almost inevitable that such cases would receive much publicity in the local media. . . . Through using that legal recourse one would have lost much of one's ability to 'pass' as heterosexual." Joseph Harry and William B. DeVall, *The Social Organization of Gay Males* (New York: Praeger, 1978), 202.

of the chair of the General Welfare Committee. More skirmishes followed, culminating in the arrest of fifteen GAA members who protested Mayor Lindsay's refusal to act publicly in support of the bill. The bill was voted on and defeated for the first time in January 1972. An endless cycle then followed of protests, "zap actions," clashes with police, arrests, and votes taken in which the GAA repeatedly failed to garner enough support for passage. In April 1974, on its fifth vote before the General Welfare Committee, the gay rights ordinance finally passed out of committee. At that point, approval by the council was considered nearly a sure thing, as "no bill passed by a committee [had] failed to pass the full Council in at least 35 years."[14]

With victory seeming to draw near, the GAA held a rally with one thousand supporters in Sheridan Square and organized gay "Freedom Ride" bus tours around the boroughs to gather support for the legislation by associating their cause with the African American freedom struggle. Several days later, the city council narrowly rejected the ordinance once again. Because twenty-four council members failed to support the bill, the GAA released twenty-four mice in a public session of the Finance Committee.[15] This cycle of protest and negative votes continued—for fifteen years!—until the City of New York finally passed a gay rights bill in the mid-1980s.[16] During that long struggle, even supporters criticized the liberationists for "disruptive" behavior that repeatedly set back the bill's chances. Many GAA members, however, saw the bill not as an end in itself but as "a tool toward liberation." The campaign for passage was "anti-closet," designed to "underline how the threat of loss of employment had been used to keep Gays in silent submission." Members of the GAA believed that New York City's ordinance "never was and never could be defeated," because it was "the best way of getting the message to the community: the closet is built in fear, not shame."[17]

Whether or not one accepts the GAA's claim to victory, the campaign reveals some of the ways that civil rights reform and the liberationist ethos were more intertwined than is sometimes understood when looking back on this period. It's notable as well that the Stonewall riot that launched gay

14. "Chronology of Gay Civil Rights," and "The Fight for a Civil Rights Law in New York City," Subject Files, Lesbian Herstory Archives, Brooklyn, NY (microfilm reel 85, frame 07740 and frame 07770, Thompson Gale).

15. Ibid.

16. Peter Frieberg, "New York City: Victory!," *Advocate*, April 29, 1986, 10.

17. Marty Robinson quoted in Toby Marotta, *The Politics of Homosexuality: How Lesbians and Gay Men Have Made Themselves a Political Force in Modern America* (Boston: Houghton-Mifflin, 1981), 225–26.

liberation in 1969 occurred nearly simultaneously with the *Norton* decision protecting federal workers in employment—a temporal confluence that might nudge us toward a view of gay liberation as a progression out of Frank Kameny's style of homophile politics as much as a dramatic departure from it. The historian Jeffrey Escoffier has helpfully described gay politics during these decades as a "mélange of sexual liberation, civil rights activism, alternative social activities, and feminist consciousness raising groups."[18] And even the reformist National Gay Task Force (NGTF), according to its executive director, understood at the time "that gay rights will never be won unless there is an expansion of consciousness concerning sexuality in general," so liberation and rights "go hand in hand."[19]

The expanded consciousness that emerged with gay liberation, considered here as a broader cultural zeitgeist rather than a narrow movement specific to a few large cities, did eventually begin to erode the "vicious circle" of gay politics and culture. As the NGTF director's comment intimated, laws had long failed to pass because people would not come out to fight for them, but gay people wouldn't come out without laws to protect them.[20] During the liberation era, though, first as a trickle and later as a crescendo, many gays simply tossed their former discretion away, even without a legal safety net. This revolution in consciousness, unaccompanied for many years by a related revolution in law, was facilitated by a broader skepticism during these years about jobs and career, a drive toward authenticity, and certainly by a downward economy that ironically made some feel like there was simply less to lose.[21]

The difference that liberation made was neither uniform nor linear in its progress but rather manifested in distinct ways in blue-collar and white-collar jobs, for men and women, as well as by individual temperament. Liberation—as the following pages will make clear—likely meant

18. Jeffrey Escoffier, "Fabulous Politics: Gay, Lesbian, and Queer Movements, 1969–1999," in *The World the Sixties Made: Politics and Culture in Recent America*, ed. Van Gosse and Richard Moser (Philadelphia: Temple University Press, 2003), 197.

19. Richard Goldstein, "The Politics of Liberation," *Village Voice*, June 25–July 1, 1980, 20.

20. Howard Brown, *Familiar Faces, Hidden Lives: The Story of Homosexual Men in America Today* (New York: Harcourt, Brace, Jovanovich, 1976), 236–37. Fear also kept people from using the limited legal tools that were available. See "Hiding on the Job," *Gay Liberator* 12 (October 1, 1971): 4.

21. On the rising dissatisfaction during these years with the noneconomic aspects of jobs and "debates about the human purpose and meaning of work," see Arne L. Kallenberg, *Good Jobs, Bad Jobs: The Rise of Polarized and Precarious Employment Systems in the United States, 1970s to 2000* (New York: Russell Sage Foundation, 2011), 4; *Work in America: Report of a Special Task Force to the Secretary of Health Education, and Welfare* (Cambridge, MA: MIT Press, 1973).

different things to the downwardly mobile individuals who "dropped out" to free themselves of repressive work environments than it did to those who banded together with ambitions of making queer workplaces for themselves. Some of those collective efforts eventually strove to be *upwardly* mobile, as, for example, the lesbian separatists who worked to create an alternative economy described in detail in the latter part of this chapter. The chaotic, experimental, and uneven nature of the liberation period makes it quite difficult to chart its impact coherently; it moves in fits and starts, backward and forward. One clear trend, however, was a gradual weakening of the bargain that had long governed the relationship between employers and their queer employees. The mutual pact *to try not to see* and *to try not to be seen* was now less likely to be upheld by either side.

For their part, liberationists counseled caution only as far as the interview stage, and then an easing out once on the job.[22] As an increasing number of gay people began to heed this advice, a prospective employee's appearance and manner during an interview were no longer seen as adequate predictors of how he or she would behave once hired. Where it had once been sufficient to merely screen out the "obvious types" during the hiring process, employers now turned their sights on the "nonobvious" as well.[23] For this reason, employers increasingly relied on tools to get at tendencies and traits that might not be visible to the naked eye. The GAA complained that the use of "pre-employment checks (police, credit, bonding, etc.) . . . is much more common than ten years ago, and much more complete. They always include questioning of neighbors, relatives, and friends. Psychological attitude testing, which often discloses homosexual tendencies, has become general with . . . larger private employers."[24] One sociologist also noted the increased use of polygraph

22. Dennis Sanders, *Gay Source: A Catalog for Men* (New York: Coward, McCann, and Geoghegan, 1977), 155–57.

23. For a discussion of the way that employers began to conduct surveillance of employees who were not obviously gay, see "Employment Discrimination against Homosexuals," presented by the Gay Activists Alliance, July 10, 1970, and Jim Owles to President, Retail Credit Company, December 30, 1970, both in folders 1–2, "Fair Employment," box 16, Records of the Gay Activists Alliance, Manuscript and Archives Division, New York Public Library, New York, NY.

24. Appendix, "On Economic Discrimination," circa 1970, folder 2, "Fair Employment," box 16, Records of the Gay Activists Alliance. On the expanding use of psychological tests during the postwar period—and the way they were used to screen for "sexual deviates"—see Sarah E. Igo, *The Known Citizen: A History of Privacy in Modern America* (Cambridge, MA: Harvard University Press, 2020), 136–37.

tests to uncover homosexuality among job applicants.[25] The executive director of the ACLU expressed concern about investigators who were being employed by prestigious financial institutions "to find homosexuals," remarking that increased surveillance of employees confronted many with "the impossibility of staying in the closet," ironically pushing some toward gay liberation.[26]

Liberationists welcomed the influx, inviting gays specifically to reject the terms of the bargain—exploitation for relatively safety—that had previously underlain the employment relation. "We have our humanity to win," one liberationist wrote. "How can what we pay for it be more than what we are paying now?"[27] Indeed, the calculus applied to these decisions was changing. As he contemplated an uncertain future (perhaps digging ditches?), one untenured academic who had just revealed his homosexuality proclaimed that "in whatever field my society forces me to survive, I will survive as a whole person."[28] The notion that a person might need to leave a career in order to be "whole"—that work was somehow antithetical to the realization of full human potential—suffused 1970s radicalism in general but had a particularly powerful valence for gay people.[29]

Gays weren't just "pushed" toward a liberationist stance by hostile employers, but drawn to it by the vibrancy and novelty of a gay culture that was exploding across the country during this period. As gay life became more elaborate and more appealing, it became harder to "shut off" during one's working hours. One New York City man had been wanting to march in the city's annual gay pride parade for several years, but he couldn't quite bring himself to do it. He was afraid of being seen by coworkers. By 1975's

25. Martin P. Levine, "Employment Discrimination against Gay Men," *International Review of Modern Sociology* 9 (1979): 156.

26. Statement of Aryeh Neier, Executive Director of the American Civil Liberties Union, April 18, 1974, before the Council of the City of New York, Subject Files: Sexual Privacy Project Memos, box 3001, Records of the ACLU; Aryeh Neier, *Dossier: The Secret Files They Keep on You* (New York: Stein and Day, 1974), 170.

27. Mike Silverstein, "The Gay Bureaucrat: What They Are Doing to You" (1971), in *Out of the Closets: Voices of Gay Liberation*, ed. Karla Jay and Allen Young (New York: New York University Press, 1992), 169.

28. Louie Crew, "The Gay Academic Unmasks," *Chronicle of Higher Education*, February 20, 1975, 20.

29. Survival on the job had long meant, as one liberationist framed it, that there was "always a piece missing." Transcript, folder 14, box 83, Barbara Gittings Papers, Manuscripts and Archives Division, New York Public Library. Toby Marotta further observed that it was gays with countercultural values who were most easily persuaded that it was worth the loss of "social status, professional advancement, [and] material reward" to lead an "integrated" life. See Marotta, *Politics of Homosexuality*, 315.

Gay Freedom Day, "I just didn't care anymore. If they see me, they see me," he remembered. When he attended, he found the march was "so freeing," the "most exhilarating experience" of his life. Back at work, though, there was a new urge he couldn't resist: he changed the screen savers on the office's bank of computers to read "Happy Gay Pride!" A coworker who saw him do this asked if the man was gay. "Yes, I am!" He exulted, "I just marched in the gay pride parade!" even though he expected to be fired once word got around the office.[30] Another woman was similarly inspired by a visit to a gay resort on Fire Island, realizing that "dammit, I have a right to my space on this planet." On her return to Los Angeles, she drove to the old Victorian that housed the city's gay community center. She was shaken by the fact that the community center was just down the street from the office of a former employer, and it took her twenty minutes to work up the courage to go in. But soon she was working there as an employment counselor.[31] Another lesbian began a search for an office job without altering her appearance or behavior "for a paycheck." She kept her short haircut, removed her earrings, and began to look for employment "as a fairly visible lesbian."[32] During this same period, a New York schoolteacher moved to Birmingham to care for his elderly father. Once there, he found a teaching position but refused to stop living the openly gay life he had been leading in New York.[33]

———◆———

The gay teacher in Alabama was subsequently fired, one of many whose "militancy and visibility," as a 1971 law review article put it, "makes it more difficult . . . to earn a living at the present time."[34] The 1970s—with gay political consciousness rising as the economy slumped and employers needed to shed workers from their payroll—were truly a perfect storm for gay employment prospects. "Trouble" followed "revolutionary action," as one gay San Franciscan pithily observed.[35] In some cases, members of the older generation tried to warn aspiring liberationists about the consequences of behavior that they regarded as reckless. A young editor in

30. Interview subject 35, New York, NY, 2012.
31. Interview subject 94, interview conducted via telephone, 2013.
32. Susan MacDonald, "Out of the Ghetto and Into the Office," *Lesbian Feminist*, September 1977. Eventually, she did find a position, but one that was "not ideal."
33. Interview subject 49, Atlanta, GA, 2012.
34. Irving Kovarsky, "Fair Employment for the Homosexual," *Washington University Law Quarterly* 1971 (Fall 1971): 531.
35. Rusty Brown interview, conducted by Len Evans, 1983, box 1, Len Evans Papers.

mainstream publishing, for example, started receiving invitations to lunch from prominent editors and publishing executives in New York City, just as he was about to launch publication of a new gay magazine. He was surprised to discover that his lunch companions were all closeted gay men in the industry who had learned of his plans. One by one, they urged him to publish the magazine under a pseudonym. He refused to do so, and, as his senior colleagues predicted, he lost his job and struggled to be reemployed despite his reputation as a rising star.[36] A lesbian who had a high-powered career as the business agent for the International Brotherhood of Electrical Workers didn't wait to be fired; she left her job and started cleaning houses in order to come out as a lesbian and become involved with the gay community in Boston.[37] Self-employment in general was championed by gay liberationists as a pathway to "economic self-determination" that made it possible to speak out "without fear of economic reprisal."[38]

In addition to being disproportionately self-employed, liberationists were also disproportionately out of work.[39] "In the early years of gay liberation," the writer Edmund White observed, "most homosexual demonstrators . . . were young, militant, and unemployed."[40] Approximately half of the "thousand or so homosexuals attending" a Bay Area meeting of gay liberationists were out of work, according to one account.[41] More generally, many of those who had migrated to San Francisco to live a gay life during these years were getting by on food stamps, and San Francisco's Tavern Guild confirmed that while unemployment rates in the city were high in general, they were significantly higher for gays.[42] Indeed, wherever gay people were clustered during these years, whether by city,

36. Interview subject 39, New York, NY, 2012.

37. Interview subject 80, Cambridge, MA, 2011.

38. "On Economic Independence for Gays," *Newsletter of the Homophile Action League* 2 (March–April 1970): 2.

39. Lillian Faderman, *The Gay Revolution: The Story of the Struggle* (New York: Simon and Schuster, 2015), 86, 141, 213, 218.

40. Edmund White, *States of Desire: Travels in Gay America* (London: Dutton Adult, 1980), 63.

41. Appendix, "On Economic Discrimination," circa 1970, folder 2, "Fair Employment," box 16, Records of the Gay Activists Alliance.

42. "S.F. Job Law Prospects Brighten," *Advocate*, January 1, 1972, 8. Discussion on the use of food stamps and other welfare among queer migrants has been informed by my interview with Jeffrey Escoffier, Brooklyn, NY, 2017; White, *States of Desire*, 37. On the downward mobility of gay migrants to San Francisco more generally, see "San Francisco as Another Sinking Venice," *Vector* 12 (April 1976): 20. On the attempt of Los Angeles County welfare officials to force a recipient of food stamps to conceal his homosexuality during his job search, see "Job Hunter Need Not Hide Being Gay," *Advocate*, June 9–22, 1971, 11.

neighborhood, or even occupation, problems with finding and keeping employment were often apparent. When the GAA collected testimonies of people discriminated against in employment in New York, for example, over half of the complaints came from teachers, an occupation that had always employed high numbers of both gay men and lesbians.[43] In prior decades, gay teachers had maintained an especially low profile because termination was almost a certainty if one's homosexuality was revealed, and the close association teachers had with children made them especially vulnerable to political attack.[44] But despite those dangers—and while most maintained a quiet existence—teachers began to entertain some risk. One Detroit teacher, for example, attended her city's gay pride parade, albeit wearing sunglasses, a hat, and a trench coat.[45] Others were quite a bit bolder: there were suddenly teachers who joined activist groups, appeared (undisguised) at gay events, let their names be published in local newspapers, and even told their students they were gay.[46] They were almost always fired for such "liberation activities," as were the handful of educators who transitioned and then tried to hold on to positions in a different gender from the one in which they began their teaching careers.[47] Even those who stayed away from activism could evince a changed consciousness that might cost them a teaching position. When confronted by her principal with the rumor that she was a homosexual, Peggy Burton said what would have been almost inconceivable ten years before: "So what?"

43. Jim Owles to Chancellor, New York City Public Schools, January 18, 1971, folders 1–2, "Fair Employment," box 16, Records of the Gay Activists Alliance.

44. That association was the foundation, for example, of the evangelical singer Anita Bryant's vitriolic campaign "Save Our Children," as well as California state senator John Briggs's proposed proposition to bar gay people from teaching in California schools. On Bryant and Briggs, see part 6 of Faderman, *Gay Revolution*, 321–89.

45. Folder 18, box 1, Rochella Thorpe Oral History Project Files, 1992–95, Collection 7607, Rare and Manuscript Collections, Cornell University.

46. A 1971 law review article noted that more gay teachers were "standing up for their civil rights." Neal G. Horenstein, "Homosexuals in the Teaching Profession," *Cleveland State Law Review* 20 (1971): 129.

47. "Seek Job Rights in Supreme Court," *Advocate*, July 31, 1974, 23; "Teacher Appeals Firing," *Advocate*, May 26, 1971, 4; "Lesbian Teacher Sues for Her Job," *Advocate*, October 5, 1977, 12; folders 1–2, "Fair Employment," box 16, Records of the Gay Activists Alliance; interview subject 60, Lansing, MI, 2012. Paula Grossman transitioned in 1971 and Steve Dain in 1976. Each fought termination through the courts. Neither was successful at being reinstated, but Grossman eventually won disability benefits, and Dain was awarded backpay. See "Supreme Court Turns Deaf Ear to New Jersey Transsexual's Case," *Baltimore Sun*, October 19, 1976, A8; Robert Hanley, "Transsexual Upheld on Teacher Position: Court in New Jersey Rules in Favor of Disability Benefits in Case," *New York Times*, February 17, 1978, B3; "Transsexual Loses Job Bid," *Philadelphia Gay News*, June 1978, 8; "Teacher Wins Back Pay from School Board," *Update*, June 13, 1980, 4.

She was removed from her position in a rural school in Turner, Oregon, then went to work at a nearby cannery, but also decided to "stand up for my rights." Although she initially had trouble finding a lawyer who would take her case, she filed suit against the school district.[48]

Teachers and others in heavily gay professions established caucuses during these years. Their organizing countered the idea that professional status was inherently at odds with homosexuality, and teachers were especially notable for securing a pledge of support from their union decades ahead of similar statements from traditional craft unions.[49] Another notable professional association that emerged at the outset of this period was the Task Force on Gay Liberation of the American Library Association (ALA). It was founded in 1970 by librarian Barbara Gittings, who was simultaneously working with Frank Kameny on security clearance cases. The librarians' caucus sought to claim a space within the ALA's annual meeting where gay librarians could find each other and network, create publicity that would educate the broader membership about homosexuality, and finally, lobby the entire organization to adopt a gay rights resolution. The task force achieved that goal just a year after its founding. The ALA committed both to protect gay librarians from discrimination and to help librarians disseminate materials to the public that included positive information about homosexuality.[50] To aid in this task, Gittings maintained a bibliography of books on homosexuality to distribute to libraries. The caucus also put on panels at the annual meeting with such titles as "Serving the Fearful Reader" and "Sex and the Single Cataloguer."[51]

The Gay Academic Union (GAU)—"one of the first good breezes in the rancid air of the academy"—began as a relatively informal gathering of graduate students and junior faculty on the Upper West Side in New York. The organization's first conference attracted 325 academics from around the country, and the GAU eventually inspired caucuses within

48. "Fired Because of Rumor, Rural Teacher Fights Back," *Advocate*, June 21, 1972, 1; "Fired Teacher Rejects Settlement," *Advocate*, May 22, 1974, 13.

49. On gay rights organizing within the union movement, see Miriam Frank, *Out in the Union: A Labor History of Queer America* (Philadelphia: Temple University Press, 2014). See also *Gay People in the Labor Force* 1 (undated, circa 1974): 1, in folder 31, box 140, Records of the National Gay and Lesbian Task Force, Rare and Manuscript Collections, Cornell University.

50. Larry Lee, "Barbara Gittings: Gay Rights Pioneer," *Metro Gay News* 2 (August 1977): 16–17.

51. Subject File: American Library Association, folder 35, box 164, Records of the National Gay and Lesbian Task Force.

many academic specialties.[52] There were, for example, groups for gay biologists and for gay sociologists. Similarly to the librarians, gay academics pushed their professional organizations to pass antidiscrimination statements, and those in the humanities and social sciences advocated research into gay history and culture. "If sociology's mission is to portray the true place of people within the fabric of society, it is far from the goal for gay men and . . . even further for lesbians," one sociologist lamented. "We know more about obscure tribes than about America's second largest minority."[53]

The Gay Nurses Association (GNA) was founded in 1973 after two nurses attended the second gay pride march in Philadelphia and decided to "start doing something constructive about their own liberation." They initially asked for exhibit space and program time at the next meeting of Pennsylvania nurses. That request was denied; the operating premise of the Pennsylvania nurses' organization seemed to be "that there are no gay nurses, but only gay patients." Gay Nurses Association organizers attended the convention in Pittsburgh anyway, renting a suite at the hotel in order to show interested conference-goers a filmstrip titled "The Invisible Minority."[54] The following year, the GNA managed to get a booth for the meeting of the American Nurses Association (ANA) in San Francisco, but local nurses still felt it wasn't safe to staff the booth without risking loss of both jobs and professional licenses.[55] The group nonetheless put on an extremely successful panel—eight hundred nurses crowded into a room intended for five hundred—but the *American Journal of Nursing* refused to cover the GNA in their reporting on the convention.[56]

Despite these challenges, as the caucus grew, the GNA was able to engage in effective advocacy for both gay patients and gay nurses. In one notable case, they intervened to have the license of one gay nurse, revoked in 1963 after an arrest for solicitation, restored. After an eleven-year

52. Crew, "Gay Academic Unmasks," 325; Martin Duberman, "The Gay Academic Union," in *Left Out: The Politics of Exclusion, 1964–2000* (Cambridge, MA: South End, 2002), 269.

53. Martin Levine, "The Status of Homosexuality within the Sociological Enterprise," folder 47, and "Gay Scientists," folder 15, both in box 164, Records of the National Gay and Lesbian Task Force.

54. Carolyn Innes, RN, and David Waldron, RN, "Staying Gay, Proud, and Healthy," in *Workforce: Gay Workers Issue*, September/October 1974, in folder 73, box 165, Records of the National Gay and Lesbian Task Force.

55. Caroline Drewes, "Why There's a New Group of Gay Nurses," *San Francisco Examiner*, June 13, 1974, 26.

56. Innes and Waldron, "Staying Gay, Proud, and Healthy."

hiatus, this man resumed his working life in his chosen profession. Five years after its founding, the GNA won a resolution endorsing the civil rights of gay people from the ANA.[57] As most professional caucuses did during these years, they built the organization by creating multiple ways for nurses to align themselves with the cause while minimizing career fallout. The organization was "acutely aware of the reluctance of many nurses to become active members." For this reason, the organization kept the names of members confidential, while pointing out that the mere fact it had to do so was reason enough to justify its existence.[58] "Examine your position and the risks involved with the various activities you undertake," the founders advised, but "'come out' whenever the opportunity presents itself." If being open wasn't yet viable, a nurse could give money or volunteer to help "behind the scenes." And if joining the GNA (however quietly) was still too big a step, gay nurses were encouraged to begin their process by joining "Nurses NOW," the feminist caucus that also had "human liberation" as its goal.[59]

———

If the 1970s were the years when the professions began to move toward greater openness, an opposite shift was occurring in many blue-collar settings. In prior decades, gay men and lesbians, as well as some trans men and trans women, had been surprisingly open in factory jobs, kept safe in part by a strong industrial economy that made blue-collar jobs relatively plentiful. Queer people of color, as well as white lesbians, had also been protected by the reality that they would not be promoted within the factories in which they worked. Yet by the late 1960s and increasingly through the 1970s, manufacturing jobs began their precipitous and irreversible decline.[60] Simultaneously, both social movement and government pres-

57. "Gay Nurses Alliance: History, Herstory, Growth and Development," "Business" folder, box 1, Records of the Gay Nurses Alliance, Lesbian Herstory Archives, Brooklyn, NY.

58. "Greetings in Gay Pride," letter from Carolyn Innes and David Waldron, "Newsletters, Pamphlets, and Memos" folder, box 1, Records of the Gay Nurses Alliance.

59. "Dear" letter from Carolyn Inness and David Waldron, undated, circa 1974, "Newsletters, Pamphlets, and Memos" folder, box 1, and "Helpful Hints: A Practical Plan for Progress," 3, "Business" folder, box 1, both in Records of the Gay Nurses Alliance.

60. While this trend was more associated with the 1970s, "the proportion of workers in historically unionized blue-collar occupations began declining in the late 1960s," observed sociologist Arne Kallenberg in *Good Jobs, Bad Jobs*, 33. On deindustrialization, see Jefferson Cowie, *Stayin' Alive: The 1970s and the Last Days of the Working Class* (New York: New Press, 2010); Judith Stein, *Pivotal Decade: How the United States Traded Factories for Finance in the Seventies* (New Haven, CT: Yale University Press, 2010).

sure began to force employment sectors that had excluded women and racial minorities to open up some opportunities, as well as to create pathways for women and racial minorities to become supervisors and managers.[61] This confluence was dangerous for sexual minorities in factory jobs. An African American man who worked on the line in Detroit associated an increasingly hostile environment for gays in his plant with both the politics of gay liberation *and* the sudden appearance of African Americans as supervisors on the factory floor.[62] His white gay coworker concurred that the situation at work became more difficult after gay liberation; he was more hassled then.[63]

Gay men across racial lines thus began to disappear from blue-collar jobs. In contrast to sociological studies conducted in the 1950s that associated overt homosexuality with craft, operative, manufacturing, and low-level clerical and service jobs, sociologists in the 1970s noted the paucity of gay men in manual occupations.[64] According to Joseph Harry and William DeVall, male homosexuals were opting out of blue-collar work "because they anticipate greater discrimination from blue-collar workers than from workers in other occupational strata," and because of the "greater homophobia found among blue-collar workers."[65] That rising hostility was likely associated with the perceived demands of gay liberation (and relatedly, feminism) at a time when straight men felt their own economic prospects growing more circumscribed in the manufacturing sector. This trend was also connected to the gradual decline of the fairy/trade paradigm that had, since the early twentieth century, enabled masculine men to be in close proximity to effeminate men, and even have sexual contact with them, without it endangering their own sense of normalcy.[66] Yet while the sexual negotiation had undoubtedly become more complex, physical relationships between straight and gay male factory workers were still commonplace in the 1970s—one factory worker discovered a "whole underground where tricks were made" at his plant. Sex between men

61. See especially MacLean, *Freedom Is Not Enough.*

62. Interview subject 54, Detroit, MI, 2012.

63. Interview subject 56, Detroit, MI, 2012.

64. In 1956, Leznoff and Westley argued that gays were more covert as they moved up the socioeconomic scale, and viewed operative, craft, and manufacturing positions as ones in which gays were open. Maurice Leznoff and William A. Westley, "The Homosexual Community," in *Sexual Deviance*, ed. William Simon and John H. Gagnon (New York: Harper and Row, 1967), 184–96 (reprinted from *Social Problems* 3 [April 1956]: 257–63).

65. Harry and DeVall, *Social Organization of Gay Males*, 156.

66. George Chauncey, *Gay New York: Gender, Urban Culture, and the Making of the Gay Male World, 1890–1940* (New York: Basic Books, 1994), 13–16, 76–86.

occurred most often in "the rest room, the parking lot, or other secluded place[s]." The exchange of money was an increasingly crucial part of these encounters. Paying gay men for sex enabled their straight-identified partners "to clearly demonstrate, at least to themselves, that they were not gay."[67] So did expressions of aggression and violence toward gays, which became a more pronounced element of blue-collar culture.

As a result of such violence, the number of gay men employed in factory work declined, even in relation to the overall decline in jobs in manufacturing; those who remained were also far more hidden than they had been in the 1950s and 1960s. One man remembered going back into the closet to take a job at General Motors in 1972.[68] No amount of discretion would protect effeminate men, however, who were subject to sustained harassment and even assault. An African American man who was "queenie," for example, was abused by his coworkers, who would "empty their spray guns on his pants." His situation improved only when two other African American men were hired in his department. "They were straight," one lesbian coworker remembered, "but they protected him somewhat."[69] Yet what is most striking in the accounts of lesbians who worked in factory jobs during these years is just how few gay men—whether masculine or feminine—they remembered seeing in their plants at all. "It would have been hell," one woman speculated.[70] Another blue-collar worker remembered the "secret homosexuals" at his plant, who all worked harder at their jobs to avoid detection, and the slur of being called a "lazy cocksucker."[71] Yet another man, who actually did come out at his job during these years, suffered reprisals. In the factory, which he described as "a microcosm of the total male culture," "we re-enacted the long and tragic history of gay male oppression." Not only was he unable to reach a peaceful coexistence with his coworkers, but "in spite of repeated efforts to come out in several locations, over a period of several years," he failed to obtain what he called

67. Michael Owen, "Coming Out in the Factory," *Gay Liberator*, August 1, 1973, 8.

68. Interview subject 61, Flint, MI, 2013.

69. Interview subject 62, Lansing, MI, 2013. Another woman said lesbians also fared better in plants where more African American men were employed. Interview subject 97, Buffalo, NY, 2013. Nancy MacLean similarly found that "black men, who also struggled for access, tended to be the most supportive of women's right to work" in general. MacLean, *Freedom Is Not Enough*, 282.

70. Interview subject 60, Lansing, MI, 2012; interview subject 58, Lansing, MI, 2012; interview subject 59, Lansing, MI, 2012; interview subject 89, Cambridge, MA, 2013; interview subject 97, Buffalo, NY, 2013.

71. Joe Schuman, "A Factory Worker Views Oppression," *GPU News*, July 1973, 14.

"a liberated position." He lamented that as a result of his openness, "I lost one job after another."[72]

———◆———

Lesbians who held blue-collar jobs were also probably more closeted during the liberation era than they had been before—"you kept your sexuality quiet," one remarked.[73] Still, as a woman who worked in a steel plant in Buffalo recalled, women were definitely "more visible" than gay men working in factories during these years.[74] Especially for women who were moving into men's jobs in the factory, passing as straight was nearly impossible because women who did "non-traditional work" were invariably suspected of being queer. And lesbians were, in fact, disproportionately represented among the "pioneers" desegregating previously all-male occupations.[75] "Dyke-baiting" worked to keep all women in line in these jobs, then, because lesbians so often *were* the women who pushed hardest at the boundaries of male power.[76] One lesbian who worked in a rural Michigan auto parts factory systematically moved into each of the traditionally "male" jobs in her plant in the mid-1970s. In every new position, "she was shunned" for almost a year after she started. Even the straight women complained about her, alleging that they were protected and "catered to," and that her "applying for men's jobs would destroy the whole company." After a time, however, all the women who complained followed her into men's jobs. Eventually, she opened almost every department in her plant to women.[77]

Another woman who started at GM in 1973 remembered that the women who were most abused in her plant were the lesbians who were really physically fit, who "could hang bumpers." They had moved into a male area in the plant and were getting overtime. Her own move into "material handling"—a trucking department that moved materials from plant to plant, was well paid, and very male—was made smoother by identifying a man she "just had a sense about" and asking him to train her. He patiently

72. Owen, "Coming Out in the Factory," 8–9.
73. Interview subject 58, Lansing, MI, 2012.
74. Interview subject 97, Buffalo, NY, 2013.
75. "We suggest that a significant number of the 'pioneers' in previously all female or all male occupations are gay persons," wrote two sociologists in 1978. See Harry and DeVall, *Social Organization of Gay Males*, 162.
76. See "Letters," in *Tradeswomen* 3, no. 2 (1984): 2; MacLean, *Freedom Is Not Enough*, 280.
77. Interview subject 58, Lansing, MI, 2012.

showed her everything about her new position. Within a short time, the other men in the unit accepted her. Her protector was tall and muscular and talked about his girlfriends. Later, she found out he was gay.[78]

In factories where several lesbians worked together, they could organize for their mutual safety. One woman told of taking a job as a steelworker at the Berwick Forge and Fabricating Plant in Berwick, Pennsylvania, in the late 1970s. When she started her job, there were twelve women working in the plant and nearly four thousand men. All twelve women were lesbians, "and we had seen what happened to other dykes that tried to take on the Forge." The small cluster of women banded together, developing "strategies to prevent rape and harassment." They went to their foremen and demanded that no woman be assigned to a crew that was not in eyesight of at least two other women. After two hours of negotiation, the women had been placed on separate crews but "within calling distance of each other." When the women were harassed by foremen, they went as a group to the foremen's office to ask, "if *their* wives wanted to go the Green Door Motel too." They responded to feeling threatened by adopting a violent posture themselves, such that they did "as little paper work and as much cornering" as possible, using "our anger and our unity to get what we deserved." Instead of feeling isolated or defeated, the experience at the forge was a powerful one. "Since we left the Forge," this steelworker wrote, "I've never lost the feeling . . . that I got there . . . of being able to handle effectively and forcefully any situation we have to."[79]

That sense of triumph at overcoming challenges and extraordinary personal growth on the job was also interspersed with feelings of hopelessness and despair for lesbians who went into the trades. This was even harder terrain to access. Years after women had "broken through" on factory assembly lines, the trades remained almost exclusively male and a heavily guarded territory.[80] As the historian Nancy MacLean has written, "skill was a kind of property, like the tools craft-workers owned and brought to their jobs." Gaining and keeping a foothold there required a push from the women's movement and support from the government. Feminists established training programs such as Wider Opportunities for Women (WOW), All Craft, and Advocates for Women. In 1973, Congress passed the Comprehensive Employment and Training Act (CETA), which heavily funded those and other training and support programs for

78. Interview subject 62, Lansing, MI, 2013.

79. Marge Risenhouse, "Coming of Age in Berwick, PA," Subject Files, Lesbian Herstory Archives (microfilm reel 148, frame 15560, Thompson Gale).

80. Interview subject 60, Lansing MI, 2012.

aspiring tradeswomen all over the country.[81] And, in 1978, President Carter settled a lawsuit brought by WOW by setting hiring goals for women in the construction industry.[82]

The opportunity to enter the trades strongly appealed to lesbians, and many jumped at these new opportunities. One woman remembered going to the CETA office in rural Pennsylvania and noticing that it seemed as if "only gay women need apply"; almost every lesbian she knew in her county was there seeking to enter the trades.[83] Another lesbian wrote that "government funding for jobs through CETA kept many of us alive and well during the hard economic times of the 1970s."[84] A Boston woman remembered lots of lesbians in her CETA-funded program, including many lesbian prostitutes trying to get out of "the life."[85] But middle-class lesbians in professional jobs also longed to be in the trades, both because they felt "these were skills women should have," and because they initially believed union protection might make it easier to come out. "I was this fired-up lesbian feminist," a teacher in Lansing, Michigan, remembered, but there "was no way to come out" at her school. She would have been fired, she believed. "It wasn't winnable."[86]

So she spent four years training to become a journeyman pipefitter. Fear mixed with opportunity: "These were damn good jobs."[87] In the 1970s, women still earned just 59 percent of what men did, and a journeymen pipefitter made a better living than a schoolteacher.[88] But the harassment most women apprentices faced was intense. The pipefitter remembered that her male coworkers didn't tell her what she needed to know to complete a job; left condoms on her tool box; gave her bad job assignments; put her with incompetent people so she could not learn. Despite

81. MacLean, *Freedom Is Not Enough*, 265–76. Interestingly, CETA also funded gay employment counseling during these years, such as that supported by the Los Angeles Gay Community Services Center and by Job Power in San Francisco. Memo from Larry to Charlie and Lucia, October 9, 1979, folder 58, box 166, Records of the National Gay and Lesbian Task Force; interview subject 94, interview conducted via telephone, 2013.

82. The timing of that executive order, which coincided with a recession and the devastating loss of jobs in construction, was unfortunate. MacLean, *Freedom Is Not Enough*, 269–70, 275.

83. Marge Risenhouse, "Coming of Age in Berwick, PA," Subject Files, Lesbian Herstory Archives (microfilm reel 148, frame 15560, Thompson Gale).

84. Birdie MacLennan, "Travelling Lesbians or Sisters of the Road: The 1930s and the 1970s," "Lesbian History" folder, box 2, Homosexuality/LGBT Collection, Sophia Smith Library, Smith College, Northampton, MA.

85. Interview subject 90, Cape Cod, MA, 2011.

86. Interview subject 60, Lansing, MI, 2012.

87. Ibid.

88. M. V. Lee Badgett, *Money, Myths, and Change: The Economic Lives of Lesbians and Gay Men* (Chicago: University of Chicago Press, 2001), 111.

the fact that it had been a strong motivation for her entering the trades in the first place, she decided that she could not come out in her factory. The "union rep" was himself a "dyke-baiter," and it seemed too risky. She already "faced so much harassment as a woman." At some point, she realized she had lost her hope of making a difference for women, and she "was starting to hate the men" she worked with.[89]

Another woman from a middle-class background who worked as an apprentice mechanic in the fleet garage of a municipal water company in the East Bay was also drawn to the trades by the wage and compelled by the idea of breaking barriers. But, "for the first time in my life, I decided I would be in the closet." She asked a male friend to be her "pretend boyfriend," thinking, as the pipefitter had reasoned, it was enough to face "one challenge at a time." She was the first and only woman in the fleet garage; she was skinny, and the mechanical parts of the job did not come easily to her. The men she worked with tried to actively sabotage her; unplugging wires in her workstation, putting her into positions where they thought she would fail. She was given extra tests, like removing and replacing a transmission in record flat time, which none of the men she worked with had to perform. She "prevailed at every turn," but harassment stopped only when she achieved a position in her union. She pursued a union role simply to get away from the hostile environment in the garage for a couple of days each week, but eventually she found she was good at it.[90]

Most women, whether they were of working-class or middle-class origin, did not stay in the trades. Some left within a year or two. Others lasted longer, but the proportion of women employed in the industry never got near the target goals set by the federal government.[91] The psychic costs of these positions—as demonstrated, for example, by one lesbian who never showed any weakness in front of her coworkers but regularly slipped into the bathroom to cry—are perhaps easier to tally up than the rewards.[92] On the positive side of the ledger were the skills women acquired; sometimes, they also took pride in the resilience they had shown in the face of extremely difficult circumstances. Maybe the least quantifiable but most palpable was simply the cachet blue-collar jobs carried among lesbians

89. Interview subject 60, Lansing, MI, 2012. Other interviews I conducted seem to confirm that union support was hit or miss. One woman said, "the union didn't look at us as gays; they saw us as members of the union." Interview subject 59, Lansing, MI, 2012. Some agreed that they had stewards that were very supportive; others reported that their stewards were homophobic and hostile.

90. Interview subject 75, Santa Cruz, CA, 2013.

91. MacLean, *Freedom Is Not Enough*, 286.

92. Interview subject 95, interview conducted via telephone, 2013.

during these years. To the extent that middle-class lesbians eyed these jobs—or the women who held them—with fascination, this development aligned with the broader downward mobility of the era. Refusing to seek jobs that conferred high status in the dominant society was part and parcel of the broader, countercultural antipathy to professional aspiration, but lesbians in particular seemed to take that ethos to extremes.[93] Away from the trades, this outlook likely meant there were many lesbians who did not benefit from feminist gains in the workplace as much as they might have.[94] "Gay women" likely constituted "the poorest women in the population," Edmund White observed in the late 1970s.[95]

The lesbian fixation on downward mobility also had an edge. One woman remembered going into a lesbian bar in Boston and seeing what was supposed to be utterly cutting graffiti about her in the restroom. It identified her by name and charged that she "uses her job to advance her career!"[96] Instead of advancing careers, middle-class lesbians urged each other to "give away their privilege."[97] Sometimes that meant working alongside working-class women, whether in the trades, or carrying mail, or driving a bus, as one lesbian with two advanced degrees from Harvard did during these years.[98] It also meant sharing resources and intimate bonds, including sleeping with working-class women, which middle-class lesbians had been more likely to shun in the 1950s and 1960s. Cross-class intimacy "led to on-the-spot analysis of class oppression . . . based on the experience of being hit over the head with it," the lesbian feminist writer Charlotte Bunch asserted. "Understand," she proselytized, "that there is no faster way to learn how class functions in our world."[99] Gay men, of course, had long championed cross-class sexual liaisons and also

93. "Lesbian feminists generally shared the intellectual Left's romance with the working class," according to the historian Lillian Faderman. "Women who had the skills to make a living at non-traditional jobs—carpenters, house painters, welders, were far more politically correct than professionals, who were seen as having to compromise themselves in order to advance." Lillian Faderman, *Odd Girls and Twilight Lovers: A History of Lesbian Life in Twentieth-Century America* (New York: Columbia University Press, 1991), 236.

94. Interview subject 91, Cape Cod, MA, 2011.

95. White, *States of Desire*, 65. (This volume was published in 1980 but reflects White's travels across "gay America" in the later 1970s.)

96. Interview subject 91, Cape Cod, MA, 2011.

97. Interview subject 75, Santa Cruz, CA, 2013.

98. Interview subject 89, Cambridge, MA, 2013.

99. Charlotte Bunch, "Not for Lesbians Only," in *Passionate Politics: Feminist Theory in Action* (New York: St. Martin's, 1987), 179–80 (originally published in *Quest: A Feminist Quarterly* 2 [Fall 1975]: 50–56).

fetishized working-class bodies. But only lesbians made a political project out of it.

———◆———

Much more than for gay men, jobs themselves also became a political
project for lesbians during these years, largely because of the centrality of
economic structures to their own oppression. "In an economy structured
around male breadwinners, lesbians faced a dual disadvantage," according to the historian Robert Self. As women, they were confined to lower-
paying jobs, and yet "no male provider waited to enfold them in marriage
and a family economy." But that "outsider status" also enabled them to see
women's subjugation as a systematic whole, and powerful writing flowed
from the pens of women who applied the insights of socialist feminism to
their own experience as lesbians.[100] "Heterosexual privilege is the method
by which women are given a stake in their own oppression," Charlotte
Bunch, for example, wrote in 1975.[101] When women rejected that "privilege" they potentially undermined the entire economic system, as Bunch's
lesbian feminist analysis made clear. Lesbians refused to work for men
both on the job and in the home, and they rejected "the nuclear family as
the basic unit of production and consumption in capitalist society." This
was potentially destabilizing if lesbians refused to be the "passive/part
time woman worker that capitalism counts on to do boring work and be
part of a surplus labor pool." Because they did not derive their economic
support from men, and in contrast to the notion of downward mobility,
lesbians cared deeply about wages and job conditions, and this could present more problems to the system: "Capitalism cannot absorb large numbers of women," Bunch opined, "demanding stable employment, decent
salaries, and refusing to accept their traditional job exploitation."[102]

Bunch wrote as a member of the Furies Collective, one of the many
experiments with communal living formed on the left during these years.[103]

100. Robert O. Self, *All in the Family: The Realignment of American Democracy since
the 1960s* (New York: Hill and Wang, 2012), 176, 161.

101. Bunch, "Not for Lesbians Only," 177.

102. Charlotte Bunch, "Male Supremacy Quakes and Quivers," *Furies*, January 1972, 9.

103. Doug Rossinow, *The Politics of Authenticity: Liberalism, Christianity, and the
New Left in America* (New York: Columbia University Press, 1998), 280–81. On the Furies,
see especially Alice Echols, *Daring to Be Bad: Radical Feminism in America, 1967–1975*
(Minneapolis: University of Minnesota Press, 1989), 228–41; Anne M. Valk, *Radical
Sisters: Second Wave Feminism and Black Liberation in Washington, DC* (Urbana: Uni-
versity of Illinois Press, 2008), 135–57.

The Furies were lesbian separatists who established their collective in three row houses in the Capitol Hill neighborhood in Washington, DC.[104] Their experiment together, begun in the spring of 1971, lasted only a year, but in those months the Furies produced some of the most insightful thinking about lesbians, work, and revolution that came out of the women's liberation movement. Although they were influenced by the Black Panthers, their philosophy was "mostly insular," one founder recalled, "generated out of our [own] conversation."[105] Several of the women in the collective were from working-class backgrounds, but rather than "erase differences between the [members] through downward mobility," the Furies faced them and sought to turn them to everyone's advantage.[106] The group insisted that middle-class and better-educated women in the collective take jobs at the highest level of pay they were capable of earning. Because the Furies pooled their economic resources, this meant that working-class women would be able to spend fewer hours at work in order to survive and that all of them would have more time for their revolutionary project. But even while sharing resources, and partly because well-paid jobs for middle-class women were also scarce, the demands of economic survival enervated them. "We have found that forty hours a week of our energy goes to the man," two of the Furies wrote. "Combining the reality of working to survive, our political work, plus the need to deal with our present ideology on a larger level, we see one direction that is related to all three." In their newspaper, which was widely read and widely influential in the development of a broader lesbian feminist politics during these years, the Furies called for the creation of lesbian/feminist institutions.[107] By that, they meant businesses that would support everyone who worked in them at the same time that they contributed to the movement.

When the collective on Capitol Hill dissolved, this idea was what remained. Despite the painful demise of the larger collective, almost all the twelve Furies hived off in smaller groups to realize separate pieces of this vision. The writers Charlotte Bunch and Rita Mae Brown founded an important socialist feminist journal, *Quest*. The photographer Joan Biren

104. One Fury described their separatism as being as much from straight feminists as from men, and said that the move to Capitol Hill was intended to put some physical distance between themselves and the burgeoning DC feminist movement (centered in northwest Washington). Interview with Coletta Reid, Santa Fe, NM, 2019.

105. Interview with Ginny Berson, Oakland, CA, 2019.

106. Echols, *Daring to Be Bad*, 235.

107. Lee Schwing and Helaine Harris, "Building Feminist Institutions," *Furies*, May–June 1973, 2.

created a film and media production company. Coletta Reid founded a printing press and publishing house named for the Greek goddess Diana. Ginny Berson, Jennifer Woodul, Helaine Harris, and Lee Schwing (and several others from outside the collective) created a record company called Olivia Records. Helaine Harris and Lee Schwing subsequently created Women in Distribution (or WIND) to distribute books and music to women's booksellers and other retail outlets. Lesbians were moved "to create our own world," Bunch later reflected. "Frequently, and mistakenly, that task has been characterized as cultural. While the culture gives us strength, the impetus is economic."[108]

That economic impetus was most explicitly articulated by Olivia Records, which aimed both to use music to stir a broader lesbian and feminist awakening, and simultaneously, to create an alternative lesbian feminist economy. Olivia's founders, in fact, strove to create nonoppressive jobs for women, and in keeping with their revolutionary dreams, they wanted to do it on a large enough scale to impact women's options more broadly. "We envisioned hiring thousands of women all over the country in all aspects of the business," Berson recalled. There would be sound engineers, backup musicians, performers, concert producers, distributors. They dreamed of eventually having their own woman-run recording studio and pressing plant and controlling the entire recording, production, and distribution process.[109] Their profits would first go into expanding their own operations, then, to helping other lesbian feminists build up their own business enterprises.[110] Ultimately, in partnership with other lesbian feminists, they would create economic opportunities for many more women not to be married to men. "If they cast their lot with women, they would be taken care of," Berson explained. "We were not saying directly, 'come be with the lesbians.' We were saying indirectly, 'women will take care of women.'"[111]

After spending some time ironing out their politics and goals, the Olivia Records Collective began in Washington, DC, in January 1973. As one former Furies member explained, up to that point, women's marginalization in the labor market left them doubly handicapped to take on a venture of this sort: "Women don't have the physical experience and machinery skills of working-class men, nor do we have the organizational

108. Bunch, "Not for Lesbians Only," 177.

109. Interview with Ginny Berson, Oakland, CA, 2019; "The Muses of Olivia: Our Own Economy, Our Own Song," *Off Our Backs* 4 (August–September 1974): 2–3.

110. "The History and Goals of Olivia Records," folder 2, box 14, Records of Diana Press, Special Collections, University of California–Los Angeles.

111. Interview with Ginny Berson, Oakland, CA, 2019; "Muses Of Olivia," 3.

and administrative experience of middle-class managers."[112] What the collective had instead was the fuel that feminists were burning all across the country at this moment: the "do-it-yourself" mentality applied to the idea that the world could and must be remade. To gather information, Berson and her colleagues began by writing letters to record companies posing as high school students writing papers on how records were made. They sent fundraising letters to women in the industry: Joni Mitchell, Helen Reddy, Yoko Ono. More effectively, they ran letters in the feminist and gay press: "Olivia Records needs engineers, producers, promotionists, financial managers, distributors, musicians, lawyers, and accountants. If you are a musician, send us a tape of your music. Or just send us a letter and tell us where your interest might lie."[113]

At this point, Olivia had one artist who was part of the collective, a singer-songwriter named Meg Christian. Founder Ginny Berson set up a tour for Christian for the summer of 1973, driving across the country, staying in cheap campgrounds, and "looking for anyone who knew anything." Once they got to California, they called home. They were told that a letter had arrived from a woman named Joan Lowe who was a recording engineer with her own studio in Vida, Oregon. She owned a children's record company, and she said she would be happy to talk with Olivia members about making records. So Berson and Christian drove up to Oregon. "She knew everything, and she was willing to tell us everything," Berson recalled. "She said things like 'you have to have a label,' [meaning] a physical label stuck on your piece of vinyl. Well, of course, you do! But who thought about that? And you have to have a catalog number. And that meant we were going to have a catalog." They made up the catalog number for that first album, which was "LF 901." "LF" stood for lesbian feminist; they used "901" because there were ten of them in the collective.[114]

Lowe also suggested that Olivia make a 45 record, which would be less expensive than a whole LP and could be used for promotional purposes. So, Joan Lowe flew to Washington, and Olivia recorded a 45 with Meg Christian on one side and an artist named Chris Williamson on the other. They advertised the record in the feminist press for $1.50 plus thirty-five cents for postage. Almost everyone who ordered a record also sent in an additional donation. The proceeds from the sales of the 45 helped finance

112. Coletta Reid, "Taking Care of Business," *Quest* 1 (Fall 1974): 17.

113. "The Letter Box," *Gay Liberator*, April 1, 1974, 14; interview with Ginny Berson, Oakland, CA, 2019.

114. Interview with Ginny Berson, Oakland, CA, 2019.

the collective's move to Los Angeles, where they would be closer to the recording industry.[115]

All the early decisions tended to be heavy ones, including the price of records. The collective understood "how little money women have," but if Olivia was going to create a strong economic community then "we can't squeeze our own pockets too hard."[116] At some point out on the road, they also met a woman who worked for a famous Berkeley record store called Leopold's who knew how record distribution worked. She helped them set up their own system. Olivia's idea was to avoid the industry system and find women who would sell records at house parties and by word of mouth, whether or not they could get them into stores. Having a wide network of distributors positioned in cities and towns was also envisioned as spreading a revolutionary cadre all over the country.[117]

Olivia's high point came at the end of 1975 with the release of Chris Williamson's album *Changer and the Changed* (LF 904) and the 1976 concert series with Williamson and three other stars of the "women's music" genre.[118] Berson remembered following the tour with a car full of records to sell. She would return to LA, "fill up the car again [with records], and drive to the next concert." These concerts were selling out two-thousand-seat venues, and the company helped to sustain a broader ecosystem.[119] Some twenty-five companies existed to handle concert production for the women's music scene. The collective itself was stable during this period, and Olivia had approximately seventy distributors nationally.[120]

Olivia had also been able to realize some of their political ideals in creating a nonhierarchical, working collective—their own self-made,

---

115. Ibid.

116. Jennifer Woodul, "What's This about Feminist Business," folder 12, box 14, Records of Diana Press.

117. Interview with Ginny Berson, Oakland, CA, 2019.

118. The "Women on Wheels" concert featured performers Margie Adam, Meg Christian, Chris Williamson, and Holly Near.

119. Interview with Ginny Berson, Oakland CA, 2019.

120. "Large numbers of women work on record production as musicians, arrangers, recording and mixing engineers, production assistants, album designers," one observer of the women's music industry recounted in 1978, and as "accountants, lawyers, business managers, fund-raisers, publicists, advertising people, and printers." Lynne D. Shapiro, "The Growing Business behind Women's Music," in *Lavender Culture*, ed. Karla Jay and Allen Young (New York: New York University Press, 1994), 196–97 (originally published 1978). "Women's music" and "women's culture" in these years generally referred to lesbian music and lesbian culture, but Olivia in particular was careful not to call its music "lesbian music" because it didn't want to scare women away. Interview with Ginny Berson, Oakland, CA, 2019. See also Jay, "No Man's Land," in Jay and Young, *Lavender Culture*, 52.

quasi-utopian version of a queer work world. The core members were living and working together in a way that merged work and family functions: several couples together, with the living room of their house converted to an office, set up with desks, instead of couches.[121] They created a writing space for Meg Christian on the back porch, and for a time, Chris Williamson lived in the "little playhouse" behind their main house. As much as possible, they tried to share decision making, information, and grunt work, and they also tried to pay staff members according to need.[122] Eventually there were women in the collective who were caring for elderly parents, or who had children to support. An older woman in the collective needed to save for retirement. Others needed less, perhaps only "rent . . . groceries, to put gas in the cars that we all shared, and [to pay for] karate class and a few books." The collective tried to balance those needs according to its founding principles. They also tried to avoid a "star system," despite the fact that it was foundational to the music industry. The collective did not just want to be the record company for Chris Williamson and Meg Christian, although at the time it would have been a good business decision. They wanted to move beyond the white acoustic soloist more generally; Olivia began to develop relationships with African American artists and to bring women of color into the collective.[123]

Those new artists did not sell as well, and Olivia's attempt to move beyond the model of the acoustic soloist drew the ire of current and potential customers. Playing with a band, especially with drums, was attacked as "cock rock." In addition, as the music they were recording became more complicated and had multiple tracks, Olivia needed to replace its original engineer, Joan Lowe. There were very few women recording engineers in the country, and Berson and others were thrilled to hire a woman who had worked with Jimi Hendrix named Sandy Stone. When it was later discovered that Stone was a trans woman, much of the lesbian feminist community that supported Olivia was enraged. Olivia refused to fire Stone, which hurt their business's standing with some of its main consumers.[124]

121. Interview with Ginny Berson, Oakland, CA, 2019.

122. Ibid.; Woodul, "What's This about Feminist Business?," 3, folder 12, box 14, Records of Diana Press; "Muses of Olivia," 2–3.

123. Interview with Ginny Berson, Oakland CA, 2019.

124. Ibid. See also "Sandy Stone on Living among Lesbian Separatists as a Trans Woman in the 1970s," interview with Zachary Drucker, *Vice*, December 19, 2018, https://www.vice.com/en/article/zmd5k5/sandy-stone-biography-transgender-history. Stone went on to earn a PhD from the History of Consciousness program at UC–Santa Cruz and is considered a founder of academic trans studies. Especially well known is her essay "The Empire Strikes Back: A Post-transsexual Manifesto," in *Body Guards: The Cultural Politics of Sexual Ambiguity* (New York: Routledge, 1991), 280–304.

Perhaps more than anything, though, it was their very success that made them especially suspicious to the feminists who were their lifeblood. "Women were fucked up about money," Berson said, and it made being a feminist business nearly impossible. While they were accused of making money "off of the movement," the novelty of the product they were selling began to wear off, and sales receipts for records and concert tickets diminished. Nearly every day the collective faced a choice about whether to do something because it was good politics or good business: they fought with feminist bookstores about pricing concert tickets; they avoided stars and produced records that they thought were important but that didn't have a big enough audience; they consolidated distributors' territories so fewer distributors could actually make a living, but they had to jettison the idea of a revolutionary cadre positioned in small towns across the country. Because they had never had enough capital to create their own pressing plant, they were never able to withdraw entirely from the "male economy."[125] "We realize we're not in control of the whole thing yet," one founder wrote, "but we take it one day at a time, with a vision of the whole."[126] By the end of the decade, the whole still seemed far off in the distance. The collective was frustrated and restless, and most drifted away.[127]

Diana Press, another outgrowth from the Furies, shared much of Olivia's economic philosophy but placed a much greater emphasis on owning the equipment. Whereas Olivia hoped to eventually build their own recording studio and pressing plant, Diana *began* with a print shop. In part, this reflected the owners' working-class backgrounds: "We felt it was important for working-class women to own the means of production and to know how to operate and fix machinery."[128] But it was also the ironic

125. Interview with Ginny Berson, Oakland, CA, 2019.

126. Woodul, "What's This about Feminist Business?," 5, folder 12, box 14, Records of Diana Press.

127. "The History and Goals of Olivia Records," Records of Diana Press. One of the founders hung on through the very hard years of the 1980s. In 1990, she turned Olivia Records into a lesbian cruise line. The company's annual revenue is now between twenty and thirty million dollars each year. Diane Anderson-Minshall, "Olivia Cruises: Truly Social Networking," *Out Traveler*, March 12, 2014, https://www.outtraveler.com/cruises/2014/03/12/olivia-cruises-truly-social-networking.

128. Kathy Tomyris and Coletta Reid, "Diana Press: An Overview, 1972–1979," folder 13, box 13, Records of Diana Press. Joshua Clark Davis treats the history of Diana Press in the context of feminist business in chapter 4 of *From Head Shops to Whole Foods* (New York: Columbia University Press, 2017).

result of cofounder Casey Czarnik having been arrested in a protest for stepping on (and breaking) a police officer's foot. Part of Czarnik's probation was to attend vocational training, and so she had several months of printing school under her belt when she met Coletta Reid, who was just leaving the Furies and looking for a way to apply the insights of the collective out in the world.[129] Starting a print shop was the obvious next step: the movement needed printing, and the founders were working-class women who needed jobs. "We came to the need for a women's institution out of economic necessity—that is, out of not being able to get either rewarding or high-paying jobs due to our skills and class backgrounds," they wrote. "We had no capital resources and were faced with the specter of going from dead-end job to dead-end job."[130]

Czarnik had been active in the antiwar movement in Baltimore, and she knew a group that ran a small press out of the basement of a three-story town house near Charles Street. She got involved with a group of women who were interested in turning that operation into a women's press. Reid soon joined the endeavor, but very shortly after that most of the other women dropped away, leaving just Reid and Czarnik. The basement had a small front office in the front and a long, narrow room in the back. The two women "spent a few weeks cleaning the linoleum floor of ink and building layout/paste up facilities from hollow doors we hung from the walls," Reid remembered. "We also built a table for typesetting, cabinets for negative and plate storage, and a counter for serving customers."[131] In addition, Reid secured a small amount of money from the Furies Collective when it disbanded, and with that she and Czarnik were able to purchase a twenty-five-year-old Multilith 1250 and an instant plate maker. As would be true of their later purchases as well, this was "used equipment that most men would not have taken the time or the trouble to put into working condition."[132]

Reid and Czarnik first set up an instant print business, doing short-run jobs from camera-ready copy and competing with chains such as Copy Cat and Minute Man. "We based our prices on underbidding these shops," and the two women did not worry about underpricing their own labor. Indeed, they understood from the beginning that the only capital they had was

129. Interview with Coletta Reid, Santa Fe, NM, 2019.
130. Handwritten notes, "History of Diana Press," folder 13, box 13, Diana Press Records.
131. Personal electronic communication from Coletta Reid, May 2019.
132. Kathy Tomyris and Coletta Reid, "Diana Press: An Overview, 1972–1979," folder 13, box 13, Records of Diana Press.

their labor, and they had to severely exploit themselves for the business to grow. In the beginning, they worked twelve hours a day, seven days a week and paid themselves a meager salary of $100 a month. Within six months, they had earned enough to buy a used paper cutter, and a StripPrinter for display type.[133] As they grew, they would bid for jobs and then buy the necessary equipment to complete them. They never knew how to operate a machine before they got it, and they never had anyone teach them. They were able to secure credit by incorporating, and "in five years we bought four presses we had never seen before, a paperback book binding machine, a collator, and a camera."[134]

Reid had the idea that a successful print shop could support a publishing arm for work by women that mainstream presses wouldn't touch. [135] At the end of 1972, the writer and former Furies member Rita Mae Brown came to Diana Press with just such a volume of poetry, *Songs to a Handsome Woman*. Brown offered to supply the paper if the press would supply the labor to produce the book.[136] From the outset, Diana determined to take advantage of being too small to reach the economies of scale of large presses. Those large presses used black ink and printed in standard sizes. Beginning with Brown's volume of poetry, "we decided to make our books as beautiful as possible, using specialty papers and ink, graphics and photographs, and sophisticated design." The publishing venture was never expected to do more "than pay for its own production," and the work was done on evenings and weekends. On this model, in 1973 Diana Press brought out three books and a calendar.[137] "We were both blue-collar workers manufacturing books and white-collar management running a business," Reid recalled.[138]

133. "Establish Your Own Printshop," folder 10, box 13, Records of Diana Press; personal electronic communication from Coletta Reid, May 2019.

134. "Establish Your Own Printshop," folder 10, box 13, Records of Diana Press; personal electronic communication from Coletta Reid, May 2019. Judy Grahn of the Women's Press Collective also told of the difficulty of learning to use machinery without any instruction. One male printer offered to get their Chief 22 press running in exchange for sleeping with one of the women in the press collective, Grahn recalled. "We ran him out, and began to take the machine apart to see how it worked." Judy Grahn, *A Simple Revolution: The Making of an Activist Poet* (San Francisco: Aunt Lute Books, 2012), 142.

135. Coletta Reid, interview with author, Santa Fe, NM, 2019; personal electronic communication from Coletta Reid, May 2019.

136. Kathy Tomyris and Coletta Reid, "Diana Press: An Overview, 1972–1979," folder 13, box 13, Records of Diana Press. Within a year, sales of the book covered production costs, and Brown was repaid for the paper.

137. Ibid.

138. Personal electronic communication from Coletta Reid, May 2019.

Although the work was intensive, the early years at Diana Press were probably its high point. Beginning with a fire in 1975, the later years were beset with difficulties. In 1976, Diana became very involved with the Feminist Economic Network (FEN) in Detroit, and its ill-fated purchase of a women's building. When that venture was harshly attacked by some feminists who thought FEN was a capitalist takeover of the movement that aimed to "share in the riches" rather than overthrow "the system," Diana's finances and reputation were badly wounded.[139] It lost its largest commercial customer, the feminist quarterly *Quest*. In the aftermath, four women from FEN arrived in Baltimore, moved in with Reid and Czarnik, and worked for free for six months to get Diana back on its feet. The experience of working together was transformative enough that Reid and Czarnik subsequently decided to move Diana to Oakland, where real estate was far cheaper than in Baltimore, to merge their operation with the Women's Press Collective, which was run by the poet Judy Grahn and her lover, Wendy Cadden.[140]

In the spring of 1977, the women loaded Diana Press's equipment into a huge semitrailer truck and drove across the country. The two merged presses kept the name Diana and set up shop in a former vitamin factory on Market Street in Oakland. They collective paid $650 a month for eleven thousand square feet of space. In addition to a front desk, the facility housed six presses, a full bindery, a darkroom, and editorial offices. Olivia Records, which had relocated to Oakland from Los Angeles, rented one-third of the warehouse for its operations.[141] Despite this seemingly auspicious start, the initial months in California were challenging ones. The controversy over FEN had followed them to the Bay Area, and relations with the local feminist community were strained from the start. It took much longer to get the press up and running than they had anticipated.[142] Money was extremely tight.[143]

139. Kathy Tomyris and Coletta Reid, "Diana Press: An Overview, 1972–1979," folder 13, box 13, Records of Diana Press; Echols, *Daring to Be Bad*, 276; Grahn, *Simple Revolution*, 238–39; personal electronic communication from Coletta Reid, May 2019. FEN's goal was to create a "holding company of for-profit feminist institutions that would sell stock to raise money," Reid explained. For more on FEN, see Finn Enke, *Finding the Movement: Sexuality, Contested Space, and Feminist Activism* (Durham, NC: Duke University Press, 2007), 239–51; Davis, *From Head Shops to Whole Foods*, 158–62.

140. Personal electronic communication from Coletta Reid, May 2019; Grahn, *Simple Revolution*, 240–42.

141. Grahn, *Simple Revolution*, 241–42; handwritten notes, "History of Diana Press," folder 13, box 13, Diana Press Records.

142. Kathy Tomyris and Coletta Reid, "Diana Press: An Overview, 1972–1979," folder 13, box 13, Records of Diana Press.

143. Staff notes, folder 6, box 15, Records of Diana Press.

There was also the merger of two work cultures and learning to work collectively.[144] The group divided the work into departments, and with the exception of printing and folding, which were highly skilled, they attempted to share knowledge and tasks. Most people knew at least four jobs. Everyone participated in editorial decisions.[145] The countercultural origins of Diana were clear in several other distinctive features of the work environment: The new printer they had hired was Pisces with Virgo rising, and all employees were encouraged to have their astrological charts read. "This will help us know how to work together better," Reid suggested.[146] All workers were also invited to receive self-defense instruction from Casey Czarnik, whom the collective decided to support for training for her black belt, and whose karate lessons went on the press's schedule.[147] The press's dog, Jenny, was not to be allowed to make friends with service men who came into the facility.[148] Workers were reminded that an anticlassist organization had no cleaning crew to deal with messes, so everyone was responsible for keeping their workstations neat.[149] Supervision was aimed at helping women to do well, which was "vital to our egos." It was often faster and easier for the more experienced person to just do the job herself rather than training and guiding another, but if "we keep our skill to ourselves we may as well forget growth as a group." The collective reminded everyone, "How are we to run a culture, if we can't run . . . a business?"[150]

It had taken longer than they planned, but by the fall of 1977, Diana Press was beginning to thrive again as sales of its backlist increased. The collective was able to pay its twelve members good salaries, although they were less than union wages, and less than Olivia was able to pay members of its collective. They produced a more commercial-looking fall catalog and planned for an ambitious production push.[151] They decided to do all three books Diana had planned in Baltimore, as well as several that were already in the works with the Women's Press Collective, and one they chose together: a total of eleven books. Diana had never purchased pallets

144. Kathy Tomyris and Coletta Reid, "Diana Press: An Overview, 1972–1979," folder 13, box 13, Records of Diana Press.

145. Handwritten notes, "History of Diana Press," folder 13, box 13, Diana Press Records.

146. Staff notes, folder 9, box 15, Records of Diana Press.

147. Staff notes, folder 7, box 15, and folder 2, box 17, Records of Diana Press.

148. Staff notes, folder 2, box 17, Records of Diana Press.

149. Staff notes, folder 9, box 15, Records of Diana Press.

150. "Notes on Supervision," folder 21, box 14, Records of Diana Press.

151. Personal electronic communication from Coletta Reid, May 2019; interview with Coletta Reid, Santa Fe, NM, 2019.

of paper on credit before but decided they were in good enough financial shape to do so. "For the first time, production of the books we were
publishing became our priority," rather than the print shop.[152] They also
began to plan for the purchase of a web press used in high-volume printing and to imagine a future of putting out inexpensive mass-market edi-
tions of feminist literature.[153]

Disaster struck on October 25, 1977, when Diana workers entered the
press to find it had been vandalized. "Chemicals and abrasive powders were
poured into the delicate rubber rollers and other moveable parts of our
presses," Judy Grahn remembered. Ink was poured over the desks and over
pallets of finished books. Film layout pages representing books in progress
were also drenched in ink. The vandals had been very strategic because the
"way the damage was done, with nothing actually being broken, the insurance company paid only about ten percent of the actual loss."[154] Coletta
Reid described being devastated and pushed nearly to the breaking point
by the attack. It sapped collective members' physical and emotional energy
and introduced intolerable levels of stress and strain into previously strong
relationships. The cleanup took months. Even when they thought they had
a machine in working order again, they would discover that the ink and the
chemicals had gummed up some other part that had to be dealt with.[155]
Some collective members, including founder and printer Casey Czarnik,
left the press in the aftermath of the catastrophe. Donations from women
all over the country kept the press on life support, but the following year
the collective made the fateful decision to close the publishing arm of the
business and focus on reestablishing the print shop. They chose printing
over publishing because "seven years of equipment bought off of working-
class women's labor should not be let go of easily."[156]

The print shop limped along for a while longer before Diana Press
folded altogether. Even without the vandalism, the late 1970s would have
been a challenging time. As with Olivia, the collective faced criticism from

152. Kathy Tomyris and Coletta Reid, "Diana Press: An Overview, 1972–1979"; interview with Coletta Reid, Santa Fe, NM, 2019.

153. Grahn, *Simple Revolution*, 242.

154. Ibid., 247. The vandals were never caught. One theory was that the FBI had vandalized the press, but Reid believes it was a lesbian separatist group from the Pacific Northwest who had a vendetta against the press. Grahn, *Simple Revolution*, 148–49; personal
electronic communication from Coletta Reid, May 2019.

155. Personal electronic communication from Coletta Reid, May 2019; interview with
Coletta Reid, Santa Fe, NM, 2019.

156. Kathy Tomyris and Coletta Reid, "Diana Press: An Overview, 1972–1979," folder 13,
box 13, Records of Diana Press.

some members of the lesbian community for the apparent success of the business. "We had dreams and visions that women should not have had," Reid remarked; after the vandalism, she recalled one woman commented that Diana "had gotten too big for its britches."[157] Others criticized Diana for putting out high-quality, beautiful books, which they interpreted as a sign that "Diana Press has class privilege."[158] That sort of skepticism whittled away support and hurt sales with the consumers Diana had always imagined its work speaking to most directly. Ironically, as sales lagged, one staff member suggested that straight men seemed to be buying more Diana books—they proved their "liberalness by 'supporting' women's books."[159] The mainstream publishing houses were also paying more attention to the burgeoning market for feminist and even lesbian literature; Bantam's purchase of the paperback rights to Rita Mae Brown's novel *Rubyfruit Jungle* signaled the broader trend. It was a positive development for individual authors, but a bitter pill for Diana's founders. "When New York moved into the market created by the women's presses, we found ourselves in direct competition with publishers with greater visibility and distribution."[160]

Iconic projects like Olivia and Diana changed the landscape of lesbian labor in the 1970s. While they were often criticized rather than lauded for their successes, they inspired offshoots in every direction.[161] They proselytized to encourage this, as for example, in a widely circulated position paper on feminist businesses by Olivia founder Jennifer Woodul. She acknowledged that it was ironic for lesbian feminists to use "capitalist strategies as a road to liberation" but added, "it's also terribly creative."[162] From Diana, Coletta Reid also got the word out in an influential essay, "Taking Care of Business," which suggested that feminist businesses should strive to avoid offering services that were closely associated with the female role, but instead try to develop consciousness-raising products. She was even more pointed in her

157. Interview with Coletta Reid, Santa Fe, NM, 2019.

158. Staff notes, folder 7, box 15, Records of Diana Press.

159. Administrative notes, folder 18, box 14, Records of Diana Press.

160. Interview with Coletta Reid, Santa Fe, NM, 2019; Kathy Tomyris and Coletta Reid, "Diana Press: An Overview, 1972–1979," folder 13, box 13, Records of Diana Press.

161. *The New Women's Survival Catalog* and *The New Women's Survival Sourcebook*, created by Susan Rennie and Kristen Grimstad, were another spur during these years. See Davis, *From Head Shops to Whole Foods*, 151–52.

162. Woodul, "What's This about Feminist Business?," folder 12, box 14, Records of Diana Press.

advice in her pamphlet "Establish Your Own Printshop." She counseled that women printers should not be afraid of getting credit, and she insisted that incorporation was key. Above all, "don't let your self-confidence be tied to your print shop's financial condition," she cautioned. "If you do, you're lost. You will always be on the edge financially, and that is because men control money and resources and have no interest in your survival." Women's businesses, Reid concluded, were a profound act of courage.[163]

Many were brave enough to try, and the ripples spread outward. The greatest concentration of businesses was in the music and book industries, where Olivia and Diana had pioneered. In addition to the network of distributors and concert producers, other record companies emerged, such as Holly Near's Redwood Records and Wise Women Enterprises.[164] Feminist presses mushroomed even more quickly. Some did printing jobs for the women's movement, some were only publishing houses, and a few combined these functions in the same way Diana had. Among the major players besides Diana Press were Daughters, the Iowa City Women's Press, the Women's Press Collective, Shameless Hussy Press, and the Feminist Press. With the exception of the latter, all were founded by lesbians.[165] In San Francisco, the Women's Press Project was a union shop and printing school founded in 1977 to train women printers. The prospect of formal training in a hospitable environment induced even more to try their hand at learning the trade. One Nevada City woman acquired two used multilith presses that sat on the bed of her Chevy truck as she drafted a letter to the Women's Press Project: "I wouldn't even have considered adopting these presses without the knowledge that your organization existed to provide very tangible help," she wrote, describing her dream of starting her own small press.[166]

Women's music festivals and conferences like Women in Print functioned as alternative business conventions, with workshops on lesbian business, which were also conducive to informal networking. One woman attended a session for bookstore owners, for example, and asked if it was possible to start a bookstore with just a few thousand dollars. She was stunned the next day when a woman swam up to her in the pool—*naked*—and said, "Yes, you can."[167] Actually, some women were doing it with even

163. "Establish Your Own Printshop," folder 10, box 13, Records of Diana Press.

164. Shapiro, "Growing Business behind Women's Music," 196.

165. Personal electronic communication from Coletta Reid, May 2019.

166. LD to Women's Press Project, September 12, 1983, "Correspondence 1977–1984" folder, box 1, Women's Press Project, GLBT Historical Society of Northern California.

167. Kristen Hogan, *The Feminist Bookstore Movement: Lesbian Anti-racism and Feminist Accountability* (Durham, NC: Duke University Press, 2016), 31.

less money. Bloodroot, a feminist bookstore and restaurant, began with a few hundred dollars and the owner selling books out of the trunk of her car.[168] Low capital requirements and the organic connection to feminist presses and record companies made bookstores one of the most prominent ventures. There were almost one hundred women's bookstores across the country by 1978, many of them offering services analogous to lesbian bars in the 1950s.[169] When lesbians arrived in a new town, for example, they could head to the bookstore not only to buy books and music, but also to find out about community events, medical care, and jobs.[170] As lesbian bars had in the 1950s and 1960s, women's bookstores sometimes tried to hire lesbians who found themselves in difficult circumstances.[171]

These were not, as they might appear at first glance, casual jobs for those who were dropping out of regular employment. As with Diana Press, what these undertakings lacked in capitalization they made up for by the labor of the collective. Working in the collective could be rewarding, but it was also demanding, as for example, in the way one bookstore owner described the work culture in a document she wrote for potential "Womanbooks Workers." There was, first, the general inefficiency and endless process of collective work itself, dependent as it was on consensus and the "honesty and directness of communication among the collective members, and often [requiring] meetings and efforts beyond the normal store hours." While much of the actual labor of the bookstore entailed detailed clerical work, workers should also have a "good deal of sophistication about feminist theory" and "a feeling for books in general," which helped offset the "inevitable process of boredom" that resulted from repetitive tasks. Despite the fact that the work was often boring, the commitment and intensity of focus had to be total. "Womanbooks is a demanding mistress," the owner warned, "and we alert you to the possible problem of joining us at a point in your life where you have other primary goals that you wish to pursue at the same time [that] cannot be combined with work

168. Kristen Hogan interview with Eleanor Batchelder, "Interview" folder, box 1, Papers of Eleanor Olds Batchelder, Lesbian Herstory Archives.

169. Hogan, *Feminist Bookstore Movement*, 37. Women's bookstores were enough associated with lesbians that some straight women (as well as closeted lesbians) were afraid to be seen there. For this reason, Olivia Records felt it was important to get its records into mainstream record stores—even if it meant distributors "put[ting] up with some shit" from men in those stores. "Olivia Records Distribution Information," folder 22, box 14, Records of Diana Press.

170. Batchelder narrative, "Heresies 7 Issue Collective 1978–1980" folder, box 1, Papers of Eleanor Olds Batchelder; Hogan, *Feminist Bookstore Movement*, 2–3.

171. Hogan, *Feminist Bookstore Movement*, 2–3.

here." For all this, workers could expect "personal growth" and between $5.50 and $6.50 an hour for full-time work, which should be "enough to live on if one is frugal and has a cooperative living situation of some sort."[172] But it was more work and less money than most women could receive elsewhere, and for this reason the owner expected that women would work at the bookstore for two or three years before they moved on to a different kind of job.[173]

What these unique work environments had to offer women who accepted what otherwise didn't seem like very favorable conditions was the euphoria that came with meaningful work and an integrated life. The women who founded Bloodroot put in twelve-to-sixteen-hour days, and yet, "what precious little time off we have we want to spend" at the restaurant. "There is no other world we feel nourished in, or even at ease in."[174] Sometimes work and personal life turned out to be *too* closely integrated. Many lesbian businesses were started by lovers who saw a joint business venture as an opportunity to further intertwine their whole lives. In the initial stages of building the business, these relationships made it easier to pour all their energy into the job. But the situation could be complicated for other coworkers. "The heartbeat of women working together can be violently disrupted by the deadlocking pattern of these relationships," one woman lamented. And the intensity of the enterprise often damaged the primary relationship, and its fraying could, in turn, endanger the business. "As much as we wanted the good parts to intermingle, so too did the bad." One bookstore employee reflected on "being on the verge of sleep or sex," and her lover (and coworker) "popping up with, 'I forgot to order [that] book!'"[175]

The basic formula for these businesses—to compensate for limited access to capital by working extremely hard and by living frugally and collectively—enabled them to spread quickly among women even without many financial assets. In addition to bookstores, there were women's coffee

172. "Womanbooks Workers," "Womanbooks: Notes, 1976–1980" folder, box 1, Papers of Eleanor Olds Batchelder. Judy Grahn remembered that by living in a collective and buying used clothes, she lived on less than $2,000 a year from 1970 to 1976. (This is about $9,000 in 2020 dollars.) Grahn, *Simple Revolution*, 169.

173. "Womanbooks Workers," "Womanbooks: Notes, 1976–1980" folder, box 1, Papers of Eleanor Olds Batchelder.

174. Betsey Beavan, Selma Miriam, Pat Shea, Sam Stockwell, "Bloodroot: Four Views of One Women's Business," *Heresies*, August 1978, 64–69.

175. Questionnaire, "*Heresies* 7, Issue Collective, 1978–1980" folder, box 1, Papers of Eleanor Olds Batchelder.

shops and restaurants across the country.[176] Even restaurants in smaller cities, such as the Bungalow in Lexington, Kentucky, were "strongly supported."[177] The vast majority of these "women's" establishments were lesbian run; they referred to themselves as "women owned," so as not to scare off patrons.[178] Such was the case with Mother Courage, the famous feminist restaurant in New York City, begun by lovers Jill Ward and Dolores Alexander, a former management consultant and a former *Newsday* reporter who were in part fleeing sexism and sexual harassment in their prior work environments.[179] There were also health clinics, food co-ops, auto repair shops, and all manner of retail as listed in the business directory of the *Lesbian Connection* magazine, and there were efforts to network and connect among those who were interested in "building a lesbian workforce."[180] The density of that world is evident in one lesbian's survey of San Diego. While she noted still many gaps, it had a coffee shop (Las Hermanas), several health clinics, a bookstore, a printing press, a lesbian dog-grooming business, the Feminist Federal Credit Union, a Women's Center, and, of course, a wide assortment of women's bars.[181]

The economist Lee Badgett has contrasted the economic institutions developed by lesbians to those established by gay men during the liberationist period. Businesses owned by and catering to gay men were also expanding during these years, but they were more narrowly focused on the commodification of sex, as bathhouses and bars multiplied in the "gay ghettos" of large cities. Badgett has noted that gay men involved with these

176. On the coffee shop as a lesbian feminist institution, see Enke, *Finding the Movement*, chapter 6; Alex D. Ketchum, *Ingredients for Revolution: American Feminist Restaurants, Cafes, and Coffee Houses, 1972–2022* (Montreal: Concordia University Press, forthcoming).

177. "Bits and Pieces," *Lesbian Connection*, May 1978, 17.

178. On the blurriness between lesbian businesses and women's business, see *Lavender Woman*, July 1974, 1. Alex Ketchum's directory lists as many as 196 feminist restaurants and coffee shops operating in the 1970s. She asserts that most were lesbian owned and operated. Personal electronic communication with Ketchum, July 2019. Ketchum's directory can be found at the Feminist Restaurant Project website, http://www.thefeministrestaurantproject.com/p/new-directory.html. See also Alex Ketchum, "'All Are Welcome Here?': Navigating Race, Class, Gender, Sexual Orientation, Age, and Disability in American Feminist Coffeehouses in the 1970s and 1980s," *Gender, Work, and Organization* 28 (March 2021): 594–609.

179. "Work," box 8, Dolores Alexander Papers, unprocessed, Sophia Smith Library, Smith College

180. "Lesbian Workers United," folder 77, box 167, Records of the National Gay and Lesbian Task Force.

181. Nancy Groschwitz, "Practical Economics for a Women's Community," in Jay and Young, *Lavender Culture*, 477–78.

establishments emphasized consumerism, but for lesbians, consumerism "was only half the point." The product itself—a book, a record—did matter, as it carried a politics with it. But lesbians, flipping the usual gender script, were just as focused on production; collective nonhierarchical work processes would create unoppressive jobs that freed women from dependence on men.[182] And where men's economic institutions were clustered together in urban neighborhoods, women's were scattered in small towns and rural communities as well as midsize and large cities. The centrifugal pattern of the alternative lesbian economy, as well as the small scale of the individual operations, makes it all too easy to miss its significance. It takes some altitude even to get high enough to see the imprint lesbians left on the landscape during these years.[183] Yet "by mid-decade," the historian Robert Self has observed, "lesbians had created a world of their own," as well as a truly generational way of working.[184] Yet it couldn't last. Women who had been twenty-five at the onset of gay liberation were approaching thirty-five as the 1970s drew to a close. After a decade of precariousness, they wanted—they needed—to be better paid.[185] They were also physically exhausted. As Jill Ward wrote in the note she left for patrons on the door of her Mother Courage restaurant before closing it for good, "Sorry, folks, I just can't do it anymore."[186]

———◆———

Beginning with the Furies on Capitol Hill, lesbian feminists during the 1970s engaged in the most sustained and creative rethinking of women's quest for meaningful work outside of the confines of marital heterosexuality since the settlement house movement of the early twentieth century.[187] Yet they weren't the only ones who were rethinking. Most people were neither gay liberationists nor lesbian separatists, yet they too experienced a bewildering decade of upheaval. For employers, the older norms around

182. Badgett, *Money, Myths, and Change*, 109–11.

183. Although her emphasis is on social rather than economic networks per se, Sandy Stone's metaphor of the "lesbian rhizome" is apt here. See "Sandy Stone on Living among Lesbian Separatists."

184. Self, *All in the Family*, 226.

185. Jeanne Cordova, "Lesbian Owned Businesses: Who's Surviving and How?," *Lesbian Tide*, September–October 1979, 6.

186. Arnaldo Testi, "My Failed Encounter with the First Feminist Restaurant in America," *Medium*, January 9, 2016, https://medium.com/@ArnaldoTesti/my-failed-encounter-with-the-first-feminist-restaurant-in-america-with-a-short-history-of-mother-19f97482d643.

187. Mary Ryan, *Mysteries of Sex: Tracing Women and Men through American History* (Chapel Hill: University of North Carolina Press, 2006), 167–74.

disclosure that had made employee behavior predictable were evaporating just as the "tectonic plates" that undergirded the entire economy were shifting.[188] And because a cultural revolution had happened without an accompanying legal revolution, work was increasingly uncertain as well for many gay, lesbian, and trans people for whom liberation actually meant unwanted exposure and risk. Consider, for example, the lawyer in Boston who received a mailing at her firm about a new organization forming for lesbian lawyers. The envelope was marked *personal and confidential,* but her secretary opened it anyway. The lawyer was furious, worried about her job, and strongly rebuked the woman who had sent it.[189] A mail carrier in Houston worried when a younger lesbian, who was "just freer," began working at her post office. What in years past might have been a quiet and unspoken camaraderie instead felt ominous. And the younger coworker did, in fact, end up exposing her older colleague, not because she was malicious, but "just in passing."[190] A Harvard Business School graduate noticed that coworkers called negative attention to his sexuality after the emergence of the gay liberation movement, but never before.[191] And there was the man who sent a donation to the National Gay Task Force in 1976. He was, he explained, fairly open with friends, but professionally closeted. "It galls me that I can't come out in the open to work for gay rights," he wrote, "but I'll do my best to help out financially."[192]

In the variety of responses that queer people had, there is probably only one thing that is common to them all: no one was able to completely isolate themselves from gay liberation. Even for those who would have wanted that, the broader public's heightened awareness, as well as the casual remarks of those who were "freer," made covering more difficult than it had been in years gone by. Employer scrutiny was intensifying just as state scrutiny—bar raids, entrapment, the vestiges of the Lavender Scare—was fading. Yet the state's easing up on its own surveillance and harassment was of limited significance without the availability of legal tools that gay people could take up to protect their own desired self-expression on the job. That did not happen, and when a new threat emerged—this time literally under the skin—vulnerability in the workplace took on even greater proportions.

188. MacLean, *Freedom Is Not Enough,* 290.
189. Interview subject 88, Boston, MA, 2011 (emphasis mine).
190. Interview subject 102, Houston, TX, 2013.
191. Interview subject 79, Cambridge, MA, 2011.
192. DA to National Gay Task Force, May 19, 1976, folder 7, box 98, Records of the National Gay and Lesbian Task Force.

PART III

Civil Rights in a
Neoliberal Age

CHAPTER FIVE

"Discrimination Engendered an Epidemic All of Its Own"

THE AIDS CRISIS ON THE JOB

HISTORIANS COMMONLY NARRATE the liberation-to-AIDS story as a discontinuous one of sudden rupture, when the liberatory impulse was halted in its tracks by the appearance of the AIDS virus in several American cities by the early 1980s. From the perspective of the bar and the bathhouse, this narrative is certainly accurate. But examining the early history of the AIDS epidemic from the vantage point of the workplace produces a different story. Viewed from the retail store, corporate office, or assembly line, the AIDS era actually extended some aspects of the previous period rather than breaking from them. The characteristics of the liberation era that were deepened were not those associated with emancipation, however, but those associated with risk.

The risk that tethers the two eras together is less the risk to sexual health (although that might also be significant) than it is risk on the job.[1] With regard to the latter dimension, both the liberation and the AIDS periods were a departure from the employment regime of the 1950s and 1960s. During those earlier years, as previous chapters have shown, employers in many sectors had been able to exploit the vulnerabilities that queer people presented to them as long as those employees conformed to certain norms of appearance and behavior on the job. That labor system had discretion

---

1. On gay sexual health in the 1970s—and the movement to support it—see Katherine Batza, *Before AIDS: Gay Health Politics in the 1970s* (Philadelphia: University of Pennsylvania Press, 2018).

at its heart—a mutual agreement not to see or be seen. If employees were discreet, employers would ignore them. When that bargain was challenged by liberationist impulses and gay and lesbian employees became less likely to mute their own expression on the job, employers increasingly invested in efforts to root out the potential homosexuals in their workforce.

A fragile trust, a tenuous agreement, was thus already fraying when the Centers for Disease Control (CDC) first reported on an unusual outbreak of cases of pneumocystis, a rare form of pneumonia, in Los Angeles in June 1981.[2] That summer the *New York Times* identified two "rapidly fatal" illnesses, pneumocystis pneumonia and a rare skin cancer called Kaposi's sarcoma, that were associated with the deaths of nearly fifty gay men in New York City and San Francisco.[3] During the next year, the CDC discerned patterns that strongly suggested an infectious disease that was sexually transmitted.[4] As the epidemic became more widely known, employers became even more distrustful of their gay employees than they had been during the liberation years. The value of gay workers—their twinned vulnerability and exploitability—was less and less offset by the multiplying liabilities that accompanied their employment. The stigma of homosexuality that might damage a company's reputation was greatly exacerbated by its association with contagion and fatal disease. Some companies moved their gay employees to back offices away from the public eye, fearing, as the executive director of the New York Business Group on Health observed, "a loss of business if [a company is] in any way associated with AIDS."[5] The hysteria of heterosexual coworkers, moreover, could create upheaval in an office. "One question I will never forget," reported a bank manager dealing with employees who had just learned of a colleague's AIDS diagnosis: "What if he licks my phone?"[6] Rather than deal with other employees' reactions, some companies arranged to pay medical expenses if sick employees agreed not to return to work.[7]

2. "Pneumocystis Pneumonia—Los Angeles," *Center for Disease Control Morbidity and Mortality Weekly Report*, June 5, 1981, 718.

3. Lawrence K. Altman, "Rare Cancer Seen in 41 Homosexuals," *New York Times*, July 3, 1981, A20; "2 Fatal Diseases Focus of Inquiry," *New York Times*, August 29, 1981, 9.

4. John-Manuel Andriote, *Victory Deferred: How AIDS Changed Gay Life in America* (Chicago: University of Chicago Press, 1999), 54.

5. Betty Liu Ebron and Michael S. Weisberg, "The Costs of Killer Disease Are Soaring," *Daily News*, March 8, 1987, 8; Testimony of Gary James Wood, 4, *Public Hearings on AIDS/ARC Related Discrimination (Addendum—Transcripts)*, February 4, 1986, San Francisco Human Rights Commission, San Francisco Public Library, San Francisco, CA.

6. Testimony of Kevin Wadsworth, Crocker Bank, 74, *Public Hearings on AIDS/ARC Related Discrimination*, February 4, 1986, San Francisco Human Rights Commission.

7. Irene Pave, "Fear and Loathing in the Workplace: What Managers Can Do about AIDS," *Business Week*, November 25, 1985, 126.

As the epidemic spread, there was also the terrifying prospect of exploding health-care costs at a time when 70 percent of Americans received health care through their employers, which typically paid 80 percent of costs.[8] Some insurers adopted exclusionary "redlining" practices, refusing to cover any business or occupation that was perceived to be densely populated with gay men. The Great Republic Insurance Company, for example, warned about "single males without dependents that are engaged in occupations that do not require physical exertion." Male hairdressers, waiters, florists, decorators, and antique dealers were listed among occupations said to "have provided a disproportionate share of this disease" and thus denied insurance coverage.[9] Worried about being left holding the bag for medical expenses, employers experimented with various ways of shifting costs onto sick individuals.[10]

Another response was simply to fire employees who either had or were suspected of having AIDS. The liberation period already had witnessed a significant uptick in employment discrimination, but discrimination rose even more dramatically with the onset of the AIDS epidemic. Employees could go home with a bad cold and find themselves terminated before they returned to work.[11] There were instances of gay men with birthmarks

8. Fern Schumer Chapman, "AIDS and Business: Problems of Costs and Compassion," *Fortune*, September 15, 1986, 126.

9. Bill Pritchett to All Agents, December 1985, in "Insurance General 1984–90" folder, box 3, Aetna Insurance AIDS Collection, University Archives and Special Collections, Northeastern University, Boston, MA. On the broader phenomenon of redlining by occupation or zip code to avoid insuring gay men, see Michael T. Isbell, "Private Coverage and HIV Care," *Health Care Reform: Lessons from the HIV Epidemic* (New York: Lambda Legal Defense and Education Fund, 1993), 82. Such practices would have been even more widespread in the early epidemic, but many insurance companies had restrictions in the "habits and morals" sections of their underwriting manuals and believed they had already blocked gay men and lesbians from coverage. See Marc Scherzer, "Private Insurance," *AIDS and the Law*, 4th ed. (Frederick, MD: Aspen, 2008), 416.

10. Under the federal Employee Retirement Income Security Act of 1974 (ERISA), companies with employee benefit plans could be held responsible for the medical expenses of employees with AIDS if insurance carriers refused to provide coverage. Arthur Leonard, "Employees with AIDS: What Companies Can and Can't Do," *Boardroom Reports*, November 1, 1985, 10. On shifting coverage, Chevron, for example, did this through the "'defined contribution,' which specified that for any particular ailment, the company paid a given amount and the rest was passed directly to the employee." Other companies shifted from maximum lifetime benefits to maximum yearly benefits. "American Businesses Face the Cost of Treating AIDS," *Washington Post National Weekly Edition*, June 20–26, 1988, 6A.

11. "Report on Discrimination against People with AIDS, November 1983–April 1986," City of New York Commission on Human Rights, folder 28, box 114, Records of the National Gay and Lesbian Task Force, Rare and Manuscript Collections, Cornell University, Ithaca, NY.

on their faces who were fired because bosses thought they saw the telltale sign of Kaposi's sarcoma, which usually presented as purplish lesions.[12] If employees were out sick for unusually long periods, company doctors might call their personal physicians to ask if the employee in question had AIDS. Sometimes doctors gave out information they should not have.[13]

By the spring of 1983, employer hostility was fed by an increasingly virulent and widespread backlash. "The sexual revolution has begun to devour its children," wrote the conservative commentator Patrick Buchanan in the *New York Post*. Volunteers staffing the AIDS hotline set up by the National Gay Task Force (NGTF) to counsel terrified gay men also heard vitriol and hatred on the other end of the line: "Get AIDS and die!"[14] Several organizations began to systematically document AIDS-related incidents. In addition to the NGTF, in the early years of the epidemic, the New York City Human Rights Commission, the ACLU of Southern California, and the AIDS Discrimination Reporting Project in San Francisco were all keeping track.[15]

The numbers were staggering: an ACLU study documented thirteen thousand reported incidents of discrimination in the five-year span between 1983 and 1988. As an advocate put it at the time, "Discrimination engendered an epidemic all of its own."[16] Employment outpaced all other categories of complaints, including medical services, insurance,

12. Testimony of Steven Pratt, Department of Social Services, 88, *Public Hearings on AIDS/ARC Related Discrimination*, February 5, 1986, San Francisco Human Rights Commission.

13. For example, a gay man in Council Bluffs, Iowa, was dismissed from his job at a hospital switchboard in 1983. His employer "had contacted [the] victim's physician who broke patient confidentiality and released information about the diagnosis." "AIDS-Related Discrimination," *NGTF AIDS Update*, folder 2, box 109, Records of the National Gay and Lesbian Task Force. On doctors releasing patient information to employers, see also "Report on Discrimination against People with AIDS, November 1983–April 1986," City of New York Commission on Human Rights, 4–6, folder 28, box 114, Records of the National Gay and Lesbian Task Force.

14. Dudley Clendinen and Adam Nagourney, *Out for Good: The Struggle to Build a Gay Rights Movement in America* (New York: Simon and Schuster, 1999), 484–85.

15. "AIDS-Related Discrimination," *NGTF AIDS Update*, folder 2, box 109, Records of the National Gay and Lesbian Task Force; "Report on Discrimination against People with AIDS, November 1983–April 1986," City of New York Commission on Human Rights, folder 28, box 114, Records of the National Gay and Lesbian Task Force; "The Lesbian and Gay Rights Chapter of the ACLU of Southern California," *Advocate*, May 15, 1984, 12; "AIDS Discrimination Reporting Project," *Golden Gate Business Association Newsletter*, January 1985, 5.

16. Testimony of Gary James Wood, 3, *Public Hearing on AIDS/ARC Related Discrimination (Addendum—Transcripts)*, February 4, 1986, San Francisco Human Rights Commission.

government benefits, housing, and public accommodations.[17] Firings occurred in corporate offices, law firms, schools, and hospitals, but they also reached deep into the queer work world, where gays had long accepted ill-paid, low-status jobs in exchange for safety. Waiters, beauty school instructors, retail clerks, hairdressers, and florists—service occupations associated with gay men—all lost positions because they either had AIDS or were perceived to be at risk of contracting it.[18] There was also a startling increase in discrimination against gays and lesbians more generally during the early 1980s, in what the executive director of the National Gay Task Force described as "a consistent pattern of transference" from "fear of AIDS" to fear of gay men and women.[19] In March 1984, for example, a New York City man reported that all the gay and lesbian wait staff were being fired from the South Street Seaport restaurant where he worked.[20] It is difficult to parse whether AIDS was an excuse for antigay bias, or if AIDS-phobia genuinely extended to all those associated with AIDS by homosexuality, including those were actually at low risk, such as lesbians.[21]

Whatever the precise motive, employers were strikingly forthright about firing employees for AIDS-related reasons. "You're a threat to

17. Nan D. Hunter to AIDS Policy Network, July 16, 1990, "APN Mailing—July 16, 1990" folder, box 4641, Records of the ACLU, Seeley Mudd Library, Princeton University, Princeton, NJ; ACLU AIDS Project, *Epidemic of Fear: A Survey of AIDS Discrimination in the 1980s and Policy Recommendations for the 1990s* (New York City: ACLU, 1990), 22–23.

18. Arthur S. Leonard, "Employment Discrimination against Persons with AIDS," *University of Dayton Law Review* 681 (1985): 683; Testimony of Jeff Levi, 2–3, US Congress, House, Subcommittee on Intergovernmental Relations and Human Relations Committee on Government Operations, September 13, 1985, included in Fowler letter to San Francisco Human Rights Commission, in *Public Hearings on AIDS/ARC Related Discrimination (Addendum—Transcripts)*, February 4, 1986, San Francisco Human Rights Commission. Sometimes it was gay men themselves who fired men with AIDS working in their businesses; for example, a Philadelphia florist terminated his employee with AIDS (and then visited him in the hospital). Interview with David Webber, conducted via Zoom, 2021.

19. Levi testimony, 3, *Public Hearings on AIDS/ARC Related Discrimination (Addendum—Transcripts)*, February 4, 1986, San Francisco Human Rights Commission.

20. "Summary of the Reports of Anti-gay Discrimination and Bias Documented by the Commission," October 1983–November 1985, New York City Commission on Human Rights, folder 2, box 141, Records of the National Gay and Lesbian Task Force.

21. The New York City Human Rights Commission viewed AIDS as a cover for antigay bias, observing that "although AIDS cannot be contracted from ordinary or casual contact, many homophobic individuals have unfortunately used the existence of AIDS to rationalize bias against gays under the guise of an alleged concern for health." See "Rights Agency Cites Rise in Reported Complaints of Anti-gay Bias," August 27, 1984, 3, Subject Files, Lesbian Herstory Archives, Brooklyn, NY (microfilm reel 86, frame 07890, Thompson Gale).

everyone around you," one employer told a switchboard operator.[22] The pattern was so pronounced early in the epidemic that the New York City Commission on Human Rights revealed that a formal investigation to determine "the veracity of allegations" was rarely necessary. "Respondents were very open about having fired someone with AIDS," they observed.[23] Often employers did not believe they had violated the law. In fact, in many localities they had not. But even where they arguably had, many employers would take their chances on paying a settlement in order to remove someone with AIDS from their workplaces.[24] Relatively few of those who lost jobs, moreover, ever pursued their grievances in court. Numerous observers noticed the paucity of lawsuits early in the epidemic. "Lawyers especially will be struck by the number of incidents reported to us anecdotally which could have been the basis for an anti-discrimination lawsuit," the ACLU's survey of AIDS-related discrimination in the 1980s noted, "but which apparently were not acted on."[25] In many parts of the country, few lawyers were willing to take cases because of the associated stigma. Potential complainants often lacked the physical or emotional resources to engage in prolonged litigation. As one advocate remarked, many AIDS patients "don't want the burden of a legal battle in what may be the final months of their lives."[26]

Employers could usually act with impunity then. Because bosses were highly incentivized to fire or to refuse to hire them, gays and lesbians were ever more cautious during this period, and the phenomenon of "recloseting" was noticeable during the early 1980s.[27] The drive to conceal one's "lifestyle" was especially acute for those who had been diagnosed with AIDS or who were caring for someone who was sick. One executive, for example, went through his partner's illness and death without missing a day of work. "No one at work could know that he had someone who was

22. "AIDS-Related Discrimination," *NGTF AIDS Update*, folder 2, box 109, Records of the National Gay and Lesbian Task Force.

23. "Report on Discrimination against People with AIDS, November 1983–April 1986," City of New York Commission on Human Rights, folder 28, box 114, Records of the National Gay and Lesbian Task Force. Employers were also open about their decisions not to hire those they considered high risk for contracting the illness.

24. Testimony of Gary James Wood, 4–5, *Public Hearing on AIDS/ARC Related Discrimination (Addendum—Transcripts)*, February 4, 1986, San Francisco Human Rights Commission.

25. ACLU AIDS Project, *Epidemic of Fear*, 46; William L. Kandel, "Current Developments in EEO-AIDS in the Workplace," *Employee Relations Law Review* 11 (Spring 1986): 684.

26. ACLU AIDS Project, *Epidemic of Fear*, 33–36. See also Sandra G. Boodman, "AIDS Discrimination Issue Mushrooming," *Washington Post*, November 24, 1986, A6.

27. Interview subject 18, New York, NY, 2012; interview subject 7, Washington, DC, 2013.

dying," a friend later remembered.[28] Some men who were sick paid medical expenses out of pocket rather than submit claims that would reveal their diagnosis.[29] For those who could not afford such tactics, discovery was only a matter of time, when vague symptoms and sick days became something very specific and undeniably AIDS related. Men with the disease were said "to have a look," even if they never had purplish lesions: they rapidly lost weight they didn't regain, their skin hung loosely, their complexion turned sallow.[30] As the epidemic wore on, employers became more skilled at reading visual cues. If discovery meant job loss, the potential loss of health insurance inflicted the greatest harm, but the loss of meaningful work also damaged the emotional health of those with AIDS. "Most of the people struck down by AIDS are at the beginning or at the midpoint of their work life," one guidance for AIDS practitioners advised. "They have not yet begun to see retirement as an enjoyable potential. To be robbed of their work is devastating."[31]

Some employers were quite cognizant that AIDS was not like cancer or heart disease, but struck down people in the prime of their working lives. In the early years of the epidemic the typical person with AIDS was between the ages of twenty and forty-five.[32] For that reason, the illness potentially "belonged" to employers in a way that was also unprecedented in the history of illness, and the looming loss of productivity was nearly as worrisome to employers as the prospect of rising health-care premiums.[33] A few business leaders were quick to see both a responsibility and an opportunity to halt the illness. "Since AIDS primarily strikes people who are in their peak productive years," asserted the CEO of Pacific Mutual,

28. Interview subject 46, Atlanta, GA, 2012.

29. Report on Discrimination against People with AIDS and People Perceived to Have AIDS (January 1986–June 1987), 8, folder 28, box 114, Records of the National Gay and Lesbian Task Force; Albert R. Jonsen and Jeff Stryker, *The Social Impact of AIDS in the United States* (Washington, DC: National Academy Press), 268.

30. Interview with Charles Cloniger, conducted via Zoom, 2020; Clendinen and Nagourney, *Out for Good*, 559.

31. Rhonda R. Rivera, "Lawyers, Clients, and AIDS: Some Notes from the Trenches," *Ohio State Law Journal* 49 (1989): 912.

32. National Leadership Coalition on AIDS, "Small Business and AIDS," "Business Interests" folder, box 1, Aetna Insurance AIDS Collection; Patti Watts, "AIDS Education in the Workplace: Fighting Indifference and Fear," *Management Review* 77 (April 1988): 37.

33. Ann M. Hardy et al., "The Economic Impact of the First 10,000 Cases of Acquired Immunodeficiency Syndrome in the United States," *Journal of the American Medical Association* 255 (January 10, 1986): 211; Edward H. Yelin et al., "The Impact of HIV-Related Illness on Employment," *American Journal of Public Health* 81 (January 1991): 79.

"education in the workplace should be most effective."[34] If people didn't learn about AIDS prevention at work, health experts warned, "they might not learn it at all."[35] Even the federal government, which was tragically slow to respond on almost every front, recognized this fact. By 1985, the CDC had issued guidelines on AIDS in the workplace that conveyed its core message: AIDS was not transmitted through casual contact, and employees should be allowed to perform their jobs as long as they were able to do so, even in food handling and other personal services. Health-care workers who did not perform invasive procedures, the CDC said in 1985, also "need not be restricted from work unless they have evidence of other infection or illness for which any [health-care worker] should be restricted."[36] The surgeon general followed the CDC in urging employers to educate the nation, informing workers that AIDS was not easily transmitted and that workplaces were safe, as well as "how they can guard against the disease by changing high risk behavior."[37]

That explicit conversation, however, was one most employers were not eager to have.[38] Several surveys found that employers had been largely unresponsive; even a number of years into the epidemic, most neglected to formulate policies and programs to deal with the situation.[39] Some

34. "Pacific Mutual Manual Covers AIDS Education," *National Underwriter*, November 2, 1987, 25.

35. "Many Companies Shrink from Dealing with AIDS," *Newsday*, August 9, 1987, 75.

36. "Summary: Recommendations for Preventing Transmission of Infection with Human T-Lymphotropic Virus Type III / Lymphadenopathy-Associated Virus in the Workplace," *Morbidity and Mortality Weekly Report* 34 (November 15, 1985): 691.

37. "Koop Urges Firms to Educate Workers on AIDS," *Hartford Courant*, October 14, 1987, B1.

38. One insurance company's guidance to its own employees departed from the usual norms of the corporate policy genre when it explicitly advised employees to use condoms "from start to finish of both vaginal and rectal intercourse," and warned that most people do not "put them on early enough, securely enough, or with enough room at the tip so that the semen won't break the condom." Leonardo Chait to All Personnel, "A Special Report for Executive Life Employees," March 10, 1987, folder 33, box 2, Aetna Insurance AIDS Collection. More typically, employers were warned against providing too much information to employees. See Anita W. Schoomaker, "Variations of the Corporate AIDS Policy Theme," *Health Cost Management*, March/April 1988, 9.

39. Reported estimates of the number of leading companies that had developed policies on AIDS ranged from around 5 percent to 20 percent. This was true even several years into the epidemic. See, for example, Marilyn Chase, "Corporations Urge Peers to Adopt Humane Policies for AIDS Victims," *Wall Street Journal*, January 20, 1988, 1; "Writing the Rules on AIDS," *Personnel*, August 1988, 13; Patti Watts, "AIDS Education in the Workplace," *Newsday*, April 1988, 38; "Many Companies Shrink from Dealing with AIDS," *Newsday*, August 9, 1987, 9. Organized labor was equally slow to respond. The Service Employees International Union (SEIU) had a policy on AIDS by 1983, but this was not true of

executives confessed they feared being seen as a "haven" for people with the disease and unwittingly attracting sick people into their workforce.[40] Others worried that a written policy would create contractual obligations that companies would later find confining.[41] "Putting out a written policy is risky," *Fortune* cautioned. "A policy that seems right [in the immediate] might not be sensible when costs and stresses run a lot higher."[42] But companies' reticence could of course create other problems, feeding biases that stymied productivity. For example, 37 percent of workers reported they would not share tools with a coworker with AIDS, and an even higher proportion said they would not eat in the company cafeteria if a colleague with AIDS was also eating there.[43] Elsewhere, employees refused to use the same bathroom as a coworker with AIDS.[44]

Only a handful of companies managed to be more proactive in the early days. In 1983, Wells Fargo, a San Francisco firm, developed a policy to help coworkers deal with employees with AIDS who were returning to work. That initial policy on personnel reporting and management procedures blossomed into a whole-scale educational program at the bank, and the company successfully helped several AIDS-affected employees return to work in several locations.[45] Wells Fargo soon joined with Bank of America, Levi Strauss, PG&E (Pacific Gas and Electric) and several other Northern California corporations to coordinate a response through the Business Leadership Task Force.[46] Other regional collaborations surfaced in other parts of the country. For example, New York and New Jersey businesses formed the Citizens' Commission on AIDS for New York City and Northern New Jersey, and the New England Corporate Consortium

most unions, and nondiscrimination statements (based on HIV/AIDS) in contracts were rare even by the late 1980s. George Mendenhall, "Lesbians and Gays Fight Discrimination through Unions," *San Francisco Sentinel*, May 6, 1988, 8–9.

40. "The Costs of Killer Disease Are Soaring," *Daily News*, March 8, 1987, 8.

41. Chase, "Corporations Urge Peers to Adopt Humane Policies for AIDS Victims," 1.

42. Chapman, "AIDS and Business," 127.

43. Alan Emery, "AIDS Strategies That Work," *Business and Health*, June 1989, 44.

44. "AIDS-Related Discrimination," *NGTF AIDS Update*, folder 2, box 109, Records of the National Gay and Lesbian Task Force.

45. "Employers Ponder AIDS Cost Containment Options," *Benefits New Analysis* 9, no. 3:20; Brian Lawton, Wells Fargo Bank, "AIDS: Legal and Human Resource Issues for the Employer," "General Discrimination/3" folder, box 1, AIDS Legal Referral Panel Files, Archives and Special Collections, University of California–San Francisco, San Francisco, CA.

46. Washington Business Group on Health, "AIDS: Employers' Rights, Responsibilities, and Opportunities," "AIDS in the Workplace" folder, box 3, AIDS Legal Referral Panel Records, GLBT Historical Society of Northern California, San Francisco, CA.

on AIDS Education was based in Boston.[47] Despite some coordination to ascertain best practices, many efforts remained idiosyncratic. Westinghouse's legal counsel advocated the use of *toilet seat covers* at their facilities as part of the corporation's response to the epidemic, even as the company's medical director acknowledged the measure had no medical basis.[48] The Mead Corporation took a somewhat instrumental tone, noting that "internally, the company may benefit by a reasoned display of compassion for a stricken employee."[49] Because it was far easier to do and say nothing, most of the early adopters of AIDS policies and educational programs were likely motivated by genuine compassion. When employees at Levi Strauss asked COO Robert Haas if they could hand out pamphlets on AIDS prevention in the company's atrium over the lunch hour, he said yes and then joined these employees in passing out the leaflets. That was in 1982.[50]

———————

AIDS, then, did not force everyone back into hiding. For some, like the employees standing in the atrium at Levi Strauss handing out leaflets over the lunch period, it had the opposite effect. That was even more true in the workplaces that arose specifically to meet the needs of people with AIDS, which were another by-product of the magnitude of the epidemic although one that has barely been considered in a historiography focused on activist groups like ACT UP.[51] Centering the workplace in the history of AIDS brings the health-care and legal professions specifically into the spotlight, for here the medical epidemic was joined to an epidemic of discrimination. Health care was the more immediate, for obvious reasons, and the paradigmatic example of what might be called an "AIDS

47. "Ten Principles for the Workplace," folder 4, box 3, Aetna Insurance AIDS Collection.

48. Corporate Medical Director, Westinghouse Corporation, "AIDS as a Workplace Issue," September 24, 1985, Bush Administration and the AIDS Crisis, White House Staff and Office Files, Archives of Sexuality and Gender database.

49. "Coping with AIDS in the Workplace," September 1987, "Employment" folder, box 3, Aetna Insurance AIDS Collection.

50. Interview with Robert Haas (former CEO of Levi Strauss), San Francisco, CA, 2015; Harvard Business School, "Levi Strauss and Company and the AIDS Crisis," "Corporations and Organizations—Levi Strauss" folder, box 2, Aetna Insurance AIDS Collection.

51. See, for example, Deborah Gould, *Moving Politics: Emotion and ACT UP's Fight against AIDS* (University of Chicago Press, 2009); Jennifer Brier, *Infectious Ideas: U.S. Political Responses to the AIDS Crisis* (Chapel Hill: University of North Carolina Press, 2009).

workplace" was the special care unit created at San Francisco General Hospital (SFGH) in the early 1980s to care for AIDS patients.[52]

The nation's first dedicated AIDS ward was the result of a confluence of two factors—a budget surplus in the City of San Francisco, and the dismal treatment that AIDS patients were receiving as they began to fill hospital beds across the city.[53] Many arrived with pneumocystis pneumonia, and hospital staff were shocked when they had to put so many young men on ventilators.[54] There were instances of blatant homophobia—one doctor, for example, who described the bronchoscopy he was about to perform as sticking "a tube down this fag's throat." But more often fear of infection distorted the care that hospital staff were able to give: putting on a "space suit" before entering a patient's room, leaving food on a tray in the hallway, and avoiding interaction with patients.[55] "What began as periodic instances of inconvenience and disrespect," two nurses wrote, "developed into a widespread breach of quality of care for people with AIDS."[56]

In the fall of 1982, a gay nurse named Cliff Morrison voiced his concerns to Maryanne McGuire, the director of nursing, when they ran into each other in the hospital cafeteria at SFGH. McGuire raised the idea of an inpatient AIDS unit. Morrison was initially resistant to the idea, as were many others within the gay community, because a separate unit might become something akin to a "leper colony." But Morrison soon came around. He himself was about to transfer from psychiatric nursing back to general medical / surgical nursing, and he suggested to McGuire that she make him a clinical coordinator for AIDS care. McGuire took the proposal to hospital administrators, who were "relieved" to have someone willing to take on the crisis.[57]

52. A popular account of the San Francisco AIDS ward is Carol Pogash, *As Real as It Gets: The Life of a Hospital at the Center of the AIDS Epidemic* (New York: Penguin Books, 1992).

53. Then Mayor Diane Feinstein was able to respond aggressively to the epidemic because San Francisco had experienced a budget surplus for several years in the early to mid-1980s. In 1983, for example, Feinstein budgeted 4.3 million to deal with the AIDS crisis. "A Crisis in Public Health," *Atlantic Monthly*, October 1985, 20.

54. Sally Smith Hughes interview with Cliff Morrison, in *The San Francisco AIDS Epidemic: The Response of the Nursing Profession, 1981–1984* (Berkeley: University of California Regional Oral History Office, 1999), 3:82–83.

55. Sally Smith Hughes interview with Diane Jones, in *San Francisco AIDS Epidemic*, 3:6–8.

56. Charles Cloniger and Steve Keith, "History of Ward 5B," "Nursing Orientation" folder, box 7, SFGH AIDS Ward 5B/5A Archives, San Francisco Public Library.

57. Smith Hughes interview with Cliff Morrison, in *San Francisco AIDS Epidemic*, 3:87–90, 107.

They were also open to paying for things that in another context "would never have flown," especially in a county hospital. Morrison was committed to primary nursing, the idea of an all-RN staff in which a registered nurse provided all the care to a patient. There were no nursing assistants or licensed vocational nurses changing sheets or emptying bedpans. The primary nursing model provided a high quality of care, accountability, and continuity; nurses would coordinate care and be "responsible holistically for the needs of patients." It was very expensive, yet the city said yes. In setting up the ward, Morrison was also able to arrange for a 1 to 4 ratio of nurses to patients, which was almost unheard of. Private rooms for patients were also critical to prevent cross-infection between patients who might have different opportunistic infections.[58]

Justified by a critically ill patient population with complex medical and psychosocial needs, the ward was, a nurse later reflected, "nursing the way nursing was supposed to be."[59] Remarkably, at a time when no one yet understood how the virus was transmitted, forty nurses applied for twelve positions on the unit. Morrison looked for a mix of those who had experience in hospice and critical care and those who had experience working in mental health. When McGuire looked at the staff Morrison had selected, she commented that he had chosen "all the troublemakers in this system." He saw the "strengths he was looking for." Roughly half were gay men, one-quarter were lesbians, and one-quarter were straight women, some of whom had formative ties to gay men and felt connected to gay culture. Morrison then asked the staff to make key decisions about how the work would be organized. They voted for a schedule, for example, in which three intense twelve-hour days were followed by four days away to rest and recover.[60]

Ward 5B opened in July 1983. Initially, the feeling on the job was oddly celebratory, "almost like a party."[61] For some of the gay nurses, it was the first time they had ever been completely open in their jobs. Hospitals in those days could be hypersexualized, almost "incestuous," work environments with

58. On a typical medical unit at SFGH, nurses would care for seven or eight patients. Smith Hughes interview with Cliff Morrison, 1996, *San Francisco AIDS Epidemic*, 3:125, 142, 165–67, 196. See also Smith Hughes interview with Diane Jones in *San Francisco AIDS Epidemic*, 3:24; Cheryl Clark, "AIDS Patients Find Special Care in S.F. Acute Ward," *San Diego Union*, October 9, 1988, A-3.

59. Interview with Susanna Kiely, Berkeley, CA, 2020; Smith Hughes interview with Diane Jones, in *San Francisco AIDS Epidemic*, 3:24.

60. Smith Hughes interview with Cliff Morrison, in *San Francisco AIDS Epidemic*, 3:155, 165; Jane Meredith Adams, "Life and Death on Ward 5-A," *Washington Post*, December 12, 1989, 14.

61. Interview with Alison Moed, San Francisco, CA, 2015.

young men and women interns, residents, and nurses sharing an experience of trauma and suffering in close physical proximity.[62] But that work culture, whether it was experienced as exciting or exploitative or something in-between, tended to be heterosexually charged, which exacerbated the isolation of gay and lesbian nurses. One nurse remembered making up stories about what she did on the weekend when she worked at French Hospital in San Francisco.[63] Another remembered the worry, given the interdependence of nurses, that if people knew you were gay, the "other nurses wouldn't be there for you."[64] Others recalled quietly finding other gay nurses to eat lunch with, discreetly forming a secret affinity group.[65] For most nurses, as for most professionals more generally, gay life was kept separate from work even though the liberationist ethos had begun to erode this boundary.[66]

On the AIDS ward, by contrast, work and "your outside life," in the words of one nurse, were "all one thing."[67] The culture on the ward was not merely tolerant of gay culture; it celebrated it.[68] One bisexual nurse noted that it was the "straight" part of her identity that was "closeted" at work because the norm "was so clearly gay."[69] In the early days especially, nurses were incredibly bonded with each other, with an "us against the world" feeling. Imagine a group of young, mostly gay nurses being left alone by their hospital administration to create something totally unique in the country. "There was the electricity of beginning something brand new," one nurse reflected.[70] They were buoyed by the feeling that they were coming together to care for their own community, and by the sense in the early days that AIDS would unfold like Legionnaires' disease and be quickly over. "We can lick this thing!" was the spirit on the ward.[71]

62. Interview with Kathleen O'Leary, Phoenix, AZ, 2020.

63. Interview with Marcy Fraser, San Francisco, CA, 2015.

64. Interview with Susanna Kiely, Berkeley, CA, 2020.

65. Interview with Marcy Fraser, San Francisco, 2015; interview with Bill Barrick, conducted via Skype, 2015.

66. This phenomenon for most defined nursing school as well. Susanna Kiely, for example, remembered a dual life in nursing school in San Mateo, where she was very isolated. She took classes in San Mateo but then would go up to study at the University of San Francisco and then spend evenings at bars like Maud's in Cole Valley or the Stud, which was South of Market. Interview with Susanna Kiely, Berkeley, CA, 2020.

67. Interview with Charles Cloniger, conducted via Zoom, 2020.

68. Smith Hughes interview with Diane Jones, in *San Francisco AIDS Epidemic*, 3:16; interview with Alison Moed, San Francisco, CA, 2015.

69. Interview with Kathleen O'Leary, Phoenix, AZ, 2020.

70. Interview with Steve Keith, San Francisco, CA, 2015.

71. Ibid.; interview with Alison Moed, San Francisco, CA, 2015; interview with Susanna Kiely, Berkeley, CA, 2020.

The unique culture of the ward was also shaped by its porousness. It was known as the "ward without walls"; from the beginning the staff, including Morrison, created policies that invited the community in. They immediately did away with visiting hours, for example. "If a partner wanted to spend the night, we rolled in a cot," nurse Steve Keith remembered, and said, "come on."[72] Long stays and private rooms meant that many patients made their rooms their own, bringing in crystal flower vases, champagne glasses, musical instruments and "boom boxes" to enliven these spaces. At some point, someone donated a piano. The ward also encouraged support from the community more broadly. Some of those arrangements were formal, as with the Shanti Project, a social service organization that had been created in the 1970s to support people with life-threatening illnesses. Shanti counselors were on the ward from the beginning. More informal arrangements also developed over time. A group that called itself the Godfather Fund raised money to donate toiletry kits and bathrobes for patients. Double Rainbow Ice Cream made regular donations to 5B. Certain individuals became fixtures. "Rita Rockett," a travel agent who had a history partying with gay men before the epidemic, appeared every other Sunday to cater a brunch and tap-dance for delighted patients. Richard Locke, a well-known gay porn star, appeared on the ward regularly to give massages. "He would walk into the room," and patients recognized him and "would exclaim, 'What? You??'" Cabaret singer Sharon McNight came to perform Patsy Cline songs. Birthdays, weddings, and baptisms were celebrated on the ward. Even in the midst of the epidemic, there was a "brightness" to the gay community in the early 1980s, and some of that energy made its way onto the ward.[73] The closest parallel in terms of a "communal expression of . . . pride [and] identity" was probably the ethnic hospital of the early twentieth century.[74]

The communalism of the unit was strengthened by the length of time patients were on the ward. Early in the epidemic, admissions would sometimes last several weeks, and many AIDS patients were readmitted three

72. Interview with Steve Keith, San Francisco, CA, 2015.

73. Ibid.; interview with Susanna Kiely, Berkeley, CA, 2020; interview with Alison Moed, San Francisco, CA, 2015; Jane Meredith Adams, "Life and Death on 5A," *Washington Post*, December 12, 1989, 14–15.

74. Guenter B. Risse, *Mending Bodies, Saving Souls: A History of Hospitals* (New York: Oxford University Press, 1999), 663. In this aspect, the AIDS ward was a very natural outgrowth of the late 1970s, which saw, according to the social scientist Dennis Altman, the invention of "the ethnic homosexual" as a sort of cultural category equivalent to other ethnic minorities. Dennis Altman, "What Changed in the 1970s?," in *Homosexuality: Power and Politics*, ed. Gay Left Collective (London: Allison and Busby, 1980), 61.

or four times over the course of their illness. Because of the length of hospital stays, as well as the low nurse-to-patient ratio, nurses got to know their patients and sometimes formed close relationships with them.[75] "I was always a good technical nurse," Susanna Kiely remembered, but the psychosocial aspects of her nursing practice "grew and blossomed" during her years on the ward.[76] Total involvement with patients was a by-product not only of a disease that had at that point a 100 percent mortality rate, but also of the fact that many patients with AIDS lacked traditional support systems. Some were estranged from their families before they ever got sick. Others came out to their families only when forced to do so by their diagnosis, and many feared being rejected at the moment when support was desperately needed. Those layers of vulnerability deepened the bonds nurses formed with patients, and many of the traditional boundaries between nurses and patients were discarded. Physical touch became a central part of the care work and included nurses crawling into bed to hold distressed patients. Bill Barrick remembered getting into bed to embrace a crying patient and being with him for five or ten minutes when a Shanti volunteer happened to walk by. "I had three other patients I needed to take care of, and we exchanged hand signals," he remembered. "I slipped out, and she slipped in. It was incredibly finessed."[77]

Nurses also helped patients navigate complex relationships with families, and they helped support distressed parents and siblings as they were learning all at once that their sons were gay and, in all likelihood, would soon be dead. Steve Keith got to know the brother and sister of a patient who had come to San Francisco for the first time and spent five days sitting on the ward. He didn't want their whole experience of the city to be a hospital room, so before their flight home he "loaded them in the car . . . and showed them some of the fun parts of the city," describing this as the sort of thing "you wouldn't [normally] do in a nursing job."[78] As often, though, nurses would need to strike an adversarial tone with families of origin. An RN remembered putting himself physically between a patient's mother and his group of gay friends whom she tried to order out of her son's room. "No," the nurse said to her, "you don't have the authority to do that."[79] Nurses sometimes protected patients from employers, who called the ward looking for their employees. Nurses never gave out the identities

75. Smith Hughes interview with Diane Jones, in *San Francisco AIDS Epidemic*, 3:37.
76. Interview with Susanna Kiely, Berkeley, CA, 2020.
77. Interview with Bill Barrick, conducted via Skype, 2015.
78. Interview with Steve Keith, San Francisco, CA, 2015.
79. Interview with Bill Barrick, conducted via Skype, 2015.

of people on the ward for this reason, and the board on the ward showing admissions only used first names.[80]

Nurses might also put themselves between patient and doctor, explaining that patients could refuse being poked and prodded when it wasn't going to change the trajectory of their illness. Nurses were more powerful in these contests than otherwise would have been the case because AIDS was a nurse's disease that inverted the typical relationship between doctors and nurses. "We were the experts, not them," Marcy Fraser remembered. "We would sit around and look at x-rays with them and say, 'What is this?' but it was a nurse-run operation." Even when they were allies and partners with nurses, doctors had much less to offer patients suffering with a disease for which there was no treatment. It was the comfort and pain relief that nurses gave that mattered.[81]

There was always some risk to the job: perhaps not as much as nurses off the ward imagined, but perhaps more than the 5B nurses allowed for. Before it was really known that AIDS was not spread by casual contact, nurses on the ward were "instinctively" headed there. "We were basically role-modeling one way of relating to patients," Diane Jones remembered, "which was to go in without precautions." In part, 5B nurses were reacting against what they viewed as the hysteria of nurses treating AIDS patients elsewhere who were taking extreme precautions in a way the 5B nurses found unnecessary and even homophobic.[82] On the ward, nurses were "adamant that we were going to prove to people that it was safe to take care of people with AIDS." There was an element of bravado or even denial in this, and accidental needlesticks, which could transmit the virus, were often downplayed. When a test for antibodies to the virus was developed in 1985, it was a relief for nurses to know for certain if they had been

80. Interview with Marcy Fraser, San Francisco, CA, 2015. Using first names only on the board was a defense against people coming on to the ward "looking for who was there." As the epidemic wore on, the practice wasn't always sustainable. Smith Hughes interview with Diane Jones, *San Francisco AIDS Epidemic*, 3:49.

81. Interview with Marcy Fraser, San Francisco, CA, 2015; interview with Charles Cloniger, conducted via Zoom, 2015.

82. Smith Hughes interview with Diane Jones, in *San Francisco AIDS Epidemic*, 3:12–18. In 1984, four nurses who were treating AIDS patients elsewhere in the hospital filed a complaint with the California Department of Industrial Relations because the hospital had refused to allow those nurses to wear masks and gloves whenever they came into contact with AIDS patients. The Division of Occupational Safety and Health dismissed the complaint, finding no safety problems "in AIDS patients having free access to public areas, in gloves not being worn unless a nurse came into contact with a patient's blood or body secretion, and in not wearing surgical masks in the absence of coughing." Kent Jonas, "AIDS and California Employment Law," *Labor and Employment Law News* 4 (Winter 1986): 6.

infected. Nurses on 5B (and 5A when the AIDS ward moved to a bigger space) were tested every few months, which took some anxiety out of the situation. But in 1987, one nurse on the ward had a needlestick and subsequently seroconverted. Nurses on the ward were stunned. The seroconversion "ended up being the catalyst to rectify the excessively cavalier attitude that we had," one recalled.[83] More gloves were worn, and recapping devices were designed to prevent needlesticks.[84]

The hardest part of the job, nurses found, was not managing anxiety about their own health, but rather the suffering and loss of patients. The work on 5B was messy nursing. Most of the nurses spoke at length about the nearly constant diarrhea that came with cryptosporidium, a common opportunistic infection. "You get a bed changed, all fresh. And five minutes later the patient puts his light on because it was full of diarrhea," Steve Keith remembered. "Sometimes that would happen five times before things would settle down and you could breathe."[85] Years later, when treatment involved suppressing viral loads and enhancing immune function such that people lived longer with the illness, AIDS deaths came to look more like cancer, heart failure, and other more "standard" deaths. Early AIDS deaths were as distinctive as they were brutal. Kaposi's sarcoma was disfiguring and painful. Pneumocystis resulted in oxygen hunger, "which was terrifying." One nurse cared for a man who died of Burkett's lymphoma, an extremely rare disease that before HIV had been seen only in some parts of Africa. "Your tumor doubles every twenty-four hours," and this nurse literally watched her patient's tumors growing during a twelve-hour shift. She reached his family, and miraculously they made it in time to be there with him as he died. After it was over, she walked out of the room and saw another nurse. "I fell into him, and I just cried. Because it was over." Grief was interwoven into every workday.[86]

83. Smith Hughes interview with Diane Jones, in *San Francisco AIDS Epidemic*, 3:12–15. The nurse who seroconverted is still alive. Rates of occupational transmission for health-care workers for AIDS were very low compared to those for hepatitis, which was far more contagious. San Francisco General Hospital, "Comprehensive Care of the AIDS Patient: A Workshop," May 1–2, 1987, San Francisco, CA, 104, carton 1, Brooks Linton Ephemeral Collection, Archives and Special Collections, University of California–San Francisco. By 1987, across the country, the CDC reported that nine health-care workers had been infected on the job. Steven Findlay, "Health Care Workers and Risk of AIDS," *USA Today*, May 21, 1987, 1D.

84. "Shielding Hospital Staffs from Dangerous Cuts," *Wall Street Journal*, April 26, 1990, B1.

85. Interview with Steve Keith, San Francisco, CA, 2015.

86. Interview with Anne Hughes, San Francisco, CA, 2015; interview with Bill Barrick, conducted via Skype, 2015; interview with Marcy Fraser, San Francisco, CA, 2015.

Nurses were all asked about their plan for self-care when they interviewed for the job, but in practice people found what worked as they went along. Marcy Fraser remembered a kind of silliness and "gallows humor" on the ward that was sustaining. She worked the night shift, and there was always some quiet time when patients would be asleep and no one needed her. She and her colleague Charles Cloniger would practice ballroom dancing down the halls because "we couldn't just be gloom and doom."[87] For others, regular time away was most critical for mental health. Kathleen O'Leary had an apartment on Clement Street in the Richmond district. It was a corner unit with a view of the ocean. Her first day off after several days on, "I would just sit on the couch and look out the window. I had no energy for anything else." Another nurse had a habit of taking a book and spending the day at the Osento bathhouse on Valencia Street; others went out to the Russian River. Not all coping mechanisms were healthy. Drugs, sex, and alcohol, in moderation or to excess, helped to numb the intensity of the workweek. Some 5B nurses socialized together a lot outside of work; others not at all.[88] The one collective ritual they shared to process their grief was incredibly simple. The turned a donated scrap book into what they called a "necrology." In it, they wrote the name of every patient they cared for who died of AIDS, the room they died in, and the diagnosis: "PCP"; "KS"; "Cryptosporidium"; "Cryptococcal Meningitis." Over time, they begin to add small details to better recall the dead as individuals.[89] With brief notes written in haste, the necrology scrapbook grew to encompass pages and pages of names, with funny and poignant asides:

—great mustache;
—square dancer;
—served vodka Collins in his room;
—husky/robust til the end;
—loving mom by his side;
—kimonos / wild flamboyance / predicted his time;
—heart beat for 1¼ hours after he died;
—Kevin was the sweetest;
—exacting patient;
—flamenco dancer;

87. Interview with Marcy Fraser, San Francisco, CA, 2015.
88. Interview with Kathleen O'Leary, Phoenix, AZ, 2020; interview with Susanna Kiely, Berkeley, CA, 2020; interview with Steve Keith, San Francisco, 2015; interview with Alison Moed, San Francisco, CA, 2015.
89. Interview with Steve Keith, San Francisco, CA, 2015.

—dear sweet Jack;

—elderly parents arrived just in time;

—received BA on day he died;

—taught us all about dealing with pain;

—the divine Judy![90]

For most nurses, the job was not sustainable over the long term. They had different breaking points, saw different events as signs that it was time to go. For one nurse, it was a back injury that for her represented a spiritual as well as a physical break. Or one too many needlesticks. The loss of a patient they had been especially close to, or the moment when ward nurses themselves began to get sick and die. In the early years alone, one woman nurse died of breast cancer and two male nurses died of AIDS.[91] However long they stayed, most of them identified their time on the AIDS ward at San Francisco General as the best job of their working lives. This extremely "rich environment," one nurse reflected, posed unavoidable "questions about life and death and sexuality and discrimination and drugs and addiction and family dynamics and pain and despair and hope and courage."[92] Meaningful work.

———

Just as nurses were treating the medical epidemic on the AIDS ward, gay lawyers were increasingly treating the epidemic of discrimination. The gay and lesbian legal office, as well as the handful of legal advocacy organizations that made up the fledgling gay rights field during these years, modeled new ways of lawyering as young practitioners mobilized in response to the crisis engulfing their communities. Unlike the AIDS ward, which was created totally anew, however, the phenomenon of the lesbian or gay law practice preceded the epidemic. The lawyer and activist Urvashi Vaid remembered Hunter and Polikoff in Washington, DC, as the first gay firm of which she was aware.[93] For Hunter and Polikoff, as for many other practices run by lesbians, the most relevant community was the feminist

90. Scrapbooks 1983–87, box 1, SFGH AIDS Ward 5B/5A Archives, San Francisco Public Library.

91. Interview with Susanna Kiely, Berkeley, CA, 2020; interview with Kathleen O'Leary, Phoenix, AZ, 2020; interview with Marcy Fraser, San Francisco, CA, 2015; interview with Alison Moed, San Francisco, CA, 2015.

92. Smith Hughes interview with Diane Jones, in *San Francisco AIDS Epidemic*, 3:30–37. Similar models of care were implemented in other hospitals across the country.

93. Interview with Urvashi Vaid, New York, NY, 2015.

community, but the firm was also interwoven with the broader alternative economy of Washington. Hunter and Polikoff did legal work for the food co-op, for various feminist enterprises, and for the women's bookstore, which was, Hunter recalled, "a lesbian project."[94] Katherine Triantafillou started her own gay practice in Boston in 1975, right after graduating from law school. She had an offer to go clerk for a judge in Cleveland but worried that taking that job meant giving up the openly lesbian life she was living in Boston, and "fall[ing] back into who I had been prior." So at the age of twenty-six she hung out her shingle, calling the established feminist lawyer she knew in town and asking her to refer gay cases. Triantafillou ran her practice out of her apartment. She got the courage for the venture from the ethos of feminism, which was so much about "recreating yourself and taking power back from the patriarchy," Triantafillou recalled. "These are concepts that now seem parochial, but we took it all so seriously."[95]

Those early practices were truly self-generated—there was nothing in the curriculum at law schools, for example, that prepared anyone to do this work.[96] Materials on gay issues were not included in legal indexes; there was certainly nothing like a casebook.[97] Moreover, "because gay persons know that the likelihood of a fair shake in the court system is remote, disputes are handled at the lowest possible level," the lawyer Rhonda Rivera remembered of these years. As a result, important cases were hidden in "lower courts, administrative tribunals, and lawyers' files," and unlikely to be seen by lawyers looking for previous cases for guidance.[98] One lawyer

94. Interview with Nan Hunter, conducted via Zoom, 2020.

95. Interview with Katherine Triantafillou, Boston, MA, 2011.

96. Urvashi Vaid "sat in stunned silence" to hear the topic of gay people in the law reduced to matters of "victimless crimes" (akin to prostitution) at Northeastern Law School in 1980. She and other classmates organized their own independent study. They called it "The Course That Dare Not Speak Its Name." Vaid, *Virtual Equality: The Mainstreaming of Gay and Lesbian Liberation* (New York: Anchor Books, 1995), 129–30. When regular courses began to appear in the curricula of law schools, Nan Hunter recalled, they were taught under "closet" names like "Topics in Constitutional History," because law students did not want references to homosexuality on their transcripts. Interview with Nan Hunter, conducted via Zoom, 2020.

97. As late as 1991, when the lawyer William Rubenstein approached publishers with the idea of a casebook dealing with gays and lesbians and the law, they weren't interested because so few relevant courses were taught in law schools. Rubenstein ended up publishing his case book with a nonprofit press. It sold out. Shortly thereafter, Nan Hunter and William Eskridge also published a sexuality casebook. William B. Rubenstein, "My Harvard Law School," *Harvard Civil Rights–Civil Liberties Law Review* 39 (2004): 326; Rhonda R. Rivera, "Queer Law: Sexual Orientation Law in the Mid-Eighties," *University of Dayton Law Review* 10 (1985): 462.

98. Rivera, "Queer Law," 462.

recalled using the legal research "checklist" that his professor had provided to systematically search for cases about gay people in Harvard's law library—"where no subject was too obscure for its own shelf"—and finding nothing.[99] All this made serving clients difficult, especially for solo practitioners, who were required to be masters of so many practice areas. Landlord/tenant, wills and estates, employment, "crimes against nature," public benefits, insurance, family law, immigration, and the military were among the many legal arenas where gay clients might have encountered issues.[100] In the early days, being able to phone a colleague for advice was a lifeline, and early networks, which eventually developed into gay bar associations, were key.[101]

Despite the challenges—not least of which were the morals qualification clauses for state bar admissions that worried many lawyers who were considering practicing openly—the field was growing.[102] Gay people were increasingly wanting to work with gay professionals more generally, and small law firms dedicated to serving the gay community began to "dot the landscape."[103] The emergence of local gay papers in some cities, coupled with a Supreme Court decision in 1977 that said lawyers could advertise,

99. Rubenstein, "My Harvard Law School," 318.

100. John Harbin Boddie remembered "crime against nature" cases and real estate transactions as some of the most common types of cases he handled in his gay law practice in North Carolina in the late 1970s. Lesbian practices did a lot of work for lesbian mothers who were fighting custody battles. Interview with John Harbin Boddie, conducted via Zoom, 2020. On custody fights in the 1970s and 1980s, see Daniel Winunwe Rivers, *Radical Relations: Lesbian Mothers, Gay Fathers, and Their Children in the United States since World War II* (Chapel Hill: University of North Carolina Press, 2013), 53–79.

101. The National Lesbian and Gay Law Association (now the National LGBT Bar Association) began as an informal meeting in 1987 and incorporated in 1989. (It was preceded by local gay bar associations in, for example, New York, San Francisco, and Los Angeles.) See James G. Leipold, "Stand and Be Recognized: The Emergence of a Visible LGBT Lawyer Demographic," *Southwestern Law Review* 42 (2013): 777–78; Gail Diane Cox, "Gay Lawyers Seek a National Voice," *National Law Journal*, December 12, 1988, 23.

102. John Harbin Boddie stayed out of gay bars as a law student until he had passed the bar exam because of the morals qualification for admission. Lawyer Abby Rubenfeld also remembered worrying about the morals qualification for the bar. Interview with John Harbin Boddie, conducted via Zoom, 2020; interview with Abby Rubenfeld, conducted via Zoom, 2020. "Every homosexual lawyer had heard of Harris Kimball, or someone like him," the *New York Times* opined in 1989 in reference to the Florida lawyer who was disbarred (in 1957, disbarment upheld in 1970) after an arrest for lewd conduct. E. R. Shipp, "Homosexual Lawyers Keep Fighting Barriers," *New York Times*, February 3, 1989, B11.

103. Interview with Michele Zavos, Washington, DC, 2021; William R. Rubenstein, "In Communities Begin Responsibilities: Obligations at the Gay Bar," *Hastings Law Journal* 48 (August 1997): 1114.

helped to sustain these businesses.[104] Five years after that decision, when Urvashi Vaid prepared a referral directory of openly gay lawyers doing gay legal work, she could identify one hundred such lawyers across the country.[105] Some of that momentum came not just from the liberationist ideals of the previous years, but from the way those political ideals mixed for some with the resurgence of professional ambition. After a decade marked by downward mobility, the career was creeping back in. This was a broader generational shift, but it carried lesbians and gay men along with it. A contemporary observer of lesbian politics noted that everyone who had dropped out was "dropping back in"; another remarked that every lesbian she knew was headed to law school.[106] For some of these lesbians, that transition prompted soul searching. Michele Zavos went to law school with social justice on her mind, but after years of doing political work in DC, some of it while collecting unemployment, she worried that it might be "copping out" in some way.[107] A renewed interest in careers among gay men, by contrast, may have been intensified by the epidemic itself. The effect of AIDS, concluded the anthropologist Stephen O. Murray, was to encourage gay men to invest their "energy elsewhere than in sexual marketplaces."[108]

AIDS created a lot of legal work right from the start. Many lawyers were skittish about taking on these clients because they did not want to work "on a problem perceived by some as a gay issue."[109] For this reason, openly gay solo practitioners, many of whom were women, filled a critical lacuna in the legal services landscape.[110] Some large cities also had local

104. Personal electronic communication from John Harbin Boddie, August 16, 2020. The Supreme Court case was *Bates v. State Bar of Arizona*, 433 U.S. 350 (1977).

105. Vaid, *Virtual Equality*, 130.

106. Interview with Blue Lundeen, conducted by Quinn, 1989, 253, box 1, Blue Lundeen Papers, 83-04, Lesbian Herstory Archives, Brooklyn, NY.

107. Interview with Michele Zavos, Washington, DC, 2021.

108. Stephen O. Murray, "Ethnic and Temporal Patterns of Gay Male Self-Identification and Migration to San Francisco," 1989, "W.C.—Theory—Queer" folder, box 100, Allan Bérubé Papers, GLBT Historical Society of Northern California.

109. Paul Albert, "Critical Need for Legal Assistance in AIDS-Related Issues," *Affiliate: A Publication of the Young Lawyers Division of the ABA* 12 (May/June 1987): 11. Law firms in general were no better than other employers in handling AIDS. Associates were fired, lawyers refused to depose people with AIDS (or showed up to depositions wearing masks and gloves), law offices were fumigated after a client with AIDS was present. See Michelle Gallen, "How Firms Face AIDS," *National Law Journal*, March 23, 1987, 1, 32–33.

110. It's likely that a majority of solo practitioners openly serving the gay community during these early years were lesbians. Gay men were as likely to go to big firms (while covering their queerness), a path that was less open to women in general. Interview with Michele Zavos, Washington, DC, 2021. Lesbian custody battles also created an urgent legal

gay bar associations that organized legal referrals for persons with AIDS, as well as trained lawyers to provide services on a pro bono basis.[111] AIDS-related news began "to take up a major part of each issue" of *Lesbian/Gay Law Notes*, remembered lawyer Arthur Leonard, who founded and edited the newsletter.[112] Simultaneously, guides for practitioners for dealing with AIDS began to appear.[113] Those guides made clear that AIDS lawyering was every bit as distinctive as AIDS nursing was, and as did the latter, required a far more holistic approach to clients in which their legal needs had to be considered in the context of their mental and physical health. In addition to examining their own feelings about both sexuality and death, a practitioner advised, AIDS lawyers needed to understand and trust the science. They had to accept that the virus was not transmitted casually, and show no fear, otherwise "fear would be transmitted to the client." In the early stages of illness, advising clients on how to stay covered under their health insurance was paramount. The usual advice was to not change jobs, even if it meant staying in a position the client disliked or passing up a better opportunity. Wills were another urgent legal need: one that was important to get settled before AIDS-related dementia set in, "documenting competency at every step." It was common for families of origin

---

need for lesbians that predated AIDS and may have helped spur the development of lesbian legal practices. Those practices also developed in relation to the elaborate lesbian feminist networks that were a natural constituency for lesbian lawyers in many locales. One fascinating glimpse into the way lesbian law practices were closely tied to lesbian feminist communities was the letter of support Nan Hunter (of Hunter and Polikoff) sent to Diana Press after it was vandalized (described in chapter 4). Hunter offered to hire a private investigator, and she also passed along the name of a feminist lawyer in San Francisco who had experience dealing with criminal matters. Nan Hunter to Dear Sisters, November 7, 1977, folder 3, box 4, Records of Diana Press, Special Collections, University of California–Los Angeles.

111. The AIDS Legal Referral Panel was created in San Francisco in 1983 as a committee of the gay bar association in that city, Bay Area Lawyers for Individual Freedom. See its website https://www.alrp.org/about/history; Janet Seldon and Tanya Nieman, "Lawyers *Can* Play an Important Role in the AIDS Crisis," *Affiliate: A Publication of the Young Lawyers Division of the ABA* 13 (May/June 1988): 4. In 1986, the Barristers Club of the Los Angeles bar also began to provide pro bono legal services for people with AIDS with a pool of nine volunteer attorneys. Genny McIntyre, "Barristers Hospice/AIDS Project," *Los Angeles Lawyer*, September 1988, 36–38.

112. Arthur Leonard noted that the first AIDS stories appeared in his *Lesbian/Gay Law Notes* around the summer of 1983. See Leonard, "Chronicling a Movement: A Symposium to Recognize the 20th Anniversary of the *Lesbian/Gay Law Notes*," *New York Law School Journal of Human Rights* 17 (2000): 2.

113. Abby R. Rubenfeld, ed., *AIDS Legal Guide* (New York: Lamba Legal Defense and Education Fund, 1984); *AIDS Practice Manual: A Legal and Educational Guide* (San Francisco: National Gay Rights Advocates / National Lawyers Guild, 1986).

to contest wills where a deceased son left property to a gay lover—even before AIDS, judges sometimes set aside a will because of the undue influence that the *homosexuality* of the testator had on the will. Practitioners warned that a gay couple's consultation with a lawyer was not privileged, as it would be with a married couple; the couple per se had no right to privacy in their communication with the lawyer. The numerous disabilities that gay people faced in their relationship to the law endlessly surfaced for those with AIDS.[114]

There was still more, much of it outside the usual run of wills and testaments. Lawyers needed to advise clients on how to make sure their end-of-life wishes would be carried out by doctors, who were seldom good at dealing with death, especially the death of young people. Lawyers needed to be prepared for their clients to raise the possibility of suicide, to potentially give the client the address of the Hemlock Society, and to also advise the client on the criminal aspects and the concept of accessory so no harm would be done to a surviving friend or lover.[115] As with the nurses on 5B, the incredibly rewarding nature of the work could offset the burnout only for so long. "No other group of clients has ever been as loving and life giving as the PWAs [persons with AIDS] with whom I work," a practitioner wrote, but still the victories were always pyrrhic ones. "I go to a funeral once a month. . . . I am in the hospital on the average of once a week. I see a PWA or HIV seropositive person as a new client probably twice a week. I receive a call from a PWA, an HIV seropositive person, or a loved one on the average of once a day," this Ohio lawyer wrote. "The complexity of each person's problems is unnerving." Every single interaction was "intense."[116]

———◆———

AIDS work helped build gay and lesbian law practices but probably had an even greater impact on lawyers working in the field of gay rights, which had also existed only in fledgling form before the epidemic. In 1972, a Manhattan lawyer named Bill Thom came across an appeal for the services

114. Rivera, "Lawyers, Clients, and AIDS," 883–928. See also William L. Earl and Judith Kavanaugh, "Meeting the AIDS Epidemic in the Courtroom: Practical Suggestions in Litigating Your First AIDS Case," *Nova Law Review* 12 (1988): 1203–23; Thea Foglietta Silverstein, "AIDS and Employment: An Epidemic Strikes the Workplace and the Law," *Whittier Law Review* 8 (1986): 651–80.

115. Rivera, "Lawyers, Clients, and AIDS," 897–900. The Hemlock Society was a right-to-die organization that was founded in 1980.

116. Ibid., 927.

of a gay lawyer in a newsletter. When he learned he was the *only* lawyer who had responded, he was convinced of the need to create a public interest firm that could advance gay rights. He modeled the Lambda Legal Defense and Education Fund, which was founded the following year as a nonprofit law firm, specifically on the Puerto Rican Legal Defense Fund, approved by the State of New York just a few months prior.[117] By the end of the decade, several other organizations had joined Lambda including Gay Rights Advocates and the Lesbian Rights Project in San Francisco, and Gay and Lesbian Advocates and Defenders in Massachusetts.[118]

Lambda, like its sister organizations, was in its early years severely underresourced, as well as constrained by how few lawyers would volunteer to take on gay rights cases. Lambda did relatively little gay rights litigation through the 1970s as a result, but when the organization began to share office space with the ACLU in 1979, access to the ACLU's organizational networks was a boon to Lambda's work. An even greater step forward was when Lambda was finally able to hire its first managing attorney.[119] Nashville lawyer Abby Rubenfeld, who had been in contact with Lambda on several lesbian custody cases over the years, was encouraged to apply and was offered the job. She arrived in Manhattan in January 1983, never having heard of HIV/AIDS, thinking her focus at Lambda would be repealing the sodomy laws that were used so destructively against lesbians fighting for custody of their children.[120]

The epidemic soon overwhelmed Lambda's workload, as it did for the other gay public interest firms.[121] Initially, few of those who sought assistance ended up filing lawsuits. "When a person with AIDS is fired, transferred or harassed because of his illness," one practitioner noted, "he often wishes to take the least stressful method of settlement; because of the cost in time, money, and energy, litigation is a poor investment in the

---

117. Ellen Ann Anderson, *Out of the Closets and Into the Courts: Legal Opportunity Structure and Gay Rights Litigation* (Ann Arbor: University of Michigan Press, 2009), 1–2. The three-judge panel assigned to review Lambda's application denied it, and Lambda "became its own first client, suing to establish its very right to exist." The court of appeals reversed, and Lambda was licensed to practice law in October 1973.

118. Ibid., 19, 34. The line between the private firm and the public interest firm was not always sharply drawn during these years. Both Gay Rights Advocates and Gay and Lesbian Advocates and Defenders overlapped with the private practices of their founders. See also the work of sociologist Jeff Kosbie, "Contested Identities: A History of LGBT Legal Mobilization" (PhD diss., Northwestern University, 2015), 124.

119. Anderson, *Out of the Closets*, 28–37.

120. Interview with Abby Rubenfeld, conducted via Zoom, 2020. It was often as "presumptive criminals" under state sodomy laws that lesbians lost custody of their children.

121. Ibid.; Kosbie, "Contested Identities," 261.

eyes of many PWAs."[122] When medical advancements meant that HIV-positive people lived longer and had the physical strength to fight cases in court, the docket increased exponentially.[123] But well before that, Lambda was feeling its way to a theory of discrimination that they could use with HIV/AIDS cases. An important early matter, which arose relatively soon after Rubenfeld arrived, was not an employment case at all but nonetheless involved the livelihood of the plaintiff. Dr. Joseph Sonnabend was an infectious diseases specialist who, in the late 1970s, also ran a private clinic in Greenwich Village treating individuals with sexually transmitted diseases. He was unusual among those who did this kind of work among gay men during these years, his attorney Bill Hibsher, a Lambda board member, emphasized. Other clinics set up to treat syphilis and gonorrhea among gay men tended to be run by "folks who went to offshore medical schools, were not highly trained or credentialed, but local candy store medical practices." When Sonnabend started seeing strange symptoms in men he treated in his practice, he was uniquely positioned to recognize the phenomenon, and soon he was not only providing care but independently conducting research on the illness.[124]

In early 1983, the owners of the cooperative apartment building where Sonnabend had his practice told him they were terminating his lease because he was treating men with AIDS. Sonnabend asked Hibsher if he had a case. Both Hibsher and Lambda agreed that he did. Hibsher then asked the New York State attorney general to join the case representing the people of New York, which they did. But it was not immediately obvious how to litigate the case. Hibsher recalled sitting around a table with the other lawyers trying to come up with the right strategy to challenge the harm Sonnabend had suffered. It only took about twenty minutes to realize that the "only viable option was handicap law." Because Sonnabend himself was not sick, Hibsher added two of his patients as plaintiffs. These were the AIDS activists Michael Callen and Richard Berkowitz who, along with Sonnabend, had authored the early safe-sex pamphlet *How to Have Sex in an Epidemic*.[125]

Hibsher remembered running into the lawyer representing the co-op, a man he knew, just as the case was filed. The lawyer said, "Bill, do you realize that this doctor's patients have AIDS?" He said it as though he were revealing something that Hibsher, a reputable attorney, didn't know. "He

122. Rivera, "Lawyers, Clients, and AIDS," 912.
123. See ACLU AIDS Project, *Epidemic of Fear*, 41.
124. Interview with Bill Hibsher, conducted via telephone, 2020.
125. Ibid.

could not understand why I would represent this guy who had patients with AIDS!" Despite the broader climate of social hostility in 1983, Hibsher realized that Sonnabend's chances were very good when he learned that the judge assigned to the case was a progressive man whom Hibsher had seen in years past at dinners Lambda hosted for the legal community. This judge "lived in sin" with another (woman) judge, and in 1983, "that was a relevant factoid."[126]

Hibsher's intuition about where the case was headed was correct, and late in 1983, the trial court granted a preliminary injunction that enabled Sonnabend to keep his lease. The court subsequently ruled that AIDS was a physical handicap within the meaning of the state human rights law.[127] It was the first decision in the country that relied on what was then called "handicap law" to protect persons with AIDS from discrimination, and Lambda would soon attempt to use the same theory in employment cases under federal (as well as state) law. The relevant federal law was the 1973 Vocational Rehabilitation Act, which extended the protections of Title VII of the 1964 Civil Rights Act to federal employees who were "handicapped" but "otherwise qualified" to perform their jobs. The law's coverage did not extend to most private employers. But section 503 covered businesses that held federal contracts, and section 504 extended coverage to employers that received federal funds, including hospitals.[128]

The first case, then, to test whether federal disability law could be used to protect persons who had or were perceived to have AIDS was brought in 1984 by Lambda Legal and a cooperating attorney in North Carolina named John Harbin Boddie. The plaintiff in the case, John Wesley Putnam, was a nurse at Charlotte Memorial Hospital who sought medical treatment from the hospital's physician after experiencing significant weight loss and fatigue. Despite that doctor's pledge to Putnam that he would reveal only that his patient had hepatitis B, the doctor subsequently reported to the hospital's director of nursing and personnel director that he believed the nurse had AIDS. As a result of this disclosure, the hospital placed Putnam on a medical leave of absence. Another doctor on the

126. Ibid.

127. The opinion in *People v. 49 W. 12 Tenants Corp* was not officially published but was reported in the *New York Law Journal*, October 17, 1983, 1 (83 NY Sup. Ct.) (No. 43604). Subsequently, the New York State Division of Human Rights issued a policy statement on the matter. That is published in *CCH Emp. Prac. 26165*.

128. Jeffrey A. Mello, *AIDS and the Law of Workplace Discrimination* (Boulder: Westview, 1995), 20–21. One of the earliest employment cases to rule that AIDS was protected under a state law protecting the disabled from discrimination was *Cronon v. New England Telephone Company*, 41 FEP 1268 (Mass. Super. Ct., Suffolk County, 1986).

hospital staff then arranged to give Putnam a position in his clinic that involved no direct patient contact. Putnam spent exactly one day working in this clinic before the hospital's personnel director showed up to order him to leave the premises.[129] Despite being subsequently presented with the opinion by several independent doctors that Putnam could be safely reemployed, the hospital did not budge. One month after being put on involuntary medical leave, the nurse's pay was suspended. Putnam was especially disappointed, Boddie remembered, that medical professionals weren't following the available science in their handling of him.[130]

Boddie's initial attempt to reach a settlement with the hospital was immediately rebuffed. He remembered being surprised at how dismissive the hospital's lawyers were; how "the idea that someone with AIDS could claim discrimination against the hospital seemed frivolous" to them. Boddie then sent a complaint letter to the Office of Civil Rights (OCR) within the Department of Health and Human Services (HHS), which adjudicated section 504 complaints brought under the Rehabilitation Act. Boddie heard back from the Atlanta office, who said they would investigate, and initially, all seemed to be proceeding as expected. Boddie learned that HHS usually took three or four months to issue findings in Rehabilitation Act cases, and he assumed that was the timeline.[131]

Months turned into years with no decision from HHS in Putnam's case. Boddie's understanding was that the investigation had actually been completed by the regional office but was being quashed by the political appointees who ran the OCR. Meanwhile, Boddie watched Putnam's body deteriorate. Putnam remained committed to his case and urged Boddie to keep it going after his death. A year and a half after Putnam first filed his complaint, with no response from HHS, John Wesley Putnam died at the age of twenty-seven.[132] Around the same time, in February 1986, an OCR regional manager named Hal Freeman resigned in protest over the agency's failure to process AIDS cases like Putnam's; by this time sixteen

129. John Harbin Boddie to Office of Civil Rights, Department of Health and Human Services, July 9, 1984, 250–51, in US Congress, House, Hearings before a Subcommittee of the Committee on Government Operations, *Oversight of the Office for Civil Rights at the Department of Health and Human Services*, 99th Cong., 2nd sess., August 6 and 7, 1986; interview with John Harbin Boddie, conducted via Zoom, 2020.

130. Interview with John Harbin Boddie, conducted via Zoom, 2020. The CDC had already issued guidelines stating that health-care workers did not pose a significant risk of transmission to patients in "CDC Guidelines for Health Care Workers with AIDS," *Infection Control* 4, no. 4 (1983): 326–49.

131. Interview with John Harbin Boddie, conducted via Zoom, 2020.

132. Ibid.

other AIDS-related section 504 cases were languishing. Freeman's resignation letter reported that the director of HHS's Office of Civil Rights had said that she did not want to lend "an aura of dignity" to AIDS cases. It was Freeman's conclusion that the agency's decision to move "cautiously" stemmed from "prejudice toward gay people," and also that HHS would avoid taking jurisdiction over the issue of AIDS "as long as possible."[133]

In the immediate aftermath of Putnam's death and Freeman's resignation, OCR punted to the Department of Justice, asking them for an opinion on the question of whether section 504 of the Rehabilitation Act protected persons with AIDS from discrimination. Putnam's parents entered into a settlement with the hospital and, as part of the settlement, agreed to withdraw their section 504 claim. Abby Rubenfeld wrote a letter to OCR explaining the family's decision but requested that the agency issue a determination anyway. "Given the length of time your office has been studying and investigating this case, as well as the fact that you must be close to making a finding," she urged, "I would nonetheless encourage you to pursue the matter as an agency action despite the forced withdrawal by the executors of [Putnam's] estate."[134] It was an unusual request, but one that indicated that the pressure point had shifted from law to politics. As a result of the "wide attention" given Freeman's protest resignation, as well as Lambda's likely appeals to allies in Congress, the Committee on Government Operations set oversight hearings for the summer of 1986. One day before OCR director Betty Lou Dotson testified before that committee, her office finally issued its ruling in the Putnam case. "I am sure [Putnam's] survivors will be fascinated by your conclusions," Lambda's executive director, Tom Stoddard, remarked bitterly to Dotson. The conclusion, much too late for Putnam, was nonetheless significant: Charlotte Memorial Hospital had violated section 504 of the 1973 Rehabilitation Act by "discriminatorily denying the complainant individualized consideration for possible reemployment."[135]

133. Hal Freeman to Betty Lou Dotson, Director, Office of Civil Rights, February 20, 1986, 19–24; "Statement of Hal Freeman," 72; Testimony of Betty Lou Dotson, 248: all in US Congress, House, Hearings before a Subcommittee of the Committee on Government Operations, *Oversight of the Office for Civil Rights at the Department of Health and Human Services*, 99th Cong., 2nd sess., August 6 and 7, 1986.

134. Opening Statement of Chairman Weiss, 2, and Abby R. Rubenfeld to Joan Burton, June 4, 1986, 257–58, both in US Congress, House, Hearings before a Subcommittee of the Committee on Government Operations, *Oversight of the Office for Civil Rights at the Department of Health and Human Services*, 99th Cong., 2nd sess., August 6 and 7, 1986.

135. "Hal Freeman, 52, AIDS Protestor," *New York Times*, August 20, 1988, 10; see also Testimony of Betty Lou Dotson, 248–49, and Marie Chretian, Regional Manager, to

That historic decision—the first to affirm AIDS was indeed covered under the Rehabilitation Act—was one of the only bright spots in what might be considered the nadir of the legal AIDS epidemic, which hit around 1985–86. The *other* bright spot was the ACLU's decision to finally open its Gay and Lesbian Rights Project, heavily focused on HIV/AIDS, and the arrival of Nan Hunter to run the office. But Hunter started this position the same month the Supreme Court handed down its venomous decision in *Bowers v. Hardwick*, upholding state laws criminalizing sodomy as consistent with "millennia of moral teaching." As Hunter recalled, "it was about as strong a message of contempt toward gay people by the court as one could imagine."[136] Law professor and advocate Arthur Leonard also pinpointed the mid-1980s as the moment when the "ramifications of AIDS hit the workplaces of America with full force," and "employment lawyers became concerned with the legal issues surrounding AIDS in the workplace." Rising public awareness of the epidemic exacerbated workplace problems "because the public apparently did not believe the statements by public health officials that AIDS was not spread by casual contact." The arrival of a reliable test for antibodies to the HIV virus, which should have been a boon by limiting the epidemic's spread, felt ominous as some employers hoped to use it to remove seropositive individuals from their workplaces or to screen out potential hires.[137] Ben Schatz, who had joined National Gay Rights Advocates in 1985 to work full time on HIV-AIDS, remembered an "avalanche" of calls during this period, five to ten a day, "from all over the country."[138]

The Department of Justice's answer to the query posed by the Office of Civil Rights within HHS was a grim middecade capstone. The

---

Dr. [redacted], 259–67, both in US Congress, House, Hearings before a Subcommittee of the Committee on Government Operations, *Oversight of the Office for Civil Rights at the Department of Health and Human Services*, 99th Cong., 2nd sess., August 6 and 7, 1986. The unpublished decision is now known as *Doe v. Charlotte Memorial Hospital*. "Putnam" became "Doe" at the wishes of John Wesley Putnam's parents after he died. (Putnam's parents are now deceased.) Putnam himself was very proud of his legal fight and hoped it would be known as the "Putnam case." Interview with John Harbin Boddie, conducted via Zoom, 2020.

136. *Bowers v. Hardwick*, 478 U.S. 186 (1986); interview with Nan Hunter, conducted via Zoom, 2020.

137. Arthur Leonard, "AIDS and Employment Law," *Hofstra Law Review* 14 (1985–86): 11–13. As late as 1987, the Gallop Poll reported that roughly a quarter of respondents believed that AIDS could be transmitted by food handlers, by sharing a drinking glass, or by being sneezed on. Linda Villarosa, "When Someone at Work Has AIDS," *Dealing with AIDS* (UAW Human Resource Center, 1988), box 2, Aetna Insurance AIDS Collection.

138. Kosbie, *Contested Identities*, 261, 229.

forty-nine-page opinion, written in 1986 by assistant attorney general
Charles C. Cooper, conceded that discrimination based on physical disability caused by AIDS might violate the Rehabilitation Act for those who
were "otherwise qualified" to perform their jobs, but with a significant
catch. The Cooper memorandum asserted that the law would not protect persons with AIDS or those infected with the virus that caused AIDS
"if discrimination was based on fear of the individual's 'real or perceived'
ability to spread the disease."[139] Even if that fear were irrational, DOJ
concluded, a discriminatory action (based on fear) was legitimate. As a
result, as Arthur Leonard testified before Congress, "an employer who is
aware of the Justice Department opinion and who wants to remove from
his workforce someone infected with this virus or who has ... AIDS would
merely have to state convincingly that he is afraid of contagion in order to
not be covered by the statute according to the Justice Department." "So its
practical effect is to tell employers how [to] lawfully get rid of people with
AIDS."[140] Leonard's conclusion was correct. Lawyers observed that firings
surged in response to the memorandum.[141]

The next year, in 1987, the Supreme Court moved closer to resolv-
ing the discrepancy that existed between the Cooper memorandum and
HHS's (albeit reluctant) decision against Charlotte Memorial Hospital in
the Putnam case. The landmark ruling did not involve AIDS, but another
contagious disease. In *School Board of Nassau County v. Arline*, the court
ruled in favor of a Florida schoolteacher who had been removed from her
post because of tuberculosis. Specifically, the court affirmed the decision
of the court of appeals that a contagious disease was a handicapping condition under the Rehabilitation Act, whether the condition was an existing
or past impairment, and it rejected the claim that discrimination against a
person with a contagious disease could be lawful if it was based on fear of

---

139. Eric Eckholm, "Ruling on AIDS Provoking Dismay," *New York Times*, June 27,
1986, 17; Arthur S. Leonard to Hon. Robert Windom, Assistant Secretary of Health,
Department of Health and Human Services, July 11, 1986, "AIDS in the Workplace, 86–87"
folder, in Director's Subject Files, Record Group 443, National Archives and Records
Administration, College Park, MD.

140. Arthur S. Leonard to Hon. Robert Windom, Assistant Secretary of Health, Department of Health and Human Services, July 11, 1986, "AIDS in the Workplace, 86–87" folder,
in Director's Subject Files, Record Group 443; Statement by Professor Arthur S. Leonard,
New York Law School, 82–87, and Testimony of Mr. Leonard, 310, both in US Congress,
House, Hearings before a Subcommittee of the Committee on Government Operations,
Oversight of the Office for Civil Rights at the Department of Health and Human Services,
99th Cong., 2nd sess., August 6 and 7, 1986.

141. "Employers Ponder AIDS Cost Containment Options," *Benefits News Analysis*, 18,
undated, "Economic Issues" folder, box 2, Aetna AIDS Insurance Collection.

contagion. The court explicitly refrained from considering *asymptomatic* carriers of infectious diseases, which was the issue that drove the odious Cooper memorandum, but many analysts at the time viewed the decision as extending coverage to persons infected with the AIDS virus.[142] The court asserted that to be protected under the statute an individual still had to be "otherwise qualified," meaning that "the person with a contagious disease could not pose a 'significant risk' to others in the workplace [that] could not be eliminated by reasonable accommodation."[143] That understanding, and its specific application to those infected with HIV, was codified by Congress in the Civil Rights Restoration Act (CRRA) of 1988. This law, which amended section 504 of the Rehabilitation Act, asserted that when a "handicap" discrimination claim was based on an infectious disease, the only relevant questions were, in the words of one legal scholar, "the actual threat to others posed by the presence of the individual in the workplace and the individual's ability to perform the job."[144]

These developments seemed to point toward a straightforward legal analysis, and more robust protection, for individuals claiming discrimination based on AIDS, HIV infection, or the perception of either.[145] But limitations in coverage for those who did not work for employers who received federal funds or who were not covered under state or local laws meant that protection was spotty on the ground.[146] An even greater prob-

142. See Arthur S. Leonard, "AIDS in the Workplace," 112–13, "Sec. 504" folder, box 4457, Records of the ACLU; Chai R. Feldblum, "Workplace Issues: HIV and Discrimination," in *AIDS Agenda: Emerging Issues in Civil Rights*, ed. Nan B. Hunter and William Rubenstein (New York: New Press, 1992), 274–75.

143. Feldblum, "Workplace Issues," 275. On the court's development of a test based on four factors to determine the standard of "otherwise qualified," see Mello, *AIDS and the Law of Workplace Discrimination*, 28–29.

144. Mello, *AIDS and the Law of Workplace Discrimination*, 34–35. On the CRRA, enacted over President Reagan's veto in 1988, see Chai Feldblum, "Civil Rights Restoration Act of 1988 Coverage of Contagious Diseases under Section 504," "Memo to Affiliates, 6/13/88" folder, box 4645, Records of the ACLU. In the fall of 1988, the Department of Justice rescinded the Cooper memorandum and declared that the law applied to asymptomatic carriers. "The impairment of HIV infection cannot be meaningfully separated from clinical AIDS," Assistant Attorney General Douglas Kmiec wrote in a memo dated October 6, 1988. Kmiec memo, "US Dept. of Justice HIV Civil Rights Opinion" folder, box 6, Records of the Human Rights Campaign, Rare and Manuscript Collections, Cornell University, Ithaca, NY.

145. Feldblum, "Workplace Issues," 276.

146. A survey conducted by National Gay Rights Advocates in September 1986 revealed that one-third of states did not forbid AIDS-based discrimination. Leonard, "AIDS in the Workplace," 114. The ACLU also reported "widespread anomalies" in coverage. See "The Gaps in Anti-discrimination Law," in Executive Summary document, ACLU AIDS Policy Update, July 16, 1990, "APN Mailing—July 16, 1990" folder, box 4641, Records of the ACLU.

lem than gaps in coverage, however, was each potential plaintiff's impending and nearly inevitable death. Employers knew that time was on their side, and defendants regularly ran the clock out on dying men. "I became an expert in what are called 'Dead Man's Statutes,'" Katherine Franke, who ran the AIDS and Employment Project during these years, remembered, which govern "who inherits a claim when [the plaintiff] dies."[147] Family members—and in extremely rare cases, if arrangements had been made, friends, lovers, or other advocates—could continue a lawsuit.[148] But in practice, grieving parents (or grieving partners, or grieving friends) rarely had the energy or the will to continue these lawsuits. But when they did—"I do want to make very clear that a civil rights complaint does survive a person's death!" pronounced one lawyer, suing Raytheon for firing a man who subsequently died of AIDS—the likelihood of prevailing in court was rising.[149]

The main exception, even a decade into the epidemic, was health-care workers, who continued to be among the most vulnerable of employees with HIV/AIDS.[150] One study found that as late as 1990, 73 percent of HIV-positive health-care workers feared losing their positions, even after the CDC had established guidelines for "universal precautions" that advised treating *all* blood, rather than only blood from members of high-risk groups, as potentially infectious in health-care settings. Those employees' fears were, in fact, well grounded. One physician, for example, vowed to fight for reinstatement of his medical license after it was suspended in the wake of his AIDS diagnosis. He conceded his fight was mostly for psychological reasons. "I earned my license," he stated, and

---

David Webber, who founded the AIDS Law Project in Philadelphia, further noted that state and local laws were limited by anemic enforcement provisions. Interview with David Webber, conducted via Zoom, 2021.

147. Interview with Katherine Franke, conducted via Zoom, 2020. See also Art Leonard, "AIDS, Employment and Unemployment," *Ohio State Law Journal* 49 (1989): 944.

148. Law professor Katherine Franke noted that in San Francisco, for example, the Human Rights Commission sought a regulation to allow persons other than biological relatives to carry a case forward. Interview with Katherine Franke, conducted via Zoom, 2020.

149. Gloria Barrios, "AIDS and Employment," *Whitter Law Review* 9 (1987): 260. Barrios represented a quality control analyst who was fired by Raytheon Corporation in 1984 and died in 1985.

150. In nonhealth employment it was becoming increasingly settled "as law and policy that there is no infection control reason to exclude persons with AIDS or HIV infection." Mark Barnes, Nicholas Rango, Gary R. Burke, and Linda Chiarello, "The HIV-Infected Health Care Professional: Employment Policies and Public Health," *Law, Medicine, and Health Care* 18 (Winter 1990): 312.

"intend to die with it in my hand."[151] For gay nurses with even less social power, the "AIDS legal crisis" remained all the more inseparably bound with the "AIDS medical crisis."[152]

The clearest illustration in the late 1980s was the case of Kevin Leckelt, a licensed practical nurse who had worked for several years at Terrebone General Medical Center (TGMC) in Houma, Louisiana, when his lover of eight years was admitted to the medical center with AIDS-related complications. In the wake of that admission, Leckelt's employers began to insist that the nurse get tested for HIV and bring them the results. Leckelt was afraid of losing his job if he tested positive, stalled for some days, and subsequently was placed on a leave of absence. He eventually refused outright to get a test. As a result, TGMC, which had not determined whether or not they would terminate Leckelt's employment if he tested positive, told him he could not return to work. During this same period, the infection control practitioner at the hospital learned that Leckelt had been treated for a lymph node condition that might have been an early symptom of AIDS, had suffered bouts of syphilis, and was also a hepatitis B carrier. About a month after his standoff with the hospital began, Leckelt's partner died of AIDS. That was enough for the hospital, which fired Leckelt for insubordination in May 1986.[153]

With Lambda Legal and the ACLU representing him, Leckelt filed suit a few months later. The district court sided with the hospital, finding that Leckelt's termination was justified because a hospital "has a right to require . . . testing in order to fulfill its obligation to its employees and to the public concerning infection control and health and safety."[154] Leckelt decided to appeal. In addition to violations of equal protection and privacy under the Fourteenth Amendment, Leckelt claimed he had been unlawfully discriminated against under state disability law and section 504 of the federal Rehabilitation Act. Leckelt's legal team claimed that as long as the nurse observed the CDC's guidance on universal precautions, the risk of his

151. Benjamin Schatz, Medical Expertise Retention Program, "'May God and the Community Help Us All': Results of a Survey of HIV-Positive and 'High Risk' Untested Health Care Workers," "APN 10/21/91" folder, box 4641, Records of the ACLU.

152. "The AIDS legal crisis is a crucial part of the AIDS medical crisis," lawyer Ben Schatz testified, "and cannot be separated." Testimony of Benjamin Schatz, 7, Public Hearing on AIDS/ARC Related Discrimination, February 4, 1986, San Francisco Human Rights Commission.

153. For an excellent synopsis of the facts in the case, see "In the Courts," *Health Span* 7 (October 1990): 28–30. See also *Leckelt v. Board of Commissioners of Hospital District No. 1*, 714 F.Supp. 1377 (E.D. LA, 1989); *Leckelt v. Board of Commissioners of Hospital District No. 1*, 909 F.2d 820 (5th Cir., 1990).

154. *Leckelt v. Board of Commissioners of Hospital District No. 1*, 714 F.Supp. 1377 (E.D. LA, 1989).

transmitting the virus to patients was extremely low.[155] Judge Garwood concurred that the risk of transmission was low and reduced further by the use of universal precautions, but his analysis differed from that of Leckelt's attorneys in so far as "there is no cure for HIV or AIDS at this time, and the potential harm of HIV infection is extremely high."[156] But at the same time that the hospital had fired Leckelt, it had allowed a female nurse who had a needlestick exposure from a patient with AIDS to continue her duties. The appeals court, according to observers at the time, tolerated "this differential treatment, finding justification for the singling out of Leckelt, since he was known to be a homosexual, a group at high risk for contracting HIV and AIDS." The result "was the exclusion of an LPN from employment based on marginal evidence of risk to patients."[157] In reality, the risk of transmission from *patient to nurse* was much higher, and evidence mounted of residents and interns refusing to train and work in areas of the country with high seroprevalence rates.[158] Indeed, away from special places like ward 5B at San Francisco General, nurses like Kevin Leckelt who were able to work but lost their positions because of an actual or suspected diagnosis were an underutilized resource in the fight against the epidemic.[159]

In 1990, when Congress passed the Americans with Disabilities Act (ADA), it seemed like a turning point. That law blended the substantive provisions

155. "In the Courts," 29. On the evolution of the CDC's specific policy on HIV in the health-care workplace, see Barnes et al., "HIV-Infected Health Care Professional," 314.

156. *Leckelt v. Board of Commissioners of Hospital District No. 1*, 909 F.2d 820 (5th Cir., 1990). Some lawyers and public health experts pointed out the double standard at work in hospitals' adoption of a "zero risk" policy only for HIV/AIDS. Health-care workers' drug and alcohol use, psychiatric difficulties, fatigue, and marital troubles posed a greater danger to patients' health, but hospitals were generally willing to tolerate some of that risk. See Barnes et al., "HIV-Infected Health Care Professional," 322.

157. Barnes et al., "HIV-Infected Health Care Professional," 318.

158. Ibid., 321. "Health care workers' concerns about becoming sick and dying following occupational exposure to HIV," the National Research Council warned during these years, "may be exacerbated by worries about breach of confidentiality, loss of employment and employee benefits, and possible economic ruin." Quoted in Albert R. Jonsen and Jeff Stryker, *The Social Impact of AIDS in the United States* (Washington, DC: National Academies Press, 1993), 60. In 1987, the American Nurses Association worried about these same issues. See Mary E. Foley memo, "AIDS and the Impact on Workplace Policies," circa 1987, "Bill Rubenstein" folder, box 4456, Records of the ACLU.

159. Kevin Leckelt lived until 1999. See Find a Grave entry for him at https://www.findagrave.com/memorial/159864745/kevin-m-leckelt.

of the 1973 Rehabilitation Act with the procedural provisions of Title VII of the 1964 Civil Rights Act, so disabled persons, including those with AIDS or HIV infection, received "precisely the same well-defined equal employment opportunities provided to other protected classes under Title VII."[160] It was a momentous civil rights achievement and the culmination of a brilliant and novel partnership between gay and disability rights activists.[161] The law remedied the gaps in coverage under the Rehabilitation Act and, as a result, went a long way to quieting the legal epidemic inside the medical epidemic. Its passage—as well as the broader human need to find silver linings in cataclysmic events—has also led some commentators to the conclusion that the AIDS crises resulted in forward momentum for gay rights generally, and in employment in particular.[162] That is partially true, but only partially.

On the one hand, while the early years of the AIDS epidemic had driven many back into the closet, by the late 1980s, it was having the opposite effect. Illness forced some people out of hiding, but for some others who were neither sick nor infected, covering their queerness on the job and elsewhere was simply becoming less tenable. The idea that "silence equals death" spread beyond the members of the direct-action group ACT UP, who popularized the slogan. The impulse to come out during these years—an impulse shared by a larger, more mainstream constituency than was true during the liberationist period—had a noticeable impact on the visibility of gay life in the culture more broadly.[163] Simultaneously, AIDS turned gay issues into national issues. It was "the first time anyone had to pay attention to this community," Nan Hunter recalled; "we were writing op-eds and appearing on television shows." Important platforms opened up that had not existed before, and AIDS made gay people, the lawyer William Rubenstein observed, "'authority figures' on a legal issue of critical

160. Feldblum, "Workplace Issues," 276–77; Charles J. Nau, "The ADA and HIV: What Employers Need to Know" (Washington, DC: National Leadership Coalition on AIDS, undated), 3, "7712" folder, box 7, Records of the Human Rights Campaign.

161. Julie Kosterlitz, "Joining Forces," *National Journal*, January 28, 1989, 194–99.

162. Elizabeth A. Armstrong, *Forging Gay Identities: Organizing Sexuality in San Francisco, 1950–1994* (Chicago: University of Chicago Press, 2002), 167. (Armstrong herself has argued the opposite position, as discussed below.) For one political scientist's account that put the AIDS crisis at the center of gay rights advances, see Jeremiah J. Garretson, *The Path to Gay Rights: How Activism and Coming Out Changed Public Opinion* (New York: New York University Press, 2018).

163. Suzanna Danuta Walters, *All the Rage: The Story of Gay Visibility in America* (Chicago: University of Chicago Press, 2001), 50; interview with Urvashi Vaid, New York, NY, 2015.

importance."[164] A remarkable corollary was the place of lesbians in AIDS law and politics, especially as gay men became sick.[165]

Relatedly, gay rights organizations expanded and professionalized as a result of the epidemic. Part of that change was the entry into gay politics of "a new generation of leaders who were upwardly mobile and educated at elite institutions," according to the historian Jeffrey Escoffier. "This new leadership was often drawn from those directly affected by AIDS, who in the past might have pursued careers along more conventional lines." This cohort brought not only a different skill set but contacts and donors to the gay movement.[166] AIDS service organizations burgeoned, creating a new industry in which many openly gay people worked. By the early 1990s, there were nearly one thousand AIDS service groups across the country.[167] AIDS also had a dramatic impact on the gay legal field. Between 1985 and 1987 alone, the budgets of gay legal organizations doubled, and some even tripled. Much of that support came from bequests by men who had succumbed to the virus.[168]

That institutionalization, however, did not parlay into more robust employment protection for gay people during the decade. There is even some suggestive evidence that as employers become more aware of legal protections based on disability law for persons with AIDS—"I know it's illegal" to fire an employee with AIDS, one business owner asked, "so what am I supposed to do now?"—incidences of discrimination against gays and lesbians actually continued to rise.[169] Yet, with the exception of the public employment cases of the late 1960s and early 1970s, courts generally were not helpful in securing employment rights for gays. "Legal frames do not

164. Interview with Nan Hunter, conducted via Zoom, 2020; Rubenstein, "In Communities Begin Responsibilities," 1113.

165. Abby Rubenfeld and Nan Hunter were two very prominent figures, but there were many others. For example, "few realize that many of the AIDS lobbyists are lesbians," Chai Feldblum and Laurie Markowitz observed in 1989. "Inside the Washington Lobby," *Western Express*, February 24–March 9, 1989, 33.

166. Jeffrey Escoffier, "Fabulous Politics: Gay, Lesbian, and Queer Movements, 1969–1999," in *The World the Sixties Made: Politics and Culture in Recent America*, ed. Van Gosse and Richard Moser (Philadelphia: Temple University Press, 2003), 208. Urvashi Vaid valued the contribution of this new cohort of activists, while also offering a clear-eyed assessment of the way their entry may have made gay politics more conservative. Vaid, *Virtual Equality*, 91.

167. Vaid, *Virtual Equality*, 91.

168. Kosbie, *Contested Identities*, 258.

169. George Suncin, Chair, Human Rights Commission City and County of San Francisco, to Colleagues, February 16, 1988; Human Rights Commission, "Report on Sexual Orientation and AIDS Discrimination, 1986–87, folders 11–12, box 114, Records of the National Gay and Lesbian Task Force.

lend themselves to gay rights claims concerning employment," explained the political scientist Ellen Anderson, "except in those jurisdictions with gay rights laws on the books."[170] But those jurisdictions were few and far between, and legislative victories for gays in the AIDS era were rare.[171] After 1982, when Wisconsin became the first state in the nation to pass a law protecting gay people in employment, momentum on antidiscrimination law stalled completely until 1989, when Massachusetts became only the second state to pass a gay rights law.[172]

In most places in the years in between, legislative initiatives foundered as a rapidly growing antigay political movement—which had cut its teeth opposing local ordinances like the one the evangelical Anita Bryant campaigned against in Florida in the late 1970s—discovered the rising power of AIDS-phobia in its campaigns.[173] By the mid-1980s, the debate over gay rights was "completely shaped by AIDS," and once the specter of the virus was deployed in any given campaign, antidiscrimination bills were handily defeated.[174] A fairly common tactic was the one used by Republican state senator John T. Doolittle in California against proposed gay rights legislation there. Doolittle warned the legislature against taking an action that would require the "hiring of homosexuals" to be the "hygienist who cleans your teeth, the health-care workers who man the hospitals, the people in restaurants who prepare and serve your food."[175] AIDS was an even stronger fund-raising tool for the right than abortion was, Nan Hunter remembered, and it "brought anti-gay politics to a new level."[176]

---

170. Anderson, *Out of the Closets and Into the Courts*, 174. The political scientist Katie Zuber similarly observed that employment cases were the most prevalent form of discrimination cases filed by LGBTs, but also the most likely to lose in the courts. Katherine Zuber, "Lobbying to Lawsuits: Optimistic Biases and Tactical Transitions in the Movement for LGBT Equality" (PhD diss., State University of New York–Albany, 2017), 37.

171. Terry Gross interview with AIDS lawyer David Webber on *Fresh Air* radio program, February 21, 1986, https://freshairarchive.org/guests/david-w-webber; Peter Freiberg, "Washington State County Oks Job Rights," *Advocate*, January 21, 1986, 13.

172. William Turner, "'The Gay Rights State': Wisconsin's Pioneering Legislation to Prohibit Discrimination Based on Sexual Orientation," *Wisconsin Women's Law Review* 23 (Spring 2007): 91–131; Peter Cicchino et al., "Sex, Lies, and Civil Rights: A Critical History of the Massachusetts Gay Civil Rights Bill," *Harvard Civil Rights–Civil Liberties Review* 549 (1991): 549–631.

173. On the antigay campaigns of Anita Bryant and also California state senator John Briggs, see Clendinen and Nagourney, *Out for Good*, 291–311, 377–90.

174. Ibid., 526.

175. Chris Bowman, "A Vote for Gay Rights," *Coming Up!*, March 1984, 34.

176. Interview with Nan Hunter, conducted via Zoom, 2020.

In the midst of an unprecedented crisis, gay rights activists responded with a political strategy of their own: they "de-gayed" AIDS. "De-gaying meant removing the stigma of homosexuality from the stigma of AIDS in order to win the access and attention we needed," activist and lawyer Urvashi Vaid remembered. This was a deliberate political choice—the term was actually coined by two gay activists middecade—and one that seemed appropriate to the circumstances.[177] They were dealing with a disease that had life-or-death consequences and was never confined to gay men. But in practice, "de-gaying" meant not only separating the AIDS movement from gay rights, but consciously setting the gay rights agenda aside so the campaign focused on AIDS could succeed. "This is not a gay rights bill," the ACLU's Chai Feldblum insisted of legislation that eventually became the ADA. "If I fired you," she clarified, "because I said people who are gay make me nervous, are immoral, or perverse, this bill will not help you."[178] That kind of messaging was essential to the ADA's passage. So was language contained in the bill specifying that homosexuality and bisexuality, along with "pedophilia, compulsive gambling, and pyromania," were excluded from the definition of disability.[179]

De-gaying AIDS had broader consequences than helping to get legislation passed. In the analysis of sociologist Elizabeth Armstrong, it produced a competing field that overtook gay civil rights.[180] Probably no one felt that more acutely than the lesbian lawyers who saw the other legal crisis of the 1980s—lesbian custody battles—backburnered as time and money was poured into AIDS. These were issues that became "internally difficult," the lawyer Katherine Franke remembered, compounded by the feeling that none of the lesbians "ever thought any of the guys would show up for them."[181] A decade of work went into pressing ahead on AIDS-specific issues, Urvashi Vaid wrote, "while avoiding gay and lesbian rights issues."[182]

For gay employment prospects, then, the AIDS era began and remained something of a disaster, certainly in the medium term when AIDS stirred the religious right to new levels of efficacy; bolstered antigay politics inside

177. Vaid, *Virtual Equality*, 75.

178. Julie Kosterlitz, "Joining Forces," *National Journal*, January 28, 1989, 199.

179. Cicchino et al., "Sex, Lies, and Civil Rights," 555.

180. Armstrong, *Forging Gay Identities*, 156.

181. Interview with Katherine Franke, conducted via Zoom, 2020; interview with Abby Rubenfeld, conducted via Zoom, 2020.

182. Vaid, *Virtual Equality*, 75.

state legislatures, Congress, and the White House; and sucked resources away to fight on even more pressing fronts.[183] If there is any solace to be found during these gruesome years, it is somewhat harder to see. But the difficulty of forward momentum in the federal government, in the states, and in the courts may have encouraged reformers to look to other sectors. The most obvious—given especially the channel through which health benefits flowed in the American context—was the corporation.[184] Gay rights advocates sometimes saw the corporation as "less labyrinthine and impenetrable than government bureaucracy," observed the historian Jonathan Bell, and perhaps more "open to change."[185] The pivot to private-sector solutions, which synced gay rights perfectly with a broader neoliberal turn in American political culture during these years, may have been less a matter of elitist opportunism than the result of the steady evaporation of other political possibilities. That story, which begins not at the top of gay rights bureaucracies but organically at the company grass roots, is the subject of the next and final chapter.

183. We will never know with certainty, but I strongly suspect that more gay people suffered adverse employment actions during the AIDS crisis than during the Lavender Scare of the 1950s. On the religious right, see especially chapter 1, "The Battle Lines Are Drawn," in Chris Bull and John Gallagher, *Perfect Enemies: The Religious Right, the Gay Movement, and the Politics of the 1990s* (New York: Crown Books, 1996), 1–38.

184. Christy Ford Chapin, *Ensuring America's Health: The Public Creation of the Corporate Health Care System* (New York: Cambridge University Press, 2017).

185. Jonathan Bell, "Between Private and Public: AIDS, Health Care Capitalism, and the Politics of Respectability in 1980s America," *Journal of American Studies* 54 (February 2020): 159–83.

CHAPTER SIX

Making the "Business Case"

GAY RIGHTS INSIDE THE
POST-FORDIST CORPORATION

ONE OF THE FEW TOOLS that the first generation of gay legal practitioners had in the early years was Rhonda Rivera's exhaustive study of the legal status of gay people, which she published in the *Hastings Law Journal* in 1979.[1] Rivera's study, which she began almost inadvertently and researched over several years, became a canonical piece of legal scholarship that served as a roadmap for many in the years before a legal treatise even existed. Two decades after it was published, the editors at the *Hastings Law Journal* contacted Rivera to ask if she was interested in updating her classic article to reflect progress in the law since she originally wrote her piece. Rivera's response was to say that she wasn't sure "exactly what 'progress' had occurred." She eventually produced an updated version, which also reflected on her original essay, but she stubbornly maintained her "glass half-empty" position.[2]

Rivera's pessimism is instructive, and it applies especially well to the arena of employment, where legal protections remained thin at best by the century's end. Not everyone could see it as clearly as Rivera, though.

1. Rhonda R. Rivera, "Our Straight-Laced Judges: The Legal Position of Homosexual Persons in the United States," *Hastings Law Journal* 30 (March 1979): 799–956. By the early 1980s, there was also Arthur Leonard's *Lesbian/Gay Law Notes*, which first appeared in 1980. See Leonard, "Chronicling a Movement: A Symposium to Recognize the 20th Anniversary of the *Lesbian/Gay Law Notes*," *New York Law School Journal of Human Rights* 17 (2000): 2.

2. Rhonda R. Rivera, "Our Straight-Laced Judges: Twenty Years Later," *Hastings Law Journal* 50 (1999): 1186–87.

She reported that the editors of the law review in particular were "taken aback" by her dismissal of their notion of "progress," instead viewing changes in the circumstances of gay people as "self-evident." Of course, the editors were also not entirely wrong to point to forward momentum for gay people (on the job and in other arenas as well) during the last decades of the twentieth century—in some workplaces, for example, greater modes of expression were indeed becoming possible across this span of years. Where they perhaps erred—and fell down in Rivera's estimation—was not so much in observing that a change had occurred, but rather when they zeroed in on the law as its source.[3]

This chapter attempts to explain the progress that the editors of the *Hastings Law Review* were so confident about, while essentially siding with Rivera that legal change was not its main motor. The opening of the American workplace to queer people by the end of the twentieth century, this chapter will argue, moved less through legal mandates than it did through the market. The turn of the gay rights movement to business, as well as business's response, may not surprise contemporary readers as LGBT politics and neoliberalism are at present often seen as highly compatible, with the corporate sponsorship of gay pride parades in major American cities regularly characterized, and sometimes derided, as "rainbow capitalism."[4] Yet if the congenial relationship between big business and LGBT rights now seems predictable, it's also true that looking back in time, almost no one would have foreseen it. Indeed, the prediction in the 1970s—at least among gay rights activists—was that the Congress was just *five to ten years* away from passing a gay civil rights bill that would cover employment.[5] But that legislation (and here one starts to appreciate Rivera's glass-half-empty viewpoint) was never enacted.[6] The federal

3. Ibid.

4. See, for example, Alex Abad-Santos, "How LGBTQ Pride Month Became a Branded Holiday and Why That's a Problem," *Vox*, June 25, 2018, https://www.vox.com/2018/6/25/17476850/pride-month-lgbtq-corporate-explained. See also James Surowiecki, "Unlikely Alliances," *New Yorker*, April 25, 2016, https://www.newyorker.com/magazine/2016/04/25/the-corporate-fight-for-social-justice. On neoliberalism and gay rights, see Lisa Duggan, *The Twilight of Equality: Neoliberalism, Cultural Politics, and the Attack on Democracy* (Boston: Beacon, 2003); Peter Drucker, *Warped: Gay Normality and Queer Anticapitalism* (Chicago: Haymarket, 2015).

5. *It's Time: Newsletter of the National Gay Task Force*, "Gay Rights Publications" folder, box 4, Costanza Files, Jimmy Carter Presidential Library, Atlanta, GA. See also Chai Feldblum, "The Federal Gay Rights Bill: From Bella to ENDA," in *Creating Change: Sexuality, Public Policy, and Civil Rights*, ed. John D'Emilio, William B. Turner, and Urvashi Vaid (New York: St. Martin's, 2000), 149–87.

6. Still true as I write this in 2021.

government's continued failure to extend meaningful protection to gay workers was especially clear in comparison to the accelerated pace of change among large businesses. Not only did workplace rights for gays and lesbians advance more quickly in the corporate sector than in the federal government (and, arguably, in the states as well), but corporate America also outpaced the nonprofit sector and even the labor movement.[7] Nancy Wohlforth, one of the founders of the AFL-CIO's LGBT constituency group Pride at Work, remembered going to her colleagues in the 1990s and saying, "Chevron has DP [domestic partner] benefits, Bechtel has DP benefits. And unions don't?"[8] To make sense of this phenomenon, scholars have criticized "neoliberal equality politics" as a kind of business co-optation of the gay rights movement.[9] While that critique is in many ways astute, it overstates the role of "the corporation" as an actor, underplays the corporate grass roots, and more generally neglects a deeper consideration of a relatively underexplored historical puzzle: Why is it that gay workplace rights advanced more quickly in the corporate sector than in any other site?

One way to answer that simple question is to examine two axial moments in the movement for gay workplace rights: first, the formation at Bell Labs of AT&T LEAGUE, the nation's largest company-recognized gay "employee resource group" (ERG); and second, the software designer Lotus's decision to offer domestic partner (DP) benefits to the same-sex partners of its employees. Lotus was the first large, highly visible, for-profit company to do so. These two cases focus on the late 1980s and early 1990s, and that timing suggests that the AIDS crisis was one causal engine for what transpired inside these businesses. The fact that these changes occurred first in high-tech companies was also no accident, so part of this story is about the particularity of that sector, the individuals within it, and the social movement they created inside their industry. But it is also

---

7. Nicole C. Raeburn, *Changing Corporate America from the Inside Out: Lesbian and Gay Workplace Rights* (Minneapolis: University of Minnesota Press, 2004), 255. Raeburn has argued that at the end of the twentieth century, the corporate sector was also ahead of states and localities in "gay inclusive" policies and practices. She noted that by 2004, for example, only ten states and 130 localities but nearly half (42 percent) of the Fortune 500 provided domestic partner benefits.

8. Interview with Nancy Wohlforth, Washington, DC, 2013. As will be discussed below, the very first DP benefits were pushed by public unions in municipalities. But they did not match the scale or speed (or often the range of benefits) offered thereafter by the corporate sector. As Wohlforth observed, "non-union places were usually ahead of union places in terms of gay rights."

9. Especially trenchant is Duggan, *Twilight of Equality.*

necessary to step back from the singularity of that sector to examine some of the broader structural factors associated with late capitalism that made it possible for workplace rights to rapidly spread beyond these early innovators to much of the rest of the Fortune 500. Both micro and macro levels of analysis, the contingent as well as the structural, are critical lenses for writing new histories of capitalism and labor.[10]

———◆———

Perceptions of the historical relationship of gay people to employment have been heavily shaped by the specter of the Lavender Scare, in which civil servants suspected of homosexuality were purged from their jobs as potential security risks.[11] Outside of the government—as discussed in earlier chapters—the relationship between employers and gay workers is more accurately characterized not as a witch hunt, however, but rather as a bargain in which employers tried not to see homosexuality among employees, and those employees tried not to be seen. The lack of formal legal protection made LGBT people vulnerable in occupational settings, but many who could blend in survived by adhering to this agreement, which mostly required discretion rather than an elaborate performance of straightness. Not looking too closely also enabled employers to benefit from the assets queer employees brought to their jobs. Gay liberation and AIDS began to break this bargain over the course of the 1970s and 1980s, as employees became less willing (and sometimes less able) to be invisible and employers responded with varying levels of bewilderment. This emergence from the shadows occurred sporadically across much of the labor market, but also systematically, for example, with the wave of gay and lesbian professional

10. Seth Rothman made a compelling argument for histories of capitalism that connect the contingent and the structural in *Scraping By: Wage Labor, Slavery, and Survival in Early Baltimore* (Baltimore: Johns Hopkins University Press, 2008). But I have been concerned by the frequent expression of relief in "state of the field" roundtables on the history of capitalism that social and cultural history have been set aside and historians can get back to the "real work" of political economy. Sven Beckert struck a related note in his synthetic essay on the history of capitalism, which referred to questions of identity as "sidelining" structural analysis, and work on race, ethnicity, and gender as "wandering further afield." See Beckert, "The History of Capitalism," in *American History Now*, ed. Eric Foner and Lisa McGirr (Philadelphia: Temple University Press, 2011). Historians of capitalism need a broad and eclectic view of the subject(s) of their histories as well as the scale on which they work. One recent model is Gabriel Winant's *The Next Shift: The Fall of Industry and the Rise of Health Care in Rust Belt America* (Cambridge, MA: Harvard University Press, 2021).

11. David Johnson, *The Lavender Scare: The Cold War Persecution of Gays and Lesbians in the Federal Government* (Chicago: University of Chicago Press, 2004).

caucuses that formed in the late 1970s and early 1980s and "constituted one of the areas of greatest growth" in gay organizing during those years.[12]

At first, this growing openness remained fairly rare in the corporate sector. Gays in corporate America who were overt during these years tended to be only those "gray-collar" clerks, typists, and computer operators who occupied "back office space" away from the public eye.[13] The National Association of Business Councils, an umbrella organization of gay business groups, voted not to include the word "gay" in its name because "many of our members are not out of the closet and would feel more at ease" if joining did not entail disclosure.[14] Tellingly, even San Francisco's Golden Gate Business Association had employed a similar calculus in selecting a name that whispered discretion.[15]

The corporate sector was thus an obvious target for the first nationwide mainstream gay rights organization. Formed in the mid-1970s, the National Gay Task Force (NGTF) applied pressure to big business through a survey it conducted of the hiring policies of the Fortune 500. While only one-third of the companies queried bothered to respond, remarkably, most of those that did stated they did not discriminate. But the director of a San Francisco employment agency was skeptical about that finding, suggesting it was mostly "lip service" and that many companies would not knowingly hire or promote homosexuals during these years.[16] "Lip service" certainly seemed to characterize AT&T's 1975 antidiscrimination policy. AT&T had

12. Memo from John to Ginny, "Report on Gay Professional Caucuses," October 7, 1982, folder 2, box 164, Records of the National Gay and Lesbian Task Force, Rare and Manuscript Collections, Cornell University, Ithaca, NY. On the formation of professional caucuses by gay librarians, nurses, social workers, and psychiatrists, see "Gay Workers Out of the Closet," special issue of *Workforce*, September–October 1974.

13. Women, minorities, and gays were all disproportionately represented in the back-office space in corporate America. The Golden Gate Business Association worried about a development plan in San Francisco that moved a lot of the back-office space to outlying areas, fretting that it would isolate gays in the suburbs. "What the Downtown Plan Means to Gays and Lesbians," *Golden Gate Business Association Newsletter*, June, 1985, 2.

14. David Petersen, Minutes of the National Association of Business Councils, November 1979, folder 39, box 167, Records of the National Gay and Lesbian Task Force.

15. Bay Area Career Women (BACW), a network of lesbian businesswomen, was even more cautious. They learned a great deal from observing the Golden Gate Business Association (GGBA) in action but also felt they didn't completely fit in with GGBA because BACW "placed greater emphasis on the confidentiality of our members." See "National Lesbian Network Is Launched," *Bay Area Career Women Newsletter*, August–September 1987, 1, Selected Newsletters and Periodicals from the Gay, Lesbian, Bisexual, Transgender Historical Society of Northern California, San Francisco, CA (microfilm reel 3, frame 23000, Primary Source Microfilm).

16. "Homosexuals in Management," *Industry Week*, July 23, 1979, 57.

one of the earliest formal policies banning discrimination against gays and lesbians by a major corporation, which was issued by a fairly conservative CEO. The origin of the policy is somewhat murky, but it was drafted in the context of the consent decree that AT&T had entered into two years prior with the Equal Employment Opportunity Commission (EEOC) to settle a large class action sex discrimination lawsuit, and the resulting nervousness within AT&T about civil rights litigation of any kind.[17] AT&T's 1975 policy was probably even more directly related to picketing by gay activists at Northwestern Bell in Minnesota in response to that subsidiary's earlier declaration that it "would not hire known homosexuals" and similar protests in San Francisco in reaction to PT&T's refusal to hire gays.[18] For the next several years, AT&T was involved in costly lawsuits defending its position that gays were not protected under the sex discrimination provisions of Title VII.[19] The negative publicity surrounding these state and federal cases, and the possibility that one California case might protect coming out at work as free speech, ultimately led the corporation's EEO office to issue a "strong recommendation letter" in 1979 urging that the company's existing (1975) policy of nondiscrimination based on "sexual preference" be included in all company personnel manuals and annually reviewed by all employees.[20]

Despite this recommendation, the company's nondiscrimination policy was not widely known by employees at the time. Many years later, one Bell Labs employee remembered discovering AT&T's policy in a NGTF pamphlet and wondering why it was never included in company EEO statements.[21] So even for the employees of Bell Labs—the research arm of the company that was more diverse, less corporate, more progressive, and had more in common with Silicon Valley than the rest of AT&T—the policy had

17. Benton Williams, "AT&T and the Private-Sector Origins of Private-Sector Affirmative Action," *Journal of Policy History* 20 (2008): 542–68.

18. Richard Zoglin, "The Homosexual Executive: What It's Like to Be Gay in a Pin-Striped World," in *Gay Men: The Sociology of Male Homosexuality*, ed. Martin P. Levine (New York: Harper and Row, 1979), 76 (the original version was published in the July/August 1974 issue of *MBA*).

19. For an excellent analysis of the state and federal lawsuits against PT&T, see chapter 6 of Katherine Turk, *Equality on Trial: Gender and Rights in the Modern American Workplace* (Philadelphia: University of Pennsylvania Press, 2016), especially 166–71.

20. Despite a groundbreaking if narrow decision in *Gay Law Students v. PT&T* in 1979, other state courts did not follow suit, and lower state courts in California issued conflicting interpretations. "For gay people," Katherine Turk concluded, "the courts were an unreliable route to workplace justice." Ibid., 171. See also Memo from Assistant Vice President to Vice Presidents–Personnel, "Strong Recommendation Letter," December 7, 1979, Steve Mershon Papers (in author's possession).

21. Interview with Steve Mershon, Maplewood, NJ, 2015.

little immediate impact. Instead, as employee Henry Baird remembered, "everyone was in the closet." Baird arrived at Bell Labs in 1984, after having been involved with gay liberation, and through a friend of a friend he knew of a senior manager who was gay. Baird asked this manager if he could safely be out at Bell Labs. The man replied, "under no circumstances. It's very hostile." In fact, it was so hostile that when Baird would pass this manager in the hallway, "he would refuse to acknowledge me," Baird remembered, adding, "that was his reality in 1984. I didn't want to be like that."[22]

Baird was not the first to feel that way. A few years before, a small group of gay employees at the Holmdel, New Jersey, facility of Bell Labs had begun meeting in the evenings. They went to their management in 1982 to ask that they be formally recognized as a Bell Labs Club.[23] Among the reasons the Holmdel management gave for rejecting the Lesbian and Gay Awareness (LGA) Club was the group's stated objective of changing company policy.[24] Apparently, the members of the LGA group were not aware that company policy was technically already with them, and neither were their managers.

Although AT&T's nondiscrimination policy was initially not the tool it might have been, at Bell Labs gay employees had something else. The Murray Hill, New Jersey, facility had created the Unix operating system in the 1960s, and by the early 1980s had developed a program called "Unix-to-Unix-Copy," which enabled computers to be networked together and for users to send mail by creating an address that consisted of a user name connected by an exclamation point (pronounced "bang") to the name of an adjacent machine.[25] The applicability of this new technology for gay employees was immediately apparent, and someone at the Murry Hill facility created a secret list that was called research!gg. "Gg" stood for "gay group," and initially there were just ten people on the list. By 1986 there were fifteen subscribers, and the next year there were seventeen, but the list was beginning to spread out from Murray Hill to other Bell Labs facilities across the country.[26]

22. Interview with Henry Baird, Bethlehem, PA, 2015.

23. GH to Mrs. Helen T. Eidberger, "Formation of LGA, a Lesbian and Gay Awareness Club," October 29, 1982, Mershon Papers.

24. H. T. Eidberger to GH, Request for Lesbian and Gay Awareness Club, December 16, 1982, Mershon Papers.

25. Interview with Henry Baird, Bethlehem, PA, 2015.

26. Minutes of the meeting of the LEAGUE Communications Committee, 1993, and Henry Baird's June 2006 talk at Lucent Bell Labs Research, both in Henry Baird Papers (in author's possession).

The list grew so slowly because almost no one was out in the company, and in order to find the list, you had to identify someone on it as gay and be willing to broach a conversation with them. In the early years, many Bell Labs employees remained in the dark. Steve Mershon, for example, was very reserved during these years and did not know any gay people. In his work at Bell Labs, first at Holmdel and later at the Summit, New Jersey, facility, he mostly kept to himself. A feeling of affinity for women and minorities—and an amorphous connection to a civil rights imaginary—led him to volunteer to maintain the diversity bulletin board, putting up articles about women's and African Americans' issues. The diversity committee eventually approached Mershon. No one had ever done this good a job with the bulletin board before, they said, and they invited him to join their committee. The group was not talking about gay topics at this point, and Mershon was terrified of ever being known as gay, but just being on the committee made him feel "a little safer."[27]

His other outlet during these lonely years was the computer. While he didn't know about the research!gg list, the Usenet newsgroup was also available then in technical companies like Bell Labs. This predecessor to the internet enabled very primitive text-only forums on a variety of topics that were arranged hierarchically under prefixes such as "soc" for social, or "sci" for science, or "comp" for computer related. Mershon discovered Usenet and began to read the "soc" forums. There were forums for hiking and camping that helped him to feel less isolated. Somewhat randomly, he came across a forum called "soc.motss" and started reading it. He had read only a few posts before he realized what he had found: *gay people*!" he exclaimed.[28]

At that time, Mershon believed that gays and lesbians would be "weirdos," not people like him. With some level of dread, he started reading the messages on soc.motss, soon determining that the "motss" acronym stood for "members of the same sex." Because there were still no personal computers, access to the forum was through workplace terminals. So Mershon would stay late at night to read the forum. He kept the door closed as he read, "ready to hit a key to hide all of this." Despite Mershon's sense at the time that the forum was "too hot to handle," the conversation mostly consisted of people telling their coming out stories, or talking about being

27. Interview with Steve Mershon, Maplewood, NJ, 2015.

28. Ibid. (emphasis mine). Soc.motss was created in 1983 by programmer Steve Dyer. See David Auerbach, "The First Gay Space on the Internet," *Slate*, August 2014, https://slate.com/technology/2014/08/online-gay-culture-and-soc-motss-how-a-usenet-group-anticipated-how-we-use-facebook-and-twitter-today.html.

afraid in the workplace, or strategizing about how to get a security clearance approved.[29]

No one had to register on soc.motss to read the forum, and unless a person posted, their anonymity was preserved. For this reason, many more read than posted. Mershon continued passively reading the forum after hours, until one day he saw a post from a coworker who also lived in his apartment building. Finally, then, Mershon knew someone who was gay, and he took his first awkward steps toward coming out by simply sending the man an email that said, "I liked your post on soc.motss." The man soon introduced Mershon to a small unofficial group of AT&T employees called LEGIT (Lesbians and Gays in Telecommunications) that had formed after Bell Labs denied formal recognition to the Holmdel LGA Club in 1982. "I went and stood outside the house where the meeting was being held for about ten minutes before I could walk in," Mershon remembered. Once in the door, he immediately saw someone he knew and thought, "My secret is out. Now what?" The meeting was uncomfortable for Mershon, but he sat through it, eventually deciding that "it was a start."[30]

Virtual networks were creating similar clusters across the country. Four years after its founding at Murray Hill, the research!gg list had fifty subscribers from across the company.[31] Some of them had been meeting in an informal group in Denver and were among the approximately five hundred thousand people who attended the 1987 March on Washington for Lesbian and Gay Rights. They came home deeply changed, having had their first experience feeling powerful as gay people, surrounded by other gays in the subways, on the train, on the airplane.[32] In the aftermath of the march, employees of Denver's facility decided to organize a formal group that they named Lesbian and Gay United Employees (LEAGUE). They wrote an anonymous letter and found an outside associate who would carry it to their senior management.[33] When four members of the group finally met with management some months later, managers were undoubtedly relieved that the organizers had a go-slow approach in mind. The executives acknowledged the step their employees had taken in

29. Interview with Steve Mershon, Maplewood, NJ, 2015.

30. Ibid.

31. Henry Baird's June 2006 talk at Lucent Bell Labs Research, Baird Papers.

32. Estimates of the number of people at the march vary widely and go as high as 650,000. See Amin Ghaziani, *The Dividends of Dissent: How Conflict and Culture Work in Lesbian and Gay Marches on Washington* (Chicago: University of Chicago Press, 2008), 123.

33. "Reaching Out at AT&T," *Gay/Lesbian/Bisexual Corporate Letter*, September/October 1992, 4.

coming out to them and thanked them "for making this meeting comfortable for us." One executive presciently asked whether or not the organizers really wanted him to tell other managers of LEAGUE's existence at a meeting the following week. "You realize the risk you're taking? Suddenly people will be looking around them wondering *who* these people are," he warned. "Do you people want this?"[34]

Denver LEAGUE answered—despite the varied openness of their membership—that "with half a million people marching in Washington," it was "time to begin the process."[35] Coming out in the workplace was never simply an individual act but a collective experience, as one person's decision to be seen could beam a light around an entire office. By the late 1980s, several years into the AIDS crisis, after the mass catharsis of the 1987 March, and with gay AT&T employees joined in an increasingly elaborate quasi-private electronic network, the situation was at a tipping point not only in Denver but also on the East Coast. The ripples made their way back to the Diversity Committee at the Summit facility where Steve Mershon was still quietly serving. Controversy was stirred when two men whom Mershon didn't know came before the Diversity Committee to complain about finding "faggot" graffiti in the men's restroom. Mershon was "terrified and excited" that, as a result, the Diversity Committee was preparing to take up gay issues. "What would I do as a deeply closeted man?"[36]

The two men were advised that they should form an employee group so they could potentially be represented on the Diversity Committee. Mershon was assigned to help the two men plan the group and did so as a "supportive ally," without revealing himself. Mershon felt the corporation was scared of the idea and advised caution. Meetings should be held off the premises, and there should be "no surprises." "Don't go to parades," he advised. In the summer of 1988, the two men submitted their proposal for LEAGUE-Summit.[37]

Several months later, the division head had still not made a decision, and Mershon was increasingly worried that the group would be denied company recognition. He spent an agonized late summer weekend in his office composing and recomposing an email to the division head explaining why he should approve the group. Because of his work on the bulletin board, as well as his time reading soc.motss, Mershon was relatively well

34. Posting on soc.motss, "LEAGUE at AT&T Denver meets with Top Level Managers," March 7, 1988, Mershon Papers (emphasis mine).

35. Ibid.

36. Interview with Steve Mershon, Maplewood, NJ, 2015.

37. Ibid.

informed about gay issues and "poured his heart into the email." After several pages, he took a leap and wrote: "I can speak from personal experience. I'm gay . . . and terrified of anyone finding out."[38]

Well-versed in corporate hierarchy, Mershon knew that the first thing an upper-level manager would do after receiving a communication like this was to send it down the chain of command for input. So Mershon took the initiative and copied it to everyone in his chain of command. He signed his full name around three a.m. on Monday morning, and "finally, I hit send." Mershon went home for a few hours of rest but didn't sleep. He returned to the office the next morning to wait for the response. It took a little while before email messages began to appear on his computer. "Most said they didn't understand the issue, but they supported me." Mershon never heard back from the division head, but within a week the formation of the Summit group had been approved. LEAGUE had its second chapter.[39]

After LEAGUE-Summit, the steady emergence of new LEAGUE chapters—in New Jersey, in Florida, in the Midwest, in the South—might in retrospect appear like dominoes falling over in quick secession. But internal documents from the organization reveal how laborious the process actually was. LEAGUE's guidelines on how to form a chapter emphasized cultivating ties with other ERG's and being inclusive by ensuring that women, racial minorities, bisexuals, and straight allies had a place in the organization. Most important was a go-slow approach. "Work within the system," the guidelines advised. "Be sensitive to management fear of backlash. Be willing to move cautiously . . . if management is hesitant."[40] That approach proved necessary, since company support, while officially pledged, was spotty on the ground. One employee in Largo, Florida, sent Mershon an email after his manager forbade him from using company equipment to communicate with LEAGUE, warning it would be his last communication.[41] In July 1989, LEAGUE–South Jersey applied for recognition as a Bell Labs Club. Board members raised "multiple concerns," and the chapter was approved only several months later in a split vote.[42] In the summer of 1989, the Summit chapter requested permission to be allowed to celebrate Gay Awareness Week in the same spirit that Bell Labs celebrated Black History Month and Women's History Month. "Sorry, the answer is no," the executive responsible for the decision responded. "I

38. Ibid.
39. Ibid.
40. "Suggestions for Forming a New LEAGUE Chapter," Mershon Papers.
41. RG to Steve Mershon, "LEAGUE Info," November 1991, Mershon Papers.
42. Timeline document, Mershon Papers.

don't think we are ready, or at least I'm not ready, to have a celebration of Gay Awareness Week at the Division in Summit."[43]

But it wasn't just management that needed LEAGUE to speak in muted tones—so did gay employees who were worried about what association with LEAGUE would mean for their careers. For this reason, membership lists were confidential, and all members agreed "to respect and maintain the privacy of other members of the organization."[44] Email was not simply a novel and highly efficient mode of communicating across the country; it was absolutely critical to the continued growth of LEAGUE because it enabled a cautious multitude to observe and learn about the organization anonymously before taking any steps that brought them into view of their colleagues. For the first year, one "secret" member of LEAGUE was "what we called a 'muffin'": a covert reader of the chat line, "never joining in on discussions and extremely anxious that someone may walk into my area while I had a LEAGUE posting on my monitor." But over time, this individual eventually started offering his moral support for colleagues on the LEAGUE forum. "LEAGUE became an extended family of faceless allies, but allies nonetheless."[45]

What made LEAGUE members especially nervous was the company's difficulty in saying the words "gay" or "lesbian" out loud, as well as the way the policy protecting gays seemed to be regularly omitted from the EEO clause in company publications.[46] "How can we eliminate the deafening silence?" LEAGUE members asked in their first meeting with a new head of the Affirmative Action office.[47] One early and dramatic success was convincing Arno Penzias, the Nobel Prize–winning head of research at Bell Labs, to hire a man named Brian McNaught to do training on "homophobia in the workplace." While this was the moment when diversity training was taking off across industry, few offerings focused on homosexuality. And McNaught, a serious Catholic who had been fired for being gay by the Catholic newspaper he worked for in Detroit, was a charismatic, even magical, messenger.[48] He made attendees of his trainings aware of the

43. Barry Karafin to RJ, April 28, 1989, Mershon Papers.

44. Text of recorded Audix message, May 1990, Mershon Papers.

45. "Opening Doors: A Collection of Stories from Employees at AT&T," June 1995, 13–14, Mershon Papers.

46. Stephen Mershon to Anne Fritz, "Lesbian and Gay Employees," March 16, 1990, Mershon Papers.

47. Questions for Anne Fritz, April 18, 1990, Mershon Papers.

48. Barbara Presley Noble, "The Unfolding of Gay Culture," *New York Times*, June 27, 1993, 23; Margo Harakas, "The Gospel of Brian McNaught," *Ft. Lauderdale Sun Sentinel*, January 19, 2005, 1E.

policy and argued that business efficiency was hurt by discrimination, but mostly he told his own story. Because some of his trainings at Bell Labs (and later throughout AT&T) were required for employees, his audiences were straight as well as gay. Some resented being there; McNaught remembered hearing "stop this shit!" from the back of the room at one of his trainings. But for many, the experience was fascinating and eye-opening.[49] One person apologized for his delay in returning the evaluation form after the training, saying, "I needed to think about it," and adding, "it will stay with me for a long time."[50] Another concluded that "the seminar is very good" but expressed his concern that "more support for the gay men and lesbian women in the workplace" could actually lead to an "increase in the percentage of people in these categories."[51] Indeed, some of McNaught's evaluations seem to suggest this suspicion might have had merit. "Hi, Brian. I am the black girl in the front row who pays your invoice," one attendee wrote. "Please send me the name of night clubs or vacation places for lesbians."[52]

McNaught's workshop was soon a regularly scheduled event throughout AT&T.[53] And with extremely supportive individuals in both AT&T's and Bell Labs's EEO offices, LEAGUE seemed to have reached a tipping point by 1990. A significant marker was the publication of a full-page story about LEAGUE in *Bell Labs News*, complete with a large photo of Steve Mershon, whose involvement with the group had induced him to become more open about his sexuality.[54] That publicity caused the email list to grow, and more chapters were soon formed. A few months later, LEAGUE was featured in a story in the *New York Times*.[55] But the increased publicity came with costs as well. Harassment, which had been an issue since LEAGUE began, increased with greater visibility. LEAGUE members had their posters torn down, received obscene phone calls, endured the sight of "kill a fag now" scribbled on restroom walls, and had their coworkers warned to keep away from them by supervisors if they "planned to

49. Interview with Brian McNaught, Ft. Lauderdale, FL, 2015.

50. JG evaluation, folder 14, box 3, Brian McNaught Papers, Rare and Manuscript Collections, Cornell University.

51. Donald Baker to Mr. Donald Liebers and Robert L. Martin, folder 14, box 3, McNaught Papers.

52. SA to Brian McNaught, folder 29, box 3, McNaught Papers.

53. Handwritten timeline, and "Summary of 1989 Affirmative Action Meetings," April 10, 1990, both in Mershon Papers.

54. Karen Delgado, "An Invisible Minority," *Bell Labs News*, July 17, 1990, Mershon Papers; interview with Steve Mershon, Maplewood, NJ, 2015.

55. Claudia Deutsch, "Gay Rights, Issue of the 90s," *New York Times*, April 28, 1991, F23.

go anywhere in the company." One log of these hostile and intimidating events took up four single-spaced pages.[56]

Moreover, backlash spread beyond the company. By the spring of 1991, Christian radio stations were broadcasting about AT&T's support for LEAGUE and the company panicked, waffling in its commitment to gay pride events.[57] AT&T's official position, they said, was "support" not "sponsorship." They asked employees to make the activities "low-key," and not to refer to the scheduled events as "Gay Pride." Finally, the company announced that they would pull the calendar of events for Pride Week that had been scheduled to run in *Bell Labs News*, which was, as one executive explained, "a pretty public newspaper."[58] Even for the "go-slow" and "work within the system" approach advocated by LEAGUE members, this was a blow. The symbolic power of a company-sponsored Pride Week went far beyond its material expression: the few card tables set up in the foyer, the brown-bag discussions over the noon hour. This was the company's most meaningful affirmation of its gay employees, as well as a critical way for LEAGUE to send a message to the unknown number of their colleagues who would never risk the LEAGUE chat line on a work computer. Just a year before, for example, a man in Mershon's building who avoided LEAGUE had also not felt comfortable attending a screening of a video featuring Brian McNaught as part of 1990's Pride Week. The closest he could come was strolling slowly down the corridor as the video played, trying to catch as much as he could as he passed by. The snippets he overheard convinced him that had to see the video. He later called Steve Mershon and asked, without identifying himself, if Mershon would send it to him. Mershon was happy to oblige, but the man couldn't think of an "entirely safe way" to get the video. After deliberating, the man decided to "throw caution to the wind." He called Mershon a second time and gave him a post office box and his "New York name." Though his plan was to "cut all ties" with LEAGUE after he got the video, instead the man watched the video no fewer than four times, had dinner with Mershon, and decided to join the organization.[59] But would he have done so a year later, if the company was withdrawing its support just as he was working up the courage to reach out?

56. "Compilation of Harassment," July 25, 1991, Mershon Papers.

57. "Christians Target AT&T Gay Policy," clipping from *Texas Times Herald* circulated on AT&T letterhead, May 14, 1991, Mershon Papers.

58. Anne Fritz, Overview of Understandings, May 1, 1991, and David Boyce to Stephen Mershon, June 3, 1991, both in Mershon Papers.

59. JD to Brian McNaught, August 17, 1990, folder 27, box 3, McNaught Papers.

Understandably, then, LEAGUE hoped to persuade management to run their Pride calendar in *Bell Labs News*. They used recent incidents of harassment to highlight the need for a week of special events, and they had a tense meeting with the company's Public Relations director in which they pointedly asked, "Are you embarrassed by the policy?" which essentially meant, are you embarrassed by us?[60] The company did not reverse course on the calendar, but LEAGUE's sense that they could "nonetheless get a lot out of the situation," proved prescient.[61] Publicity did not die down; in subsequent months, articles in *Personnel Journal* and *Fortune* mentioned LEAGUE.[62] New chapters continued to form. And LEAGUE began to speak in more assertive tones, increasingly demanding that the company market directly to gay consumers.[63]

Perhaps connected to an interest in the gay market—AT&T did send its first direct mail campaign to seventy thousand gay consumers, "Let Your True Voice Be Heard," in 1994—company support was expanding.[64] This was most evident in the establishment of an annual company-funded LEAGUE conference, which brought an eager network together who had previously known each only through the email list. The event was a huge boost to LEAGUE membership. And because individuals had to be out to managers to get funding to attend, the company was finally creating incentives for its own employees to come out. There was still work to do. Chief executive officer Bob Allen flatly refused to appear at LEAGUE conferences, for example. Efforts to get the company to extend DP benefits also met resistance, and AT&T lagged behind as other tech companies paved the way on this issue. But working within a relatively conservative Fortune 500 company, LEAGUE was a one-thousand-member organization with thirty chapters across the nation and a national conference. Just five years after its founding, it was the largest and arguably the most successful gay employee resource group in the country. And it had achieved that without the assistance of "higher level managers who are gay, lesbian, or bisexual" because those individuals remained afraid to associate with LEAGUE, or

60. KJ to Ethel Battan, May 24, 1991, and handwritten notes, meeting with LEAGUE members and David Boyce, May 31, 1991, both in Mershon Papers.

61. "Info for Our Meeting with Boyce," undated, Mershon Papers.

62. George Kronenberger, "Out of the Closet," *Personnel Journal*, June 1993, 41–45; "Gay in Corporate America," *Fortune*, December 16, 1991, 42–56.

63. WA to K., February 18, 1993; "Diversity Insert," September 7, 1993; "Second Annual LEAGUE Conference," June 1993 LEAGUE newsletter; 1994 "League Conference Notes": all in Mershon Papers.

64. Lynn Jones, "AT&T Targets Gays and Lesbians," *Direct*, August 1994, 25.

really be out at all.[65] What the company's grass roots had was a new technology, perfectly suited for their moment and circumstances, and a steely determination to change the system from within.

———————

When AT&T employees asked the company to recognize LEAGUE as an officially sponsored ERG, they were in essence asking the company to treat them like other civil rights constituencies. Within AT&T, there were well-established ERGs for women, for Latinos, and for African Americans. But when employees began to demand equal benefits for domestic partners—at AT&T and elsewhere—they were demanding to be treated like straight people. That demand, which encapsulated a shift from a political strategy that emphasized difference to one that emphasized sameness, first emerged far from the corporate sector at the *Village Voice* in 1982. The *Voice* had long had an unofficial policy of providing benefits for the unmarried partners of heterosexual employees, and when shop steward Jeff Weinstein discovered that, he used it to bargain for "spousal equivalent" benefits for gay employees in contract negotiations.[66] Weinstein's union, District 65 of the UAW, was generally unable to expand the benefits to other units in New York City, but Weinstein's achievement shaped the political imaginary elsewhere.[67] In Berkeley, California, the municipal workers' union convinced the city to become the first municipality in the country to extend DP benefits in 1984.[68] A handful of other progressive cities across the country followed suit. Most municipalities offered "non-cost" benefits, which most often was a means to register one's partnership with the city, and qualify for bereavement and sometimes sick leave. But Berkeley, West Hollywood, and Santa Cruz, and later Seattle and Laguna Beach, offered health benefits as well.[69] For those cities,

65. Stephen Mershon to Mr. Martersteck, Mr. Leonard, and Mr. Blinn, "1994 Diversity Plan," February 10, 1994, Mershon Papers.

66. Interview with Jeff Weinstein, New York, NY, 2014.

67. Martha McDonald, "Domestic Partner Benefits Changes," *Business and Health*, October 1999, 11–22; interview with Jeff Weinstein, New York, NY, 2014.

68. Desma Holcomb, "Domestic Partner Health Benefits: The Corporate Model vs. the Union Model," in *Laboring for Rights: Unions and Sexual Diversity Across Nations*, ed. Gerald Hunt (Philadelphia: Temple University Press, 1999), 106–7; Daniel Boggan to Honorable Mayor and Members of the City Council, "Proposed Policy Establishing 'Domestic Partnerships,'" folder 33, box 4, Records of the Human Rights Campaign, Rare and Manuscript Collections, Cornell University.

69. Lambda Legal Defense and Education Fund, "A National Overview of Domestic Partnership Legislation," *Domestic Partnership: Issues and Legislation* (New York: Lambda Legal, 1992) (in author's possession).

finding an insurer was a challenge. In West Hollywood, for example, eighteen insurers declined to provide coverage before the city finally decided to insure itself.[70]

While progress in municipalities was fairly slow, by the early 1990s cities and a few universities appeared to be the only arenas where DP benefits were gaining any traction. "No movement of significance," reported the publishing company the Bureau of National Affairs in 1991, "has occurred among private sector employers with respect to offering benefits for domestic partners."[71] Yet within months, organizing efforts in several corporations burst into public view, and partner benefits in the private sector soon far surpassed anything that had occurred in the public sector. As in many of the municipalities that had led the way, the AIDS crisis was a catalyst. In the midst of the epidemic, the San Francisco Chamber of Commerce established a working group to study how firms were meeting the needs of employees with "nontraditional families" in areas such as bereavement leave.[72] But a far more direct push came from employees themselves.

A variety of factors made Lotus—the Cambridge, Massachusetts, software company—especially fertile ground. As at Bell Labs, gay employees at Lotus were connected through a secret email group; you had to know someone to get on it. They also enjoyed extremely strong support from the EEO office. At Bell Labs, LEAGUE's strongest champion had been Ethel Batten, an African American vice president of human resources who had cared for a beloved nephew while he was dying of AIDS.[73] At Lotus, gay employees had Janet Axelrod, who was Jewish and had spent her youth at Communist Party–inspired summer camps outside of New York City, and then participated in women's liberation and antiwar activism as a student at Barnard. In the early 1980s, Axelrod was in Cambridge and unemployed when she was somewhat randomly connected with a man named Mitch Kaper who was starting a business and needed someone to help. He was thirty, she was twenty-nine, and when she went to work in his house, Axelrod became Lotus's first employee.[74]

70. Catherine Iannuzzo and Alexandra Pinck, "Benefits for the Domestic Partners of Gay and Lesbian Employees at Lotus Development Corporation," report for Simmons College Graduate School of Management, 1991 (in author's possession).

71. "Benefits for Domestic Partners," *Bureau of National Affairs Pension Reporter* 8 (1991): 946.

72. Statement by Richard Morten, Vice President of San Francisco Chamber of Commerce, April 25, 1989, accessed at Levi Strauss corporate headquarters, San Francisco, CA.

73. Interview with Ethel Batten, Union, NJ, 2015.

74. Interview with Janet Axelrod, Cambridge, MA, 2015.

From those humble origins, Lotus grew quickly, especially once the spreadsheet software "Lotus 123" was introduced. Then, Axelrod remembered, it was as if the company was "printing money," which "led to a certain looseness." Kaper entrusted her with more responsibility as the company grew, and Axelrod, as vice president of human resources, had leeway to try to create what she called "an entitled workforce." Lotus was quickly perceived as a good place to work, "especially if you were slightly off the grid. If you weren't a white guy in a suit, this was your place."[75] Polly Laurelchild, a lesbian who had spent part of the 1980s working in women's music production, took a job at Lotus because she needed money to fix her teeth. "It was head and shoulders better than any other [corporate] environment," she remembered.[76] Its appeal to gays and lesbians was only enhanced in 1986, when Lotus became the first company to fund the AIDS Walk and Axelrod wrote a policy including sexual orientation in the company's nondiscrimination statement. She also eliminated the dress code.[77]

The dress code was not trivial to lesbians, many of whom had struggled with professional attire in the years before pantsuits were widely accepted for women in corporate settings. AnnD Canavan remembered having to "do legs" before she came to work at Lotus; there, she wore Hawaiian shirts and jeans or khakis every day of the week.[78] This wasn't simply a matter of comfort—casual wear made it easier to identify other lesbians. Lesbians had often felt even more compelled than gay men to maintain a culture of covering in the workplace, largely because of their greater vulnerability as women workers.[79] So lesbians could be harder to spot than gay men, even for those who were looking. But the fact that Lotus was attracting unconventional employees and making it safe for them to express that difference through dress meant that "it was more obvious than it had ever been."[80] Lesbians, as well as gay men, weren't yet out in large numbers, but they

75. Ibid.

76. Interview with AnnD Canavan, Margie Bleichman, and Polly Laurelchild, Brookline, MA, 2015.

77. Interview with Janet Axelrod, Cambridge, MA, 2015.

78. Interview with AnnD Canavan, Margie Bleichman, and Polly Laurelchild, Brookline, MA, 2015.

79. On the greater emphasis placed on discretion at work by lesbians relative to gay men, see *Bay Area Career Women*, August–September 1987, 1. Kathleen Dermody, a president of AT&T LEAGUE, also suggested that lesbians were especially vulnerable and reluctant to be out in the workplace. See, "Harassment Gone? Think Again," in *Bell Labs News*, November 25, 1991, 6.

80. Interview with AnnD Canavan, Margie Bleichman, and Polly Laurelchild, Brookline, MA, 2015.

had moved to a different place on the continuum of discretion. Margie Bleichman was astonished on her first day at Lotus to go to a meeting of the team that was developing the "HAL" software. Only women were at the meeting, and many of those around the conference table were obviously lesbians.[81]

That sense of excitement generated the notion that Lotus could become some sort of utopia for gay and lesbian employees. Canavan, who founded the secret email list several years earlier, sent out an announcement to ask if anyone wanted to work on getting Lotus to approve DP benefits. Her original idea was that the campaign should convince the company to allow employees to put any person they wanted to designate on their insurance. Her brother had HIV, and she wanted to insure him. Since benefits constituted 40 percent of employee compensation, the logic was very simply equal pay for equal work.[82] The group started to meet in 1989. Initially it was ten people, then eight, but after the tedious nature of the committee work became apparent, the membership dwindled down to just three women: Canavan, Bleichman, and Laurelchild.[83]

Despite the progressive atmosphere at Lotus, the campaign was surprisingly long. Over two and a half years, the trio researched the few models that existed elsewhere. Through the gay employee's virtual network they discovered that a hospital in New York had authorized DP benefits in response to the threat of a lawsuit but kept it very "hush, hush." So they called Montefiore Medical Center, Ben and Jerry's Ice Cream, and Levi Strauss in San Francisco, which at that point had only a bereavement leave policy. Then they approached management with their proposal. They were never told no, but forward momentum was elusive, as meeting after meeting was filled with nonanswers and corporate jargon. Finally, after more than a year, Bleichman wrote a very strongly worded email that said, in essence, "we are being yes'd to death." Janet Axelrod also intervened, arguing to the CEO well before it was axiomatic that offering employees DP benefits made good business sense because it would put Lotus way out ahead as an "employer of choice" for progressive people across the industry. This novel argument gained a lot of traction in just a few years.[84]

81. Ibid.

82. The 40 percent statistic was from the benefits and compensation firm Hewitt Associates. See "Benefits for Live-in Mates of Workers Face Obstacles," *Wall Street Journal*, July 25, 1989, B1.

83. Interview with AnnD Canavan, Margie Bleichman, and Polly Laurelchild, Brookline, MA, 2015.

84. Ibid.; interview with Janet Axelrod, Cambridge, MA, 2015.

Yet there was still a considerable distance between approval from the corner office and getting a working policy. Lotus hired an outside consultant who understood the partner benefits issue. But even with him at the table, the situation was static. Management kept saying, "This will be so costly." Finally, the consultant suggested that "they talk about AIDS," and everyone in the room seemed relieved. Once AIDS could be openly discussed, it was easy to dispel concerns about the cost of the illness: AIDS care was mostly palliative, and the disease was actually far less expensive than maternity, heart disease, and some cancers. Because Lotus was primarily self-insured, they needed mostly to convince themselves that they could afford to take this step, and those statistics nearly secured the policy.[85]

The one remaining obstacle was getting Lotus's stop-loss insurer on board. Like most companies that self-insured, Lotus only did so up to a maximum dollar amount and then had a stop-loss policy with an insurer to cover expenses in excess of that cap. At Lotus during these years, stop-loss insurance kicked in at $140,000. So the first step in convincing the insurer was demonstrating that the cost of AIDS care was almost always well below $140,000. Moreover, the Lotus team assured the insurer that the risk of fraud was minimal. Domestic partners had to sign an affidavit that made them liable for each other's debts and was actually more stringent than marriage. Most importantly, because some municipalities had been offering DP benefits for a few years, there was hard empirical data that showed that benefits for same-sex couples were not more expensive than benefits for heterosexual couples. Strikingly, the company that provided the actuarial data did so on the condition that it remain anonymous because it did not want to be known as the "gay/lesbian insurer."[86]

In September 1991, Lotus finally announced that it would offer health and other benefits for domestic partners. Understandably nervous about the reaction, it had hoped to do so "quietly." But the news was electric, traveling first along the nodes of gay electronic communication inside technical companies that had sustained the politics that made the breakthrough possible in the first instance. Within minutes, "I got [the news] from ten different people," said a gay manager with Xerox in California.[87] At Lotus, so many employees posted a response to the new policy on the electronic

85. Interview with AnnD Canavan, Margie Bleichman, and Polly Laurelchild, Brookline, MA, 2015.

86. Polly Laurelchild to Margie Bleichman and AnnD Canavan, "Process Summary," November 4, 1991, in folder 36, box 38, Records of the Human Rights Campaign.

87. "A Cutting-Edge Issue: Benefits," *Fortune*, December 16, 1991, 50.

bulletin board that the system crashed. Many of the initial responses were skeptical, ranging from concerns about what impact the new policy would have on the cost of premiums to fears that the policy would attract gays to the company.[88]

A media frenzy followed: the three women who shepherded the policy into existence found themselves "media stars," as the story was widely covered in the mainstream news outlets. Other businesses wanting to explore the policy began calling. Then letters arrived from across the country and around the world.[89] And while some customers shredded their Lotus disks and sent them back to the company, over time the public response was 6 to 1 in favor of DP benefits.[90] One VP remembered getting a call from an anonymous executive at a large financial institution who would place the call only with his office door closed. He said he had been in the closet all his life and thanked Lotus for the policy. "It means there is hope," he said.[91]

When the frenzy had settled, very few employees opted for the policy. Even three years later, only twenty of Lotus's thirty-two hundred employees had signed up for the benefits.[92] Unlike some of the municipalities whose DP policies preceded Lotus's, the software company made benefits available only to same-sex couples, not to unmarried opposite-sex ones. They reasoned that the issue was one of antigay discrimination, not creating policy alternatives to marriage.[93] Yet gay employees were unlikely to use the policy in high numbers for a wide range of reasons. Signing up for DP benefits meant coming out at work, at least to management, and in the early years this was not something many employees were ready to do. In addition, while health benefits for married partners were not taxed as income, the IRS determined that DP benefits had to be imputed and taxed as income. Opting for the benefits increased the employee's tax burden. Perhaps most significantly, gay couples were less likely to follow the breadwinner-caregiver (or primary-secondary earner) models that still characterized many heterosexual marriages. Each member of a same-sex

88. Bruce Shutan, "Gay Partner Benefits Facing New Scrutiny," *Employee Benefit News*, January 1992, 32.

89. Iannuzzo and Pinck, "Benefits for the Domestic Partners."

90. Ibid.; David Jefferson, "Gay Employees Win Benefits for Partners at More Corporations," *Wall Street Journal*, March 18, 1994, A1–2; Jennifer Laabs, "Unmarried with Benefits," *Personnel Journal*, December 1993, 67.

91. Iannuzzo and Pinck, "Benefits for the Domestic Partners."

92. Jefferson, "Gay Employees Win Benefits."

93. Interview with Janet Axelrod, Cambridge, MA, 2015.

partnership was more likely to have independent access to health benefits than each member of an opposite-sex partnership.[94]

As data spread that debunked myths about the costs of insuring persons with AIDS, insurance companies began to drop their opposition to extending coverage. Several large corporations then began to offer DP benefits. Most followed Lotus's example and made the benefits available only to same-sex partnerships. The early adopters were mostly in the tech sector—Silicon Graphics, Apple, Sun Microsystems, Oracle.[95] As the policy spread, the fact that fewer than 1 percent of a company's employees were likely to sign up made it easier to do "the right thing." When IBM acquired Lotus in 1996, it quickly became the largest employer to offer health benefits to the same-sex partners of employees. IBM did so at the same moment that it also announced major layoffs.[96] The seeming paradox of IBM adding DP benefits while it was downsizing its workforce was paralleled by a more general trend of the benefit being added at the same time that corporations were "reducing coverage for nonemployees."[97] It was an almost entirely symbolic benefit that carried with it the potential for significant gains in employee loyalty from a population that was still unaccustomed to having powerful entities stand with them. "My dedication to the company changed completely when it extended domestic partnership benefits," a man recalled of his job at Microsoft. "I don't intend on using them," but they "mean more to me than the monetary value of the benefit."[98]

———

Looking at the early corporate adoption of DP benefits from a bird's-eye view, it seems to resemble successive waves as companies appeared to be moving at a steady pace to match their competitors, sector by sector. But the view from the ground reveals that even in loose Silicon Valley, and even as time went on, corporations needed to be persuaded. Most of the initial companies to enact partner benefits did so in response to

94. Jefferson, "Gay Employees Win Benefits."

95. The entertainment industry—HBO and Warner Brothers—followed. "DP Trend Accelerates as Leading Firms Add Benefits," *Gay/Lesbian/Bisexual Corporate Letter* 2, Fall 1993, 1.

96. "IBM Benefits Go to Partners," *Business Insurance* 30 (1996), 2.

97. "Cutting-Edge Issue," 50.

98. James Woods with Jay Lucas, *The Corporate Closet: The Professional Lives of Gay Men in America* (New York: Free Press, 1993), 251.

the demands of ERGs.[99] At Sun Microsystems, for example, yet another group of employees connected by a secret email list pushed for several years for both DP benefits and an antidiscrimination statement. "Company executives didn't have personal animosity, but they didn't want to be first," one organizer remembered. "They were very concerned about what shareholders would think."[100] It was an even harder struggle at the staid Hewlett Packard, where members of the Gay and Lesbian Employees Network (GLEN) went to their CEO with substantial data about the low cost of DP benefits. After he refused their proposal, they asked for permission to meet individually with his executive staff. They decided not to go before these staff members with statistics and graphs but instead to develop and perform a "readers' theater" compiled from the actual experiences of gay employees at the company. Eventually, they wore down the opposition.[101] Even the board at socially liberal Apple turned down DP benefits twice before finally approving them, again pushed at every step by a well-organized group of employees who had initially joined together over a quasi-secret company email list.[102]

Progress was aided too by the fact that employees were networked not only within companies but across the tech sector. Untold numbers of people were reading soc.motss during these years, and they were not only commiserating about the pain and discomfort of being closeted in their companies, but passing along organizing strategies to change the status quo.[103] That those networks were so dependent on access to computers in the workplace meant that while alliances formed easily across companies, they rarely crossed class lines. At Sun Microsystems, for example, it was difficult to reach LGBT employees on the manufacturing side of the company, who "shared computers, had less privacy and less access."[104] In general, companies that were persuaded to extend benefits in order to "attract the best and the brightest" employees were also not thinking about

99. Raeburn, *Changing Corporate America*, 3; Daniel B. Baker, Sean O'Brien Strub, and Bill Henning, *Cracking the Corporate Closet: The 200 Best (and Worst) Companies to Work for, Buy from, and Invest in If You're Gay or Lesbian—and Even If You Aren't* (New York: Harper Business, 1995), 15.

100. Interview with Marc Stein, conducted via telephone, 2015.

101. Interview with Kim Harris, conducted via telephone, 2015.

102. Interview with Elizabeth Birch, Bethesda, MD, 2015; interview with Bennett Marks, conducted via telephone, 2015.

103. Auerbach, "First Gay Space on the Internet," 1. (Auerbach's article suggests that 3 percent of Usenet readers were reading soc.motss by the early 1990s—this would be approximately eighty-three thousand people.)

104. Interview with Marc Stein, conducted via telephone, 2015.

blue-collar employees on the line. So benefits were often extended at company headquarters, not in the factory.[105]

On the white-collar side of the industry, however, the grassroots campaign quickly scaled up to a broader workplace movement. Groups like Digital Queers and High-Tech Gays organized to protest the denial of security clearances.[106] In the fall of 1991, 150 people attended the first Lesbian and Gay Workplace Issues Conference in San Francisco. Under the auspices of the NGTF's Workplace Project, 330 people participated in a workplace conference at Stanford University in 1993. The tech industry was well represented, but so were Pacific Gas and Electric (PG&E), Chevron, and Pacific Bell. The group convened again under the name "Out and Equal" at Stanford the following year.[107] Around the same time, two publications appeared—*Working It Out* and *The Gay/Lesbian/Bisexual Corporate Newsletter*—to channel the energy of workplace activists. The Wall Street Project promoted shareholder actions for gay rights. For ten years it waged a highly publicized campaign against Cracker Barrel after the restaurant blatantly fired eleven gay and lesbian workers across the Midwest and South.[108]

One of the most significant innovations of this burgeoning workplace movement was the deployment of standardized criteria for evaluating a company's climate for gay and, eventually, transgender employees. Those standards had been developed years earlier by NGTF and included several benchmarks for business: a written nondiscrimination policy that included sexual orientation; domestic partner benefits; recognition of gay affinity groups; diversity training that included sexual orientation; sensitive marketing; and support for AIDS causes.[109] It was the brainchild of author Grant Lukenbill and financial adviser Howard Tharsing to systematically collect information from corporations on the benchmarks and then make them available to gay consumers in a "Gay/Lesbian Values

105. Interview with Desma Holcomb, Toronto, Canada, 2014.

106. High-Tech Gays won an important legal challenge in 1987, when a federal district court ruled that it was a violation of equal protection guarantees for the Department of Defense to engage in more extensive investigations of gay employees who applied for security clearances (than it did of other applicants). See "Homosexuals Win Case on Security," *New York Times*, August 22, 1987, 8.

107. Flyer, "The NGLTF Workplace Project," Steve Mershon Papers; "Going National," *Gay/Lesbian/Bisexual Corporate Newsletter* 1 (November/December 1992): 4.

108. Interview with Grant Lukenbill, conducted via telephone, 2015; Raeburn, *Changing Corporate America*, 43.

109. Interview with Grant Lukenbill, conducted via telephone, 2015; Raeburn, *Changing Corporate America*, 142–43.

Index."[110] Lukenbill added a metric for transgender issues and maintained the list through the 1990s, when it was taken over by the Human Rights Campaign Fund and reincarnated as the Corporate Equality Index.[111] A company's rating provided another pressure point for employees and accelerated the extension of progay workplace policies beyond Silicon Valley and the other leading sectors, such as entertainment and financial services, toward a broader adoption by more of the Fortune 500.[112]

It's difficult to overstate how fast moving this all was. In 1989, the committee of business people convened by the San Francisco Chamber of Commerce considered the adoption of partner benefits as a possibility "several decades from now."[113] Yet within ten years, eighty-three of the largest corporations in the country had made DP benefits available to same-sex partners of their employees.[114] Many more had antidiscrimination policies in place or had recognized gay employee groups. The contrast to the federal government—where an increasingly sophisticated lobbying operation was unable to achieve similar results with antidiscrimination legislation—was sharp. Less sharp but still clear was the contrast with the labor movement, where grassroots activism by organizations such as Boston's Gay and Lesbian Labor Activists' Network (GALLAN) and New York's Lesbian and Gay Labor Network (LGLN) was fueled by the same 1987 March on Washington that sparked gay organizing at Lotus and Bell Labs. In the labor context, as Pride at Work founder Nancy Wohlforth observed, with the exception of some progressive unions, grassroots gay

110. Grant Lukenbill, *Smart Spending: The Gay and Lesbian Guide to Socially Responsible Spending and Investing* (Los Angeles: Alyson Books, 2000).

111. In the 1990s, as the Corporate Equality Index gained visibility, workplace advocacy became a greater focus for the Human Rights Campaign Fund (later just the Human Rights Campaign, HRC) than it had been for the National Gay and Lesbian and Task Force (NGLTF). For a nuanced examination of NGLTF and HRC during these years, see Stephen Engel, *Fragmented Citizens: The Changing Landscape of Gay and Lesbian Lives* (New York: New York University Press, 2016), especially chapter 4.

112. Interview with Grant Lukenbill, conducted via telephone, 2015; Raeburn, *Changing Corporate America*, 142–43. In addition, San Francisco's 1996 Equal Benefits Ordinance provided another incentive by requiring that businesses that contracted with the city provide equal benefits. Ninety percent of those who adopted DP benefits to comply were small companies, thus spreading the momentum beyond large corporations. See Marc A. Rogers, "Contracts with Equality: An Evaluation of the San Francisco Equal Benefits Ordinance," report of the Institute for Gay and Lesbian Strategic Studies (IGLSS), 27, folder 21, box 38, Records of the Human Rights Campaign.

113. Peter Hanson to Domestic Partnership Study Group, June 7, 1983, San Francisco Chamber of Commerce, accessed at Levi Strauss corporate headquarters, San Francisco.

114. Raeburn, *Changing Corporate America*, 3.

rights organizing was stymied by an "old boys network" at the top.[115] In the building trades, as the historian Miriam Frank remarked, the organization of openly LGBT union caucuses by the end of the 1990s "was not even a notion."[116]

What do the cases of Lotus and Bell Labs reveal about why progress was faster in the corporate realm? One answer has to do with the particularities of the tech sector, where the movement for workplace rights enjoyed its earliest successes. While the management of Silicon Valley companies was certainly white and male, these were not established enterprises run by an "old boys network." The environment within them was countercultural and initially somewhat topsy-turvy in terms of gender; early computer programming was, for example, dominated by women.[117] Most of these companies, moreover, had a high tolerance for nonconformists. Margie Bleichman at Lotus remembered "the guy who had the hamster in his cubicle."[118] Elizabeth Birch, who was general counsel at Apple during the 1980s, described those years as typified by the brilliant programmers with "earrings and purple hair." Birch's assertion that if you were gifted "no one cared" seemed to apply to at least a limited extent to the trans woman Lynn Conway, an extremely talented computer scientist whose research inaugurated a revolution in microchip design.[119] After she transitioned from male to female in the late 1960s, she was fired by IBM and later denied employment by RCA, but she continued to reveal her identity to the personnel office everywhere she subsequently worked. This disclosure was necessary in order to get a security clearance; her past would inevitably be revealed in the investigation, so she needed the personnel office behind her. Although she restarted her career several levels below where she had been at IBM, all her subsequent employers hired her despite her quiet revelation, and over time she worked her way back up the ladder.[120] Even for those without purple hair, like Henry Baird at Bell

115. Interview with Nancy Wohlforth, Washington, DC, 2013.

116. Miriam Frank, "Lesbian and Gay Caucuses in the U.S. Labor Movement," in Hunt, *Laboring for Rights*, 100.

117. Interview with Lynn Conway, Ann Arbor, MI, 2015; interview with AnnD Canavan, Margie Bleichman, and Polly Laurelchild, Brookline, MA, 2015.

118. Interview with AnnD Canavan, Margie Bleichman, and Polly Laurelchild, Brookline, MA, 2015.

119. Interview with Elizabeth Birch, Bethesda, MD, 2015; Jeremy Alicandri, "IBM Apologizes for Firing Computer Pioneer for Being Transgender . . . 52 Years Later," *Forbes*, November 18, 2020, https://www.forbes.com/sites/jeremyalicandri/2020/11/18/ibm -apologizes-for-firing-computer-pioneer/?sh=6980f22967d5.

120. Interview with Lynn Conway, Ann Arbor, MI, 2015. On Conway's contribution to the Very Large Scale Integration (VSLI) revolution of the 1970s, see the University of

Labs, something about computing drew LGBT people. "There was a sense in which high-tech people worked . . . in isolation among well-educated young people who were . . . open-minded and liberal."[121] All these factors made the computer industry, in the words of the diversity trainer Brian McNaught, "the new florist's shop."[122]

Yet an experimental culture of openness did not in and of itself make it safe for people to be out; in any of these companies only a few dared to be open during the 1980s. This is why, as scenarios at Bell Labs and Lotus demonstrate, rudimentary electronic mail and computerized bulletin boards were so critical. Those Unix-based technologies allowed employees in the industry to sidestep the problem that had long plagued gay politics more generally—that of the phantom constituency. It was a classic catch-22: "Until protections exist and societal attitudes change many gays rightfully fear coming out," the legal scholar Barbara Case observed in 1989. "But unless gays let politicians know they exist, their strength as a group remains hidden, making it difficult to gain legislative support."[123] For this reason, the founder of the nation's first gay lobbying organization complained, "it was almost impossible" to get gay and lesbian professionals involved in gay politics during these years.[124] "It used to be that the more strongly a person identified himself or herself as gay," a career consultant explained to *Personnel Journal* in 1995, "the less likely that person would be to identify himself or herself as professional."[125] There was, in fact, a sharp opposition between having a career and being "political."

So, in the years before email enabled surreptitious gay organizing within business, a man wrote a letter to the executive director of the National Gay Task Force urging her to contact Prudential Insurance, his employer, to argue that the company should adopt a nondiscrimination statement protecting its gay employees. He provided detailed instructions about winning arguments but then concluded, "I hope you will cover my

Michigan's *Engineering Research News*, https://news.engin.umich.edu/2018/10/computing-pioneer-to-receive-honorary-um-doctor-of-science-degree/.

121. Interview with Henry Baird, Bethlehem, PA, 2015.

122. Interview with Brian McNaught, Ft. Lauderdale, FL, 2015.

123. Barbara Case, "Repealable Rights: Municipal Civil Rights Protections for Lesbians and Gays," *Minnesota Journal of Law and Inequality* 7 (December 1989): 448. See also Barney Frank, *Frank: A Life in Politics from the Great Society to Same-Sex Marriage* (New York: Farrar, Straus and Giroux, 2015), 96.

124. Steve Endean and Vicki Eaklor, eds., *Bringing Lesbian and Gay Rights into the Mainstream: Twenty Years of Progress* (New York: Routledge, 2006), 34. Endean was the founder of the Human Rights Campaign Fund.

125. Shari Cauldron, "Open the Corporate Closet to Sexual Orientation Issues," *Personnel Journal* 74 (August 1995): 44.

traces as you pursue this."[126] Just a few years later, gay employees were banding together and making the case to their employers themselves. They were politicized by the AIDS crisis, and they had also watched their colleagues who worked in technical fields lose security clearances and sometimes jobs.[127] But what seemed to make as much difference was the way that quasi-private electronic communication, in spaces like soc.motss and League!gg, enabled them to stealthily move toward a safe, quiet, but critical mass. We now recognize the more general phenomenon of communities finding each other, and the vast political possibility that this enabled, as the power of social media. No one knew to name it that way then. "What if we had only had the courage and the wit to notice it at the time and push it further and faster earlier?" Henry Baird wondered about the early years of gay organizing within Bell Labs, which had at that time "the best email in the world."[128] Perhaps no one could see the broader phenomenon because the work to simply find one another, formulate demands, and finally come out enough to approach management was all consuming, and (in the same way the internet later changed temporalities) also proceeding at a breakneck pace. That was on display as gay affinity groups and DP benefits spread rapidly across Silicon Valley in the early to mid-1990s. By that time, companies that had once been the experimental edge of the economy had become its leading sector, and more staid, long-established companies outside of high tech looked at Silicon Valley as a model. Some of Silicon Valley's ways of doing things, including policies that affirmed gay employees, leapfrogged relatively quickly to other parts of the Fortune 500. As they did, electronic communication remained a vital tool, helping queer people to find and acknowledge one another while simultaneously respecting particular norms around privacy and discretion. "Email—and Why You Need It," was the front-page story in the winter 1993 edition of the *Gay/Lesbian/Bisexual Corporate Letter*.[129] In the early years, it was sometimes information technology (IT) employees in companies in other parts of industry who began to organize their gay coworkers as activism moved across a wider swath of corporate America.[130]

126. AK to Jean O'Leary, January 12, 1977, folder 7, box 98, Records of the National Gay and Lesbian Task Force.

127. That security clearances were a topic on soc.motss from the beginning suggests an interesting link between discrimination in the public sector and activism in the private sector among knowledge workers. See also chapter 3.

128. Interview with Henry Baird, Bethlehem, PA, 2015.

129. Ronald Hayden, "Email—and Why You Need It," *Gay/Lesbian/Bisexual Corporate Letter*, Winter 1993, 1.

130. This was the case, for example, in the mid-1990s at the Chubb Group, and around the same time at Shell Oil, and probably many other companies during these

Besides the IT department, the diversity office often helped to translate Silicon Valley personnel practices for queer employees to the rest of corporate America. In addition to the advent of electronic mail and related communication technologies, another major factor that helped spread LGBT policies through corporate America was the shift from affirmative action to diversity that occurred from the 1980s and into the early 1990s. That shift was prompted first by Ronald Reagan's election to the presidency, which brought an abrupt end to the use of affirmative action policies to redress discrimination against women and minorities.[131] Enforcement virtually halted during these years, but affirmative action law already had established a huge presence inside personnel and human resources offices in both the public and the private sectors. In corporate America, EEO officers acted quickly to salvage their programs, primarily by adopting diversity rhetoric and "disassociating" it from civil rights law and compliance.[132] Diversity was about business efficiency and becoming an employer of choice, they maintained, rather than an onerous legal requirement. They argued that the most competitive businesses in the future would be the ones that were best equipped to tap into the resources of an increasingly diverse workforce. These proselytizers were aided in 1987 by the publication of *Workplace 2000*, a report commissioned by Reagan's Department of Labor, which projected increasing percentages of immigrants and racial minorities by century's end.[133] By the early 1990s, diversity consulting was a booming business as corporations spent millions to hire consultants and trainers and linked management compensation to diversity benchmarks.[134]

The push by gay employees for workplace rights during the late 1980s and early 1990s was thus perfectly timed with the rise of diversity management within industry. It was also perfectly aligned with it. Going back to

years where IT employees would have been the first exposed (through soc.motss and groups like Digital Queers) to what was happening in Silicon Valley. On Chubb, see "Hello" note, June 26, 2001, folder 64, box 23, McNaught Papers; on Shell Oil, see transcript of "Diversity Best Practices Conference Call," August 16, 2000, 29, folder 3, box 23, McNaught Papers.

131. See Erin Kelly and Frank Dobbin, "How Affirmative Action Became Diversity Management: Employer Response to Antidiscrimination Law," *American Behavioral Scientist* 41 (April 1998): 960–84; Nancy MacLean, *Freedom Is Not Enough: The Opening of the American Workplace* (Cambridge, MA: Harvard University Press, 2006), 300–314.

132. Lauren B. Edelman, Sally Riggs Fuller, and Iona Mara-Drita, "Diversity Rhetoric and the Managerialization of Law," *American Journal of Sociology* 106 (May 2001): 1589.

133. See Kelly and Dobbin, "How Affirmative Action Became Diversity Management," 960–84.

134. Heather MacDonald, "The Diversity Industry," *New Republic*, July 5, 1993, 22–25.

the 1970s, gay organizations had disavowed any interest in affirmative action on the grounds that it was impractical. How would quotas or targets be set when no one had any idea how many gay people there were? And how could gay people claim affirmative action without actually coming out?[135] What they articulated instead came to be known as the "business case."[136] Antigay discrimination actually "penalized *the employer* by depriving the company of qualified workers and impairing the productivity of gay employees already on the job," the National Gay Task Force asserted.[137] Rather than "reasoning from race" in making workplace claims, in other words, gay employees increasingly engaged in market talk.[138] By the 1990s the argument had crystalized that gay people would most effectively advance their interests in the corporation by always bringing the focus back to business.[139] And what was good for gay workers in this instance was probably also good for EEO officers— incorporating gays who were excluded from civil rights laws into diversity initiatives made the curtailment of affirmative action policies instead feel like an expansion. Diversity rhetoric, the sociologist Lauren Edelman noted, included "a wide array of characteristics not explicitly covered by any law." It represented a "weakened ideal of civil rights," but with a far broader impact.[140]

The older model of EEO and civil rights enforcement had sometimes benefited LGBT employees, but usually only indirectly.[141] The benefit

135. See Michael Morris to Ken Oshman, December 28, 1979, "Sexual Orientation Ordinance," especially the section titled "Gay People and Affirmative Action," 7–8 in "G/L Civil Rights—Various States, 1978–83," folder 33, box 4, Records of the Human Rights Campaign; and the note reading, "Quotas not appropriate [as] presence of openly gay employees is required," in "Notes Out of ICCR," December 10, 1974, folder 41, box 97, Records of the National Gay and Lesbian Task Force.

136. Conference Agenda for LEAGUE and EQUAL, 1996, Internal Files: Executive Director Kerry Lobel, series 1, folder 56, box 22, Records of the National Gay and Lesbian Task Force. The language of the "business case" was commonly used among gay rights advocates during these years.

137. "The NGTF Corporate Survey," circa 1983, folder 3, box 98, Records of the National Gay and Lesbian Task Force.

138. "Problem Solving," *Working It Out: The Newsletter for Gay and Lesbian Employment Issues*, Summer 1992, 5; Serena Mayeri, *Reasoning from Race: Feminism, Law, and the Civil Rights Revolution* (Cambridge, MA: Harvard University Press, 2014).

139. On the analogous way advocates for nonsmokers' rights used the "business case" to argue for nonsmoking policies in the workplace (as good for the bottom line), see Sarah E. Milov, "Clearing the Air and Counting Costs: *Shrimp v. New Jersey Bell* and the Tragedy of Workplace Smoking," in *Shaped by the State: Toward a New Political History of the Twentieth Century*, ed. Brent Cebul, Lily Geismer, and Mason B. Williams (Chicago: University of Chicago Press, 2019), 218–40.

140. Edelman et al., "Diversity Rhetoric and the Managerialization of Law," 1590, 1632.

141. Lesbians of course benefited directly from these laws as women, and queer people of color as racial minorities.

could be felt more directly in states with antidiscrimination laws, which were nonetheless still fairly anemic at these lower levels of governance. Local and state civil rights laws underprotected gay people, in other words, because clauses were often written in severely compromised language (explicitly disapproving of homosexuality, for example) or slipped in so quietly that few knew about the change in the law that had occurred.[142] Diversity policies—even as they represented a weakened and privatized civil rights—were, by contrast, a direct, and sometimes even dramatic, improvement for gays and lesbians. As time went on, they explicitly included gay issues in the menu of diversity initiatives spreading through the company. As importantly, diversity initiatives brought LGBT employees strong allies in the EEO offices of corporate America. It was not an accident that Ethel Batten was a hero to the founders of LEAGUE and that Janet Axelrod was held in similarly high esteem by the organizers at LOTUS. As the sociologist Frank Dobbin observed, EEO policy was made on the ground by personnel managers.[143] Notably, the Lambda Legal Defense and Education Fund advised those hoping to persuade their companies to offer DP benefits during these years to find a "friendly human resources officer."[144]

So, in seeking an explanation for the pace and responsiveness of big business to gay workplace rights, we find that rudimentary email first provided the technical basis for hidden people to organize, while the shift from affirmative action to diversity gave these early organizations natural allies in the corporations' EEO offices. But, in addition to the technology that fueled organization and strategically placed allies, these activists were also *pushing against a door that opened*. Why did the "old boys network" at the top of corporate America then respond when counterparts inside government and the labor movement did not?

Corporations have no obligation and nothing to gain from making their records available to historians, which makes it hard to look inside

---

142. State laws represented "the strongest political compromise that gay rights advocates were able to obtain," legal scholar Jane Schacter wrote in 1994. She noted that such laws limited the protection that extended to gays and lesbians; some went further in disclaiming any "approval" of homosexuality or in *explicitly making a linkage between homosexuality and child abuse.* Jane Schacter, "The Gay Civil Rights Debate in the States: Decoding the Discourse of Equivalents," *Harvard Civil Rights–Civil Liberties Law Review* 29 (1994): 287; Barbara Case, "Repealable Rights," 441–57.

143. Frank Dobbin, *Inventing Equal Opportunity* (Princeton, NJ: Princeton University Press, 2011).

144. Lambda Legal Defense and Education Fund, *Negotiating for Equal Employment Benefits: A Resource Packet* (New York: Lambda Legal, 1994), 3 (in author's possession).

their heads. Yet at the risk of speculating about societal changes that are still ongoing, one possibility is that corporations responded relatively quickly to the claims of LGBT employees because those employees fit the template of late capitalism so well. Historians and economic sociologists are just beginning to understand the "third industrial revolution" that emerged in the 1970s and divided the Fordist era that came before from the post-Fordist one that came after.[145] That shift was driven by globalization and the outsourcing of jobs, the decline of manufacturing and the rise of the service economy in the US and Europe, technological innovation, financialization, and changing investment patterns, among other factors. As Jacob Hacker has written, it was characterized as well by the demise of a social contract "whose influence belied its less-than-complete reach."[146] That old contract, which governed the economy from the end of World War II into the mid-1970s, was defined by employee loyalty to the company and a tamping down of labor militancy in exchange for high wages, decent benefits, and job security. In blue- and white-collar settings, jobs for "breadwinners" were often for life, and the idea of the family wage was sacrosanct. The key words of the Fordist regime were attachment, stability, and security.[147]

Yet many were, as Hacker has suggested, excluded from the benefits of Fordism. In fact, the Fordist economy was divided between core and peripheral sectors, and the periphery was defined by low wages and job insecurity, a combination now referred to as precarity.[148] That sector of the economy was heavily African American, female, immigrant, and also visibly queer. "While the division between a predominantly white, male, and highly unionized work force and the 'rest' was useful . . . for labor control," the geographer David Harvey has explained, "it also meant a rigidity in labour markets" that created difficulties for employers. When heightened

145. Gerald Davis, *The Vanishing American Corporation* (Oakland: Berrett-Koehler, 2016), 168.

146. Jacob Hacker, *The Great Risk Shift: The New Economic Insecurity and the Decline of the American Dream* (New York: Oxford University Press, 2006), 65.

147. On post-Fordism / flexible capitalism, see especially, Hacker, *Great Risk Shift*; David Harvey, *The Condition of Postmodernity: An Enquiry into the Origins of Cultural Change* (Cambridge, MA: Blackwell, 1990); Alison Pugh, *The Tumbleweed Society: Working and Caring in an Age of Insecurity* (Oxford: Oxford University Press, 2015). The stability of Fordism came with its own set of costs, of course. As Pugh has observed, as appealing as it might seem, the old contract was reserved for "skilled white men and . . . rooted in deep inequalities—of gender, of sexualities, of class, of race" (186–87).

148. Harvey, *Condition of Postmodernity*, 138. Harvey used the terms "monopoly" and "competitive" to distinguish between the core and the peripheral sectors of the Fordist economy.

competition and labor surpluses made it possible to do so in the 1970s, employers began to look for an escape from these expensive, lifelong commitments to primary workers and their families. In the ensuing years, the "core" who could still rely on such permanent full-time employment continued to shrink, and part-time, temporary, and subcontracted work became far more prevalent.[149] Businesses also shed much of the responsibility they once claimed for the care of the families of employees.[150]

Missed in this extensive discussion of what the sociologist Gerald Davis has labeled "the death of the career" is the recognition that gay workers actually may have been harbingers of precarity in the "core" sector all along.[151] Although these workers could sometimes benefit from the stable high-wage employment of the Fordist era, they were more often a reserve labor force within the system, vulnerable to being pushed out with even minor downturns in the business cycle. One midcentury observer wrote, for example, about the various degrees of "economic precariousness" he observed among the homosexuals he knew, who were "gainfully employed now because times are still good, but candidates for economic hardship should times become hard."[152] His remarks were not class specific; the observation held true all the way up the socioeconomic ladder. Often readily discoverable if an employer cared to look, gays and lesbians were guest workers of the corporate office—unattached, contingent, and in a sense, deportable.[153] Their vulnerability made them exploitable in particular ways, and as a result they brought distinct and valuable assets to the companies they worked for. They worked hard for the company but also knew that being overly ambitious

149. Ibid., 150.

150. "Cutting-Edge Issue," 50.

151. Davis, *Vanishing American Corporation*, 123.

152. Report of Alfred Gross for the Quaker Emergency Service Civil Readjustment Committee, December 31, 1947, "Sex Offenders—1947" folder, box 1962, Records of the Society for the Prevention of Crime, Rare Books and Manuscripts Library, Columbia University, New York, NY.

153. "Deportable" is meant in the sense that even as late as 1996, "public and private sector employers in most places can and do discriminate against gay men and lesbians in the workplace with impunity." Norma Riccucci and Charles M. Gossett, "Employment Discrimination in State and Local Government: The Lesbian and Gay Male Experience," *American Review of Public Administration* 26 (June 1996): 176. And while some legal protections existed at state and local levels, in practice, those ordinances sometimes made employees more rather than less vulnerable. Barbara Case documented, for example, how filing a discrimination complaint in one city generally meant coming out and attracting attention that made one more vulnerable if one ever moved away from that municipality. In those circumstances, many people abandoned claims partway through the process. "The gay victim of discrimination . . . stands to lose more through publicity than would be gained by a settlement." Case, "Repealable Rights," 456.

about their career trajectory exposed them to risk.[154] Yet they were simultaneously available to put in extra hours or work split shifts, travel for the company on a moment's notice, or be transferred to a different part of the country.[155] Those who were partnered behaved as if they were single.[156] As a rule, they were flexible workers in the Fordist regime, accepting far more tenuous ties to the workplace than did the typical "organization" man or woman, forging identities and lasting attachments *outside* the workplace.[157]

When flexible capitalism arrived, LGBT employees thus fit the new paradigm extremely well. It is hard to know if employers got these ideas about reconfiguring work—about treating, say, even white professional men like casual, unattached labor—from observing the quasi-visible, quasi-knowable gay men and lesbians in their industries.[158] At the very least, there is an intriguing overlap between the earliest companies to make flexible capitalism the model of their employment relations and those that also were the first to advance gay rights. Those developments happened nearly simultaneously in Silicon Valley. And the last sectors to recognize the rights of their LGBT employees? Those were the "old economy" or heavy-industry sector, which was also the most removed from flexible modes of production.[159]

———◆———

Did the corporation co-opt gay rights? Did gay rights co-opt the corporation? In attempting to evaluate that question—which is really a question

154. This is a very common theme in many interviews I have done with LGBT employees born in the 1930s and 1940s about their working lives. See also "What Price Promotion?," in which a lesbian working for a Silicon Valley defense contractor declined a promotion because it would have meant having to get a higher-level security clearance that could expose her. "What Price Promotion?," *Bay Area Career Women*, April–May 1985, 1.

155. Joseph Harry and William B. DeVall, *The Social Organization of Gay Males* (New York: Praeger, 1978).

156. Even domestic partnership didn't change that because many gays and lesbians really never felt secure enough to claim the benefits.

157. Daniel Bell, "The Post-industrial Economy," *Educational Forum* 40 (1976): 575–79; Vicki Smith, "New Forms of Work Organization," *Annual Review of Sociology* 23 (1997): 315–39.

158. Louis Hyman has argued that the idea came from the advent of temporary agencies (who not incidentally employed a lot of queer people). Intriguingly, he also has noted the importance of undocumented workers in Silicon Valley especially who (like temps) "enabled employers to imagine a workplace without obligations, without regulations, and without oversight." Louis Hyman, *Temp: How American Work, American Business, and the American Dream Became Temporary* (New York: Viking, 2018), 112. On the analogy I draw between queer and immigrant work, see chapter 2.

159. Raeburn, *Changing Corporate America*, 14.

about how historians should think about corporate America's remarkable turn toward gay rights in the last decades of the twentieth century, as well as how they should assess the most privatized of all American social movements—it's important not to overlook the people who first set these changes in motion. Seeing the founders of LEAGUE and the Lotus trio as activists is a helpful reminder that progress in the corporate sector did not come from the voluntary initiative of employers, as the "appropriation" framework implies, but only at the behest of newly mobilized clusters of employees. And while the men and women of LEAGUE and Lotus may not look or sound like what we think of as gay activists in the liberation / ACT UP era, "zapping" recalcitrant employers and decrying corporate neglect from the streets, they took huge risks and were courageous in their context. "We were strong, we were sturdy, we were forthright, and we didn't cry in public," Henry Baird remembered tearfully, but "you didn't really feel safe. You felt you were making a little progress on the edges, but it could all vanish. . . . It could all go backwards."[160]

Like all activists, their politics look messy in hindsight and may have had some unintended consequences. While gay rights movements have employed "tactical dexterity"—lobbying, litigation, shareholder activism, and direct action—gay advocates also "negotiated directly with employers to obtain internal policies against discrimination" in a way that no other civil rights constituency has done.[161] That special dependence on the corporation was born out of the particular vulnerabilities created by state abandonment.[162] No other minority group has had so little claim on formal legal protection on the job, so gays argued quite persuasively that closeted and fearful people could not be productive workers. The business case was accepted relatively quickly. Indeed, the speed and visibility with which corporations came to embrace gay rights may actually have helped to undermine the larger case for antidiscrimination legislation, as the supposed power and affluence of the gay community was always marshaled as "exhibit A" in the case against such laws.[163] What the corporation offered

160. Interview with Henry Baird, Bethlehem, PA, 2015.

161. Nan Hunter, "Civil Rights 3.0," in *A Nation of Widening Opportunities? The Civil Rights Act at Fifty*, ed. Samuel Bagenstos and Ellen Katz (Ann Arbor: University of Michigan Press, 2015), 48, 58.

162. A related and useful discussion is found in Matthew Dean Hindman, *Political Advocacy and Its Interested Citizens: Neoliberalism, Postpluralism, and LGBT Organizations* (Philadelphia: University of Pennsylvania Press, 2019).

163. Chai Feldblum, Written Statement, 145–48, US Congress, House, Hearings before the Subcommittee on Government Programs of the Committee on Small Business, *The Employment Non-discrimination Act of 1995*, 104th Cong., 2nd sess., July 17, 1996.

instead was patchwork protection that made it possible for middle- and upper-class gays to go from being the least to the most visible part of the community over the course of the postwar era.[164] People of color and trans people, as well as many southerners, rural residents, and others living outside of progressive states, were nearly as vulnerable as they had always been. This seems then to lend credence to Lisa Duggan's influential critique of "neoliberal equality politics" as "compatible with the continued upward redistribution of resources."[165]

But, perhaps, that may be true mostly in the short run? In the longer term, the unprecedented shift in cultural attitudes that has occurred in the last thirty years seems inconceivable without the corporation, which (until very recently) was virtually the only national entity on the scale of the state that stood with queer people. The likely impact of that relationship extended well beyond those who worked in the corporate sector. It's hard to imagine marriage equality or the repeal of the military ban, for example, without the Fortune 500's trumpeting of gay workplace rights for the preceding several decades.[166] Open military service and same-sex marriage were conservative goals to be sure, but they nonetheless serve as a reminder that private-sector advances may come back to reform state policies that have a very broad reach.[167] That dynamic was also clearly at play when President Obama issued an executive order protecting federal workers and the EEOC pushed litigation to establish that LGBT employees were covered under Title VII's prohibition on sex discrimination—a legal theory just recently affirmed by the Supreme Court.[168]

164. "Middle-class and wealthy gay people are far more likely to be visible than are working-class and poor queers," Urvashi Vaid wrote in 1995. Vaid, *Virtual Equality: The Mainstreaming of Gay and Lesbian Liberation* (New York: Anchor Books, 1995), 256. That was a reversal of patterns at midcentury. See, for example, Maurice Leznoff and William Westley, "The Homosexual Community," in *Sexual Deviance*, ed. William Simon and John H. Gagnon (New York: Harper and Row, 1967), 184–96 (reprinted from *Social Problems* 3 [April 1956]: 257–63).

165. Duggan, *Twilight of Equality*, xii.

166. "A growing number of organizations appear to be successfully tackling what the Pentagon portrays as unsolveable," the *Washington Post* chided in a 1993 article that described, for example, how employers were by then accommodating gays while the military still refused. Lee Gomes, "Many Employers Make Room for Gays in Ways the Military Won't," *Washington Post*, February 21, 1993, H2.

167. I use the word "conservative" in the sense that these reforms were about expanding access to traditional institutions rather than transforming them. Political scientist Stephen Engel has emphasized "the need to grapple with the way private sector developments affect public or state recognition of the status of LGBT persons." Engel, *Fragmented Citizens*, 6.

168. *Macy v. Holder*, No. 0120120821, 2012 WL 1435995 (E.E.O.C., April 20, 2012); *Baldwin v. Fox*, No. 0120133080, 2015 WL 4397641 (E.E.O.C., July 15, 2015); *Bostock v. Clayton County, Georgia*, 590 U.S. ___, 140 S. Ct. 1731 (2020) (No. 17-1618).

What that expanded legal protection will actually mean in the context of ever-growing economic precarity remains an open question, and one taken up in greater detail in the epilogue. More immediately, that these citizens—long denied fundamental rights—did not refuse "the opportunities afforded within neoliberalism's limits" in no way diminishes their courage but rather illuminates the ways that civil rights have sometimes moved through market logics, for better or worse.[169]

169. Hindman, *Political Advocacy and Its Interested Citizens*, 118.

Epilogue

IN THE SPRING OF 2018, I participated in an innovative program of the New York Historical Society called "Think and Drink with Historians." For this series, the Historical Society invited scholars to its museum and library in Manhattan to present their research to New York City elementary and secondary schoolteachers and then engage them in an informal conversation over wine. In my talk, I outlined much of what has become the first chapter of this book. Then, as I settled in with a glass of chardonnay, I expected to field the standard questions about how I conducted my research, or how I planned to develop subsequent chapters to move the story forward. Instead, my audience, which turned out to be made up almost entirely of LGBT teachers, was primarily interested in talking with one another. Many of them, they revealed to their colleagues, were closeted in their respective schools. They wanted to talk about the difficulties of navigating that situation, as well as their worries that they were letting down the queer kids in their classrooms by not being more open.

As a spectator to this unexpectedly intimate conversation, I was initially surprised that many of the teachers in attendance suggested that they were not out in their jobs. Across the country, of course, teachers still deal with homophobic and transphobic parents and school boards. But teachers also enjoyed the earliest labor movement support of any occupation.[1] And this was *New York City*. As I reflected on it later, however, I came to feel more perplexed about why I had expected these teachers to feel comfortable at work. Their experience, after all, lines up well with recent studies, which estimate that nearly half of LGBT workers in this country are not open at

---

1. Miriam Frank, *Out in the Union: A Labor History of Queer America* (Philadelphia: Temple University Press, 2014), 6–7.

their places of employment.[2] What those New York City teachers revealed about how they managed their working lives is also consistent with one of the central themes of this book about the long history of queer vulnerability in the workplace. Yet despite being steeped in this longer history, the fact that I initially felt surprised by this lingering insecurity is itself a testament to how deeply engraved in our popular consciousness certain myths about LGBT people have become. Historical and even contemporary evidence of queer precarity has been consistently overlooked and underplayed. Instead we are regularly presented with images that underscore the privilege of LGBT people, particularly their wealth and even their social power. Those images leave a deep imprint, even on those who study these issues and should have a critical vantage on them.

What has correctly been identified as the "myth" of gay affluence has several points of origin.[3] The most ironic source is gay people themselves. Unable to secure meaningful employment protection from the state, LGBT employees increasingly appealed to their employers directly. They made a case for support from their employers based on their own value and productivity as workers. They understandably bolstered this claim with another about their increasing economic clout, sometimes emphasizing a unique market position as childless people with high discretionary incomes. While this *may* have been true for the select segment that was making the pitch, it certainly wasn't true of the broader LGBT community. Market researchers in search of advertising dollars simultaneously pointed to unrepresentative surveys of the readership of gay publications to highlight "only the most 'desirable' members of the market."[4] While data greatly overstating the economic position of LGBT people has been repeatedly debunked by economists, the right wing grabbed hold of it and has never let it go.[5] For several decades, numerous attempts to pass

2. For 2018 data, see the website of the Human Rights Campaign, https://www.hrc.org /resources/a-workplace-divided-understanding-the-climate-for-lgbtq-workers-nationwide. The Pew Research Center reported in 2013 that one in five LGBT Americans reported experiencing employment discrimination. Pew Research Center, *A Survey of LGBT Americans: Attitudes, Experiences, and Values in Changing Times* (Washington, DC, 2013).

3. M. V. Lee Badgett, "Beyond Biased Samples: Challenging the Myths on the Economic Status of Lesbians and Gay Men," in *Homo Economics: Capitalism, Community, and Lesbian, and Gay Life*, ed. Amy Gluckman and Betsy Reed (New York: Routledge, 1997), 65–72.

4. Katherine Sender, *Business Not Politics: The Making of the Gay Market* (New York: Columbia University Press, 2004), 7–8. See also Urvashi Vaid, *Virtual Equality: The Mainstreaming of Gay and Lesbian Liberation* (New York: Anchor Books, 1995), 253–56.

5. The economist Lee Badgett shows that, contrary to the myth of gay affluence, gay men have earned between 11 percent and 27 percent less than heterosexual men. Lesbians

antidiscrimination laws have been countered by social conservatives who have claimed that LGBT people are elites who neither need nor deserve protection. That sentiment even made its way into Justice Scalia's dissent in the landmark 1996 Supreme Court civil rights case (*Romer v. Evans*) that decided the fate of Colorado's Amendment 2, a ballot measure that attempted to deny civil rights protections to gay people. In his dissent, Scalia referenced the "high disposable income" of gay people, and their disproportionate political power as evidence that gays and lesbians were not disadvantaged like other groups covered by civil rights laws.[6] But even before Scalia wrote those words, gay civil rights advocates already understood that every serious attempt to win antidiscrimination legislation, whether at state or federal levels, had to begin by thoroughly surveying and documenting the discrimination queer people faced, even if this was experienced internally as a somewhat ridiculous exercise. Such discrimination was, as activists vented in the 1970s, "*self-evident*."[7]

Nonetheless, it has been a necessary task, and when I embarked on this book I envisioned this research as hopefully contributing to this larger project: to demonstrate that the harms that gay people had suffered in employment were not "merely cultural" ones of "misrecognition" but also fundamentally economic, and that queerness mattered greatly in how gay people went about making their livelihoods.[8] Understanding that fact has

---

may actually earn at slightly higher rates than straight women, but they "work more hours and weeks every year than their heterosexual counterparts" for that slight gain. Lesbians still "face a large gender gap compared with men," and same-sex female households are significantly poorer than households with a male earner in them (gay or straight). See M. V. Lee Badgett, *The Economic Case for LGBT Equality* (Boston: Beacon, 2020), 53–54; Peter Drucker, *Warped: Gay Normality and Queer Anticapitalism* (Chicago: Haymarket Books, 2014), 259.

6. *Romer, Governor of Colorado, et al. v. Evans et al.*, 517 U.S. 620, 116 S. Ct. 1620 (1996) (No. 94-1039) (Scalia, J. dissenting).

7. Gay Activists Alliance, "A Homosexual Bill of Rights Presented to the New York State Legislature," folder 40, box 165, Records of the National Gay and Lesbian Task Force, Rare and Manuscript Collections, Cornell University, Ithaca, NY (emphasis mine). On the need to document discrimination in order to pass gay rights laws, see "Gay Civil Rights Legislation in Massachusetts," 1979, Lesbian Herstory Archives, Brooklyn, NY, Subject Files (microfilm reel 85, frame 07830, Thompson Gale); US Congress, House, Hearing before the Subcommittee on Employment Opportunities of the Committee on Education and Labor, *Civil Rights Amendments Act of 1979*, 96th Cong., 2nd sess., October 10, 1980; Pat Califia, "Documenting Discrimination: Michael Shively," *Advocate*, November 25, 1982, 17; US Congress, House, Hearing before the Subcommittee on Select Education and Civil Rights of the Subcommittee on Education and Labor, *Employment Discrimination against Gay Men and Lesbians*, 103rd Cong., 2nd sess., June 20, 1994.

8. On this point, see the provocative exchange between Judith Butler, "Merely Cultural," and Nancy Fraser, "Heterosexism, Misrecognition, and Capitalism: A Response to

obviously meant attending to hiring and firing, but it also requires thinking across a broader range of metrics: it's been about segmented opportunity, as well as curbed ambition, in addition to the psychic fear that
many people took with them to their jobs every day. Above all, it requires
understanding, as the liberationists so clearly did, that legal and cultural
sanctions against homosexuality did not function to keep queer people
out of certain kinds of work but rather to make them exploitable *on* the
job.[9] Homosexuality was less totally repressed under capitalism than it
was leveraged by employers.

———◆———

The history of transgender workers diverged somewhat from this pattern,
and for much of the twentieth century it tended to be a story of outright
exclusion. "A lot of the marginalization" that trans people have faced has
been because "they can't get jobs," observed Mara Keisling of the National
Center for Transgender Equality.[10] In the contemporary moment, trans
people are twice as likely as the general population to be unemployed,
and rates of extreme poverty for trans people are four times the national
average.[11] But the picture becomes even bleaker if we look back in time.
From the moment surgical intervention first became available well into
the 1980s and 1990s, a decision to transition medically (as well as socially)
was usually accompanied by severe downward mobility. "Out trans people
were not tolerated even in the most liberal work environments," one trans
woman remembered. It was "just automatic" that you lost your job. For
those in professional jobs who transitioned before they retired, the best-
case scenario involved leaving the occupation one had been trained in and
seeking employment several rungs below—a trans woman, for example,
might start over as a secretary or office assistant.[12] Trans men tended to
work in low-status, low-wage work before transition and stay in those jobs

---

Judith Butler," both in *Adding Insult to Injury: Nancy Fraser Debates Her Critics*, ed. Kevin
Olson (Brooklyn, NY: Verso, 2008), 42–69.

9. "Hiding on the Job," *Gay Liberator*, October 1, 1971, 4.

10. Claire Martin, "Going from Marginalized to Welcomed at Work," *New York Times*,
March 19, 2017, BU4.

11. "The Struggle of Transgender Workers," *New York Times*, July 9, 2015, 26.

12. Interview with Donna Cartwright, Baltimore, MD, 2013. For trans women, moving
into a much lower paid "women's" job was sometimes heralded by doctors and even other
trans people as a sign of a "successful" transition, as a well as a strategy for blending in.
Janis Walworth, *Transsexual Workers: An Employer's Guide* (Bellingham, WA: Center for
Gender Sanity, 2003), 93; Joanne Meyerowitz, *How Sex Changed: A History of Transsexuality in the United States* (Cambridge, MA: Harvard University Press, 2002), 233.

post-transition. Jude Patton, who transitioned in the 1970s in California, remembered parties he hosted for other trans men during those years. Nearly all his associates, he remembered, had working-class jobs, often in factories.[13] Trans women who held working-class jobs before they transitioned often ended up in sex work. Many of them, one observer remembered, "never made it out of their thirties and forties" because of violence, drugs, suicide, or disease. "The AIDS casualty rate was high."[14]

For those who survived through this period, as the trans woman judge Phyllis Frye declared, employment was *the key*. "If a transgender can earn enough money to pay for food and a place to live, all other obstacles can be handled in time," she wrote. "Hormone therapy, electrolysis, and new clothes can be obtained later, but only if the transgender is not on the street and hungry."[15] It was touch and go for Frye, who sold Amway cleaning products to gay bars while she struggled to find employment as a lawyer.[16] After being fired from IBM in 1968 in the wake of her transition, computer engineer Lynn Conway—whose subsequent breakthroughs in microchip design would "power smartphones and computers"—also remembered a period of desperation when she struggled to put food on the table.[17] She eventually found a low-level job as a contract programmer,

13. Interview with Jude Patton, conducted via Zoom, 2020. While distinguishing the work trajectories of trans men and trans women, Patton remembered a kind of convergence at the bottom of the labor market for both. Trans men's career trajectories tended to be relatively flat ones in which they worked in marginal jobs before and after transition; trans women who were employed in professional jobs before transition often faced severe downward mobility after transitioning. Today, the sociologist Michelle O'Brien observes that it is usually trans women who have the most difficulty passing and face the most severe employment discrimination. Michelle Esther O'Brien, "Trans Work: Employment Trajectories, Labour Discipline and Gender Freedom," in *Transgender Marxism*, ed. Jules Joanne Gleeson and Elle O'Rourke (London: Pluto, 2021), 48.

14. Interview with Donna Cartwright, Baltimore, MD, 2013.

15. Phyllis Randolph Frye, "The International Bill of Gender Rights vs. *The Cider House Rules:* Transgenders Struggle with the Courts over What Clothing They Are Allowed to Wear on the Job, Which Restroom They Are Allowed to Use on the Job, Their Right to Marry, and the Very Definition of Their Sex," *William and Mary Journal of Race, Gender, and Social Justice* 7 (October 2000): 175.

16. Deborah Sontag, "Once a Pariah, Now a Judge: The Early Transgender Journey of Phyllis Frye," *New York Times*, August 29, 2015, A1; Jenny B. Davis, "10 Questions: Groundbreaking Transgender Judge Happily Passes the Torch in Post-Caitlyn Age," *ABA Journal*, May 2016, https://www.abajournal.com/magazine/article/10_questions_groundbreaking _transgender_judge_happily_passes_the_torch_in_p.

17. Jeremy Alicandri, "IBM Apologizes for Firing Computer Pioneer for Being Transgender . . . 52 Years Later," *Forbes*, November 18, 2020, https://www.forbes.com /sites/jeremyalicandri/2020/11/18/ibm-apologizes-for-firing-computer-pioneer/?sh =6980f22967d5; interview with Lynn Conway, Ann Arbor, MI, 2015.

which was then considered a women's job. Because "there was a gender issue about keyboards," which seemed a lot like typewriters, men didn't want to touch keyboards. That strange fact gave Conway a toehold from which, undetected, she was subsequently able to rebuild her career.[18]

The situation improved incrementally, and by the 1990s some progressive employers would help transgender employees "disappear" within their companies.[19] The employee would work "behind the scenes" with human resources to take a leave of absence, and eventually the company would transfer the employee to a new location where they could appear as their true gender without anyone knowing about their past.[20] The strategy involved severing ties not only with existing coworkers but with everyone who knew the employee pre-transition, including other trans people.[21] This approach, which simply enlisted company support in the way trans people had long gone "stealth" on their own, was an arduous path even for a deeply desired outcome. Eventually some trans people began to work with their companies to stay on the job while they transitioned. In many workplaces, it was helpful that gay and lesbian employees had begun to have conversations with employers a decade or so earlier. Donna Cartwright, a copyeditor at the *New York Times*, went to her management to tell them she planned to transition. Thinking she might be fired, she told them, "You have dealt with this before with gay men and lesbians; this is just a further extension."[22] In some workplaces, trans people consciously leveraged the same formula that gays had, accepting lesser pay for the sake of greater expression on the job. When one trans woman (who at that point was still living as a man) found herself downgraded in a major reorganization of her company, she went to her management and said she would accept the downgrade, "but," she told them, "I am going to start coming to work as Pamela."[23]

These sorts of negotiations—"we weren't waiting on the laws," one trans woman remembered—gradually evolved into formal protocols and

18. Interview with Lynn Conway, Ann Arbor, MI, 2015. See also Jason Resnikoff, "The Paradox of Automation: QWERTY and the Neuter Keyboard," *Labor* 18 (December 2021): 9–39. In order to manage security clearances, Conway was quietly and strategically "out" to personnel directors in the companies she worked for.

19. In an earlier attempt, "Jane Doe" asked Boeing to reassign her to another part of the country in her new gender. They did not do that, and in 1985 she was fired for wearing a pink pearl necklace to work. See chapter 4 of Polly Reed Myers, *Capitalist Family Values: Gender, Work, and Corporate Culture at Boeing* (Lincoln: University of Nebraska Press, 2015), 129–52.

20. Interview with Mary Anne Horton, conducted via Skype, 2016.

21. Ibid.; Walworth, *Transsexual Workers*, 93.

22. Interview with Donna Cartwright, Baltimore, MD, 2013.

23. Interview subject 106, interview conducted via telephone, 2014.

guidelines for best practices.[24] Transitioning at work is typically a lot more involved than coming out as gay or lesbian, which could be as simple as putting a partner's picture on one's desk. To transition at work, by contrast, "you needed an intricate plan," as one trans woman observed. "You have to tell people your new name, ask them to use [different] pronouns, figure out how to roll this out, when you will appear at work for the first time dressed as the other sex, what bathroom you will use."[25] Personnel documents had to be altered, and more recently, efforts have been made to get employers to cover gender affirming surgery and hormones. As with the "business case" that gays and lesbians had made for domestic partner benefits in the late 1980s and early 1990s, some trans activists were able to persuade employers that the medical costs associated with an employee's transition were much less expensive to the company than the toll that "untreated transsexualism" took on employee productivity and effectiveness.[26]

———

In beginning to affirm the rights and needs of trans people on the job, the corporate sector was on pace with and in some aspects possibly even ahead of the broader gay rights movement, which had for years treated the transgender community as a political liability rather than an ally.[27] By the end of the first decade of the twenty-first century, however, the major gay rights organizations had formally brought transgender issues into their purview.[28] Meanwhile, the success of LGBT rights claims within the

24. Interview with Mary Anne Horton, conducted via Skype, 2016; "Workplace Guidelines for Transgender Employees," Company Policies, 2003 folder, box 54, Records of the Human Rights Campaign, Rare and Manuscript Collections, Cornell University. Particularly important was a 2008 Harvard Business School case study by Gary Loren and Brian Elliot, "When Steve Becomes Stephanie," *Harvard Business Review* 86 (November 2008): 35–39, 131. See also "Accommodating Sex Transformations," *HR Magazine*, October 2009, 59–63; Patricia Graves, "How Should a Company Handle Issues Related to the Use of Workplace Restrooms for a Transgender Employee?," *HR Magazine*, August 2012, 28.

25. Interview with Donna Cartwright, Baltimore, MD, 2013.

26. Interview with Mary Anne Horton, conducted via Skype, 2016.

27. Phyllis Randolph Frye, "Facing Discrimination, Organizing for Freedom," in *Creating Change: Sexuality, Public Policy, and Civil Rights*, ed. John D'Emilio, William B. Turner, and Urvashi Vaid (New York: St. Martin's, 2000), 451–68. See also Shannon Price Minter, "Do Transsexuals Dream of Gay Rights? Getting Real about Transgender Inclusion," *New York Law School Journal of Human Rights* 17 (2000): 153.

28. In 2007, however, the Human Rights Campaign supported federal antidiscrimination legislation (ENDA) that had been stripped of protection for transgender people.

corporate sector reached a remarkable apogee in 2015 in the aftermath of North Carolina's passage of the Public Facilities Privacy and Security Act (HB-2), which both banned local ordinances that protected LGBT people from discrimination and restricted access to bathrooms on the basis of sex assigned at birth. The response to HB-2 was swift. PayPal decided it would not build a global operations center in the state; Deutsche Bank similarly halted plans to add 250 jobs to bank operations there. Executives at eighty companies signed a letter calling for repeal of the law. That pressure was ultimately successful.[29] While a striking development on its own terms, the dramatic intervention by the Fortune 500 also seemed to provoke renewed skepticism among leftists and progressives who have fretted, for as long as Bank of America and Apple Computer have sponsored floats in annual gay pride parades, about the corporate seduction of LGBT rights movements. Those critiques are varied, but many are layered on the substratum belief that individual rights movements (i.e., "identity politics") have undermined collective rights struggles for economic justice.[30] The most pointed criticism, coming from a queer leftist perspective, has elaborated on Lisa Duggan's influential critique of gay rights as a balkanized movement oriented, at best, toward "legal and electoral systems for inclusion," and, at worst, toward a privatized gay culture "anchored in domesticity and consumption."[31] Queer studies is permeated, one political scientist has observed, with such "language about depoliticized or neoliberalized subjects."[32]

In response, more than three hundred organizations came together to demand that transgender-inclusive language be put back in the bill. After the legalization of gay marriage in 2015, the historian Susan Stryker observed a "rapprochement between trans activism and the liberal gay and lesbian movement," including the Human Rights Campaign. Susan Stryker, *Transgender History: The Roots of Today's Revolution* (New York: Seal, 2017), 188–93, 225.

29. Big business had a similarly antagonistic response to the Religious Freedom Act in Indiana, which would have legalized discrimination against LGBT people in that state, as well as to similar legislation in other states. James Surowiecki, "Unlikely Alliances," *New Yorker*, April 25, 2016, https://www.newyorker.com/magazine/2016/04/25/the-corporate-fight-for-social-justice.

30. Nelson Lichtenstein, *State of the Union: A Century of American Labor* (Princeton, NJ: Princeton University Press, 2002).

31. Lisa Duggan, *The Twilight of Equality: Neoliberalism, Cultural Politics, and the Attack on Democracy* (Boston: Beacon, 2003). See also Alexandra Chasen, *Selling Out: The Gay and Lesbian Movement Goes to Market* (New York: St. Martin's, 2000); Myrl Beam, *Gay, Inc.: The Non-profitization of Queer Politics* (Minneapolis: University of Minnesota Press, 2018).

32. Matthew Dean Hindman, *Political Advocacy and Its Interested Citizens: Neoliberalism, Postpluralism, and LGBT Organizations* (Philadelphia: University of Pennsylvania Press, 2019), 39.

There is certainly a grain of truth in these rhetorically powerful accounts, but they also abstract a fair amount from the historical context. In my view, the history of the modern LGBT rights movement is not a matter of privileged people sidling up to business or legitimating neoliberalism, but rather a matter of vulnerable people (and a fledgling but growing movement) exhausting every possible avenue open to them. Years and years of efforts to achieve protection in employment from the state—much of it attempted in the wake of the retrenchment of civil rights that characterized the broader Reagan/Bush era—had yielded relatively little gain beyond state-level protections in some liberal states.[33] So the interesting historical question is not why LGBT people began to negotiate directly with employers; the answer seems obvious, especially in the wake of the AIDS crisis. But why did business respond in the way that it did? While that had something to do with the persuasiveness of the business case that employees made to their companies, I contend that it had as much to do with the historical relationship between employers and their queer employees, who had long been viewed as "unattached," contingent, and flexibly deployable, the very opposite of Fordism's prototypical breadwinners. The values that had been associated with queer workers since midcentury, *in primary- as well as secondary-sector jobs*, perfectly aligned with the demands of late capitalism. "Fordism's non-normative subjects," in Melinda Cooper's striking term, thus became post-Fordism's normative ones.[34] A position that was once marginal has in some sense become the center, and we should perhaps think of queer workers less as outliers than as harbingers of axial shifts in employment relations across the second half of the twentieth century.

Nonetheless, coming to terms with what is surely the most marketized of all civil rights movements involves understanding that its engagement with business, while effective in some ways, led in a certain direction. Above all, it reinforced patchwork protection, which has provided more privileged segments of the workforce with the most recourse against harms in employment directed against LGBT people. Queers of color, trans people, and working-class queers are considerably more vulnerable

33. And, as Nan Hunter has argued, state civil rights laws tend to underprotect in general. Nan D. Hunter, "Sexuality and Civil Rights: Re-imagining Anti-discrimination Laws," *New York Law School Journal of Human Rights* 17 (2000–2001): 572–73. This is especially true in the gay rights context, however, as many have been reluctant to out themselves to claim protection in one locale if it meant potentially becoming more vulnerable elsewhere. Barbara Case, "Repealable Rights: Municipal Civil Rights Protections for Lesbians and Gays," *Minnesota Journal of Law and Inequality* 7 (December 1989): 456.

34. Melinda Cooper, *Family Values: Between Neoliberalism and the New Social Conservatism* (New York: Zone Books, 2017), 143.

to employment discrimination and harassment, and yet they have fewer tools to respond to it.[35] No wonder that "middle class and wealthy gay people are far more likely to be visible than are working class and poor queers."[36] The activist Urvashi Vaid made that observation at the end of the twentieth century, but it is probably even more true now, and as this book has shown, it represents a striking reversal from the mid-twentieth century, when queer people were far more visible in working-class occupations than in most professional settings.[37] For the queer steelworkers she studies, to take just one contemporary example, the ethnographer Anne Balay concludes, the world has gotten "less rather than more accepting."[38]

As the most privileged sectors of the community have moved increasingly into the public eye while the most vulnerable have become harder to see, the odds of outmaneuvering social conservatives, who attack proposals for antidiscrimination legislation covering LGBT employees as elitist "special rights," have remained low.[39] Indeed, regarding the prospect of enacting such legislation, the legal scholar Nan Hunter writes, over the past twenty years "the needle has not moved."[40] Fortunately, the courts have their own rhythms and logics, including the tendency to over time consolidate broader social and cultural change. To be clear, the path through the courts also seemed for years to be glacially slow; this book has pointed to the many junctures at which a cultural revolution for gay people happened without a concomitant legal revolution, so the workplace continued to exist as a somewhat retrograde space that was for many sharply bifurcated from "personal life." In particular, a consensus

35. Badgett, *Economic Case for LGBT Equality*, 38; Martin Duberman, *Has the Gay Movement Failed?* (Oakland: University of California Press, 2018), 71–72.

36. Vaid, *Virtual Equality*, 256.

37. One liberationist's assertion at the beginning of the 1970s that blue-collar settings were the most tolerant of homosexuality reads now like a final missive from a rapidly fading culture. "Hiding on the Job," *Gay Liberator*, October 1, 1971, 4. "Many of us know of the gay activist in Detroit who came out on the job at Chevrolet two years ago," the *Gay Liberator* further reported in 1971, "with really no ill consequences." That statement, which lines up with evidence in chapter 2, contrasts sharply with Ron Wood's experience at Chrysler in the late 1990s, and with the stories Anne Balay tells in her contemporary ethnography of gay steelworkers. See "Coming Out at Chrysler," *New Yorker*, July 21, 1997, 38–49; Anne Balay, *Steel Closets: Voices of Gay, Lesbian, and Transgender Steelworkers* (Chapel Hill: University of North Carolina Press, 2014).

38. Balay, *Steel Closets*, 58.

39. Jeremiah J. Garretson, *The Path to Gay Rights: How Activism and Coming Out Changed Public Opinion* (New York: New York University Press, 2018), 179.

40. Nan D. Hunter, "Civil Rights 3.0," in *A Nation of Widening Opportunities: The Civil Rights Act at 50*, ed. Ellen D. Katz and Samuel R. Bagenstos (Ann Arbor, MI: Maize, 2015), 50.

that hardened early around a narrow meaning of "sex" in Title VII of the 1964 Civil Rights Act proved difficult to dislodge.[41] Beginning in the 1970s, cases brought by gay and transgender plaintiffs under Title VII were dismissed as inconsistent with Congress's intent when it enacted the law.[42] After the Supreme Court ruled in 1989 that discrimination based on sex stereotyping was sex discrimination under Title VII, movement lawyers were eventually able to persuade some courts that employment actions that harmed transgender persons, and sometimes gender nonconforming gays and lesbians, were actionable under the law.[43] Such rulings were issued beginning in the early 2000s.[44]

The gender stereotyping argument was thus a legal wedge for some LGBT plaintiffs that began to pry some courts away from precedents that had earlier excluded LGBT workers from claiming coverage under Title VII's prohibition on sex discrimination. Another breakthrough came when movement lawyers pivoted toward an even more straightforward argument that discrimination against trans people was inherently (in legal parlance, *per se*) sex discrimination because "transgender status is defined by a difference between a person's gender identity and their sex assigned at birth."[45] Under this logic, it would be impossible to discriminate against a trans person without considering their sex. That argument was first successful in a 2008 decision.[46] Then in 2012, the EEOC ruled that discrimination based on gender identity "*inherently* takes sex into account in a

41. By 1975, the EEOC declared homosexuality outside of the purview of Title VII, and courts immediately followed suit. But what became the "common sense" of Title VII "masked far more multifarious approaches to Title VII on the ground in the decade prior." Brief of Historians as *Amici Curiae* in Support of the Employees in *Bostock v. Clayton County*; *Altitude Express, Inc. v. Zarda*; and *R. G. & G. R. Harris Funeral Homes v. EEOC*, Nos. 17-1618, 17-1623, 18-107 (U.S. July 3, 2019).

42. For example, *Voyles v. Ralph K. Davies Medical Center*, 403 F.Supp. 456 (N.D. Cal., 1975) (No. C-75-0861 SW).

43. This argument became possible only after the Supreme Court decided in 1989 that Title VII's prohibition on sex discrimination encompassed discrimination on the basis of gender stereotypes. See *Price Waterhouse v. Hopkins*, 490 U.S. 228 (1989) (No. 87-1167).

44. Alexander Chen, "Gay Rights and Trans Rights Are Indivisible: SCOTUS Just Showed Why," *Slate*, June 18, 2020, https://slate.com/news-and-politics/2020/06/gay -transgender-rights-indivisible-supreme-court.html; Katie R. Eyer, "Statutory Originalism and LGBT Rights," *Wake Forest Law Review* 54 (2019): 82n85.

45. Chen, "Gay and Trans Rights Are Indivisible." One of the origins of the textualist argument was, interestingly, same-sex marriage litigation (*Baehr v. Lewin*) from the state of Hawaii in the early 1990s. Chai Feldblum, "What Got Us to the Bostock Moment," *Medium*, June 2020, https://medium.com/@chaifeldblum/what-got-us-to-the-bostock -moment-5d4cb0f7ce54.

46. *Schroer v. Billington*, 577 F.Supp. 2d 293 (D.D.C., 2008) (No. 307-08).

manner that violates the law," and in 2015, the EEOC found that the same theory also applied to sexual orientation.[47] The per se argument increasingly found its way into court cases concerning both gay and transgender employees, and as changing cultural attitudes gradually penetrated the judiciary, some judges opened their minds to the clear logic of the argument. But federal courts also continued to issue conflicting rulings.[48]

That was the landscape when the Supreme Court agreed to hear three consolidated cases (two plaintiffs were gay and one was transgender) to determine if Title VII's coverage extended to LGBT employees. In the wake of Justice Anthony Kennedy's retirement and the court's further drift to the right, LGBT rights advocates were generally not optimistic; some even worried the court might roll back sex discrimination protections more broadly. But the increasing embrace by conservative jurists of what the legal scholar Katie Eyer calls "truly" textualist modes of judicial interpretation was unexpectedly a boon for LGBT rights.[49] The key issue was not whether or not Congress intended to include gay or transgender people in the law when they enacted Title VII in 1964.[50] Rather, the key issue was the plain meaning of the text, however broad. "It is only by ignoring the words of the statute—in favor of what judges have imagined Congress would have expected or anticipated, that such discrimination has been treated as outside the statute's scope."[51]

Even though some justices asked during oral argument about the "upheaval" that such a decision might produce, the court ruled 6 to 3 in the summer of 2020 that Title VII's ban on discrimination "because of sex"

47. Feldblum, "What Got Us to the Bostock Moment"; *Macy v. Holder*, No. 0120120821, 2012 WL 1435995 (E.E.O.C., April 20, 2012); *Baldwin v. Fox*, No. 0120133080, 2015 WL 4397641 (E.E.O.C., July 15, 2015).

48. Katie R. Eyer, "Sex Discrimination Law and LGBT Equality," *American Constitution Society for Law and Policy*, August 2017, 11–13.

49. Eyer, "Statutory Originalism and LGBT Rights," 66. Note, though, that it is also possible the court could have reached this decision without recourse to textualism. The Second Circuit's decision in *Zarda* (concerning one of the three plaintiffs in *Bostock*) ruled that sexual orientation was potentially covered under Title VII's prohibition barring discrimination based on sex on three separate grounds: the text of the statute, sex stereotyping, and associational discrimination. *Zarda v. Altitude Express, Inc.*, 883 F.3d 100 (2nd Cir., 2018) (15-3775).

50. "Under the modalities of statutory interpretation dominant in the 1970s and 1980s—under which subjective congressional expectations or intent were viewed as a proper basis for excluding applications of a textually broad statute—this arguably could (and often did) prove fatal to the claims of LGBT employees." See Eyer, "Statutory Originalism and LGBT Rights," 84.

51. Ibid., 85.

applied to LGBT employees.[52] In a short, dry opinion that almost entirely ignored the historic oppression of LGBT workers, Justice Neil Gorsuch adopted the logic of the textual, per se argument that it was impossible to discriminate against LGBT people without considering sex. In the majority opinion in *Bostock*, Gorsuch first asked readers to consider two employees—one male, one female—who were both attracted to men. If the employer fired the man because he was attracted to men but did not fire the woman because she was attracted to men, then "the employer intentionally singles out an employee to fire based in part on the employee's sex." Alternatively, Gorsuch considered an employer who fired a trans woman who had been assigned a male gender at birth. If the employer fired that person while retaining an otherwise identical female employee who had been assigned a female gender at birth, then "the employer intentionally penalizes a person identified as male at birth for traits and actions that it tolerates in an employee identified as female at birth." Gorsuch also swept away any consideration of what Congress wanted. The law was "written in starkly broad terms," Gorsuch asserted. "It has repeatedly produced unexpected applications."[53]

———————

Writing directly in response to opponents of the gay and transgender plaintiffs who wrote that Congress did not "hide elephants in mouseholes," Gorsuch responded that the elephant—the finding that the phrase "because of sex" encompassed "LGBT"—was *never* hidden in a mousehole. "It has been standing before us all along," he opined.[54] Yet thinking about how long it took the court to fully acknowledge something that seems so obvious in retrospect, it is worth considering *Bostock* as a fitting capstone to the trajectory of LGBT employment rights more generally. Nearly everything about this trajectory is distinctive or unexpected.[55] In the courts, for example, gay employment rights seem to have arrived almost as a by-product of transgender rights, which led the way. The irony

52. Adam Liptak and Jeremy W. Peters, "Justices Appear Split over Cases of L.G.B.T. Protections at Work," *New York Times*, October 9, 2019, A1; *Bostock v. Clayton County, Georgia*, 590 U.S. ___, 140 S. Ct. 1731 (2020) (No. 17-1618).

53. *Bostock v. Clayton County, Georgia*, 590 U.S. ___, 140 S. Ct. 1731 (2020) (No. 17-1618).

54. Ibid.

55. Among the unexpected elements was that marriage equality arrived five years ahead of the court's employment decision. The court's decision legalizing gay marriage is *Obergefell v. Hodges*, 576 U.S. 644, 135 S. Ct. 2584 (2015) (14-566).

here was that for years trans people had been told by a segment of gay rights advocates that including gender identity in antidiscrimination legislation would doom any given bill to fail.[56] Unforeseen as well was the way that that the Supreme Court decision came from the pen of a very conservative jurist, applying a legal method that had been developed and advanced by earlier legal conservatives (notably Antonin Scalia). In reaching its decision in *Bostock*, moreover, the court purported to be indifferent to the broader revolution in social values that had reshaped American life (and guided the court's other LGBT rights decisions in areas other than employment).[57] While legal scholars will continue to debate whether or not *Bostock* "vindicates" textualism's objectivity—and if there were other, better routes for the court to take—textualist methodology in this instance appears to have broken a precedential stranglehold that had for years prior made the courts fairly unreceptive to the claims LGBT plaintiffs made under federal sex discrimination law.[58]

Until this recent breakthrough, the situation in the courts was paralleled by the limited protection that was afforded by state legislatures, as well as the lack of momentum toward achieving federal legislation.[59] The

56. This sentiment led to the exclusion of trans people from coverage under the Employment Non-discrimination Act (ENDA) legislation on multiple occasions. See Frye, "Facing Discrimination, Organizing for Freedom," in D'Emilio, Turner, and Vaid, *Creating Change*; Stryker, *Transgender History*, 188–93.

57. *Bostock appears* to stand in contrast to the court's other major LGBT rights decisions (*Romer v. Evans, Lawrence v. Texas, Windsor v. United States, and Obergefell v. Hodges*), which acknowledged applying, according to Cary Franklin, "new insights and societal understandings." Franklin, "Living Textualism," *Supreme Court Review* 2020 (2021): 120.

58. Cary Franklin argues that rather than being objective, textualism conceals the "shadow decision points" whereby judges produce outcomes that align with their values. Franklin, "Living Textualism," 126. The contrasting argument that *Bostock* may vindicate textualism as objective is found in Tara Grove, "Which Textualism," *Harvard Law Review* 134 (2020): 265–307. The debate among antidiscrimination scholars and advocates over textualism is also taken up by Katie Eyer, who concludes that it is "simultaneously conservative in its aspirations and potentially radical in its legal effects." Eyer, "The But-For Theory of Anti-discrimination Law," *Virginia Law Review* 107 (December 2021): 1621.

59. On the cusp of the court's ruling, only twenty-one states had laws protecting gay and trans employees from discrimination; another two states protected gay workers only; and another thirteen states had executive orders or personnel regulations prohibiting discrimination based on sexual orientation or gender identity in public employment. Several states offered no protection to gay or transgender workers. In the spring of 2020, the Williams Institute estimated that half of the country's LGBT workforce lived in states without laws protecting them from employment discrimination. See its website, https:// williamsinstitute.law.ucla.edu/publications/lgbt-nondiscrimination-statutes/.

vacuum left by the state (courts and legislatures, state and federal) had already led some LGBT people to pursue a path to rights directly through their employers, and business's responsiveness further shaped the broader culture and may even have helped to change the minds of conservative judges, however much they might protest the idea that social change was a driver.[60] By whatever path the court got there, we should view the culminating decision in *Bostock* as signifying the end of a regime of federal anti-homosexualism, whose emergence and consolidation spanned the better part of a century.[61] As importantly, *Bostock* heralds the moment when LGBT people have been finally brought into the federal civil rights regime to which they have long sought access.[62]

Yet the timing is less than auspicious. As historians Reuel Schiller, Nancy MacLean, and others have pointed out, civil rights protections for women, racial minorities, and (now) LGBT people mean less as the conditions of work in general deteriorate under late capitalism and as the power of organized labor has diminished.[63] Beyond these larger structural issues, social scientists and legal scholars have thoughtfully explored the limitations of rights paradigms for advancing social justice, and a voluminous literature cautions us not to romanticize rights.[64] The formal equality that

60. It is noteworthy that two hundred corporations filed an amicus brief in support of the gay and transgender plaintiffs in *Bostock*—in essence inviting more regulation in their support of LGBT rights. Brief of 206 Businesses as *Amici Curiae* in Support of the Employees in *Bostock v. Clayton County*; *Altitude Express, Inc. v. Zarda*; and *R. G. & G. R. Harris Funeral Homes v. EEOC*, Nos. 17-1618, 17-1623, 18-107 (U.S. July 3, 2019).

61. Margot Canaday, *The Straight State: Sexuality and Citizenship in 20th Century America* (Princeton, NJ: Princeton University Press, 2009).

62. Title VII exempts small firms from coverage. LGBT people working for employers with fewer than fifteen employees in states without antidiscrimination laws protecting LGBT workers remain vulnerable. However, some legal advocates note that states without such protections are still likely to follow the court's ruling in *Bostock*. See, for example, Alex Reed, "Beyond *Bostock*: Employment Protections for LGBTQ Workers Not Covered by Title VII," *New York University Journal of Legislation and Public Policy* 23 (2021): 538–86.

63. Nancy MacLean has written of a "world that at last acknowledges the justice of equal opportunity for all, yet does so amidst spiraling inequality of rewards." MacLean, *Freedom Is Not Enough: The Opening of the American Workplace* (Cambridge, MA: Harvard University Press, 2006), 347; Reuel Schiller, *Forging Rivals: Race, Class, Law and the Collapse of Postwar Liberalism* (New York: Cambridge University Press, 2015), 222.

64. See, for example, Richard Thompson Ford, *Rights Gone Wrong: How Law Corrupts the Struggle for Equality* (New York: Picador, 2011); Ellen Berrey, Robert L. Nelson, and Laura Beth Nielsen, *Rights on Trial: How Workplace Discrimination Law Perpetuates Inequality* (Chicago: University of Chicago Press, 2017); Lauren B. Edelman, *Working Law: Courts, Corporations, and Symbolic Civil Rights* (Chicago: University of Chicago Press, 2016).

civil rights laws support can eliminate overt discrimination, they reason, but does little to tackle social stratification and hierarchy.[65] In the worst-case scenario, as three legal scholars have recently pointed out, legal equality "reinscribes the invidious hierarchies it was created to ameliorate."[66]

Under the weight of these criticisms, antidiscrimination law has become "unfashionable" in the academy.[67] Yet, even with these cautionary notes in mind, I am optimistic about the difference that *Bostock* will make. Some of the reasons are those that champions of civil rights laws have long held: the deterrent effect the ruling may have on some employers; the social legitimacy that comes from being seen by the court; the related impact on rights consciousness. But Title VII's remedies will also work *directly* to address the problems that both gay and trans workers still regularly face—problems of overt, or first-generation, discrimination.[68] The prevalence of overt discrimination, as well as the particular segments of our community it is most often directed at, belies the oft-cited notion that LGBT employment rights are "middle-class" issues or that civil rights are not also about remedying social stratification and economic injustice.[69] As this book has shown, the economic exploitation of queer people was historically licensed by law. That licensing initially came in the form of aggressive state policing, from which employers were able to benefit. Later it was in the form of the state's enduring refusal to make antigay and transgender discrimination illegal, to sanction and authorize the vulnerability that remained even after state harassment had receded. Civil rights laws are thus not irrelevant to or separate from social stratification, as reflected

65. Ford, *Rights Gone Wrong*, 9–10.

66. Berrey, Nelson, and Nielsen, *Rights on Trial*, 19.

67. Olatunde Johnson, "Leveraging Antidiscrimination," in Katz and Bagenstos, *Nation of Widening Opportunities*, 211.

68. To the extent that civil rights laws are best suited for "ending exclusions and categorical inequalities," and to the extent that "LGBT equality has been overwhelmingly framed as being about ending exclusions," Nan Hunter concludes, LGBT rights are an "easy fit" for a civil rights paradigm. Hunter, "Civil Rights 3.0," 48–49. The concept of first- and second-generation discrimination is from Susan Strum, "Second Generation Employment Discrimination: A Structural Approach," *Columbia Law Review* 101 (March 2001): 458–568.

69. Vaid, *Virtual Equality*, 271. In time, we will know more about the full impact of the law—especially what kind of tool it will be if, as happened with discrimination directed against racial minorities and women, overt discrimination takes on a more covert form that will be harder for the law to reach. The potential for *Bostock*'s "but for sex" principle to apply to many forms of discrimination (instances that may be coextensive with "second-generation" or more covert discrimination) is discussed in Eyer, "But-For Theory of Antidiscrimination Law."

in simply being able to get and keep a job. It is why, when the decision in *Bostock* was announced, one trans man wrote, "To understand our joy, you have to understand . . . [our] seemingly endless worry over jobs."[70]

———

Yet for all that the *Bostock* decision may potentially mean, it has almost nothing to say about the lived experiences of queer people on their jobs. In that aspect, it is fundamentally out of sync with the aims of this book and the way I have attempted to intertwine a history of both vulnerability and meaning in queer work lives across the second half of the twentieth century. So I'll end not with Justice Gorsuch's opinion, but rather by attempting to situate one of the three plaintiffs in her employment: Aimee Australia Stephens was born in Fayetteville, North Carolina, and began her working life in the mountain town of Mars Hill, where she attended a small Baptist college and earned a degree in religious studies in 1984. As a college student, Stephens needed a job, and "in that small mountain town," she recalled, "the funeral home was the only thing available." She

70. Evan Urquhart, "The Joy of Having a Job," *Slate*, June 16, 2020, https://slate.com /human-interest/2020/06/trans-job-discrimination-scotus-bostock-decision.html. In his critique of formal legal equality, legal scholar Dean Spade has emphasized the violence done to trans people by the "administrative governance that typically comes from state agencies like departments of Health, Motor Vehicle, Corrections, Child Welfare, and Education, and federal agencies like the Customs and Border Protection, U.S. Immigration and Customs Enforcement, the Bureau of Indian Affairs, the Bureau of Prisons, and the Food and Drug Administration." Dean Spade, *Normal Life: Administrative Violence, Critical Trans Politics, and the Limits of the Law* (Durham, NC: Duke University Press, 2015), 11. *This* should be the focus of political struggle, Spade argues, not antidiscrimination laws that target "aberrant individuals with overtly biased intentions" (42–43). I take Spade's point, but *Bostock* could potentially apply to all federal laws that prohibit sex discrimination (enumerated in appendix C of Justice Alito's dissent in *Bostock*), as well as strengthening state laws that prohibit sex discrimination, and thus reaches some of the issues that particularly concern Spade. The symbolic impact of *Bostock*'s affirmation of transgender employees should also influence the decision making of bureaucrats who shape administrative regulations that affect trans people. Full protection for the transgender community would build on *Bostock* to enact a federal law (such as the Equality Act) that would extend antidiscrimination protections to public accommodations and federally funded programs. *Bostock*, in other words, may not be *everything* that LGBT people need, but it does provide a baseline of protection that did not exist before. See Chris Johnson, "Is the LGBTQ Fight Finished after the *Bostock* Ruling?," *Washington Blade*, June 24, 2020, https://www .washingtonblade.com/2020/06/24/is-the-lgbtq-fight-finished-after-bostock-ruling-not -so-fast-advocates-say/.

started vacuuming floors and dusting and eventually began to help in the embalming room. After graduation, Stephens spent a year in seminary and then a year pastoring a Baptist church, which subsequently folded. While Stephens had thought she "might be standing in a church preaching, leading God's people," she "soon found out there were other callings that were just as important, and one of those was funeral service." Stephens took a job at a funeral home in Charlotte and later returned to Fayetteville to begin a two-year program in mortuary science at the technical college. When she graduated, she took a position with a funeral home in Alliance, North Carolina, and later at a funeral home in Raeford, North Carolina. Stephens discovered that her employer was not paying her insurance as they had committed to do, and she took a job with a removal service to earn a higher wage. Eventually, Stephens purchased the Carolina Mortuary Services, an embalming and body removal service. Unfortunately, her business venture coincided with the corporate consolidation of the funeral industry, when large companies bought out small family-run funeral homes and increasingly did their own removals. As a result, as Stephens remembered, "the bottom . . . fell out of the business."[71]

Stephens, who had known something was fundamentally different about her from the time she was a small child, was still presenting as male during this period. Stephens had also married, and when her wife needed to be closer to her family, the couple returned to Fayetteville. There, she took a job managing an auto parts store. Several years later, when that marriage fell apart and Stephens moved to a small town in Michigan to begin a life with a woman she had known since childhood, the auto parts company transferred her. Later Stephens moved on from that position to work as a mechanic with a few different employers in the area, but here too she found that automotive work was "drying up in terms of decent money." Stephens's wages barely covered her benefits, and she began to investigate getting licensed in Michigan for mortuary work, which required passing the state exam and completing a six-month apprenticeship. She started putting out résumés and making cold calls and in the fall of 2007 took an apprenticeship with R. G. and G. R. Harris Funeral Homes, which had locations in Livonia, Detroit, and Garden City. Her apprentice wage was $10 an

71. Deposition of Aimee Stephens, December 11, 2017, 8–12, and Deposition of Aimee Stephens, December 16, 2015, 32–33, *EEOC v. R. G. and G. R. Harris Funeral Homes*, 884 F.3d 560 (6th Cir., 2018) (No. 16-2424). Stephens's depositions were provided to author by the EEOC. On consolidation in the funeral industry, see Thomas Lynch, "Funerals-R-Us: From Funeral Home to Mega Industry," *Generations* 28 (Summer 2004): 13.

hour. When her six months were completed, she was offered a position as funeral director at the Garden City location, making $40,000 per year.[72]

The funeral director role was quite varied. In the course of her work, Stephens's tasks included collecting doctors' signatures for the death certificate; gathering permits; removing the body from the hospital or home; embalming, "cosmetizing," dressing, and "casketing" the body; arranging flowers in the visitation room; setting up chairs for the funeral; directing parking at the funeral; greeting people as they came into the building; and going out to the cemetery to help with arrangements there. Stephens took great pride in her work. If she went to remove a body from a home, she always made sure the bed was made and she would lay a rose on top of it. Most important to her was to make sure the body was as well prepared as it could be so that families might have closure. She was, one coworker recalled, "an incredible embalmer." The man who replaced her at Harris heard after the fact about her embalming work and positive interactions with families. Her wife, Donna, remembered that she was "meticulous," "making sure that makeup, hair, and clothes" for the deceased "were properly done"; "families requested her" specifically to prepare the bodies of their loved ones. Adding to the satisfaction that Stephens found on her job were the friends she made at work, especially three women colleagues she regularly met for lunch or dinner. In addition, in 2011, her salary was raised to $50,000.[73]

While her work life was going well, her inner life was in turmoil. By this time Stephens had come to understand herself as transgender, and she had told her wife, Donna. Stephens had also sought therapeutic help and begun electrolysis, but she was still living a "double life" as far as work was concerned. The burden of her secret was increasingly too heavy to carry, and in the fall of 2012 she stood in her backyard with a gun pointed at her chest. She couldn't bring herself to pull the trigger—"I realized I liked me too much"—and decided then and there that she would transition fully, including at work. She quietly told the coworkers she was closest to; for the most

72. Deposition of Aimee Stephens, December 11, 2017, 13–19, *EEOC v. R. G. and G. R. Harris Funeral Homes*, 884 F.3d 560 (6th Cir., 2018) (No. 16-2424).

73. Deposition of Aimee Stephens, December 11, 2017, 20–27, *EEOC v. R. G. and G. R. Harris Funeral Homes*, 884 F.3d 560 (6th Cir., 2018) (No. 16-2424); excerpts from Deposition of Wendie McKie, January 22, 2016, 22, and excerpts from Deposition of Troy Shaffer, November 13, 2015, 37–38, *EEOC v. R. G. and G. R. Harris Funeral Homes*; interview with Donna Stephens, conducted via telephone, 2021. One of the managers at Harris concurred that Stephens was "a very good embalmer . . . very, very thorough" and that families were "very pleased" with her work. Excerpts of Deposition with David Cash, January 22, 2016, 32, *EEOC v. R. G. and G. R. Harris Funeral Homes*.

part, they were supportive. She spent the next six months drafting and revising a letter to her boss and coworkers. Once completed, it was a perfectly crafted, heartfelt expression. "I have known many of you for some time now, and I count you all as my friends," Stephens began. "I am writing this both to inform you of a significant change in my life and to ask for your patience, understanding, and support, which I would treasure greatly."[74]

The letter then explained that Stephens would soon be going on vacation and that when she came back it would be as "my true self, Aimee Australia Stephens, in appropriate business attire." She acknowledged that the news might be distressing but said that she needed "to do this for myself and my own peace of mind and to end the agony of my soul." Optimistically, she concluded that "the best is yet to come. I hope we enjoy it together. It is my wish that I continue my work at R. G. and G. R. Harris Funeral Homes doing what I have always done, which is my best!"[75]

Stephens gradually showed the letter to additional coworkers. But the conversation with her boss in the chapel of the funeral home did not go nearly as well. Two weeks after that meeting, Aimee Stephens was fired from her position as funeral director at Harris Funeral Homes. Perhaps because she was so gifted at what she did, Stephens was shocked by the news.[76]

That shock and anger led Aimee and Donna Stephens to the ACLU and then to the EEOC to begin the seven-year legal battle—joined by two gay plaintiffs also fighting their terminations—that culminated in the *Bostock* decision. In the immediate, however, the couple was financially devastated by the funeral director's firing. They sold two vehicles, a camping trailer, and a piano to cover their bills. Still, there were times when they didn't eat,

74. Deposition of Aimee Stephens, December 11, 2017, 32–37, *EEOC v. R. G. and G. R. Harris Funeral Homes*, 884 F.3d 560 (6th Cir., 2018) (No. 16-2424); Meagan Flynn, "A Transgender Woman Wrote a Letter to Her Boss: It Led to Her Firing—and A Trip to the Supreme Court," *Washington Post*, April 30, 2019, https://www.washingtonpost.com /nation/2019/04/30/transgender-woman-wrote-letter-her-boss-it-led-her-firing-trip -supreme-court/; interview with Donna Stephens, conducted via telephone, 2021; "Dear Friends and Co-workers," exhibit A, in Brief in Opposition for Respondent Aimee Stephens in *R. G. & G. R. Harris Funeral Homes, Inc. v. Equal Employment Opportunity Commission* (No. 18-107); *Bostock v. Clayton County, Georgia*, 590 U.S. ___, 140 S. Ct. 1731 (2020) (No. 17-1618).

75. "Dear Friends and Co-workers," exhibit A in Brief in Opposition for Respondent Aimee Stephens.

76. Deposition of Aimee Stephens, December 11, 2017, 37–41, and Deposition of Aimee Stephens, December 16, 2015, 84, *EEOC v. R. G. and G. R. Harris Funeral Homes*, 884 F.3d 560 (6th Cir., 2018) (No. 16-2424); exhibit 23, EEOC Memo for File, March 25, 2014, *EEOC v. R. G. and G. R. Harris Funeral Homes*, 201 F.Supp. 3d 837 (E.D. Mich., 2016) (No. 14-13710); interview with Donna Stephens, conducted via telephone, 2021.

Donna Stephens recalled. Her kindhearted boss would sometimes notice the strain on her and ask, "Do you need some money?" Aimee Stephens was severely depressed after being fired: "Do I not matter anymore?" "Am I not important?" she wondered. "It's like . . . going from being somebody to nobody."[77] Still, she summoned the energy to mount an extensive job search, sending out forty to fifty résumés to area funeral homes. Stephens was turned down after every interview despite her thirty years of experience. She surmised one difficulty may have been that her certification was under her previous (male) name, although none of the prospective employers said anything outright. When that door seemed to close to her, Stephens took a part-time job at a Chicken Shack restaurant. She was earning $7.45 an hour. Eventually, she got a somewhat better position as a histology assistant at a local hospital, performing the cutting during an autopsy. She was overqualified for the position and making just $14 an hour. But her wife remarked that in both positions, at the Chicken Shack and at the hospital, "they accepted her as Aimee Stephens."[78]

Stephens worked at the hospital for about six months until she developed end stage renal disease that made it impossible for her to continue. It is difficult to say whether her termination and the consequent stress and depression accelerated the kidney disease with which she had long struggled. The meetings with lawyers, depositions, and media appearances that accompanied her lawsuit against Harris Funeral Homes occurred in the midst of regular dialysis treatments and bouts in the hospital.[79] Stephens was barely well enough to travel to Washington to attend the oral argument before the Supreme Court, but with her wife, Donna, at her side, she mustered the strength to appear. She wore a black suit that day, which seemed to symbolize her lost career as a funeral director.[80] Tragically,

77. Deposition of Aimee Stephens, December 11, 2017, 41–52, *EEOC v. R. G. and G. R. Harris Funeral Home*s, 884 F.3d 560 (6th Cir., 2018) (No. 16-2424); interview with Donna Stephens, conducted via telephone, 2021.

78. Deposition of Aimee Stephens, December 16, 2015, 10–11, 108–13, and Deposition of Aimee Stephens, December 11, 2017, 46–47, *EEOC v. R. G. and G. R. Harris Funeral Homes*, 884 F.3d 560 (6th Cir., 2018) (No. 16-2424); interview with Donna Stephens, 2021.

79. Deposition of Aimee Stephens, December 11, 2017, 45, 51–52, *EEOC v. R. G. and G. R. Harris Funeral Homes*, 884 F.3d 560 (6th Cir., 2018) (No. 16-2424); interview with Donna Stephens, 2021.

80. Katelyn Burns, "The Supreme Court Is Finally Taking On Trans Rights: Here's the Woman Who Started It All," *Vox*, October 7, 2019, https://www.vox.com/latest-news/2019/10/7/20903503/trans-supreme-court-decision-employment-discrimination-aimee-stephens; Masha Gessen, "Remembering Aimee Stephens, Who Lost and Found Her Purpose," *New Yorker*, May 20, 2020, https://www.newyorker.com/news/postscript/remembering-aimee-stephens-who-lost-and-found-her-purpose.

Stephens died just five weeks before the Supreme Court issued its opinion in *Bostock*, not knowing the change she had made.[81] That decision is a lasting part of her legacy. Yet her story is also a poignant reminder of how much work matters to our sense of self, belonging, and well-being, and shows as well how Stephens's quest for rights was layered on top of a longer struggle for a "good job" that would keep body and soul together. One supporter stood outside the Supreme Court on the day of the oral argument with a sign that read "*We are all Aimee Stephens*."[82] As this statement simply and powerfully suggested, Stephens's experience was singular yet also universal, and continues to carry meaning for so many of us caught between the promise and the perils of a life's work.[83]

81. Aimee Ortiz, "Aimee Stephens, Plaintiff in Transgender Rights Case," *New York Times*, May 12, 2020, B12. The plaintiff Donald Zarda also died before the court's decision. Gerald Bostock was the only plaintiff of the three who was alive to hear the outcome.

82. Melissa Nann Burke, "Hundreds Rally For Transgender Rights during Arguments before High Court," *Detroit News*, October 8, 2019, https://www.detroitnews.com/story /news/politics/2019/10/08/transgender-bias-arguments-supreme-court-aimee-stephens -garden-city-funeral-home/3902175002/ (emphasis mine).

83. On the notion of a "life's work," see Vicki Schultz, "Life's Work," *Columbia Law Review* 100 (2000): 1881–964.

ACKNOWLEDGMENTS

THOUGH THE RESEARCH COMMENCED many years prior, I began the intensive writing phase of this book just after the election in November 2016, as the country slid into the darkest and saddest period certainly of my adult life, and, my nearly eighty-year-old mother would say, of hers as well. I was still writing (the chapter on the AIDS epidemic, to be precise) when Covid-19 arrived in the United States. As I chase down the last remaining footnotes and draft these acknowledgements—the final tasks in completing the manuscript—we are experiencing another Covid surge from a new variant, uncertain as to when or how the global pandemic will end. In between, we have witnessed the murder of George Floyd, unprecedented wildfires and other ominous signs of climate change, a vicious wave of hate directed at Asians and Asian Americans, as well as a violent insurrection at our nation's Capitol. Women's autonomy as represented in the right to a safe and legal abortion hangs by a thread. Through all that, I have been drafting this book. So what am I thankful for as I complete this task? I am grateful to have been where I was in the life cycle of a long project when all this calamity landed in our collective laps. In contrast to many colleagues who were embarking on research and saw their work shut down by Covid-19 as archives closed, or those with small children whose lives were turned upside down by parenting responsibilities, I was able to get lost in writing. It has been such a balm and a comfort, and I imagine I would be in far worse emotional shape than I am if this project had not demanded so much of my focus during the past (otherwise unremittingly awful) several years.

There are also many people to thank. At the top of the list are the more than 150 informants who agreed to speak with me and shared stories about their working lives. I could not have written this book without these conversations, and I suspect when I look back on them at the end of my own career, these interviews will stand out as the most meaningful aspect. I'm so grateful not only for the history these conversations helped me to uncover, but for the opportunity they provided for intergenerational connection to other gay, lesbian, bisexual, and transgender people. I hope I have treated these informants and their stories with the sensitivity and care they deserve.

In the wake of Covid-19, our long physical separation from our work-places has made many of us especially aware of how important the culture and community that happens on our jobs is for us. So, for this book on workplaces, let me acknowledge those colleagues especially who make my own place of employment a good one, and whose stimulating presence has surely made me a better historian. First, this book has been in progress long enough that it's been supported by three department chairs (and one act-ing chair). For their generosity and care, thanks to William Chester Jordan, Keith Wailoo, Michael Gordin, and Angela Creager. Also in Dickinson Hall, special thanks to David Bell, He Bian, Michael Blaakman, Divya Cherian, Jacob Dlamini, Yaacob Dweck, Laura Edwards, Shel Garon, Tony Grafton, Molly Greene, Katja Guenther, Judy Hanson, Tera Hunter, Alison Isenberg, Matt Karp, Kevin Kruse, Mike Laffan, Beth Lew-Williams, Rosina Lozano, Federico Marcon, Erika Milam, Judie Miller, Yair Mintzker, Isadora Mota, Katya Pravilova, Jenny Rampling, Marni Sandweiss, Max Siles, Jack Tan-nous, Emily Thompson, Xin Wen, Natasha Wheatley, Sean Wilentz, and Peter Wirzbicki. While he was still at Princeton, Jon Levy and I cotaught an undergraduate seminar on the history of the American workplace that was foundational for me in orienting myself to a new subject of inquiry. I thank Jon for that collaboration. Two (now emeritus) faculty also deserve mention for their many brilliant insights that shaped my thinking along the way, as well as the distinctive models their respective careers provide for ways of being in the profession: Dirk Hartog and Dan Rodgers. Dean Jill Dolan has been for years another source of kindness and inspiration on this campus. Janet Chen merits special acknowledgement for the support and solidarity that have characterized our fifteen years of working together. She also once returned from a research trip to Taiwan with a really fancy bottle of Taiwan-ese whiskey for me tucked into her suitcase. That is a good colleague!

Graduate students are also a critical part of my workplace, and while cognitive decline is a fact of aging (for most of us anyway), I like to believe their sparky, buoyant, and brilliant presence helps to slow the process. Their sense of joy and resilience and intellectual curiosity is a constant inspiration, as is the kindness they continually show to one another. There are far too many to mention them individually, but special thanks to the students over the years who took my graduate seminars on the history of the state, on work and inequality, and on the history of women, gen-der, and sexuality; or who cluster around the Modern America Workshop; or who more recently joined my "Pandemic Writing Group." They have helped me develop intellectually and personally as much as (if not more than) I have helped them.

Intellectual communities—and the debts we incur through them—of course transcend our home institutions. Among the many riches of a life in the great city of Philadelphia are the wonderful historians who reside there who have also helped me muddle through problems in my work and shared urban conviviality more generally: Lori Ginzberg, Kathy Peiss, Kathy Brown, Karen Tani, Brent Cebul, Bob Lockhart, and especially Sophia Lee and Serena Mayeri. I have benefited as well from participation in a "Mid-Atlantic" writing group (including a few "emergency" sessions!) with Jennifer Mittelstadt, Johanna Schoen, and Regina Kunzel. During the years I was writing this book, I also took part in two intensive collaborations. One was the volume *Intimate States*, which I coedited with Robert Self and Nancy Cott. During this same period, Nancy Cott also led a team of four of us in drafting a historians' amicus brief in the *Bostock* case, which was before the Supreme Court in 2019. Working with Nancy, Anna Lvovsky, and Serena Mayeri on that was truly an honor, as was the endeavor with Robert and Nancy. These collective labors on questions that are so closely related to the topic of this book greatly refined my thinking here.

Although I'm sure Stephanie McCurry does not remember this, she helpfully leaned over to me at a dinner in Princeton just as I was embarking on this project and told me to resist the pressure to write a "fast" second book and to write the book I wanted to write, however long that took. Her advice was so important to my feeling okay about my process and pace as I went along. I also thank Mary Lindemann, whom I have never met, for her related call for "slow history" (like slow food!) in her recent presidential address for the American Historical Association, which has been similarly steadying.[1]

Nancy MacLean, Barbara Welke, and Joanne Meyerowitz—three historians I admire tremendously—have all done a lot to support my work in the world, for which I am profoundly grateful. Among other things, that support led me to fellowships that provided critical time to research and write. In addition to sustained research support from my own institution, I thank the American Council of Learned Societies, the National Endowment for the Humanities, and the Radcliffe Institute for funding this project. While at the Radcliffe, archivists at the Schlesinger Library were endlessly patient about letting me basically camp out for a year in the library at the very beginning of my research process. I'm grateful as well to archivists at the GLBT Historical Society of Northern California,

1. The address was published as Mary Lindemann, "Slow History," *American Historical Review* 126 (March 2021): 1–18.

the Rare and Manuscript Collections at Cornell University, the Lesbian Herstory Archives (especially Rachel Corbman), the San Francisco Public Library (where Tim Wilson kindly scanned records to save me an eleventh-hour trip to the West Coast after the book was in production), the Manuscripts and Archives Division of the New York Public Library, Seeley Mudd Library at Princeton University, the Jimmy Carter Presidential Library, the National Archives, the Library of Congress, the Reuther Library at Wayne State University, the Labor Archives at San Francisco State University, the Baker Business Library at Harvard University, the University Archives and Special Collections at Northeastern University, Archives and Special Collections at the University of California–San Francisco, Special Collections at the University of California–Los Angeles, the Rare Books and Manuscripts Library at Columbia University, the Sophia Smith Collection at Smith College, Archives and Special Collections at the Thomas J. Dodd Research Center at the University of Connecticut–Storrs, Special Collections and Archives at Central Connecticut State University, and the Tamiment Library and Robert F. Wagner Labor Archives at New York University.

The only thing better than finding something in the archives yourself is having someone send you a relevant find from their own files. No one did this more than Stephen Vider, but I also benefited from the generosity of Tim Stewart-Winter, Anna Lvovsky, Scott D'Orio, Regina Kunzel, Clay Howard, Robert Self, Dan Ewert, Miriam Frank, Siobhan Somerville, Will Kuby, Landon Storrs, Brooke Depenbusch, Shane Lin, Nancy Cott, David B. Long, and Nancy Polikoff. Miriam Frank (and the Tamiment Library) generously allowed me access to her oral histories ahead of the collection opening to the public. Steve Mershon deserves special thanks for loading his own personal archive into the back of my car and trusting me as I drove away with it. (He was also patient when I kept it for longer than I said I would.) Marjorie Bryer, Liz Faue, Susan Cahn, Martin Meeker, David Minto, Jennifer Luff, Heather Love, Gary Gerstle, Natalia Molina, Jonathan Bell, Christopher Phelps, Ellen Herman, and Amy Dru Stanley all helped me think through my ideas (or research strategies) at various stages. David Hollander, Princeton's smart, kind, and extremely skilled law librarian, has been enormously resourceful throughout in helping me to track down legal sources. Dale Price of the EEOC provided me access (with the family's permission) to the transcripts of the depositions of Aimee Stephens, and Donna Stephens generously shared memories of her late wife with me. My graduate students Teal Arcadi and Casey Eilbert provided excellent research assistance, as did several undergraduates:

Nora Aguiar, Zoe Tucker, Liz Pinto and Phillip de Sa e Silva. For their assistance in locating interview subjects, thanks to: Rhonda Wittels, Bruce Williams, Brooke Trent, Tom Weber, Sarah Savino, Daniel Rivers, Tim Retzloff, Arden Eversmeyer, Sophia Lee, Shannon Minter, Marta Ames, Kate Masur, Karen Miller, Amy Bronson, Desma Holcomb, Miriam Frank, Alix Genter, Ellen Herman, and Jay Kaplan.

Talks and workshops in front of both academic and nonacademic audiences gave me an opportunity to test out ideas as they developed, as well as to plot next steps. I'm so grateful for critical feedback from audiences at the University of Minnesota, SAGE New York, SAGE Atlanta, the University of California–Berkeley, the University of Colorado–Denver, Duke University, New York University, Northwestern University, Virginia Commonwealth University, the University of Virginia, Tulane University, the Levi Strauss Corporation, the University of Chicago, the University of Iowa, Columbia University, Wayne State University, Dickinson College, the University of Pennsylvania, the University of Richmond, Temple University, the New York Historical Society, Yale University, University College London, and Princeton University.

Most important of all was the insightful feedback I got at various stages from readers of the full manuscript. While I was not able to solve every problem they pointed out, this book is much better because of the extraordinary time and care several colleagues took with it. Thanks to two anonymous readers and Serena Mayeri for Princeton University Press, as well as to Joanne Meyerowitz, Stephen Vider, Sarah Milov, and Sophia Lee. I felt a bit guilty when my graduate student Maia Silber asked if she could read the manuscript just *after* she finished her generals exam. She assured me it would be helpful to her in thinking through her dissertation prospectus. I don't know if that really turned out to be true, but she provided incisive comments anyway, as I knew she would. The brilliant Grey Osterud appeared in the very late stages with exceptional editorial assistance. She's a force! And the last set of eyes were those of Greta Krippner, who read the manuscript just as I was putting it into production, caught some remaining errors, and generally helped me to be at peace with letting it go.

Princeton University Press has been wonderful to work with, once again. Initial conversations with Eric Crahan and Brigitta van Rheinberg convinced me that they understood the aims of this project. My editor Bridget Flannery-McCoy has been patient, encouraging, and responsive throughout. Kathleen Kageff was a dream copyeditor, who made that (usually stressful) process as smooth as possible. Thanks also to Alena Chekanov, Ellen Foos, and Sara Lerner, who managed the book's production expertly. Karl Spurzem designed a beautiful cover. Above all, it's a great pleasure to work with a publisher that remains so clearly committed to the mission of an academic press, and that has so strongly promoted the leadership of women in university press publishing.

It's conventional in academic acknowledgements to save the intimate ties closer to home for the end, and I won't break with the tradition. Our commuting lifestyle—two different jobs in two different cities—would be impossible without the kindness of our neighbors who on occasion pick up the mail, keep an eye out for storm damage, and let the plumber in. Thanks to Kaitlin and Michael Caruso, William Whiting, Martha Peech, Pat Circolo, Lesley Siegel, Hilary Skinner, Michael Rusch, and Shilpa Shah. For their sustaining love and friendship across many years, my thanks to Janet Chen, Sarah Milov, Sarah Song, Kate Masur, Pippa Holloway, Jennifer Rubenstein, Susan Curry, and Lisa Misher. I'm so grateful for my parents and siblings and the way we came together during the pandemic, and for the love and support from Northern California from Rachel's mom, who never gets off the phone without asking, "How is the book coming?"

By the time this book appears, Rachel Spector and I will have crossed the thirty-year mark together. She is the opposite of a hoarder who has nonetheless watched our basement fill up with books and boxes of documents with little more than a shrug of resignation. In this and everything, she has tolerated my excesses (I have quite a few), and cheerfully followed me into the assorted passions and pursuits (with varying degrees of enthusiasm) that have filled the hours when I was not working. I'm so proud of her own long career with the Department of Interior (and grateful for the way her job has made wilderness more a part of the culture of our partnership). She is a steadfast companion; a "medicinal" presence, as a friend once remarked; and a wonderful chef. I'm so lucky to have her by my side.

I would be equally lost without my twin sister, Greta Krippner, who keeps me up-to-date by sending the latest jazz releases, and also made our family read together Emily Wilson's new translation of the *Odyssey* during the pandemic. ("The ultimate story of family separation!" she reminded us.) She is full of schemes like this; a great mom to Esme; runner of half marathons; obsessive fan of Ezra Klein. Another "slow-cooking" academic, I admire her work as a sociologist and her grounded way of being in the profession. For years, she has helped me to find the joy not just in our family but in our work as well. Along with Rachel, she is the light of my life, and so this one is for her, with love and gratitude.

A NOTE ON THE TYPE

———◆———

THIS BOOK has been composed in Miller, a Scotch Roman
typeface designed by Matthew Carter and first released by
Font Bureau in 1997. It resembles Monticello, the typeface
developed for The Papers of Thomas Jefferson in the 1940s
by C. H. Griffith and P. J. Conkwright and reinterpreted in
digital form by Carter in 2003.

Pleasant Jefferson ("P. J.") Conkwright (1905–1986) was
Typographer at Princeton University Press from 1939 to 1970.
He was an acclaimed book designer and AIGA Medalist.